TEACHERS AND TEXTS IN THE ANCIENT WORLD

Teachers and Texts in the Ancient World presents a comprehensive and accessible survey of religious and philosophical teaching and classroom practices in the ancient world. H. Gregory Snyder synthesizes a wide range of ancient evidence and modern scholarship to address such questions as how the literary practices of Jews and Christians compared to the literary practices of the philosophical schools and whether Christians were particularly noteworthy for their attachment to scripture.

Teachers and Texts in the Ancient World will be of interest to students of classics, ancient history, the early Christian world and Jewish studies.

H. Gregory Snyder is Assistant Professor of religion at Davidson College, North Carolina.

D0217648

RELIGION IN THE FIRST CHRISTIAN CENTURIES

Edited by Deborah Sawyer and John Sawyer,
Lancaster University

Too often the religious traditions of antiquity are studied in isolation, without any real consideration of how they interacted. What made someone with a free choice become an adherent of one faith rather than another? Why might a former pagan choose to become a 'god-fearer' and attend synagogue services? Why might a Jew become a Christian? How did the mysteries of Mithras differ from the worship of the Unconquered Sun, or the status of the Virgin Mary from that of Isis, and how many gods could an ancient worshipper have? These questions are hard to answer without a synoptic view of what the different religions offered.

The aim of the books in this series is to survey particular themes in the history of religion across the different religions of antiquity and to set up comparisons and contrasts, resonances and discontinuities, and thus reach a profounder understanding of the religious experience in the ancient world. Topics to be covered will include: women, conversion, language, death, magic, sacrifice and purity.

Also available in this series:

WOMEN AND RELIGION IN THE FIRST CHRISTIAN CENTURIES
Deborah F. Sawyer

THE CRUCIBLE OF CHRISTIAN MORALITY
J. Ian H. McDonald

SACRED LANGUAGES AND SACRED TEXTS
John Sawyer

DEATH, BURIAL AND REBIRTH IN THE RELIGIONS OF ANTIQUITY
Jon Davies

TEACHERS AND TEXTS IN THE ANCIENT WORLD

Philosophers, Jews and Christians

H. Gregory Snyder

London and New York

First published 2000
by Routledge
11 New Fetter Lane, London EC4P 4EE

Simultaneously published in the USA and Canada
by Routledge
29 West 35th Street, New York, NY 10001

Routledge is an imprint of the Taylor & Francis Group

© 2000 H. Gregory Snyder

Typeset in Garamond by RefineCatch Limited, Bungay, Suffolk
Printed and bound in Great Britain by
TJ International Ltd, Padstow, Cornwall

British Library Cataloguing in Publication Data
A catalogue record for this book is available from the
British Library

Library of Congress Cataloging in Publication Data
Snyder, H. Gregory, 1959–
Teachers and texts in the ancient world : philosophers,
Jews, and Christians / H. Gregory Snyder.
p. cm. – (Religion in the first Christian centuries)
Includes bibliographical references and index.
1. Philosophy, Ancient. 2. Philosophy – Study and teaching –
History. 3. Christian education – History – Early church,
ca. 30–600. 4. Jewish religious education – History.
I. Title. II. Series.
B177 S59   2000
180 – dc21   99–088076

ISBN 0–415–21765–2 (hbk)
ISBN 0–415–21766–0 (pbk)

Plate 1 Philosopher, courtesy of the Ostia Museum.

CONTENTS

PLATES

PREFACE

"Book! you lie there; the fact is, you
books must know your places. You'll do
to give us the bare words and facts, but
we come in to supply the thoughts."

Stubb, *Moby Dick*

While no one is likely to confuse the second mate of the *Pequod* with
a scholar or intellectual, Stubb's remark about books is admirably
direct and most relevant to the present study. Pierre Bourdieu says
much the same thing in a more sophisticated idiom:

> Re-siting reading and the text read in a history of cultural
> production and transmission means giving oneself a chance
> of understanding the reader's relation to his or her object
> and also of understanding how the relation to the object is
> part and parcel of that object.
>
> (Bourdieu 1990: 101)

However it is stated, Bourdieu's (and Stubb's) insight is one of the
fundamental convictions lying behind this book. Written texts presume users and contexts of use; they are embedded in a wide variety
of human transactions. They should not and cannot be understood as
isolated objects. Therefore, I have attempted to provide not another
"history of the book," but rather a contribution towards a "history of
the reader," or a "history of the reader–text relation."

This study was initially motivated by a curiosity about the "suspicion of written texts" supposedly widespread in the ancient world.
In certain fields, especially in biblical studies, this has become something of a scholarly commonplace. As a first step in getting at what

people thought about written texts – surely too complex to be summed up in a single phrase – it seemed wise to discuss how texts actually functioned for their users. The present book is the fruit of that preliminary step. A comprehensive treatment of the reader's relation to written texts in the ancient world would also require that we pay close attention to explicit statements about the strengths and weaknesses of writing, e.g., that books escape from the control of their authors and the proper context for their interpretation, that a fixed text of any kind cannot stand in a dialogical relation with the reader, and so on. The promise of this comprehensive study will be the subject of future work.

By attempting to give an account of teachers and texts within a total of eight different school/group settings, I have embarked on a very broad enterprise. Specialists in one or more of the areas covered here will no doubt think of subjects that should be added or taken away from the individual chapters, or of relevant secondary literature that might have been explored. Nevertheless, for the project to be useful, it is not necessary to give a comprehensive treatment of all of the areas treated; the goal has been to illustrate the range of possible relationships between teachers, texts, and students. That being said, I believe that reasonable coverage has been provided in most areas.

The nature of the project also requires that I reconnoiter terrain that will be familiar to many readers. Classicists may find the story of Andronicus to be old news; similarly, students of Judaism and Christianity will probably not require an introduction to pesher commentary at Qumran. Still, in order to have all the requisite material in view, and to address readers with different areas of expertise, I have found it necessary to err on the side of including, rather than excluding, relevant subjects.

Stubb's remark is true of books in general, and it is also true of this particular book: many people have come in to supply much of what is seen and much of what is unseen. Bentley Layton and Heinrich von Staden served as advisors on the dissertation that lies behind this book; in addition to the concrete assistance they have provided, both of them have been models of personal and professional integrity. I have also learned a great deal by watching Wayne Meeks ask sensitive and subtle questions of the ancient world, and this work bears the impress of his approach throughout, not to mention many discrete suggestions offered in conversation and correspondence. Steven Fraade has provided expert advice on Chapter 5. Allen Hilton has been a faithful conversation partner on many subjects, in particular, the material on Paul and Acts. Harry Attridge, Stan Stowers and Wayne Meeks evaluated this study in its dissertation form and all of them offered perceptive criticism and advice. Bob Kraft, Natalie Kampen, Ann Ellis Hanson, Seth Schwartz, and Roger Bagnall have graciously responded to my queries with sage advice on several topics. I am also grateful to Bob Scott and the staff of the Electronic Text Center at Butler Library, who were always quick to supply me with advice on things electronic, to Karl Plank, Chair of the Religion Department at Davidson College and to Tom Poundstone, Chair of the Religious Studies Department at St Mary's College of California, for generously supporting the project. Finally, my thanks go to authorities at the Ostia Museum, the British Library, the Papyrus Collection at the Staatliche Museen zu Berlin Preussischer Kulturbesitz, and to the Israel Museum, for their kind permission to reproduce photographs of items in their collections.

Finally, I am grateful to Richard Stoneman and also to John Sawyer for accepting this book into the Religion in the First Christian Centuries series. It has been my aim to produce a volume that will engage the attention of scholars without discouraging readers having a more general interest in teaching and literary practices in antiquity. While the present work carries a somewhat heavier proportion of scholarly apparatus than its companion volumes, my hope is that those readers who have profited from other fine titles in the series will find this one to be worthy of its peers. Rob Curtis at Routledge has very capably shepherded this project in the long path that lies between manuscript and book.

The idea for this book and our four-year-old son Stephan entered the world at about the same time, and both have simultaneously vied for attention. Managing both of these tasks would have been more difficult without the kindly assistance of my mother-in-law, Anna Procyk. My father has also aided this project materially in several ways. My wife Motria has also read the entire manuscript and made many useful suggestions. She has been wonderfully supportive throughout, and it is with great pleasure that I dedicate this study to her.

ABBREVIATIONS

Bibliographic nomenclature for periodicals may be found in *L'Année philologique* or in the *Oxford Classical Dictionary*. For papyrological and epigraphical publications, I generally follow the abbreviations to be found in Liddell–Scott–Jones.

Unless otherwise noted, I have used the Loeb Classical Library (LCL) editions of Greek and Latin authors. Texts in the Oxford, Sources chrétiennes or Teubner editions have also been consulted when appropriate.

ANRW	Hildegard Temporini and Wolfgang Haase (eds) *Aufstieg und Niedergang der römischen Welt*, Berlin and New York: Walter de Gruyter, 1972–present
CAG	*Commentaria Aristoteles Graecarum*
CIJ	*Corpus Inscriptionum Iudaicarum*
CMG	Corpus Medicorum Graecorum
Corpus	*Corpus dei papiri filosofici greci i latini*, 5 vols, Florence: Leo S. Olschki
CPJ	*Corpus Papyrorum Judaicarum*
DJD	Discoveries in the Judean Desert
DJDJ	Discoveries in the Judaean Desert of Jordan (early version of DJD)
EAH	Τὸ Ἔργον τῆς Ἀρχαιολογικῆς Ἑταιρείας
K	C. G. Kühn's edition of Galen
LAB	*Liber Antiquitatum Biblicarum*
LCL	Loeb Classical Library
Life	Porphyry's *Life of Plotinus*
LSJ	Liddell–Scott–Jones, Greek–English Lexicon
OCT	Oxford Classical Texts
OGIS	*Orientis Graeci Inscriptiones Selectae*
PG	Patrologia Graeca (Migne)

RAC   *Reallexikon für Antike und Christentum*
RE   *Realencyclopädie der klassischen Altertumwissenschaft*
SC   Sources chrétiennes
SEG   *Supplementum Epigraphicum Graecum* (Amsterdam)
SIG   *Sylloge Inscriptionum Graecarum*
SVF   *Stoicorum Veterum Fragmenta*
TAM   *Tituli Asiae Minoris*

GENERAL INTRODUCTION

About the time that Seneca was advising Lucilius on the use of books, when Cornutus and Persius were hunched over their writing tables, while the slaves at the Villa of the Papyri saw to the maintenance and expansion of the soon-to-be-buried library at Herculaneum, other groups in Rome were also busy appropriating texts. Christians and Jews in their small conventicles scattered around the city of Rome and elsewhere around the Mediterranean were, like members of philosophical schools, consumers of texts. In all these gatherings, large and small, public and private, written texts were part of the everyday business of teaching and learning. We have a vivid representation of one such occasion in a grave relief from Ostia, found on page vi of the prelims of this volume. Elevated above his audience, the speaker raises his right hand in a teaching gesture, while holding a closed bookroll in his left. The beard and bookroll suggest a philosopher rather than a rhetorician.[1] Indeed, the presence of a written text is probably not a prop that would be favored by orators, who prized *ex tempore* utterance and freedom from any reliance on script.[2] In a standing position, he is at a disadvantage for reading, since most readers preferred to sit when handling a roll.[3] The rapt attention of the figures to the teacher's right, and the apparent debate prompted by his remarks among those on his left testify to the effect of his speech on the hearers. Here we have a person who through his mastery of texts has integrated the wisdom of previous thinkers and who produces on his own authority a synthesis of his knowledge. Still, a book is present, even if closed. Strikingly, while this teacher has moved beyond reliance on texts, he is in the process of becoming a text himself: in the foreground, two scribes busily commit the words of the speaker to tablets.

As in this instance, texts were only components of complex interactions within school settings, interactions that I have called

1

"textual performances." In order to be brought to life, a text required a performer and almost always presumed the presence of an audience. This audience may have partaken in the performance to a greater or lesser degree. Such a performance necessarily took place in a specific environment on a concrete occasion, and this too bears significantly on the overall performance. And in the ancient world, even the text itself, whatever it may be, is simply one particular version of a work, say Aristotle's *Topics*, that might vary significantly from other recensions: perhaps it is the full text, perhaps it is a paraphrase, an epitome, or a commentary like *PFay*. 3, which contains the *Topics* along with interspersed paraphrase.

The term "textual performance" may suggest something akin to a dramatic reading, and while it was often the case in the ancient world that public reading happened this way, I use the term in a broader sense. The language of performance reminds us that in most cases written texts were brought to life by readers or teachers addressing an audience, just as music is brought to life by musical performers. In some cases, teachers coached students as they sought to give a proper performance of a text, assisting in phrasing and elocution. Proper performance required practice. When a student in Epictetus' class boasts of his ability simply to "read Chrysippus," we see that the ability to read a text smoothly can be taken as evidence that one has understood it.[4] When Aulus Gellius says that a poor reader "murders the thought," we see the same assumption at work: an ability to phrase and articulate the text properly demonstrates understanding.[5] We also know of occasions where "textual performers" would display books in public and ask onlookers to select random passages to be explained. Galen thought of this as a type of performance similar to his publicly staged dissections of goats and pigs.[6] And so reading as it actually happened in the ancient world shares many significant aspects with modern notions of performance.

The idea of performance is also useful because in many cases, audiences who listen to a musical performance or who witness a dramatic production are having something brought before them that they could not acquire on their own. Nowadays, it is a small thing for most (perhaps all) of the people reading this book to appropriate a written text. But for a multitude of reasons, this would not have been the case in the ancient world, particularly with challenging philosophical and religious writings. An individual able to serve as a guide to a School's texts would have seemed an obvious necessity to most people. The following quote from Augustine illustrates the point:

> When I was only about twenty years of age Aristotle's book
> on the 'Ten Categories' came into my hands. Whenever my
> teacher at Carthage and others who were reputed to be
> scholars mentioned this book, their cheeks would swell with
> self-importance, so that the title alone was enough to make
> me stand agape, as though I were poised over some wonder-
> ful divine mystery . . . Other people told me that they
> had understood it only with difficulty, after the most
> learned masters had not only explained it to them but also
> illustrated it with a wealth of diagrams.[7]

Augustine notes with obvious pride that he was able to understand
the book without such help. In any case, people in antiquity would
have viewed such unbrokered access to a text in the same way that
most people today would look at a person who decided to represent
him- or herself in court. It is a rare person who would stroll into a
law library to solve a legal problem or to learn about the law. First,
such texts are not widely available, being found only in specialized
collections or in the hands of legal practitioners. Second, even with
access to such collections, most people would be incapable of excav-
ating material relevant to the situation at hand. Third, the texts are
written in a particular jargon that requires special training to understand. The analogy to legal literature is particularly apt because in
modern legal debate appeal to precedent has special weight, just as
it did in ancient philosophical and religious argument. Just as an
attorney builds a compelling case by appeal to precedent, just as a
judge decides a case by considering relevant decisions, so ancient
philosophical and religious teachers built their cases on appeals to
the texts and traditions of their School, whether it was Taurus the
Platonist reading from his teacher's notes, Philodemus of Gadara
citing texts of Epicurean founders, or Paul of Tarsus making appeal
to the Septuagint. In groups where written texts were central, individuals able to serve as text-brokers accordingly occupied a position
of power and prestige.

Finally, thinking of reading in terms of performance causes us to
question certain habits of mind encouraged by the ubiquity of print
and high literacy. For example, we often use the name of an author
as a euphemism for the books of that author: we say "Aristotle"
when we mean Aristotle's books. We presume that Aristotle reduced
to print form – desiccated, if you will – can be rehydrated and
restored to full-blown Aristotle without suffering any losses in the
transition, and our language reflects this assumption. But what if we

were to reserve that use of "Aristotle," not for the written text containing Aristotle's words, but for those words brought alive on specific occasions by a performer for an audience? When a teacher asks her students, "What does Aristotle say?" and then reads a relevant portion of text, followed, perhaps, by a short explanation, or another bit of text, when students and teacher discuss and clarify the issues, is it not then that we can more aptly claim to hear "what Aristotle says"? It is at moments such as these that we have a heightened chance to encounter Aristotle's thought. And strictly speaking, it is only then that utterance is produced – that "Aristotle" *says* anything – or that this utterance is *heard*. Of course, we have to do here with an interpretation of Aristotle, but the same is true for the solitary reader; the "Aristotle" that emerges from both reading transactions is every bit an interpretive product.

All this points to an intellectual bias that privileges written texts as self-sufficient vehicles of meaning while remaining blind to the complexities involved in appropriating these texts on specific occasions. This reflexive habit of mind has been the subject of criticism for some time, though it has yet to appear on the list of endangered opinions. In his call for a "sociology of texts," Donald McKenzie writes, "each reading is peculiar to its occasion, each can be at least partially recovered from the physical forms of the text, and the differences in readings constitute an informative history."[8] In a similar vein, John Dagenais describes how the formal aspects of manuscript evidence are often overlooked by modern textual critics:

> Tens of thousands of medieval manuscripts exist, not as "vehicles for readings" to be discarded in the process of edition-making, chopped up into lists of variants and leaves of plates, but as living witnesses to the dynamic, chaotic, error-fraught world of medieval literary life that we have preferred to view till now through the smoked glass of critical editions.[9]

No doubt our failure to attend to the forms of texts stems from our own experience as readers. The format of the modern book is for the most part conventional, and our way of appropriating knowledge from it, entirely habitual and therefore largely invisible. With their standardized layout, modern books appear uncircumstanced and inviolate, unaffected by conditions of use and appropriation.[10] Not only do we often fail to understand the subtleties involved in our own reading transactions – how they are constrained by the forms of texts – we are also prone to import these assumptions into our understanding of ancient reading transactions. This makes it especially challenging for modern people to appreciate how ancient readers felt when approaching their texts. To understand this, we need to gain a feel for an age where knowledge committed to texts was fluid and malleable, ephemeral at times, hard to find and difficult to interpret.

In pursuit of this goal, we will explore the many different kinds of textual encounters that occurred in religious and philosophical groups. We will examine a range of literary activities that these groups performed on and with their central texts: collecting and distributing them, defining and maintaining canons of authoritative works, writing commentaries, as well as excerpting, epitomizing, or otherwise rewriting them. In a few instances, we are fortunate enough to possess actual manuscripts, as with the papyrus commentaries on Aristotle and Plato or the Dead Sea Scrolls. Paleographic details and the organization of information on the page often hold precious clues about the role these texts played in study situations. Most importantly (and interestingly), we shall be on the lookout for explicit remarks about the use of texts in teaching situations, and how teachers deployed these writings in the business of teaching.

All of the groups to be examined may be described as "text-centered."[11] By this term, I mean to include those groups who were fundamentally concerned to study, maintain, transmit a discrete set of authoritative texts. Such texts may be oral: rabbinic Jews are one example of a group who organized themselves around a text that was not, in principle, committed to writing. For the present, however, we will consider groups who would have pointed to a corpus of writings as especially important for their group identity. Within this class of text-centered groups we shall examine individual members, all of whom perform certain operations on their books. To different degrees, these groups sought to catalogue and organize their texts, maintain them by textual criticism, epitomize, paraphrase, or expand them, write commentaries upon them, and finally, to study them in private and corporately. If we ask which groups in the ancient world engaged in these activities, we find that both religious and philosophical groups are candidates for study: Jews and Christians, Stoics, Epicureans, Aristotelians, Platonists, all come under this heading. More might have been included – Pythagoreans, for example, or the medical schools; for now, I have elected to treat representatives of the four main philosophical Schools, as well as Jews and Christians.

By treating these groups together, I do not mean to imply that they would have all viewed their central texts in the same way, i.e., that a Stoic would have accorded the same status to the writings of Chrysippus that a Jew would have accorded to the Torah. This possibility is not precluded of course, but the comparison does not rest on that assumption.[12] Instead, I approach the evidence, not by asking about attitudes towards the texts and whether they are venerated sufficiently to merit the appellation "scripture," but rather about how they functioned within the group, and the various manipulations to which they were subjected. Indeed, such a study of the function and use of texts should serve as a prolegomenon to any claims about "attitudes" that members might have taken towards their corpus of writings.

There is also the pressing question of whether religious and philosophical groups are similar enough to sustain fruitful comparison. Certainly we find important differences, in intellectual commitments, in ritual behaviors, and in social organization.[13] Even pagan observers such as Galen noted that Jews and Christians acquiesced to "undemonstrated laws," not to the dictates of reason as befitted those taking a scientific approach to things.[14] It is important, however, to note that Galen does not reserve the term "school" for groups choosing the proper scientific mode of doing business, while classing Jews and Christians under a different heading. They are all classed as "sects" (*haireseis*) or "schools" (*diatribai*). They do not sacrifice this appellation by carrying on dogmatically. Indeed, many if not most physicians and philosophers are content to appeal simply to the undemonstrated pronouncements of founder-figures and so behave unphilosophically, to Galen's mind.[15] So while it may be the case that according to Galen, true philosophers would operate differently than the followers of Moses and Christ, in practice, they do not. And while Galen obviously thinks of himself as a model for philosophical inquiry, many of his commitments would strike moderns as quite religious in character: Asclepius won his undying loyalty by saving the famous physician from a fatal condition due to an abscess.[16]

These remarks of Galen are not the only evidence demonstrating that the boundary between philosophy and what we today think of as religion was rather undefined. Joining a philosophical sect amounted to a kind of conversion: moral and spiritual transformation was the goal.[17] Epicureans gathered together in groups for the purpose of "attaining salvation through each other."[18] The Stoic philosopher Cornutus expresses this hope for his manual of Stoic etymologies, that by it,

> young men be introduced to piety but not to superstition, and taught to sacrifice and to pray, to worship and to take oaths in proper fashion and appropriate moderation in whatever situation may arise.[19]

Here in particular, we are in the presence of something more akin to religion than philosophy, given our modern understanding of those terms. As others have observed, philosophical groups were more than intellectual think-tanks; they were groups dedicated to cultivating a particular way of life.[20] Like religionists, philosophers were often viewed askance for their idiosyncratic commitments and choices of lifestyle. Impressed by his teacher Sotion, the young Seneca ceased to eat meat. However, his father, who "detested philosophy," feared that this habit might be taken as evidence of membership in a foreign cult (*superstitio*), and compelled him to resume his normal diet.[21]

Still, the issue will hardly be decided by adducing anecdotal evidence on either side of the question, showing members of religious groups acting philosophically, or philosophers acting religiously. Part of the problem lies rather with the modern categories "philosophy" and "religion," and the social *loci* for the pursuit of these activities, namely, "school" and "church." Loveday Alexander observes,

> Deeper than any awareness of apparent differences of structure is the gut feeling that, at bottom, "going to school" and "going to church" are two entirely different kinds of activity ... the comparison seems to be an attempt to assimilate two fundamentally different phenomena.[22]

I suggest that a significant portion of the unease lies within the language we use to describe these entities and the concepts rooted therein. Taxonomies of knowledge informed by Enlightenment categories have traditionally separated religious and philosophical discourse, indeed, set them at odds, and the nagging sense of incommensurability we feel is a function of our own patterns of thought, etched as they are by these reflexive ideas about the differences between "school" and "church." Wafting along in the train of these terms is a host of images: on the one hand, the chalk-board, the lectern, not to mention a long history of humanistic learning often standing in opposition to ecclesiastical hegemony; on the other hand, 1500 years of popes and pageantry, dogma and ritual that have left us with a dense cloud of images and pre-reflective notions connected with the idea of church. Mortarboard and miter, so similar in many respects, seem to be set orthogonally against each other, and these predispositions cannot help but infect our understanding of "school" and "church." As such, both terms may cause us to misjudge the ancient evidence.

If this is indeed the case, we would be well advised to scrap both terms entirely when talking about the ancient world. Strictly speaking, in the period of interest, the term "group" is probably preferable for both of these entities, school and church, as it is not freighted with pre-existing conceptions. It carries the right level of ambiguity; when necessary, it can be honed by adding the adjective "religious" or "philosophical." Whenever possible, I have attempted to favor this usage. Still, it is not necessary to go quite so far as to avoid the term "school" altogether. What is required, however, is to broaden the term in significant respects. No institution should be presumed. A school may be comprised of one teacher and one student. It may perish with its teacher, or it may survive under a successor. Nor should it be understood necessarily as "academic" in our modern sense of the term. So in spite of the risks, I have continued to employ "school" as a group designation, though it should be understood in the loosest and most general sense. I use the term "School" (capital "S") for the broader movement (Stoics or Epicureans) of which a "school" (lower-case "s") is a part. Thus a "School" is comprised of a congeries of "schools," which may have different degrees of identification with or attachment to the larger School. I will observe this distinction throughout the volume.

A kindred objection might also be raised: philosophers (and their students) belonged for the most part to the learned and elite classes; the same cannot be said for Jews and Christians. "There are those among us," says Justin, "who do not even know the forms of letters, who are uneducated and barbarous in speech."[23] The early Christians could not deny the charge, nor should we. Still, not all members of the various philosophical Schools were uniformly wealthy. Among the members of the Epicurean School, for example, are found some individuals who were manual laborers or who had not learned letters.[24] Conversely, among Jews, individuals such as Philo can hardly be described as impoverished, nor were the first Christians

8

drawn exclusively from the lumpenproletariat as was once believed.[25] This being said, the comparison I seek to make does not depend on forcing philosophers, Jews, and Christians into the same social class. All these groups were committed to distinctive forms of life and thought, all of them drew on texts as sources of authority, and all of them featured teachers who facilitated this process. It is this likeness that justifies the comparison.

Finally, readers familiar with the state of philosophy and philo- sophical groups in the Hellenistic and especially in the Imperial ages will wonder whether my strategy of dividing the evidence under the traditional rubrics of Stoic, Epicurean, Aristotelian, and Platonist potentially misrepresents the complex mixture of intellectual com- mitments that characterized these groups. Did Platonists read only Plato? Did Aristotelians read only Aristotle? Traditional doxo- graphic divisions become increasingly problematic during the first and second centuries CE and beyond.[26] Porphyry, for example, refers to Trypho, the "Stoic and Platonist"; he also observes that the writ- ings of Plotinus, whom I have treated as a Platonist, are filled with concealed Stoic and Peripatetic doctrines.[27] At an earlier period, we find Seneca reading and benefiting from the writings of Epicurus. He is, however, quick to apologize for "crossing over into the enemy's camp"; the pride he takes in his boundary-crossing guerrilla raids on Epicurean texts suggests that strongly felt divisions and allegiances did exist. We also find a highly developed sense of group loyalty in Plutarch, who writes polemical tracts against rival Schools, and as we shall see in Chapter 4, the curriculum of the second-century Platonist Alcinous does not include any documents other than Plato's dialogues. Lucian premises his satire *Philosophies for Sale* on the recognizable differences between the philosophers of various Schools. So while an approach based on doxographic categor- ies runs the risk of presuming too much theoretical consistency in human thought and behavior, it does appear that there are discern- ible joints in the ancient evidence, even if there are no impermeable boundaries. Indeed, it will become evident that these different groups manifest different ways of handling their texts.

Granting, then, that the comparative strategy I propose is intel- lectually respectable and fruitful, how may we characterize the com- plex ways in which written texts were embedded in the lives of such groups? The question is not new, of course. Some have argued that the very existence of a School might be imperiled by the loss of its writings.[28] Others have relativized the importance of books within the school setting.[29] Still others have stressed the importance of scripture for Christian groups by describing them as textual communities, or by claiming that Christianity was "constitutionally oriented to texts."[30] There is a certain vagueness in these remarks: were Christians more "textual" than Stoics? Might we not say that Epicureans were also "constitutionally oriented to texts"? Similar comments apply to the medical schools as well: medical research in antiquity depended upon the exegesis of texts, not scientific experiments. To one degree or another, most ancient school groups were constitutionally oriented to texts, or could be described as textual communities. Obviously, talking about "less" or "more" is too crude; finer distinctions are required if we wish to make fruitful comparisons. A synoptic look at the different ways texts were employed in different schools will furnish us with a richer understanding of this particular aspect of group life.

The contours of the available evidence will guide the study, and this results in a certain irregularity in organization. It does not seem, for example, that Stoics particularly cared to define a canon of texts for their School, nor did they write commentaries. As a result, the treatment of commentary among Stoics occupies a vanishingly small place. We are fortunate, however, to have a very frank and immediate look at procedures in Epictetus' school thanks to Arrian's notes; we also have Seneca's correspondence with Lucilius, some of which touches on the subject of reading. As a result, Epictetus and Seneca account for most of the evidence treated in Chapter 1. In Chapter 2, we will examine the textual habits of Epicureans. Here, the Herculaneum finds yield a rich trove of evidence. *PHerc.* 1005 in particular merits special attention: one of its major concerns is Epicurean textual practices. In sharp contrast to Stoics and Epicureans, Aristotelians of the second century were extremely assiduous commentary writers, and an examination of their practices in this area is featured in Chapter 3. Platonists (Chapter 4) also wrote commentaries on the works of Plato – not as many, it seems, as Aristotelians wrote on Aristotle's works, but some traces of the activity remain. We also have portraits of teachers using texts in the person of Taurus and of Plotinus. Finally, in Chapter 5, we shall examine several groups within Judaism that exhibit distinctive textual practices: the Qumran sectarians, scribal culture in Palestine (exclusive of Qumran), and the early Christians. I have also devoted a section to the works of Philo, even though he cannot be considered a representative of a well-defined group. Very often, the shape and extent of the evidence reflects historical accident, not ancient culture, and it will be part of the task to discern when a lacuna in the evidence reflects differences between Schools or simply the vicissitudes of preservation. If a well had not sunk above the town of Herculaneum, had a goatherd not thrown a rock into a cave in Palestine, Chapters 2 and 5 of this book would look quite different.

In general, the time boundaries for the present study run from the first century BCE through the second century CE, though these limits are somewhat permeable. On occasion, particularly enticing bodies of evidence require that we trespass these boundaries. For example, I have looked at the literary activities of certain Epicureans during the second century BCE; I have also strayed into the third century CE in order to examine Porphyry's account of Plotinus and the use of written texts in his class.

Some books revolve around one central axis; they offer the reader one main course. For better or for worse, the present work is not that kind of book. I do not argue for one central thesis. Instead this book is more akin to a buffet that offers a cluster of items. Useful conclusions are reached on a number of separate points – on Epictetus' pedagogical procedures, on the correlation between interest in books and social class, on Philo as a writer, on the role of *Jubilees* at Qumran, the portrayal of scribes in the Gospels – conclusions that are generated by the broad comparative perspective I have adopted. Still, in the course of this investigation, there is a bass chord behind the whole that emerges fully in Chapter 5, namely, the idea of teachers as "text-brokers." The appropriation of texts in the ancient world almost always involved some type of mediation by a trained specialist. Even highly literate individuals employed readers who would perform texts while their patron bathed, ate, or traveled. The mechanics of reading, however, have been much studied and are not the central focus here. I am interested in other aspects of textual appropriation: in particular, how a member of a "text-centered group" would have been introduced to the texts of the School in question. Generally, this involved the figure of a teacher who mediated a transaction between a student and a body of traditions captured in textual form.

Two significant omissions in my treatment should be acknowledged at the outset. The first concerns the rabbinic evidence. A complete study of Jewish groups in the second century CE should take account of this material. The activity of Judah ha-Nasi in codifying the Mishnah might be fruitfully compared to the editorial work of Andronicus, Thrasyllus, and Porphyry. Indeed, the stress on orality within this tradition would provide an interesting point of contrast between groups organized around oral texts and groups organized around written texts. Much of the evidence for first- and second-century Jewish teachers, however, derives from sources written two or three centuries after the incidents they describe. In so far as it was in the interest of the rabbis to legitimize their practices by grounding them historically, these reports are suspect. Careful and critical use of this material would enrich this study, but there is much to discuss even if the rabbinic evidence is held in abeyance.

A difficult problem arises with the Christians of the second century: when, exactly, do the books of the New Testament become the central textual axis of Christian groups, and when did they attain their present form? Obviously, this happened incrementally: some books achieved scriptural status sooner in some places, later in others. Some books that held scriptural status for a time were later removed from canon lists. One would need to begin with Origen and extend into the post-Constantinian era to allow for a time lapse similar to that which separated first-century Stoics, Epicureans, and others, from the writings of their founders. Thus in order to maintain an apt synopsis of the uses of texts by these groups, I have limited myself to the earliest phase of the Christian movement, when Christians had not yet added new scriptures to the collection they shared with Jews. Even with these constraints, some very interesting results are obtained that illuminate certain aspects of the New Testament and early Christian literature.

Nomenclature

In what follows, there will be much discussion of epitomes, excerpts, anthologies, and various kinds of abbreviated literature. Ancient readers were familiar with these types of literature, for which a rich (and very untidy) vocabulary developed.[31] Here is the terminology I have adopted for the present study:

Abbreviate: to delete large portions of a written text, leaving some parts unchanged. The result is a skeletal version of the original work.

Anthologize: to bring together a collection of excerpts drawn from one or more written sources. In principle, one might speak of a "one-work anthology" in which a set of excerpts is taken from a single book, appearing in the order in which they appear in the longer version, and in principle, an anthology like this would be identical to an abbreviation.

Epitomize: to reduce the size of a text by paraphrasing. An epitome is a shortened version of an original text. The process of epitomizing may also be brought to bear on a more or less defined collection of works which gives expression to a body of dogma. This type of epitome embraces a body of thought rather than one specific written *Vorlage*. Epicurus' epitomes, for example, present a body of thought in reduced and simplified form.

Excerpt (verb and noun): "To excerpt" is to traverse a text gleaning pieces of special interest. An excerpt is a single fragment of a text. A compilation of excerpts drawn from one or more works is an anthology.

Paraphrase (verb and noun): to take a piece of a work and rephrase it in different language. Writers of commentaries and epitomes employ this technique frequently. One could paraphrase a text and come up with one of shorter, equal, or longer length. The end result of this process is a paraphrase.

Re-present: this describes a complex of activities including epitomizing, expanding, adding material, adding comment. The term is used chiefly in Chapter 5 with reference to a type of literature termed "re-presented Bible."

1

"NOT SUBJECTS OF A DESPOT": STOICS

While on holiday in the country, Cicero wished to consult some books not in his possession, so he repaired to the library of his friend Lucullus. There, he found Marcus Cato "surrounded by piles of Stoic books."[1] Stoics were apparently famous for their literary production: Plutarch describes Chrysippus as a man who put down absolutely everything that came into his head, while Lucian satirizes the bookishness of Hermotimus, an aspiring and rather ingenuous adherent of Stoicism.[2] Members of the School had a reputation, it seems, for being eager producers and consumers of books.

In this and subsequent chapters, I will generally follow a basic template when approaching the literary practices of the Schools, moving from less invasive to more invasive procedures. So I will consider whether the group(s) in question bothered to collect and organize their School texts, and whether they sought to maintain them through textual criticism. Then, we shall ask about the practice of commentary. Following this, we will explore more invasive procedures that involve "re-presenting" the texts: altering them either by epitomizing, paraphrasing, or expanding. Finally, we shall pursue the question of use, exploring any available testimony that promises to shed light on the way that members of these groups used books in their gatherings.

Placing the Stoics up against this template, we find it possible to vault quickly over the first few sections. While it would be rash to claim that no Stoics cared to organize and preserve their texts or to write commentaries upon them, the lack of evidence about these types of activities suggests that Stoics simply did not pursue these practices as avidly as members of other Schools. There is little evidence that Stoics thought it important to establish a recognized canon of the works of their founders, or to engage in textual criticism on these works; nor did they write commentaries on the texts of

Zeno, Chrysippus, or Cleanthes. The Suda, a tenth-century encyclo-
pedia of ancient words, writers, and writings, attributes a four-
volume commentary to a certain Aristocles of Lampsacus, but
Aristocles is otherwise unknown and the Suda is notoriously unreli-
able in such matters.[3] They preferred, it seems, to comment on
Homer; perhaps Homer should be considered a school text for
Stoics. Some Stoic writers and teachers repackaged the writings of
their founder-figures: Cornutus' *Epidrome* is one example, and this
will be treated before we broach the subject of use. What we do have
in relative abundance is evidence from Epictetus and Seneca about
the role of written texts within two very different kinds of teaching
situations. In his notes from Epictetus' class, Arrian shows how
written texts functioned in one philosopher's classroom. Seneca's
correspondence with Lucilius yields a glimpse of the role of books
in another philosopher's private reflection and moral formation. The
Diatribes of Musonius Rufus will occupy us briefly, but the material
from Epictetus and Seneca offers the most promise.

"Things handed down to us": re-presented texts

As this study proceeds, it will become evident that adherents of
many of the Schools (and schools) under investigation epitomized,
anthologized, commented upon, and freely rewrote their central
texts. As noted, however, there is very little evidence for these practices in the case of the Stoics. One partial exception is Cornutus'
Compendium of the Traditions of Greek Theology, or *Epidrome*, a book
containing etymological remarks on ancient myths that the author
has culled from earlier Stoic texts and traditions and re-presented in
convenient handbook form.[4] A contemporary of Seneca, L. Annaeus
Cornutus was the author of numerous philological, philosophical,
and rhetorical works; he was also a mentor to Persius and Lucan.[5]
Apart from the *Epidrome*, we possess only fragments and echoes of
many lost works: one directed against Aristotle's *Categories*, a book
on the soul, commentaries on Virgil, a treatise on figurative language, an unknown number of books on rhetoric, on Latin orthography, and finally a two-volume work, probably on Stoic physics.[6]
His exile (or death, according to some sources), probably took place
between 63 and 65 CE.[7]

At the conclusion of the *Epidrome*, Cornutus expresses his hopes
for the book:

Although this [the subject matter of the work as a whole]

has been said at greater length and in greater detail by the older philosophers, it was my desire to hand them on to you in this condensed form in our days. For a ready knowledge of these matters even to this brief extent is useful.

The goal is that "young men be introduced to piety but not to superstition, and taught to sacrifice and to pray, to worship and to take oaths in proper fashion and appropriate moderation in whatever situation may arise."[8] In short, Cornutus hopes that readers of this work might become properly educated citizens, neither departing from their cultural heritage, nor accepting it in a naive and superficial way. Encouraging as it does the proper practice of piety, sacrifice, and prayer, the enterprise is thoroughly religious in character – hardly philosophical by modern standards.

At first glance, the *Epidrome* does not exhibit the features of a Stoic school text; none of the Stoic fascination with dialectic is in evidence, for example. Instead, the author uses etymology to interpret ancient myths in terms of Stoic physics. Information about the origin and structure of the universe is concealed within the names of mythological characters. Here is how the text begins:

> The "Heaven (*ouranos*)," my child, encloses in its circle the earth, the sea, and all things upon the earth and in the sea. And that is why it obtained its designation: because it is the upper boundary (*ouros*) of the universe and delimits (*horizōn*) nature. There are some, however, who say that it is called *ouranos* from its "tending to (*ōrein* or *ōreuein*)," i.e., guarding, entities . . . . Yet others derive it from "to be seen above (*horasthai anō*)."[9]

The etymology of Hera, for example, derives from the Greek term for air (*aēr*). So when the myth-makers report that Zeus punished Hera by hanging her from the ether, attaching heavy weights to her feet, it means that air is stretched downwards, anchored by earth and sea (*Epidr.* 26.14–15). Kronos is said to devour his children since Time (*chronos*) likewise devours all things (*Epidr.* 7.4–5); Apollo (the sun) and Artemis (the moon) are both represented as archers because of their far-ranging rays (*Epidr.* 65.1–4). Ancient poets, says Cornutus, are simply discussing Stoic physics in a mythopoetic idiom.

Careful study shows that the *Epidrome* owes extensive debts to earlier Stoic literature. Judgments about sources are problematic,

however, since Cornutus never gives a citation for any of his etymologies. Zeno, Chrysippus, and Cleanthes are clearly among his
sources, as are other Stoic teachers.[10] Cornutus' decision not to
explicitly name his sources is puzzling: it would have been a simple
matter to insert, "Chrysippus said," or "Zeno wrote," and by doing
so to create an aura of hoary venerability for his remarks. It may be
that the genre of the work is incompatible with extensive citation of
sources, i.e., it is a school handbook, rather than a scholarly treatise.
Alternatively (or additionally), these observations may have been
considered "school property," relieving any need for explicit
citation. He is almost certainly drawing on works similar to the
Epidrome, texts which he would have inherited from his own
teachers. Written traditions within the Stoic School appear to
have been in a rather amorphous state, consistent with the lack of
attention to activities such as commentary and canonization. Indeed,
Seneca says as much when he speaks of the "unruly multitude
(*turba*)" of Stoic writings:

> Suppose we should desire to sort out each motto from the
> general stock (*ex turba*); to whom shall we credit them? To
> Zeno, Cleanthes, Chrysippus, Panaetius, or Posidonius? We
> Stoics are not subjects of a despot: each of us lays claim to his
> own freedom.[11]

Stoics were certainly not unique in circulating their texts in frag-
mented and partial forms; compared to the other School literature
we will encounter, however, Stoic writings were indeed a very unruly
mob, as Seneca says.

The only time that Cornutus does mention one of his predecessors,
it is for the sake of disagreement. In a discussion about Heracles,
Cornutus makes a dig at Cleanthes:

> And it is indeed possible to understand the twelve labors as
> pertaining not to the hero but to the god, as Cleanthes did.
> But it does not appear to be necessary to always give priority
> to that inventor of ingenious arguments.[12]

The remark about ingenious arguments carries a pejorative air, and
echoes the many criticisms directed at Stoics for their seemingly
endless fascination with intricate and eristical arguments.

While it is not evident from the *Epidrome*, we know that Persius
bequeathed all of his 700 volumes of Chrysippus to Cornutus;

presumably, these documents were used and prized by both men. So we may safely infer that the writings of Chrysippus and perhaps Cleanthes, too, were found in Cornutus' house, and that they must have played some role in the education that went on there. The *Epidrome*, however, is not a way of approaching the texts of Zeno, Chrysippus, or Cleanthes as ends in themselves. Instead, it culls material from various Stoic sources in order to provide a tool for the proper understanding of something else; namely, ancient myths. In this case, Stoic texts are cannibalized rather than rewritten.

"See how well I read": texts in use

Musonius Rufus

While the *Diatribes* and Fragments of Musonius Rufus are also of obvious interest for the philosophy of the Late Stoa, they are of slight importance in providing evidence for the use of texts in teaching environments. Their editor has reworked and polished them to such a degree that many of the interesting and informative details about pedagogical procedures in Musonius' school have been lost:

> Lucius is consciously playing the role of Xenophon to his Socrates and so consistently transforming what must have been scenes of vivid discussion full of the rapid give and take of debate into rather conventionalized essays on ethical questions that the portrait of Musonius loses sharpness and vigor.[13]

It was the unusual, rather than the usual, that merited preservation, whereas we are more interested in the day-to-day regimen of teaching and learning.[14] We shall see that Chrysippus was a very real presence in Epictetus' classroom; we would not know that Chrysippus even existed, based on Musonius' *Discourses*, which feature two references to Zeno, one to Cleanthes, and none to Chrysippus. Nor do we find any references to books by these authors.[15]

Nevertheless, in spite of appearances, Musonius probably spent a great deal of time guiding his students through technical material. It was the business of philosophy to discriminate good arguments from bad ones, and this required the study of logic. Philosophy must confer on its devotees "the ability to remain superior to others in debate, to distinguish the false from the true, and to refute the one and to confirm the other," and it is practically assured that Musonius drilled his students in these skills.[16] Epictetus reports that Musonius chided him for overlooking the missing member in a syllogism.[17] But while it is virtually assured that Musonius dealt with technical material, it seems that he did not use classic Stoic texts in a systematic way as a vehicle for this kind of instruction.

It is entirely possible that Musonius would have cited Stoic authors as authorities, but this brief glimpse at his pedagogy suggests that it was Musonius himself who was the chief center of authority in the class, not the written texts of founder-figures. In fact, Musonius claims that the ideal classroom situation would be found in the fields, with students observing their teacher bearing up under hardship and toil. "What is there to prevent a student while he is working from listening to a teacher speaking about self-control or justice or endurance?"[18] That philosophical instruction could take place in such a setting (even ideally), where the trappings of texts, tablets, and notes would have no place, suggests that written texts and detailed explication of them were not of paramount importance for Musonius' pedagogy.

Epictetus

Happily, Arrian's notes from Epictetus' class provide us with a fairly unvarnished account of life in a Stoic school. Relative to his teacher Musonius, Epictetus devoted significant amounts of attention to the reading and discussion of Stoic texts.[19] It is not an easy matter, however, to discern exactly which texts were considered central. After a brief discussion of the authors and writings found in Epictetus' class, we will explore the fourfold method that he used for the examination of texts.[20]

Many different works and writers are mentioned in the *Discourses*, but without doubt Epictetus prizes the writings of Chrysippus above all others. Other philosophers, most prominently Socrates and Diogenes, are often used for illustrative purposes, but the works of Chrysippus form the backbone of the curriculum. Epictetus mentions him more frequently than any other author, and portrays him as the "exegete of nature," which is high praise in Stoic circles.[21] It is from him that one learns "what is the administration of the universe, and what place therein the rational animal has" (1.10.10). "What," asks Epictetus, "does Chrysippus provide for us?" Speaking for Chrysippus, he answers,

> That you might know that these things are not false from
> which serenity arises and tranquillity comes to us, take my
> books and you shall know how conformable and harmonious
> with nature are the things which render me tranquil
> (1.4.28–30).

Chrysippus' discoveries are as beneficial for the soul as the gifts of
Triptolemus, the founder of agriculture, are beneficial for the body.
This is our "great good fortune," and Chrysippus is lauded as "our
great benefactor who points the way."[22] Although Epictetus often
derides mere book knowledge of Chrysippus that is not translated
into action, there can be no mistake about the importance of
Chrysippus and his books in Epictetus' school.

We do not know precisely which texts of Chrysippus were used or
in what form they were present in the classroom. Epictetus
explicitly mentions his treatise on the Paradox of the Liar, *On Things
Possible*, and also various "Introductions."[23] When a confident student asks Epictetus to test him on his knowledge of "the treatise
concerning choice" (1.4.14), there is no explicit remark that the
work is by Chrysippus, but it is not an unreasonable assumption,
given the fact that Chrysippus and his books are discussed in the
immediate context (1.4.5–9), and that boastful students tend to
parade their ability to interpret this particular author (e.g., 1.4.9).[24]
Diogenes Laertius lists a great many works by Chrysippus that
would have provided a rich palette for the entire range of logical
analysis that went on in class – works on ambiguous terms, hypothetical arguments, and on famous paradoxes and fallacies.[25]

Unfortunately, we know very little about the physical presence of
such texts in Epictetus' classroom. Presumably, many of his students,
who were wealthy enough to travel to Nicomedia for study, would
have been able to afford books. Persius, we have seen, gathered 700
volumes of Chrysippus in his personal library. On one occasion,
Epictetus mentions that a book such as *On Choice* could be had for
five denarii (1.4.16). It is probably safe to assume that Epictetus
himself would have possessed many of Chrysippus' treatises. But we
rarely catch a glimpse of the texts themselves in class. One exception
is apparent at 1.4.14, where we find a brash student saying, "take
the treatise on choice and see how well I can read it."[26] Here, it
appears that the teacher is being challenged to pick a spot in
the book for the student to explain. The remark presupposes the
presence of a text.

As for other texts that might have been present in Epictetus' classroom, we know that the writings of Zeno of Citium, the founder of the Stoic School, are also on Epictetus' list of recommended reading. He once chides a student for preferring the erotic poets Aristeides and Evenus to Chrysippus and Zeno (4.9.6), and he quotes Zeno's call to the philosophic life with approval (1.20.15–16). Nevertheless, Zeno's writings are employed only anecdotally; they appear to have had inspirational value, but when it came to technical matters, Chrysippus was the author of choice. Several other authors are mentioned, among them, Cleanthes, who is mentioned in the company of Zeno, Chrysippus, and Socrates (1.17.11–12). Epictetus knows of a treatise by Cleanthes on the same subject as Chrysippus' *On Things Possible*, (2.19.9), and he quotes parts of Cleanthes' Hymn to Zeus on several occasions.[27] Of lesser value were Stoic authors such as Antipater and Archedemus, whose works were esteemed by certain students. Epictetus refers to them only when criticizing those who think that reading a difficult book is what it means to be a philosopher.[28] A certain Crinus was proud of his ability to understand Archedemus; this knowledge did not keep him from suffering apoplexy when surprised by a mouse.[29]

While Epictetus tends to dismiss other philosophical Schools,[30] he often refers to non-Stoic philosophers for pithy, hard-hitting remarks on the high calling of the philosophic life, resistance to societal pressures and fearlessness in the face of death. Chief among these are Diogenes and Socrates, both of whom Epictetus held in high regard. Students would have been familiar with sayings of Diogenes and Socrates from grammar school days, when they learned composition by copying their aphorisms.[31] As with Zeno, the sayings and deeds of Diogenes were of great inspirational value, but nowhere is it implied that any piece of writing from Diogenes had a formal place in the curriculum. The works of Antisthenes, Diogenes' teacher, are mentioned on a few occasions, though his chief claim to fame seems to have been his association with Diogenes.[32] His books were in circulation, for students could boast about their ability to imitate his style (2.17.36). When he talks about Socrates, Platonic texts are almost always in the background.[33] The manner of quotation is close enough for us to assume that Epictetus was familiar with Platonic writings, but generally short and loose enough to give the impression of casual quotation without reference to a text.[34] Epictetus also refers to Plato (apart from Socrates), though such references are relatively sparse.[35] Students were obviously familiar both with Xenophon and with Plato, for some prided themselves on being able to imitate their style (2.17.35).

As with a great many ancient authors, Epictetus makes reference to Homer, but his way of reading hints at conflicting evaluations of the poet. He can deride people for piling up quotations from Homer which have nothing to do with the moral life (e.g., 2.19.10). But he also assumes that Homer's poems can be read as moral allegories, and that Homer meant to convey an ethical message.[36] As such, his reading list may have overlapped slightly with Cornutus'. There is no evidence, however, that texts of Homer were examined in class. Epictetus' allusions to the poet would have been familiar to students who had been steeped in Homer throughout their school career.

A few authors do not appear that one might otherwise have expected to find. No mention is made of Diogenes the Babylonian, of Boethius, Panaetius, or of Posidonius, all figures from the Middle Stoa.[37] We cannot infer that they were never used or discussed, only that they do not even appear in negative characterizations, as do the works of Antipater and Archedemus.

Finally, Epictetus himself does not appear to have written anything that was intended either for distribution or for use in the classroom.[38] This is interesting, given that most figures in the Early and Middle Stoa were prolific authors, not to mention Epictetus' near-contemporaries, Seneca and Cornutus. One could surmise that this antipathy to writing was in conformity to the example of Socrates, or to that of his teacher Musonius, who also wrote nothing.[39] Oddly enough, Epictetus believed that Socrates did write: "Did not Socrates write? – Yes, who wrote as much as he?"[40] According to Epictetus, Socrates wrote because "it was not possible for him to always have someone at hand refuting his opinions or someone whose opinions he himself might refute," and so "he refuted himself" by committing ideas to paper (2.1.32–3). Here, a written text provides a technology for having a conversation with oneself in the absence of a dialogue partner. In any case, Epictetus may well have followed Socrates' example. Since he recommends that his students have wholesome thoughts "ready at hand by night and by day; write them, read them," there is little doubt that Epictetus did the same.[41] It seems very unlikely, however, that he would have committed his teachings to a systematic treatise.

We turn now to a discussion of the way these texts might have been used in Epictetus' classroom.[42] Taking a cue from 4.4.14, it appears that the analysis of texts consisted of four phases: "But we stop with having learned what is meant, being able to explain it to someone else, analyzing the syllogism, and examining the hypothetical argument."[43] This I take to be a provisional scheme for different stages in the analysis of a text. The first involves a basic reading, ascertaining grammatical and syntactical sense. Second, comes the explanation of terms; third, the analysis of logical arguments; and fourth, proposing one's own arguments and premises.[44] This procedure may even have been familiar to students from their study of grammar: Varro speaks of the four parts of grammar, namely reading, exposition, correction, and judgment.[45] I shall address each of these stages in turn.

The standard mode of instruction began with the reading of a selection of text, probably chosen by the teacher. In some cases, Epictetus himself did the reading: "Once when a certain Roman citizen accompanied by his son had come in and was listening to one of his readings (*anagnōsma*), Epictetus said, 'This is the style of my teaching'" (2.14.1). This obviously presumes a public reading to the entire class. Interspersed explication may also be implied. Elsewhere, the same term refers to one's course of private reading, as it does at 3.26.39 and 4.4.17. The same mixed usage is also observed with *anagnōsis*, referring to a public reading in 1.26.13, but private reading in 4.4.40.[46]

An interesting term for reading which appears to be the special province of the teacher is represented by the term *epanagignōskein*. It is quite rare in the extant corpus of Greek writings. Usage favors the sense "authoritative reading": e.g., that by a teacher.[47] Epictetus employs the word for his own reading of a text, which he might prepare before class: "As soon as day breaks I call to mind briefly (or perhaps, "jot down notes about") what it is necessary for me to explain in detail."[48] The *epi-* prefix suggests an "on top of" sense: i.e., a correcting and deepening of a previous reading, presumably one given by a student. The process is probably analogous to the way in which a modern teacher of Greek or Latin, after letting students try their hand, might read through a text, touching on the possible senses of words, parsing on the fly, bringing out the nuances of particles, etc.[49] In *Encheiridion* 49, Epictetus addresses an imaginary interlocutor concerning the interpretation of Chrysippus:

> If, however, I admire the mere act of interpretation, what have I done but turned into a grammarian instead of a philosopher? The only difference, indeed, is that I interpret Chrysippus instead of Homer. Far from being proud, therefore, when somebody says to me, "Read (*epanagignōskein*) me Chrysippus," I blush the rather [*sic*], when I am unable to show such deeds as match and harmonize with his words.

Here, the term is roughly parallel to "interpret" (*exegeisthai*) and presumably carries some extra explanatory sense beyond *anagignōskein*.

Even without any added explanatory comments, a smooth, mistake-free reading would have been a great aid to the understanding. A reading that featured proper accent and division of words, together with skillful phrasing and emphasis would have had a much greater impact on the hearers than a clumsy or inarticulate reading. Aulus Gellius relates an amusing story proving this point. Toying with a self-proclaimed scholar, whose pretensions he wants to expose, Gellius claims not to know how to read a difficult text: "'How on earth can I read,' I replied, 'what I cannot understand? Surely my reading will be indistinct and confused, and will even distract your attention.'" When the "scholar" takes up the text to read, his incompetence is exposed: "Ignorant schoolboys, if they had taken up that book, could not have read more laughably, so wretchedly did he pronounce the words and murder the thought" (*NA* 13.31.5–9). So a decently phrased and articulated reading might even have been considered a kind of explanation.[50] A bad reading, on the other hand, was a major impediment to understanding. On hearing an uneducated fellow (*apaideutos*) reading Euripides' *Bacchae*, Demetrius the Cynic snatched the book out of his hands and tore it up: "It is better for Pentheus to be torn to tatters by me once for all than by you repeatedly."[51] The need for a proper reading was probably particularly acute in Epictetus' class, since Greek was probably not the first language of many of his students.[52]

This remark about *epanagignōsis* suggests several interesting questions: did Epictetus pick subjects or texts for discussion somewhat at random, or was there a curriculum or trajectory of sorts that he followed? Was it necessary for him to read over a chosen text because that happened to be the text the class was reading at the moment, or because he as a teacher deemed it necessary that a given subject be treated? Strange to say, we are ignorant of this rather basic fact about procedures within the philosophical classroom. Reading through a text would provide structure to a class: students and teacher would know that for the next two weeks, say, they would be working their way through a single text. But this approach seems to presume the existence of a local bookstore where students could acquire identical copies of Chrysippus' treatises, which is hardly likely. Presumably, the teacher had a copy of the text (or texts) being examined. It may be that the teacher proposed discrete pieces of text for analysis, and that students copied these down on wax tablets for later transcription. Cicero's son required a secretary for just this purpose: "But I beg of you to see that a secretary is sent me as quickly as possible – best of all a Greek; for that will relieve me of a lot of trouble in writing out lecture-notes" (*ad Fam.* 16.21.8). Students in a modern classroom may be expected to read ahead of time the material that will be covered in lecture. In the ancient world, it is more likely that the main responsibility of students on any given night after class was to write up and assimilate the material *after* it had been delivered. So students may not have come into class with a copy of Chrysippus, but they may well have left class with one, or at least, with annotated portions of such a treatise. The teacher, therefore, did more than simply explain a text already in the hands of students; in all likelihood, the teacher delivered the text itself to students in the process of teaching. And of course, the teacher's own text probably derived from his teacher. So while students might have gathered a text here and there from various sources, the textual spine of a philosophical education in Epictetus' school probably consisted of the transcriptions of texts analyzed in class. As a delivery vehicle for the text, as its articulator and exegete, the teacher exercises a high degree of authority *vis-à-vis* the text. It is no exaggeration to describe a teacher in this position both as a text provider and as a text-broker.

Students were also required to read to the rest of the class. When Epictetus was not reading or lecturing, students might have read on an individual basis to Epictetus, or to each other.[53] During such times, Epictetus may have taken the opportunity to quiz students individually (2.1.30). On one occasion, an older student has set a younger student to reading a passage that was too difficult. Epictetus catches the older student snickering and gives him a sharp rebuke: "You are laughing at yourself," he says. "You did not give the young man any preliminary training, nor did you discover whether he could follow these arguments, but you use him as a mere reader" – i.e., as a slave whose task it is to read (*anagnōstēs*) (1.26.13). Obviously, some responsibility for teaching was given to the older students. The practice of farming out teaching responsibilities is also familiar from Quintilian:

> I now know that this form of teaching (coaching in reading) is practiced by the Greeks, but is generally entrusted to assistants, as the professors themselves consider that they have no time to give individual instruction to each pupil as he reads.[54]

So it appears that students sought to give a smooth and intelligible reading of the book being studied, with the teacher providing *epanagignōsis*, or an "expert reading." This was the first step in textual analysis.

The reading of a given text was followed by definition and interpretation of terms. In a text already cited, where the presumptuous Roman drops into the classroom, Epictetus claims that the details of any skill, whether shoemaking, carpentry, or music, are boring to the layperson. Likewise, the mechanics of philosophy will be tedious for the uncommitted bystander. What are these tiresome details in the case of philosophy? Epictetus responds in the following diatribal exchange:

> If you enter upon this task, I will say that in the first place you ought to understand the meaning of terms. – So you imply that I do not now understand the meaning of terms? – You do not. – How comes it, then that I use them? – Why, you use them as the illiterate use written speech, as the cattle use external impressions; for use is one thing, and understanding another. But if you think you understand terms (*onomata*) propose any term you please, and let us put ourselves to the test, to see whether we understand (2.14.14).

Apparently, the reading of a text would be followed by a discussion of basic terms, which were to be closely examined and developed in ways that went beyond ordinary usage.[55] *Exegeisthai* is the term generally used to describe this process. As with reading, both teacher and student might have presented explanations of a text to other members of the class, and these explanations would no doubt have been subjected to criticism and debate.[56] On one occasion, a student, overly infatuated with the details of philosophy at the expense of its greater aims exclaims, "I will explain (*exegeisthai*) Chrysippus for you as no one else can; his language (*lexis*) I will analyze so as to make it perfectly clear" (3.21.7). While this student is reproved for confusing the methods of philosophy with its goals, the exchange demonstrates that competence in exegesis was part of the training.

The third stage included what seems to fall more properly within the domain of logic; namely, the analysis of arguments. This was an area of endeavor for which the Stoics were famous (or infamous). Lucian, for example, satirizes the Stoic preoccupation with "crooked problems," and even Epictetus himself admits that "the books of the

Stoics are full of quibbles" (1.29.56).[57] Facility in logic and the ability to analyze arguments were obviously points of pride for many Stoics, and opponents of Stoicism took pains to cudgel them over inconsistencies whenever the opportunity arose.[58] Though one modern critic has proposed that "Epictetus put little emphasis on logic," it is obvious at many points in the *Discourses* that this is simply not the case.[59] While Epictetus stated repeatedly that such logical niceties were not ends in themselves (as apparently they were among some students), he strenuously maintained that the philosopher must be able to "state the true, eliminate the false, and to suspend judgment in doubtful cases" (1.7.5). Several kinds of activity might fall under this heading. One such was the analysis of syllogisms. Epictetus recalls an occasion from his days as a student of Musonius Rufus, when he received a stern rebuke for failing to discover an omission in a syllogism (1.7.32).[60] Another aspect of analysis was the investigation of statements with "equivocal premises," statements which are intended to mean one thing at one step in the argument, another at another.[61] Most probably, teachers and students devoted significant effort to the examination of these types of statements and arguments. It is not too surprising that Arrian has passed over this type of technical material.

A fourth stage in the analysis of texts that is closely linked with the third stage deals with "hypothetical statements." In addition to 4.4.14, cited above, Epictetus distinguishes "changing arguments" from "hypothetical arguments": "Many people," he says, "do not realize that the study of changing arguments, hypothetical arguments, arguments which become valid by being posed, and all arguments of this kind, has a bearing on proper function."[62] Examining and proposing hypotheses or hypothetical statements is an activity that appears often in the *Discourses*.[63] It may have involved fashioning one's own premises and arguments, based on the model provided by the text, perhaps formulating premises under which a fallacious argument might become true, or extending an argument by adding a premise.[64] It was also something that a student might have read out loud to the rest of the class for discussion and critique.[65] While it would take us away from the point at hand to examine this in detail, Epictetus considered it a valuable exercise. Skill in these matters will prevent the student from "being led astray by those who use sophistries in the guise of demonstrations. That is the reason for our study and exercise" (1.7.12).

Such is the outline of the fourfold approach to texts taken in Epictetus' class. Obviously, it would be a mistake to press Epictetus into any rigid schema. He was ever quick to give extemporaneous "sermons" on topics that struck his fancy or that arose in class – indeed, this is precisely the material which Arrian has preserved. Epictetus was not one to subject himself to a set curriculum. Still, this fourfold approach may be taken as a pedagogical scaffolding that was generally followed.

Having discussed the role of teacher and texts in Epictetus' classroom, it remains to draw attention to two uses of books that Epictetus condemns. First, students are occasionally censured for attempting to imitate the style of certain authors.[66] Students who read with an eye for imitating a particular kind of style typically receive a strong rebuke. "The small art of selecting trivial phrases and putting them together, and of coming forward and reading or reciting them gracefully" (3.23.26), this sort of dalliance is scorned by Epictetus. Indeed, it is hard to imagine that such an activity could have been pursued in class; most probably, it was an extracurricular activity that took place in a student's own time. Writing was apparently a part of the curriculum, and encouraged. Students were to have noble thoughts "ready at hand by night and by day; write them, read them, make your conversation about them."[67] But too much emphasis on stylistic niceties for the purpose of winning praise is antithetical to the goals of philosophy (3.23.32–8).

Second, students often confused literary prowess with moral progress. We have seen Epictetus rebuking students who prided themselves on their ability to read Chrysippus "all by themselves" (1.4.9). His objections presuppose a widespread tendency on the part of students to prize and to parade conspicuous mastery of texts. This, it seems, passed for erudition, the ability to read and to explain a text with ease, or to compose in the style of an ancient author. It was not enough for Epictetus; for him, books were merely tools, just like the jumping weights of the athlete or the measuring devices of the craftsman.[68] Proper philosophers valued moral progress, not display. The degree to which Epictetus had to exert himself to make this point shows that he was paddling against a strong current.

Examining the use of written texts in Epictetus' classroom demonstrates the difficulty of making simple claims about the status of written texts in his pedagogy. Epictetus certainly projects a robust sense of his professorial authority; he does not seem to have been the type who would have relegated himself to secondary status behind an authoritative text. He even goes so far as to liken the teacher to an oracle (2.21.10). The practice of referring to students as "slaves" also suggests a strongly hierarchical authority structure that existed between teacher and student.[69] Nevertheless, we have seen that Chrysippus and the subject matter of his works (though not, perhaps, the actual treatises themselves) occupied a prominent place in the curriculum. In fact, it is precisely because texts were so heavily used that the methods of philosophy were often confused with the goals, and mastery of books became an end in itself.

Given the pride of place occupied by Chrysippus in the curriculum, would it be accurate to say that the works of Chrysippus functioned as a kind of "scripture" in Epictetus' school?[70] To say that students would have understood Chrysippus' works as "holy" misses the mark. As we have seen, Chrysippus himself is called the "exegete of nature," and a provider of food for the intellect, just as Triptolemus provided food for the body. This is high praise, but we find no evidence of any particular reverence for the texts themselves; no interest, for example, in establishing the proper text of Chrysippus, or in preserving or collecting his works, or in writing commentaries on them. Indeed, the actual texts being used in Epictetus' class appear to have been rather amorphous. They probably consisted of excerpts taken from Chrysippus' works relevant to the topic at hand. There is nothing to suggest that all students would have been expected to have worked their way through, say, Chrysippus' *Treatise on Logic*, as we might expect students of a Peripatetic to have read Aristotle's *Categories*. The curriculum in Epictetus' classroom was most likely structured around a series of topics proposed by Epictetus, rather than a set of texts. To elucidate and illustrate these topics, Epictetus would have used texts – more than anecdotally, to be sure – but in such a way that texts were conformed to curricula, not vice versa.

From a functional standpoint, however, the label "scripture" carries a grain of truth. The mastery of Chrysippus was considered (by students, at least) to be an achievement of the highest possible order, and considerable energies were devoted to this end. Many Christian bishops of a later day would have been delighted had their parishioners been as devoted to their scriptures as the students of Epictetus were to the works of Chrysippus.[71] Yet one gets the impression that it was often enough to *appear* to have mastered Chrysippus, rather than to have actually done so. Strutting this capacity, real or pretended, boosted the prestige of the performer within the structure of values ambient in the classroom, and probably outside the class as well. This emphasis on conspicuous erudition is quite intelligible, nested as it was in a culture that valued and rewarded the public display of expertise and the visible signs of mastery. During his guerrilla raid on the Trojans, Diomedes finds himself at an impasse: better to kill more sleeping Thracians or to steal their shining armor and carry it off in triumph? (*Il.* 10.503) Better the concrete gain or the visible show? In the culture we are studying, the choice was not a simple one.

Seneca

Seneca's correspondence with Lucilius opens a window on a different kind of teaching situation, one which takes place entirely through the medium of written texts. A great variety of moral exhortation is found in this correspondence, and much of it concerns how one ought to use books in the process of character formation. In Seneca's own case, private reading was a crucial component of his moral development:

> You cannot conceive what distinct progress I notice that each day brings to me. And when you say: "Give me also a share in these gifts which you have found so helpful," I reply that I am anxious to heap all these privileges upon you, and that I am glad to learn in order that I may teach . . . I shall therefore send to you the actual books; and in order that you may not waste time in searching here and there for profitable topics, I shall mark certain passages, so that you can turn at once to those which I approve and admire.[72]

Although this passage is followed by remarks that "the living voice and the intimacy of a common life will help you more than anything fixed in writing," there is little doubt about Seneca's confidence in the written medium: he trusts that his letters will have good effect, both on Lucilius, and on future generations.[73]

Beyond the fairly banal claim that reading bulks large in Seneca's pursuit of moral excellence, it is possible to expand on specific aspects of his reading habits. In Epictetus' *Discourses*, we glimpsed the role played by Stoic texts in an actual classroom situation. Here, we will explore the ways in which a philosopher/teacher might deploy written texts for his own edification in a private, as opposed to a public setting. As such, the evidence from Epictetus and Seneca may be seen as complementary.

With respect to the mechanics of reading, very little sets Seneca apart from other intellectuals of his day. Reading in the ancient world almost always involved vocalizing the text, even when done privately, and there is no reason to suspect that it was otherwise with Seneca.[74] He seems to presume this practice when he says that physicians sometimes tell their patients to read more loudly than is normal in order to exercise the lungs, and he himself recommends that Lucilius modulate his volume, reading vehemently or softly as his spirit leads, for the purpose of developing his vocal capacities.[75] We do not know, however, whether such a dramatic style typified the reading experience, or whether it was employed only occasionally for the sake of exercise. Seneca deplores the fashion for the sing-song modulation of tone practiced by some readers, the "raising and lowering of the voice by scales and specific intonations" (*Ep.* 15.7). It was also common practice for wealthy individuals to listen to texts read to them by slaves. Pliny, for example, relied heavily on his reader Encolpius – "who else . . . will hold my attention as he does?" (Pliny, *Ep.* 8.1). There is no evidence, however, that Seneca habitually "read" texts this way, or that he utilized a literary assistant in the way that Cicero employed Tiro.[76] In fact, he indicates that hearing something read is less conducive to understanding than reading it oneself: "I shall discuss the book more fully after a second perusal; meantime, my judgment is somewhat unsettled, just as if I had heard it read aloud, and had not read it myself."[77] If anything is unusual about Seneca's reading habits, it would be the absence of any such literary assistant. Finally, there are no indications that Seneca read any of his own works publicly, or that he participated heavily in public literary culture after the fashion of Pliny.

Writing up collections of excerpts from one's reading was common practice. The Elder Pliny, for example, was accompanied at all times by a secretary responsible for reading or taking dictation.[78] The scarcity of books and the difficulty of locating passages of interest made such literary distillations extremely useful and therefore quite valuable: Pliny the Elder was offered 400,000 sesterces for his notebooks, even when they were still incomplete (Pliny, *Ep.* 3.5). Seneca, like other scholars of the period, probably collected such excerpts in the course of his reading, and could consult or distribute them when required. Indeed, it appears that in Seneca's case, reading nearly always entailed writing. On an excursion to the country, Seneca remarks that he was never without his writing tablets.[79] At *Ep.* 39.1, in response to a request by Lucilius, Seneca remarks, "I shall indeed arrange for you, in careful order and narrow compass the notes (*commentarii*) which you request." Whether these are just excerpts from books, Seneca's own reflections on such excerpts, or excerpts with added remarks is unclear.[80]

Unfortunately, the use of excerpts tends to promote bad reading habits. Seneca warns Lucilius against the tendency to sample lightly from too many authors and advises him to concentrate on learning a few standard authors well, rather than knowing many authors only superficially:

> Be careful, however, lest this reading of many authors and books of every sort may tend to make you discursive and unsteady. You must linger among a limited number of master-thinkers, and digest their works, if you would derive ideas which shall win firm hold in your mind.[81]

Then, as now, students often found it convenient to approach difficult authors through abridgments or epitomes, avoiding a direct encounter with the original. At *Ep.* 39.1, Seneca alludes to the existence of the *breviarium* and the *summarium*, an abridgment and outline of chief points, respectively: "The former is more necessary to one who is learning a subject, the latter to one who knows it. For the one teaches, the other stirs the memory." Lucilius even asks for notes (*commentarii*) of this kind, and though Seneca complies, he urges Lucilius to read the authors themselves.[82] With philosophers from other schools, choice tidbits may be few and far between, and here it may be permissible to employ such literary shortcuts, but, on the whole, Seneca is wary of too much dependence on notes. "For this reason, give over hoping that you can sample lightly from the wisdom of distinguished men. Look into their wisdom as a whole; study it as a whole" (*Ep.* 33.5). Too much reliance on excerpts gives rise to mental habits unworthy of a mature thinker:

> to chase after choice extracts and to prop his weakness by the best known and the briefest sayings and to depend upon his memory is disgraceful; it is time for him to lean on himself. He should make such maxims and not memorize them. For it is disgraceful even for an old man, or one who has sighted old age, to have a notebook knowledge (*ex commentario sapere*; *Ep.* 33.7).

Similarly, as bees gather pollen and synthesize it to create honey, so the process of reading and reflection should give rise to new thoughts, not just the recycling of old ones (*Ep.* 84.3–5). However, Seneca does not take his own advice completely to heart. His own practice of ending his letters with an aphorism drawn from other

writers is indicative of the anecdotal habit of thinking that he dis-
courages in Lucilius: "I have got you into bad habits" (i.e., by always
ending with a quote, *Ep.* 17.11); "Now you are stretching forth your
hand for the daily gift" (*Ep.* 14.17).[83]

Seneca also objects to methods of reading that give priority to
grammatical and historical detail over moral content. These
approaches to texts have their specialized practitioners: the *grammaticus* and *philologus*. At times, Seneca seems to consider these two
literary offices as distinct, though he often blurs the distinction. The
grammaticus took an interest in word morphology and etymology, in
archaic terms, and in source criticism.[84] He was also concerned with
the pronunciation of syllables and the proper scansion of poetry (*Ep.*
88.4). The office of *philologus* seems to embrace tasks typically
performed by the *grammaticus*, but includes a broader expertise,
especially in history. An individual by the name of Lucius Ateius
Philologus established a reputation as a *grammaticus*, but later
assumed the title *philologus* in virtue of his wide and varied learning.
He was responsible for a work entitled *Hyle*, "Material," or perhaps,
"Stuff," collected in 800 books.[85] As an appellation, "*philologus*"
carried a slightly better cachet, just as "intellectual" might be
preferable to the more specialized and possibly pedantic term
"scholar." Some tasks, finally, might fall either to the *grammaticus* or
to the *philologus*, for example, text-critical study.[86]

Seneca appears to have had no theoretical objections to these
different ways of reading:

> There is no reason why you should marvel that each person
> (i.e., the philosopher, the *philologus*, and the *grammaticus*) can
> collect from the same source suitable matter for his own
> studies; for in the same meadow the cow grazes, the dog
> hunts the hare, and the stork the lizard (*Ep.* 108.30).

His main objection is that these reading strategies are irrelevant to
the task of moral formation. They are not misuses of texts, but
misuses of time. So when the true philosopher reads in Virgil that
"time flies," he considers the short time available for moral reform;
the *grammaticus*, on the other hand, immediately writes down in his
notebook how many times Virgil uses the term *fugit*. Philosophers
forfeit their calling when they dabble in such matters (*Ep.* 88.42).
Seneca, at least, and probably Musonius and Epictetus as well,
would not consider these activities as worthy of a philosopher. Cornutus, however, did occupy himself with such subjects, and Seneca's

anxieties over the "philologization" of philosophy suggest that many other teachers were similar to Cornutus in this regard.

Just as we explored the different texts used by Epictetus, so now we inquire after the books favored by Seneca. He claims that Stoic writings are clearly superior to those of other Schools: "such thoughts as one may extract here and there in the works of other philosophers run through the whole body of our writings" (*Ep.* 33.3). Zeno and Cleanthes, along with Socrates, Plato, the Catos, and Laelius are worthy of veneration (*Ep.* 64.10). Such names tend to occur in clusters: for example, Zeno, Chrysippus, and Posidonius.[87] But in spite of this ostensibly positive estimation of Stoic writers and writings, he is often rather dismissive of Stoic founder-figures, Zeno in particular. He quotes Zeno infrequently, and on the few occasions when he does, it is for the purpose of showing how absurd his syllogisms are when brought to bear on moral questions.[88] The mincing distinctions of Chrysippus also come up for sardonic asides.[89] "A great man, no doubt, but yet a Greek, one whose acumen is so finely pointed that it gets blunted and often folds back on itself" (*De Ben.* 1.4.1). He disagrees with Chrysippus on technical matters (e.g., that the act of walking has a particular kind of ontological essence), though he applauds Chrysippus' independence of mind and willingness to disagree with his teacher Cleanthes (*Ep.* 113.23). He does quote with high approval the "Hymn to Zeus" of "our Cleanthes," which he renders in Latin (*Ep.* 107.10). However, he prefers the solid moral teaching of the Catos, Laelius, or Tubero, to the overly precious Greeks. Obviously, certain nationalistic sentiments inform these judgments.

He demonstrates a similar independence of mind in his positive estimation of Epicurus, and by his frequent quotation of Epicurean material.[90] He occasionally offers an apology for doing so, and claims that truth is the property of all people and ought not to be considered the property of any one particular sect (*Ep.* 8.8). He even seems to value Epicurus for his style, which to Cicero, at least, would be a sign of aesthetic depravity.[91] There can be little doubt that Seneca considers himself rather broad-minded for venturing outside the literary canon of his own school:

> I shall show, too, that the Stoics also accept this doctrine (that leisure for the purposes of study is to be pursued), not because I have made it my rule to set up nothing contrary to the teaching of Zeno or Chrysippus, but because the matter itself suffers me to adopt their opinion; for if a man always

follows the opinion of one person, his place is not in the senate, but in a faction (*De Otio* 3.1).

One might safely infer from this attitude that the literary preferences of many of his fellow Stoics tended to be intramural in nature. This, in turn, reflects the highly polarized relations between the various philosophical sects, and the zeal with which people clung to their schools and their texts. With respect to his reading of Epicurus, Seneca remarks that he is willing to cross over "even into the enemy's camp" (*Ep.* 2.5). Nevertheless, in spite of this jab at the narrow-mindedness of his fellow Stoics, Seneca does not exhibit a systematic preference for Epicurean writings over Stoic writings. The frequency of the quotes may indicate that Seneca was currently reading Epicurean books and gleaning useful items from them; coming at the beginning of the letter collection, these references to Epicurus also contribute to his self-construction as an independent thinker.

Finally, we should take special note of two metaphors in Seneca's writings that capture important aspects of the benefits of reading: books as good company, and books as good medicine. Both metaphors are linked to ways of doing philosophy that privilege moral reform over intellectual speculation. Reading good books stimulates moral progress because books allow a reader to keep company with the authors. Although Seneca mentions on one occasion that he has been attending the lectures of a philosopher,[92] his chief impetus towards moral development comes not from such classroom exposure, nor through conversation with other students of philosophy, but through his private reading. Seneca is clear on the benefits of uplifting relationships, and equally clear on the deleterious effects of bad company.[93] Unfortunately, bad company is more easily found than good company, especially when bad company is just oneself: "The miser, the swindler, the bully, the cheat who will do you much harm merely by being near you, are *within* you." The only way to escape the company of the corrupt self is to furnish one's mind with good companions:

> live with the Catos, with Laelius, with Tubero. Or, if you enjoy living with Greeks also, spend your time with Socrates and with Zeno. . . . Live with Chrysippus, with Posidonius: they will make you acquainted with things earthly and things heavenly; they will bid you work hard over something more than neat turns of language and phrases mouthed forth for the entertainment of listeners . . .[94]

Clearly, the fact that these are only literary companions does not prevent them from conferring great benefits. The sort of companionship that Seneca imagines is somewhat heightened compared to our modern notions of literary companionship. Reading aloud may contribute to the impression that the person whose text is read is present. We shall see that Philo Judaeus speaks in a similarly realistic way about "studying with the prophet Jeremiah."[95] Indeed, Seneca places himself among the company of uplifting literary companions by numbering himself among those who will continue to speak through their writings: "I am working for later generations, writing down some ideas that may be of assistance to them."[96] Just as Epicurus engraved the name of Idomeneus on history, just as Cicero kept the name of Atticus from perishing, Seneca will preserve Lucilius' name: "I shall find favor among later generations; I can take with me names that will endure as long as mine." He ends with a quote from Virgil, who claims that he will keep the names of his heroes from being "erased from out the book of Time" (*Ep.* 21.3–5). Beyond making himself the peer of Epicurus and Cicero, the remark illustrates his high expectations for the effect of written texts in the cultivation of the moral life, and for their capacity to influence future generations.

Seneca exhibits his optimistic attitude about written texts by his use of pharmacological metaphors:

> There are certain wholesome counsels which may be compared to prescriptions of useful drugs; these I am putting into writing; for I have found them helpful in ministering to my own sores, which, if not wholly cured, have at any rate ceased to spread (*Ep.* 8.2).

The background for this remark is Seneca's faith in the importance of precepts (*praecepta*) for the moral life.[97] Precepts are practical guides to moral action captured in proverbs, maxims, or aphorisms. "'Harmony makes small things grow; lack of harmony makes great things decay': this was a proverb by which Marcus Agrippa became the best of brothers and the best of friends" (*Ep.* 94.46–7). "Fortune favors the brave; but the coward is foiled by his faint heart"; "forgetting trouble is the way to cure it," or even "know thyself," are also examples of precepts (*Ep.* 94.27–8). They are more, however, than anodyne moralizing: once ingested, precepts work like slow-release pills, gradually transforming the soul. Their truth value works directly on the emotions just as a drug works on sickness:

> Such maxims . . . go straight to our emotions, and help us simply because Nature is exercising her proper function. The soul carries within itself the seed of everything that is honorable, and this seed is stirred to growth by advice, as a spark that is fanned by a gentle breeze develops its natural fire (*Ep*. 94.28–9).

Similarly at *Ep*. 94.47: "proverbs of such a kind, when welcomed intimately into the soul, can mold this very soul. . . . " When Horace asks, "Is your bosom fevered with avarice and sordid covetousness? There are spells and sayings (*verba et voces*) whereby you may soothe the pain and cast much of the malady aside" (*Ep*. 1.1.33–5).[98] Such sentiments strike post-Cartesian thinkers conditioned to think of separation between intellectual and physical domains as rather odd. However, we are reminded that people in antiquity generally saw the state of the soul and the state of the body as fundamentally intertwined. In the *Timaeus*, for example, Plato remarks that "bitter and bilious humors," when confined in the body, "mingle their vapor with the movement of the soul and are blended therewith, [and] implant diseases of the soul. . . . "[99] So in the ancient world, the pharmacological mechanisms of good advice are quite intelligible.

There are times, however, when Seneca appears to question the value of fixed and prepared utterances, whether written or verbal. This extends even to his letters to Lucilius. Conversation, he says, bestows more benefits than letters, because it "creeps little by little into the soul" (*Ep*. 38.1). The same can be said for the reading of books or the hearing of prepared speeches. Once, after offering to send some books to Lucilius, he remarks,

> Of course, however, the living voice (*viva voce*) and the intimacy of a common life will help you more than a fixed utterance (*oratio*). . . . Cleanthes could not have been the express image of Zeno, if he had merely heard his lectures; he shared in his life, saw into his hidden purposes . . .[100]

Conversations enter the mind and stick in the memory more effectively than one-sided presentations (*Ep*. 38.1) Furthermore, truly beneficial moral guidance requires on-the-spot assessment by the teacher:

> There are certain things which can be pointed out only by someone who is present. The physician cannot prescribe

by letter the proper time for eating or bathing; he must feel
the pulse (*Ep.* 22.1).

General rules can be committed to writing, but specific recom-
mendations can only be made on the basis of personal contact.

Nevertheless, in spite of these apparent qualms, Seneca has no
thoroughgoing pessimism about the capacity of the written word
as a vehicle for truth. First of all, written precepts do not depend
on being verbally inculcated in order to be effective. Second, even
in the absence of the author, a piece of writing can be powerfully
moving. Seneca describes a reading of Quintus Sextius the Elder,
heard after a dinner party:

> By the Gods, what strength and spirit one finds in him! This
> is not the case with all philosophers; there are some men of
> illustrious name whose writings are powerless (*exanguia*).
> They lay down rules, they argue, and they quibble; they do
> not infuse spirit because they have no spirit. But when you
> come to read Sextius, you will say: 'he is alive; he is strong;
> he is free; he is more than a man; he fills me with a mighty
> confidence before I close his book.'[101]

So written texts do have the capacity to infuse the spirit of the
author, assuming the author has spirit to infuse, and chooses an
honest and straightforward style. In fact, a person's style, whether
verbal or written, is a mirror in which his or her character is
reflected, for good or for ill (*Ep.* 114.5–8).

This treatment of Seneca's textual habits shows how a Roman
intellectual used written texts for his own private moral formation.
In contrast to Epictetus, the teacher in this case *is* a text: Seneca
cannot be present to "feel the pulse." Nevertheless, in spite of the
obstacles, this enterprise in epistolary pedagogy indicates that for
Seneca, wherever a text and an individual are gathered, moral
improvement can result. This implies a fundamental confidence on
Seneca's part about the efficacy of written texts as a vehicle for
teaching. His letters to Lucilius may therefore be described as an
attempt to create an "inscribed classroom": a literary construct to be
sure, but one which is provided with a great deal of classroom
furniture.[102]

Cornutus

Continuing with the question of use, it would be a misrepresentation of the Late Stoa to examine Musonius, Epictetus, and Seneca as though they were typical of the entire movement. In fact, they were probably exceptional in their methods. Many other Stoic philosophers were plying their trade, and their methods may stand in contrast to the figures seen thus far. One such is Hierocles, whose work appears to have been more along the theoretical lines of the Early Stoa.[103] Chaeremon was a Stoic philosopher and grammarian affiliated with the library in Alexandria, who was described by Eusebius as a *hierogrammateus*, or "sacred scribe."[104] Eusebius mentions him along with Cornutus as a person from whom Origen learned the art of allegorical exegesis.[105] All of these individuals might come up for examination. But Cornutus is the single individual about whom we have more than a trace of information.

External testimony about Cornutus' pedagogical procedures is rather sketchy.[106] Persius was sixteen when he came to study with him, having completed grammatical and rhetorical studies with other teachers. Cornutus' school was thus a place for relatively advanced students. In addition to Lucan, we know of two older men, both physicians, who frequented Cornutus' house: Claudius Agathurnus and Petronius Aristocrates, both of whom were also pursuing philosophical studies.[107] We do not know whether these men were students of Cornutus, or simply philosophical compatriots. Philosophy was apparently one of the subjects, for Persius records that Cornutus had sowed "the seed of Cleanthes" in the ears of his students, and the rest of the Fifth Satire, being a call to philosophic conversion, is certainly inspired by Cornutus' example.[108] Suetonius, too, remarks that Persius gained "some knowledge of philosophy" from Cornutus.

Cornutus stands out for the intensely personal style of his teaching. Epictetus and Seneca deplored philological pursuits of the sort fancied by Cornutus, but they might well have been envious of the teaching evaluation written for him by his student Persius:

> It is a joy to me to show you, beloved friend, how large a portion of my soul is yours. Strike it and note carefully what part of it rings true, what is but paint and plaster of the tongue. It is for this that I would ask for a hundred voices: that I may with clear voice proclaim how deeply I have planted you in the recesses of my heart, and that my words

may render up all the love that lies deep and unutterable in my inmost soul.[109]

Persius may even have taken up residence with Cornutus:

> With you, I remember did I pass long days, with you pluck for feasting the early hours of the night. We two were one in our work; we were one in our hours of rest, and unbent together over the modest board.[110]

"Unbent" suggests that a great deal of time was spent hunched over books in the posture of study. In any case, it is reported that Persius "never left his side."[111] For his part, Cornutus returned the affection, and served as Persius' literary executor after the latter's premature demise. So it appears that Cornutus has configured his "school" rather differently than the classroom of Epictetus and the epistolary classroom of Seneca. The exact role of a document like the *Epidrome*, however, is unclear; it seems rather jejune for students such as Persius or Lucan. In so far as Cornutus' "school" includes older men of the medical profession, it looks rather like a philosophical salon.[112] However, with respect to Persius, Cornutus plays the role of a kindly *Doktorvater*.

Conclusions

All the teachers treated in this chapter employed texts in one way or another. Of the four figures studied, Epictetus appears to have invested the most effort in the interpretation and study of classic Stoic texts as part of philosophical training. Indeed, one concrete result obtained in this chapter is the isolation of four stages of textual analysis that characterized Epictetus' pedagogy. I have argued that these may be characterized as reading, explanation, analysis, and argument. Seneca seems to have placed more stress on ethics rather than logic, at least as far as reading went, and Cornutus probably devoted more time to the study of Virgil, if the titles in his *oeuvre* may serve as a guide. Musonius stressed the importance of logic and argument, but written texts played no obvious role in his classroom, which might just as easily be set in a field or on a farm. While all of these authors value Stoic writings to various degrees, their worth is relativized. For Epictetus, Stoic texts were only means to an end, not an end in themselves. Seneca, while occasionally according such figures and their writings a token respect, often belittles their contributions. And in the narrow compass where it is possible to judge, Cornutus too seems to have exercised a good deal of freedom with School writings. Authorities are not cited by name, and on the one occasion Cleanthes is mentioned, it is for the sake of disagreement.

We found no evidence at all that Musonius, Epictetus, Cornutus, or Seneca, would have bothered to write commentaries on the works of Zeno or Chrysippus, or to carry out any kind of textual work on them. Cornutus was more philologically inclined, but his textual efforts were centered on Virgil. In fact, we find very little evidence of commentaries or books designed to explain or expand on classic Stoic texts. The existence of such commentaries would make a significant statement about the codification and authority of Stoic texts, but such activity is barely attested among Stoics. Nor do we observe any systematic gathering or organizing of the works of Stoic founder-figures. In sum, the writings of the Stoic School, relative to the other groups we will examine, are in a somewhat amorphous state. This may be why, in the middle of the second century, Galen can claim that all of Chrysippus' books have been lost.[113]

Based on this evidence, what can be said about the "bookishness" of Stoics generally? Both Seneca and Epictetus bemoaned the philological trend in philosophy; both were suspicious of trivial book-learning. It is hardly likely that these men would concern themselves with trends in rival Schools; in all likelihood, the philologization of philosophy was worrisome since it was a problem within their own ranks. This worry probably reflects a tendency within Stoicism that is now lost to us. All we have is the look of concern, as it were, on the faces of Epictetus and Seneca, and we can only make inferences about the situation that gave rise to such concerns. With his literary and antiquarian concerns, Cornutus is probably representative of many Stoic teachers active at the time. Persius and Cornutus, it appears, spent many an hour together in literary pursuits, perhaps in the study of one or more of the 700 treatises of Chrysippus owned by Persius, but also, no doubt, in the study of Virgil and Homer. And so while Stoics in general would have been seen by their peers as quite bookish, it does not follow that Stoic texts were at the center of their attentions. Seneca and Cornutus (Romans both) belittle the work of Cleanthes and Chrysippus. Although Seneca is a highly literate figure there is a palpable weariness and cynicism about bookish erudition that causes him to claim, "wisdom is not to be found in letters" (*Ep.* 88.32). Later in the second century, Marcus Aurelius vents a similar sentiment:

"away with the books!" (*Med.* 2.3); "away with the thirst for books!" Not all books, apparently: he thanks his teacher Rusticus for supplying him with a copy of Epictetus' *hypomnēmata*, or commentaries (probably just the *Discourses*). But while this sentiment is true of Seneca and Epictetus and Marcus Aurelius, one suspects that their voices were in the minority. So philological pursuits were probably the order of the day in many Stoic teaching circles, and Stoics may be aptly described as bookish. However, their attentions were not focused on the study and maintenance of a defined group of authoritative texts.

Finally, these results equip us to address a claim recently advanced by David Sedley; namely, that Stoics were characterized by a "virtually religious commitment to the authority of a founder figure," and that they were "ruled by a set of canonical texts."[114] In fact, for Stoics during the Roman period, both of these claims may require some adjustment. Sedley admits that Seneca is a "puzzling exception" to the pattern of philosophical allegiance he finds among the Epicureans; as we have seen, Seneca is rather dismissive of Zeno. But while the other teachers we have examined are ostensibly more respectful, veneration for Zeno and his ideas does not make itself strongly felt in their extant writings. Musonius mentions him twice; Epictetus invokes him more often and appears to hold him in high regard, but does not single him out for particular honors. His name is often mentioned in a list of others, e.g., Diogenes and Socrates (good company, to be sure, though not Stoic), or with Cleanthes and Chrysippus.[115] Diogenes and Socrates are mentioned on many occasions as paradigms of virtue, while Zeno is not; there are relatively few places where Zeno is mentioned apart from Diogenes and Socrates.[116] And apart from Zeno's maxim about the ends of philosophy (*Disc.* 1.20.15–16), it does not seem that his writings are an object of study in Epictetus' classroom – certainly not to the degree that the works of Chrysippus were objects of study. Cornutus appropriates material either directly or (more probably) indirectly, from the writings of Zeno, Chrysippus and Cleanthes, but the names of these men do not surface in his extant work. Furthermore, as we have seen, Cornutus accuses Cleanthes of being rather too precious in his arguments. None of this quite adds up to a "virtually religious commitment to the authority of a founder figure." Students in Epictetus' class and perhaps even Epictetus himself might have felt a greater attachment to Chrysippus. Nevertheless, Epictetus continually reminds his students that Chrysippus and his books are only means to an end, not an end in themselves.

And what shall we say about the "canonical set of texts" proposed by Sedley? Epictetus uses some assemblage of Chrysippus' works, and students in his course probably took down much of this material during lecture. Some of them had no doubt managed to procure copies of Chrysippus' works from other sources. However, it does not appear that the "atomic units" here are individual treatises that might be gathered into a discrete set of works; at least, we find hardly any mention of named treatises in the text of Epictetus, Seneca, Cornutus, or Musonius. Epictetus mentions a treatise by Chrysippus entitled *On Things Possible* and "Introductions." As such, it is probably the material with which Chrysippus deals, rather than the treatises *per se*, that is of primary importance. So even in Epictetus, who out of all the teachers examined holds Chrysippus in highest regard, we find little evidence of a "canonical set of texts." As for Seneca, he tends to suggest other reading materials, and Cornutus, as far as we know, focused his attention more on Virgil than on Zeno. So for Stoics under the Empire, claims about "religious commitment to a founder figure" and a "canonical set of texts" are questionable at best.

Scholars interested in the role played by texts in the Hellenistic philosophical schools have proposed that it is not the founder-figures that are the center of gravity in a given school, but rather the individual teacher. In particular, John Dillon has drawn attention to this phenomenon in the case of the Middle Platonists:

> The chief vehicle for the transmission of Platonic doctrine during all this time is not so much a series of written and published treatises as the oral tradition of the schools, embodied, perhaps, in notes written up by either teacher or pupil . . . but only rarely taking a public form even theoretically observable to us. To talk of the 'influence', then, of Antiochus, Posidonius or Arius Didymus on the scholasticism of the mid-second century AD is grossly to oversimplify the situation. They are indeed there, as remote influences, but the chief influence upon a philosopher is that of his own teacher, and the works of Plato and Aristotle as seen through his eyes, and his chief influence in turn was his teacher, and so on . . . [117]

The evidence gathered in the present chapter confirms the general truth of this statement as applied to the Stoics.

It is certainly true to say that texts and teachers can both serve as *loci* of authority in a given school, and we may imagine different ways these two might be related. A teacher might function as the servant of a School's texts; here, it is the texts themselves that are in the foreground. Or the teacher may exercise various degrees of freedom with respect to the texts of the School, even to the point of disregarding them. The Stoic teachers examined here seem to conform more closely to the second model, where text and teacher stand in partial tension. Not all Stoics fit this model; Hierocles, for example, may have directed attention back to the classical formulations of Cleanthes and Chrysippus. But one feels that even though Epictetus spent much time in the study of Chrysippus, he exercised a kind of veto power over the written text. In other words, Epictetus might indeed have said that in some matter of detail Chrysippus was wrong. It is difficult to imagine an Epicurean teacher saying to students, "the books of Epicurus are filled with quibbles" (*Disc.* 1.29.56). But to that particular body of evidence we now turn.

2

"SALVATION THROUGH EACH OTHER": EPICUREANS

Among ancient school groups, Epicureans show a remarkable reverence for their founder-figures and the written texts the founders left behind. For Philodemus, writing in the first century BCE, tilting against these authorities on any issue was a grave offense:

> For if Epicurus and Metrodorus, as well as Hermarchus say clearly that it [sophistic rhetoric] is an art (*technē*), as we will note in what follows, those writing against them are open to the charge of parricide.[1]

This was still true in Numenius' day, in the mid-second century: among Epicureans, "innovation is an impiety and something to be condemned."[2]

Consonant with this reverential attitude, many Epicureans showed a keen interest in the writings of their founder-figures, and it is the task of the present chapter to examine the range of these activities. The library unearthed at the Villa of the Papyri in Herculaneum allows us to glimpse the contours of an Epicurean book collection as it existed in the year 79 CE, the year Mount Vesuvius erupted. Close paleographical study shows that the first century BCE was a time of particularly intense activity at the Villa of the Papyri; however, the simple fact that the books were maintained and used during the first century CE makes the Herculaneum library a valuable witness to that period as well. Unlike the Stoics, some (but not all) Epicureans lavished a great deal of philological attention on Epicurus' literary corpus, weeding out spurious works and repairing textual problems. Like the Stoics, Epicureans are not conspicuous for their use of commentaries; they were quick, however, to cast the works of Epicurus and the other founders into digested and simplified form. And finally, there is another striking use of a written text that requires special mention; namely, the inscription of Diogenes of Oenoanda.[3]

A few books between friends: the collection and distribution of written texts

The discovery of an Epicurean library at the so-called Villa of the Papyri at Herculaneum has allowed scholars to write an entirely new chapter in the history of the Epicurean movement. Treatises from authors whose works had been completely lost and whose identities were known only from a few scattered remarks in doxographies suddenly came to light. By observing the contours of this collection, the kinds of texts present or absent, the kinds of operations performed on these texts, and of course, their contents, we gain a unique perspective on Epicurean literary practices.

A full description of the Herculaneum library and its contents has yet to be given, in light of the incomplete state of the excavations and the many carbonized papyrus rolls still to be examined. Nevertheless, it is possible to give a fair sample of the books discovered there and some details about their contents.

Roughly 2000 papyri have been catalogued thus far.[4] This figure does not represent the number of complete rolls: many of the pieces separately catalogued are parts of single rolls fractured by unsuccessful attempts at unrolling. Philodemus' *De pietate*, for example, is composed of ten separately catalogued fragments.[5] It has been estimated that some 1100 complete rolls comprised the original collection.[6] Roughly 750 rolls, or fragments of rolls, have been opened; 1250 are yet to be examined. Many of those that remain, however, are fragmentary and carbonized to such a degree that no writing is visible. It has been estimated that half of these cannot be unrolled.[7] Twenty-seven of the fifty-seven rolls opened between 1983 and 1989 had lost all traces of writing; only eight contained decipherable words. Of the decipherable works, some 230 Greek rolls survive, along with sixty-one rolls in Latin. Among the Greek texts were found twenty-five rolls of Epicurus, nineteen by Demetrius Lacon, 167 by Philodemus, and a few by other Epicurean writers.[8] The Latin rolls seem to be of a literary, rather than a philosophical, character, and contain juridical orations, a poem about Alexander the Great, as well as fragments of Lucretius, Ennius, and Caecilius Statius.[9] Thus, Epicurean texts constitute the vast majority of the texts recovered from the Villa of the Papyri. Furthermore, many books in the library are present in multiple copies. The 167 Philodemus rolls represent a total of only thirty-seven distinct works: fifty-eight of the rolls, for example, appear to derive from the seven books of his work *On Rhetoric*; eighteen are from the five-volume work on poetry.[10] Similarly with Epicurus' *On Nature*; it seems to have been present in the library in at least three copies, although there is no way to know whether all thirty-seven books were represented three times over. Some books of *On Nature* (or parts of them) were no doubt more popular than others, and some books may have rehashed subjects previously treated. The author of *PHerc.* 998 observes that "in the thirty-second book of *On Nature*, he [Epicurus] provides a brief statement of most of the topics examined, both outlined and condensed."[11] In fact, sixteen of the placeable fragments derive from only six books of *On Nature*.

The library appears to be stratified into distinct "editorial blocks." This fact suggests that the original collection at the Villa was assembled over a long period of time. One recent study finds seventeen such strata as well as thirty-four different scribal hands.[12] Since many of the manuscripts appear to pre-date the arrival of Epicureanism in Italy, it has been proposed that the core of the collection was assembled elsewhere and brought to the Villa sometime during the first century BCE, perhaps by Philodemus himself.[13] This original core consisted chiefly of works by Epicurus and Demetrius Lacon. The second stage of growth (from 70 to 20 BCE) is characterized by the production of manuscripts of Philodemus' works, a stage which also exhibits certain discernible strata.[14] Additions to the library continued during the rest of the first century BCE, when there seems to have been a turn back to Epicurean classics: the collection is augmented by a few more transcriptions of Epicurus' *On Nature*, along with works by Polystratus, Metrodorus, Colotes, and Demetrius Lacon.[15] It was also the time when many of the Latin texts were added to the library, among them at least one complete copy of Lucretius' *De Rerum Natura*.[16] Certain works of Philodemus also continue to surface in new copies, perhaps for the creation of doxographic manuals.[17] On the whole, however, new acquisitions appear to have ceased by the middle of the first century CE.

Even a casual perusal of the Herculaneum texts discovers readily observable differences among the various rolls. Some rolls are carelessly written and give the impression of being working copies or preliminary drafts, while others appear more polished.[18] In some cases, a preliminary copy shows evidence of additions, corrections, erasures, and transpositions of material that then appear as part of the final edition. Based on the fact that two lengthy marginal additions in *PHerc.* 1021 appear as integral to the text of *PHerc.* 164, W. Crönert inferred that the marginal additions in 1021 must have been in Philodemus' own hand, since the added material was too substantial to be merely a correction by a scribe.[19] Sometimes, manuscripts that exist in more than one copy show slightly different readings, a fact that may be observed at points where extant texts overlap; one such place is Book 25 of Epicurus' *On Nature.*[20] Occasionally these are simply copying errors; in other cases, differences between manuscripts may be traceable to "gradual adaptations" made in later editions.[21] Sometimes changed circumstances may have resulted in a new edition of an old work.[22]

One striking fact emerges from this quick scan of the collection: the relatively small number of texts actually derived from Epicurus relative to those of Philodemus. Furthermore, all the manuscripts of Epicurus seem to derive from *On Nature*, and though it is not surprising that this central work should be well represented, it is interesting that Epicurus' epitomes of his own works do not seem to be present.[23] Also lacking are any traces of the *Kyriai Doxai*, or any other collections of sayings or of apophthegmata that could be considered predecessors of later collections such as the *Ratae Sententiae* or *Gnomologium Vaticanum.*[24] Collections of letters must have been readily available at Herculaneum, but no letter collection such as that used by Seneca has been firmly identified.[25] Some Epicurean authors are noticeably absent, e.g., Apollodorus, the so-called "tyrant of the Garden" and a prolific author, supposedly responsible for over four hundred books.[26] It is tempting to speculate that the absence of epitomes and collections of sayings reflects an intellectual bias on the part of the Epicureans who used these texts. As we shall see, Zeno of Sidon and Philodemus frowned on the use of simplified literature, given its misuse by certain factions within the Epicurean movement. But taking into account the vagaries of historical preservation, such generalizations should remain very tentative. Philodemus certainly refers to many works of Epicurus and other founder-figures not recovered in the library, and these books were probably also in his possession.[27] Quite possibly, the rolls recovered from the Villa represent only a fraction of the original collection. Latin texts make up roughly five percent of the collection (sixty-one out of roughly 1100 papyri), a rather small percentage for a library on Roman soil. Cavallo believes there may have been a collection of Latin books in another area in the Villa, and based on the narrowly philosophical nature of the collection, more Greek books of general interest, also held in another location.[28]

In addition to the evidence provided by the Herculaneum library, we also have explicit testimony about the book-gathering efforts of an Epicurean by the name of Philonides. Philonides of Syrian Laodicea, active around the middle of the second century BCE, was the founder and leader of an Epicurean school in Syria, a mathematician, a figure of importance in the Seleucid court, and a zealous collector of Epicurus' works.[29] Such books might have been acquired from other Epicurean groups in Syria and Asia; in all probability, however, Philonides pursued his book-collecting with most success during his two sojourns in Athens, where he would have had access to the library at the original Epicurean school.[30] It has been proposed that Epicurus deposited his books for safekeeping in the Metroon, or state library at Athens, although this seems questionable, given the mutual antipathy between Epicurus and the governing authorities.[31] Since Epicurus bequeathed his books to Hermarchus along with his property, it would not be surprising if the Epicurean school at Athens was a repository for most if not all of the three hundred rolls which Epicurus supposedly wrote.[32]

It is a well-known fact that collecting books was not a matter of purchasing pre-existent copies, especially writings used within a school, except in rare circumstances.[33] Rather, copies of desired works were commissioned with the permission of the owner, typically a friend or colleague.[34] Although the author of a manuscript might make a copy at his own expense to give to friends, the person who desired the book usually bore the cost of copying. In all probability, Philonides had copies of hard-to-find works made during his travels to Athens. Then, of course, Philonides' own collection would have been available for copying by other Epicureans in Syria.[35] A similar situation is captured by a second-century CE papyrus fragment from Egypt, which mentions books of Metrodorus and Epicurus being sent among at least three Epicurean friends.[36] Somewhat later in the second century, Diogenes of Oenoanda goes to the trouble of carving in stone the fact that he has sent *On the Infinity of Worlds* to his friend Antipater.[37]

Fragments of *PHerc.* 1044 show Philonides involved in other kinds of literary pursuits in addition to book collecting. First, he seems to have been responsible not only for the collection of Epicurean texts, but also for their public circulation: "Philonides . . . published 125 treatises; he also left behind some books of notes with his pupils."[38] The works so issued may have been some of the texts collected on his trips to Athens, or several other texts of which he is the author, editor, or simply the owner. In fact, Philonides himself "published" notes taken from his teachers, Eudemus and Artemon:

> Furthermore, he circulated in book form two early collections of notes, one from Eudemus, the other from Artemon: from Eudemus, the notes on the sixth [book of Epicurus' *On Nature*], and a work *Concerning Scientific Ideas*; from Artemon, his work from the first up to the thirty third [book of Epicurus' *On Nature*] (a few books excepted), and also lecture notes from Dionysidorus. He also produced a treatise *Against Patareus* . . .[39]

Here, the writer makes Philonides responsible for the compilation and distribution of a variety of works. He is a purveyor rather than an author, unless he wrote the treatise *Against Patareus*. In the case of his presentation of Artemon's commentary, one need not imagine a book entitled *On the Commentary of Artemon*, but a release of that commentary, perhaps with some additions by Philonides, similar, perhaps, to Ammonius' "second edition" of the *hypomnēmata* of Aristarchus.[40]

Philodemus also possessed such note-collections, which served as raw material for several of his works.[41] Sometimes this is explicitly stated in the title.[42] In other cases, he avers that the text is based on lectures he has heard, or on other texts. In his *De Signis*, for example, Philodemus states that the text is based on the lectures of Zeno, and that he has incorporated material from Bromius, a fellow student who attended a different set of Zeno's lectures, as well as elements from "Demetrius," which may refer to Demetrius Lacon's *Encheiridion*.[43] PHerc. 1471, *On Frank Criticism*, contains the subscript, "from the lectures of Zeno."[44] So it appears that there was a great deal of informal literature circulating among Epicurean groups, much of it derived from lectures, passed from teacher to student, promulgated and collected by Epicureans such as Philonides.

Snakes in the garden: pseudepigraphy and textual criticism

In the context of the present study, when we consider the process of textual criticism, we are not interested in the goals traditionally pursued by that discipline, i.e., original readings and so forth. Instead, we seek to understand textual criticism as one feature of a part of a "textual profile": was it common for members of religious and philosophical groups to give this sort of attention to their central texts? Of course, practices will probably not be consistent within a given School. As we shall see, Zeno of Sidon was very much a philologist while Philodemus was not.[45]

Less of a popularizer and public figure than Philonides, Zeno of Sidon, active *c.* 125–75 BCE, is notable for his wide range of philosophical and philological activities.[46] He was also a beloved teacher of Philodemus, who used many of Zeno's writings in his own treatises. Two areas of particular interest to the present study are Zeno's work on spurious Epicurean texts and his textual work on Epicurus' writings.

Zeno's work exists only in fragments, but several of these showcase his philological labors. One fragment in particular sheds light on his critical approach to certain Epicurean literature:

> based on his accurate understanding of the doctrines of the Founders, he was suspicious from the start about certain books, for example, certain letters, the epitome *To Pythocles* concerning heavenly phenomena, *On Virtue, Counsels* [attributed to Metrodorus], *Testimonies*, and especially the second book *Against the Gorgias of Plato*, the books *Against the Rhetors*, attributed to Polyaenus, and *Concerning the Moon* and works [attributed] to Hermarchus.[47]

Apparently, some of the works circulating under the names of the Founders were not to be trusted. Diogenes Laertius confirms that certain scandalous letters issued under Epicurus' name were a deliberate attempt to tarnish his reputation: "Diotimus the Stoic, who is hostile to him, has assailed him with bitter slanders, adducing fifty scandalous letters as written by Epicurus; and so too did the author who ascribed to Epicurus the epistles commonly attributed to Chrysippus."[48] So Zeno was certainly justified in his suspicion. In fact, it may be a result of his efforts that none of the writings called into question here (with the possible exception of the *Letter to Pythocles*) were taken as authentic by later Epicureans.[49]

Unfortunately, Zeno's precise methods for determining the authenticity of a work remain in doubt. Critical judgments about the authorship of written texts had been raised for a long time, at least as far back as Herodotus, who expressed doubts about the authenticity of the *Cypria*, attributed to Homer. For the most part, however, such judgments were intuitive and lacked a rigorous methodology. Dionysius of Halicarnassus was the first critic known to us who specified precise categories for such literary judgments, testing a work on stylistic, artistic, and chronological grounds.[50]

Philodemus is also skeptical about the paternity of certain Epicurean texts, and his critical methods were no doubt influenced by those of his mentor Zeno. He questioned Polyaenus' authorship of *On Rhetoric*, as did Zeno, although the arguments he makes are lost.[51] In a polemic against Stoic opponents, Philodemus argues that Diogenes the Cynic was indeed responsible for the scandalous *Politeia* attributed to him, an attribution which Stoics tried hard to deny.[52] He makes his case on two grounds: first, it appears in the lists of catalogues and libraries under Diogenes' name, and second, Chrysippus, Cleanthes, and even Diogenes himself frequently refer to the text.[53] One might suppose that arguments against the authenticity of a text would show that such conditions were not fulfilled.

Apart from critical judgments on questions of authenticity, Zeno and other Epicureans also practiced textual criticism on the manuscripts of the founding figures of the Epicurean school. Demetrius Lacon, a contemporary of Zeno, has preserved evidence of this activity in an untitled work contained in *PHerc*. 1012.[54] Both Zeno and Demetrius claim that in some cases, apparent difficulties in Epicurus' thought arise from various kinds of textual corruption: ignorant copyists who miss classical allusions or who make clumsy emendations.[55] Textual critics were often aided by confused copyists, since points of difficulty were sometimes flagged by notes in the margin.[56] Apparently, even Epicurean scholars often disagreed among themselves: Demetrius remarks that "our dear Zeno" was inclined to find textual errors where some of his Epicurean colleagues might seek another explanation.[57] For critical readers, the act of reading always involved an awareness of the fallibility of the text.

At times, a textual critic might go beyond simply repairing mistakes in the text to something more akin to "pre-emptive editing":

> " . . . the removal of everything that brings suffering." Now, the reading, "everything" varies according to the manuscript; "everything" appears in some manuscripts, but doesn't appear in others. In all the bad copies is written "the elimination of that which brings suffering," not "removal," since, as would seem obvious, we are suspicious about something with the unsavory connotations of "elimination" . . . [58]

Criteria at work in this text-critical judgment are aesthetic and apologetic, rather than philological. Given the vulgarized public image of Epicureanism, such infelicitous expressions might have afforded an opportunity for detractors eager to poke fun at Epicurean doctrine. For defenders of Epicurus, the temptation to "restore" the text at this point would have been particularly strong.

The following example represents a more profound piece of textual tinkering:

> [And some would consider the following a problem in Epicurus]: "Whether a wise man will take thought for food (*trophē*)," while in fact, the texts have, "Whether a wise man will take thought for burial (*taphē*)." Perhaps encountering copies in which the alpha has fallen out, a copyist who wished to complete the word inserted the rho and the omicron.[59]

Given the standard caricature of Epicureans as pleasure-seeking gourmands, it is easy to see why such a text might provide ammunition for assaults on Epicurean doctrine. However, it is also possible to imagine that *trophē* stood in the original: Epicurus might simply have been speaking about the basic necessities of life and freedom from want, which is necessary for the pleasant life (D.L. 10.144).[60] Opponents may have canvassed Epicurus' writings looking for points to attack – Plutarch's *Against Colotes* is one example – and it makes sense that Epicurus' defenders would have tried to forestall such attacks by fixing "mistakes" in the text. However, such alterations were probably internally, not externally motivated. Given the prevalent philosophical clime, this particular remark of Epicurus' might have given offense to people within the school and so prompted the change. This suggests that in the case of the Epicureans, school texts were not simply a static body of documents to be restored, but a sinuous, evolving entity. This insight is manifestly confirmed by the use of epitomized literature among Epicureans.

Veritas, brevitas: epitomes

In addition to their philological labors, Epicureans also recast the works of their founders into a variety of forms. Epicurus himself provided the warrant for later epitomizers by reissuing and restating his thirty-seven book treatise in a number of shorter versions.[61] These were not mere popularizations aimed at outsiders, but documents for people who were already acquainted with Epicurus' philosophy.[62] As such, they were designed chiefly for study purposes within the school, for review and for memorization. According to Cicero, every Epicurean worthy of the name has committed to memory the *Kyriai Doxai* of Epicurus.[63]

In Epicurus' case, an epitome is a concise statement of a body of thought, not necessarily a distillation or condensation of a single written *Vorlage*. Among later Epicureans, we find that Philonides assumed the task of fashioning epitomes:

> And he made the epitomes of the letters of Epicurus, Metrodorus, Polyaenus, and Hermarchus, valuable for lazy youths and [epitomes] of letters arranged according to subject matter . . . [64]

According to Philodemus, the probable author of *PHerc.* 1044, the beneficiaries were lazy youths; Philonides, however, probably had a different audience in mind. Epitomes were not always concessions to the lazy: originally, Epicurus himself imagined that such summary statements of doctrine would benefit more experienced students in need of review, or could serve as an aid to committing important aspects of doctrine to memory.[65]

Other Epicureans also took it upon themselves to refashion the works of the Founders. Diogenes of Tarsus, an Epicurean of the second half of the second century BCE, compiled a work entitled Selected Remarks (*Epilektoi Scholai*) of Epicurus, as well as an epitome of Epicurus' ethical doctrines.[66] Demetrius Lacon apparently wrote a work entitled *Encheiridion*.[67] Its precise contents and form are uncertain, although on one occasion he seems to equate the terms *bybleidion* and *encheiridion*,[68] and since he mentions elsewhere that the *Kyriai Doxai* can be found in a *bybleidion*, the *Encheiridion* may be of a similar character: a compilation of selected teachings from Epicurus on physics, cosmology and ethics, pithily expressed.[69] It may also have contained stock replies to Stoic attacks on Epicurean doctrines.[70]

Other unknown Epicureans were also producing condensed or simplified versions of Epicurus' works; some of these individuals are censured by Demetrius and later by Philodemus. In one fragmentary passage, Demetrius writes,

> Those aiming for brevity, who try to accommodate the tradition of philosophical positions to the ability of their students – going almost so far as to exchange the standard

> introductory material with this teaching, – show . . .
> pleasing to the general crowd and doing this . . . Therefore,
> it is not allowed . . . for anyone to corrupt both the tradition
> about these things and the standard introductory material,
> for it is customary to do both in the service of brevity . . . [71]

Clearly, Demetrius is concerned that some teachers are diluting Epicurean teaching in an attempt to make difficult concepts accessible
to their students. Apparently, certain Epicureans who sought to
popularize their doctrines among the less educated may have taken
Epicurus' habit of epitomizing as a warrant for extensive simplification, more than Demetrius would allow.

Similar concerns are voiced by Philodemus. Those who read only
condensations and summaries come away with a shallow knowledge
of the Epicurean system:

> For in fact, the person who is familiar with us, and has even
> been instructed by us, and who claims to have actually read
> various writings and entire treatises, even if he gets a few
> things right, has only learned extracts, and is unacquainted
> with the particulars of the system. And as for those things
> which he is required to do, he looks to summaries, being, as
> they say, like someone who navigates from a book. [72]

We find still other remarks from Philodemus that suggest reservations about condensed works. *PHerc.* 1389 mentions a "summarizing
statement of arguments on many subjects" of which Philodemus
seems to disapprove. [73] In *PHerc.* 1005, he disparages the person who
flattens out the complexities of Epicurean doctrine. [74] For Philodemus, most books of a popularizing and synthetic character are
inadequate as teaching vehicles.

It may be the case, however, that a well-done epitome could have
its place. It is possible, though difficult, to distill Epicurean doctrine:

> It is only necessary, then, to adapt the majority of things we
> have talked about to just such instances of frank speech. But
> it is difficult for those trying to express ideas concisely to be
> as accurate as those who treat things exhaustively. [75]

Based on this fragment, it seems clear that Philodemus has no objection in principle to concise expression; however, striking the proper
balance between brevity and fidelity to the ideas being expressed is a

delicate matter. Without offending against proper standards of length, the author must "capture the gist of the matter at issue without omitting any of the component parts."[76] Philodemus would probably object to any simplification wrought by an author other than himself or a recognized authority such as Zeno.

It is very likely the case as well that Philodemus, like any trained intellectual, objects to what he sees as the flattening of complex and subtle matters that take training and experience to appreciate. Does this objection stem solely from concerns about the purity of the subject matter or does it arise from an elitist desire to pursue study in a way that admits only like-minded (and socially homogeneous) intellectuals to the table? If modern behavior may serve as a guide, one could imagine that both motivations are present in some degree. In any case, the evidence makes it very clear that synthesized and simplified literature was very much a part of the textual profile of the Epicurean School. Members of individual groups would have felt the presence of the Founders, not only in the form of the treatises written by the Founders themselves, but in forms customized for various purposes.

"Mali verborum interpretes": translation and commentary

The foremost attempt to cast Epicurean doctrine into another tongue is Lucretius' didactic poem, *On the Nature of Things*. Still, this is a rather different (and perhaps more interesting) enterprise than simply translating a work such as the *Greater Epitome* or *Lesser Epitome* from Greek into Latin. Presumably Lucretius might have taken the route chosen by the translators of the Septuagint; it is significant that he did not. We know of other Epicureans who popularized Epicurean doctrine in Latin; namely, Amafinius and Rabirius and others in their train. Apparently, they enjoyed some success: Cicero complains that these individuals "took all Italy by storm" with their writings.[77] We cannot say, however, whether these writers took it on themselves to actually translate Epicurean School texts; doubtless they would have very soon rendered Epicurus' maxims such as the *Tetrapharmakos* into Latin in the course of proselytizing and teaching. It may be these attempts that prompt Cicero to call them "incompetent translators of terms,"[78] but this passing remark is the only surviving evidence about translating activity on the part of Amafinius or his compatriots. No Latin renditions of Epicurus' *On Nature* or of any other Epicurean text written in Greek have yet surfaced.

With the possible exception of Artemon's commentary on the first thirty-three books of Epicurus' *On Nature*, Epicureans do not seem to have favored the use of commentaries that proceeded methodically through a single text. *PHerc*. 1012, for example, deals with points of difficulty in Epicurus' works that were particularly vulnerable to attack; it does not qualify as a continuous commentary.[79] Zeno of Sidon seems to have been responsible for *Interpretations of Things in the Founders*, which may have offered explanations of selected doctrines of the Founders.[80] But nothing has surfaced so far in the work of Demetrius, Zeno, or Philodemus that fits the description of a continuous commentary.

"Most 'scruciating idle": the use (and non-use) of books

PHerc. 1005 contains extremely valuable evidence for the use of books among Epicurean groups. The main thrust of the text is difficult to characterize on account of its fragmentary character; the title too, is lost.[81] In any event, one of the featured topics is a discussion about the use of books among Epicureans. In the course of his argument, Philodemus criticizes certain Epicureans who are either not using or who are misusing the texts of the School: "But the most shocking thing among the majority of Epicureans is this, namely, their unpardonable inactivity with respect to books . . . "[82] It is not the only occasion where Philodemus decries the shallow engagement of Epicureans with the texts of their School:

> It is amazing that those who wish to be accurate readers and interpreters of the books of the School, having ignored these things [quotes from the Founders just cited by Philodemus] as well as the things already mentioned, consequently have "proven" that according to the Founders, the wise man will be subject to anger.[83]

The remark, "most Epicureans" in the quote from *PHerc*. 1005 is suggestive: it seems that many Epicureans did not meet Philodemus' (no doubt very high) standards for literary ability. It may be that C. Amafinius and his followers are in view:

> C. Amafinius appeared as a teacher, and the common people were excited by his books and attached themselves to that school in preference to all others . . . Now after Amafinius

many Epicureans, imitating his method, had written books, and they took over all of Italy for the following reasons: their topic was not expressed subtly; and it was easily memorized and therefore found favor with the uneducated who thought it the basis of the doctrine.[84]

Amafinius was active towards the end of the second century BCE and the beginning of the first; his followers would therefore have been contemporaries of Philodemus. Cicero writes that "on their own testimony these writers claim to be indifferent to definition, arrangement, precision and style."[85] Amafinius and Rabirius, another like-minded Epicurean,

discuss matters that lie open to the view in ordinary language, without employing any technicality and entirely dispensing with definition and division and neat syllogistic proof, and who in fact believe that no science of rhetoric or logic exists.[86]

The valorization of poor style by Amafinius and others points to a distinctly populist strain within Epicureanism, and these anti-intellectual elements must have been a source of embarrassment for Zeno and Philodemus. It is this milieu within which *PHerc.* 1005 is most plausibly situated.[87]

Philodemus himself alludes to the presence of less-educated members of the School when he speaks of the responsibility that learned members have for those without formal academic training:

Those who have been fortunate to have had good Greek training and . . . who have been educated in basic studies, such people are able to understand the books. Having thought deeply about these things their entire lives, [perhaps even] having composed similar treatises themselves, with all the acuity that requires, they can at the very least teach people how to uncover obscurities of one kind or another. But those who serve as manual laborers or are ill-bred, and who have not learned letters . . .[88]

The last sentence breaks off before the author describes how the educational deficits of these members are to be remedied. But the teaching burden placed on educated members leads one to believe that those distracted by quotidian pursuits were dependent on more educated members of the community for guidance in appropriating the texts of the School.[89] It seems, however, that less-educated people can develop their critical abilities and, in fact, may have been expected to do so:

> and with respect to the reading and the writing of books, it is possible to understand them, and not to consider that type of literature which requires explanation as something worthless. With proper training, people can be taught to recognize as incompetent a writer who exceeds the proper length, or who omits necessary subjects, or someone who conducts himself in a manner unbecoming to the argument at hand.[90]

Based on this, some kind of training in reading and perhaps writing could be obtained within the School, and Philodemus recommends that members acquire the proper training to understand its literature. These remarks give the impression that Philodemus is carrying on a discussion with someone who claimed that such training was unnecessary. Philodemus seems unwilling to surrender the field to Epicureans who eschewed learning and culture altogether, and so he allows for the presence of illiterates and "less-literates" in Epicurean communities. On the other hand, he seems anxious to prove to the "cultured despisers" of Epicureanism that it is not necessary for all Epicureans to reject *paideia* as their founder did. To claim that erudition was a requirement for membership in the Garden would be to betray a fundamental tenet of Epicurus. Philodemus can, however, insist that members develop their critical capacities in order to read the writings of the School and so become well-grounded Epicureans.[91]

While *PHerc.* 1005 speaks of the necessity for such training, it does not, in its surviving portions, outline class procedures in an Epicurean school, and the evidence for such procedures is sparse. In *De Signis*, Philodemus remarks, "Zeno in his discussions with us used to set forth the arguments of our opponents as I have presented them and employed these sorts of answers."[92] It seems, however, that he has presented the arguments but removed the background noise of the classroom.[93] There is never any mention of student interaction, hint of dialogue, or diatribal elements of the sort found in Epictetus' *Discourses*. Nor in the section which follows, where Philodemus claims to draw on the notes of his fellow pupil Bromius, is there any sign of such activity. Finally, there are no references to written texts of Epicurus, Metrodorus, Hermarchus, or Polyaenus in support of any of the positions taken, let alone any indications of how such texts might actually have been studied in class. This, however, may not have been typical of Zeno's method; elsewhere, material transcribed from Zeno's class contains many references to the Founders.[94] While the text may not contain many classroom echoes, the manuscript carries evidence of careful study. It is particularly rich in paleographic detail, and this suggests active use.[95]

The treatise entitled *On Frank Criticism* is very illuminating on the subject of student–teacher relations within Epicurean groups.[96] Filled with remarks about how teachers are to reprove students and how students are to receive such criticism, it showcases the intensely collegial and communal aspect of life in an Epicurean community. But even though it is billed as a record of lectures, *On Frank Criticism* contains very little material that shows us the process of classroom instruction or the presence of written texts in class.[97] At the very least, we know that teachers must have typically posed problems for students to solve through discussion and argument among themselves, since it appears that certain students were more interested in winning arguments than in developing their character.[98] Elsewhere, we find the remark that people engaging in discussion with merely disputatious attitudes cannot share in the benefits of common study.[99]

So it appears that there were a number of distinct "textual profiles" within the Epicurean School: some groups, Philodemus', for example, featured a very high engagement with texts and in principle proclaimed it necessary for members to improve their ability to appropriate the texts of the School. In the case of Philodemus, however, it is unclear what if any concrete steps were taken towards this goal. We should hardly imagine Philodemus or anyone of his immediate circle investing their time and energy teaching illiterates how to read. There were, however, certain segments of the population from which candidates for simplified literature might have been drawn, individuals who possessed a modicum of economic power but who were denied a corresponding increase in social status.[100] In various sources, we find individuals eager to acquire the trappings of culture. Horace, for example, pokes fun at Damasippus, the antiquities merchant turned Stoic philosopher (*Sat.* 2.3); the humor lies in the clumsy attempts of new money to acquire the habits and bearing of old money. It has been proposed that in the wake of Caesar's victory in 44 BCE, a "large group of newly prosperous and partly educated" *municipales* would have had increased access to privileges previously denied to them.[101] Philosophical pursuits (a decent way for a gentlemen to wile away the hours) would have been one such perquisite. Epicurus' claim that *paideia* was not necessary for the philosophical life might have made the Epicurean School more attractive (and accessible) to many. Individuals shut out of traditional social networks might have been drawn to the "community of Friends." It may even be the case that with the concentration of political power in imperial hands, people previously involved in the business of politics found occasion for withdrawal from society and for individual pursuits.[102]

The rhetoric of stone: the inscription of Diogenes of Oenoanda

So far, we have looked at instances in which teachers and texts are presumably acting in concert. We conclude this chapter by examining one very remarkable case in which a text is allowed to stand entirely on its own, independent of a classroom context. I refer to the inscription of Diogenes of Oenoanda. At some point during the second century CE, perhaps as early as Hadrian, Flavius Diogenes, an enthusiastic but amateur adherent of the Epicurean sect, commissioned an inscription in a public stoa so as to "publicly advertise the medicines that bring salvation."[103] Only a fraction of the inscription survives, but in its original form it may have been roughly three meters high and perhaps eighty meters in length. Consisting of at least seven distinct works, including epitomes on physics and ethics by Diogenes, a work on old age, as well as letters and maxims of Epicurus, it may have contained more than 25,000 words, making it the longest Greek inscription known from antiquity.[104]

Regrettably, the exact site and configuration of the inscription is unknown.[105] It appears to have been dismantled during the construction of a defensive wall around the city in the latter part of the third century. Following this, the stones were reused in other structures and became widely dispersed. So there are many unanswered questions that hobble interpretation beyond the loss of substantial portions of text: did the inscription run along one straight wall? Was it located on a thoroughfare or in the agora where it would have received maximum exposure? How was the inscription situated with respect to patterns of movement in the town? Attempts at reconstruction have also brought another oddity to light: the bottom course of the inscription appears to have been at about eye level.

This places the top course of the inscription at roughly six feet above eye level, a fact which would seem to complicate the act of reading. As a compensating factor, the letter heights increase from roughly 2 cm to heights of 2.5–3.5 cm on the upper course.

An optimistic estimate about the efficacy of Epicurus' writings, nakedly presented to passers-by, must certainly have underlain this grand project. One wonders to what degree the message of this "document" was effective at the level of understanding, or whether most of its impact was made on account of its sheer size. Without even reading any of the text, an observer could hardly fail to be impressed. Normally, in the course of reading, the reader manipulates the book roll. Here, the text manipulates the reader, who would have had to scroll down its length to read the inscription. For both reasons, there is a striking rhetorical dimension to this particular text. The Column of Trajan offers a useful parallel. Like the inscription of Diogenes, that text manipulates the viewer, who must circle repeatedly around the column to follow the upwardly spiraling narrative. Furthermore, "reading" the column becomes nearly impossible in its upper regions. Obviously, there is value in committing this story to stone, capping it with a statue of Trajan and placing it in a public place, even if no one was actually capable of following the text. In both cases, the reader is impressed, almost bludgeoned with a "rhetoric of stone" that conveys a magnificent weight and monumentality.[106]

In any case, Diogenes is explicit about his motives, which are both philanthropic and apologetic. Seeing the frustration and futility of people's lives, and having experienced the benefits of the Epicurean system for himself, "I considered it the duty of a good man so far as it is in my power (to assist) those among them who are endowed with sense . . . (This then is the first reason for my writing)."[107] Second, he sought to defend philosophy against the charge that it is useless for daily life "and not least that I may refute those who attempt to abuse philosophy saying that it cannot be of any use."[108] Humankind suffers from a plague of false opinions, which passes from one person to another as disease travels among sheep. "By making use of this Stoa," he says, "I wanted to set out (the remedies) which bring health and safety."[109] Presumably, Diogenes believed that the inscription would have a beneficial effect on its readers, just as medications have an effect on illness. We saw above, in the case of Seneca, that the pharmacological language may be more than a likely metaphor. Seneca says that maxims properly understood

go straight to the emotions, and help us simply because
Nature is exercising her proper function. The soul carries
within itself the seed of everything that is honourable, and
this seed is stirred to growth by advice (*admonitio*), as a spark
that is fanned by a gentle breeze develops its natural fire.[110]

The soul which is bathed in helpful maxims can no more resist their
effects than diseases can resist the effects of medicine. This is a most
striking way to think about the therapeutics of texts. We cannot
know whether Diogenes had the same lively idea about the effects
of his inscription on the souls of its readers, but it is not unlikely.
A similar argument has been made for the effects of iconographic
representation in the case of Epicurean statuary: statues of Epicurus
were crafted in such a way as to "move the soul," with an eye to
gaining converts for the sect without compromising the tenet of
withdrawal from society.[111] Accordingly, both iconographic representation and written texts might have stood in for an Epicurean
presence in the noisy and crowded marketplace of ideas. The silent
but monumental presence of Diogenes' inscription would have stood
in striking contrast to the sometimes rancorous competition
between philosophers and sophists that would typically have
occurred in public places. Even those who could not read this text
might be impressed by its equanimity.

Conclusions

Based on the evidence gathered in this chapter, we see that written
texts figured prominently within teaching transactions in Epicurean
groups. Add to this "written texts in all forms," both in terms of
differently fashioned versions of Epicurean teachings, and in terms
of media. The inscription of Diogenes is most remarkable in this
regard: could a Stoic have been found who would have been willing
to commit 25,000 of Chrysippus' words to stone? It seems unlikely,
and this suggests a different estimation of the founder's writings
among Epicurean groups. Some of the activities we find documented
in the Epicurean evidence are probably present among other groups,
such as the trading and distribution of notes from lectures. But even
allowing for the vagaries of historical preservation, Epicureans seem
particularly inclined to recast and re-fashion their written texts in a
variety of forms.

But although Epicureans obviously held Epicurus' writings in
high regard, the ultimate object of their veneration seems not to

have been a written text *per se* (e.g., Epicurus' *On Nature*), but rather Epicurus' body of doctrine; this might be transmitted in any number of ways, by epitomes, by epic poems, and in distilled formulations such as the *Tetrapharmakos*. The manifold forms into which Epicurus' works were recast implies that nothing was sacrosanct about any one written statement of Epicurus' doctrine. Philodemus' concerns about those who were writing bad epitomes shows it was common practice. The absence of commentary writing on texts of Epicurus is also significant at just this point. It seemed preferable to many Epicureans to rewrite and to re-present classic Epicurean texts (if indeed we may call them such) than to comment on them.

Amafinius and Rabirius taught their brand of Epicureanism "without employing any technicality," and so found favor with the *indocti*, the uneducated. By *indocti*, Cicero probably does not mean absolutely illiterate cobblers and donkey drivers but rather Latin speakers whose facility in Greek did not allow them access to texts written by a notoriously difficult author. Still, the tendency we have observed to recast texts in various forms is probably reflective of the social diversity of the movement. New forms of literature that make previously unavailable writings available to new readers; novel ways of disseminating and appropriating information; these reflect underlying social contours. At the same time, new forms of literature can serve as important catalysts for social change. Cultural critics, or perhaps, "ethnographers of reading," have reflected on the relation between popularizing forms of literature and the social worlds in which they are embedded.[112] It appears that the different forms of Epicurean literature were caught up in and reflective of conflicts within the movement, conflicts that sometimes pitted the learned against the less-learned. We have seen that in *PHerc.* 1005, Philodemus deplores the lethargy of "most Epicureans" when it comes to using books. Certain subjects are indeed difficult, but according to Philodemus, uneducated Epicureans should strive to acquire enough literacy to give them access to basic writings of the School. But some Epicureans were content to acquire their philosophical education through forms of literature that Philodemus, at least, frowned upon.

Written records of Epicurean doctrines were important and it appears that Epicurean schools would have many different kinds of texts at their disposal. Texts, in so far as they were useful expressions of Epicurean doctrine, would have been fundamentally important. Nevertheless, these results point in a somewhat different direction than that championed by David Sedley, who remarks that one of Zeno's and Philodemus' chief concerns was to establish a canon of authentic Epicurean writings, purged of spurious works, with a repristinated text of these writings.[113] Certainly such work was considered important, though it appears that Zeno and Philodemus may not have been typical in this regard. Sedley's view seems to presuppose that the heart of Epicurean tradition was vested in texts, and that maintaining and defining that corpus was of pre-eminent importance. But there may be a certain canonical/textual prejudice informing this judgment. The variety of textual forms employed by Epicureans implies remarkable flexibility at just this point. Texts were vehicles, valuable for what they carried, but not venerated in and of themselves. Sedley very properly wants to guard "against a temptation to assimilate [ancient philosophical schools] to those of a modern philosophy department" (p. 102), but the need for a definitive set of securely edited texts may reflect modern, print-conditioned habits of mind, not ones fully shared by ancients. It appears that the burden for maintaining Epicurean traditions fell to the teachers who were capable handlers of School literature, and who could produce modified and simplified versions of it.

3

A LIBRARY LOST AND FOUND: PERIPATETICS

Looking at the mediocre character of the Peripatos in his own day, Strabo attributed its decline to the failure of Aristotelians to safeguard their texts:

> Thus it was that the older Peripatetics who came after Theophrastus did not possess the books at all – except for a few, and in particular the exoteric works – and so were not able to do any serious philosophy but merely declaimed generalities.[1]

While modern historians rightly suspect this to be a highly simplified account of the school's demise, Strabo (and presumably his first readers) considered it to be a plausible explanation for the decline of the School. In Strabo's opinion, the withering of the Peripatos was directly tied to the loss of its written texts.

When examining the different ways that Peripatetics of the first and second centuries appropriated the literature of their School, we are confronted by a striking fact and a difficult puzzle. The fact is the extraordinary amount of attention that Aristotelians lavished on their texts compared to the Stoics and Epicureans. Even when the accidents of preservation are taken into account, it appears that Aristotelians were particularly devoted to crafting, fine-tuning, and commenting upon their texts. Herein lies the puzzle: how are these literary products generated by the pedagogical practices of Aristotelian schools? This is the question to which the present chapter is directed.[2] I will suggest that many of the texts we possess reflect classroom activity, and that compared to the Stoics and Epicureans, education in Peripatetic teaching circles tended to be textually, not topically, structured.

In order to describe the modes of textual usage by Peripatetics in the Roman period, one must begin with a nod to Andronicus of Rhodes. This story has been often told, and for the present I will elide the details; the interested reader may consult several recent studies.[3] Scholars disagree over Andronicus' date and location; in any event, his *floruit* certainly falls within the first century BCE, and so within the bounds of this study.[4] Andronicus generally receives credit for fostering a revival of Aristotelian studies with his preparation and circulation of a new edition of Aristotle's scholarly treatises. His contribution may have been overstated.[5] Indeed, many philosophically informed writers of the first and second centuries CE seem to have had no knowledge of his work. Nevertheless, his editorial activity set the stage for all of the writers to be examined in this chapter.

After genuflecting briefly in the direction of Andronicus, I will revert to the template already established in previous chapters. There was almost no evidence of philological work on Stoic texts by Stoic philosophers (though there was a great deal of this activity performed on literary texts by people such as Cornutus). The Epicurean Zeno of Sidon exerted himself in this area, though Philodemus did not, and the popularizers that Philodemus opposes would hardly have done better. As we shall see, many Peripatetics were committed to philological pursuits. Perhaps this is not surprising: Peripatetics seem to have brought to their corpus of literature the same zeal for organization and description that they brought to the natural world. We shall then turn to commentary. Once again, the Aristotelian evidence in this area fairly towers over that from the Stoics and Epicureans. After dealing with re-presented literature such as paraphrases and epitomes, we shall reflect on the use of texts within a classroom setting. I will argue that continuous reading with comment by the teacher was the chief means of instruction within the school of Alexander of Aphrodisias and, perhaps, among other Aristotelian teachers as well.

Aristotle redux: Andronicus

To understand Andronicus' accomplishment, it is necessary to know something about the condition of Aristotle's books when Andronicus began his work. According to Strabo, after Theophrastus' death in 288 BCE, Aristotle's library was inherited by a certain Neleus, who removed the books from Athens to Scepsis, in Troas (northwestern Asia Minor).[6] When Neleus died, the texts came into the hands of his ignorant heirs, who failed to store them properly. After some unknown number of generations, during which time the manuscripts rotted badly, they were sold to the bookseller Apellicon of Teos, perhaps in the last quarter of the second century BCE.[7] Apellicon attempted to restore the texts by making new copies and filling gaps, but he was not a skilled philologist and the texts he produced were very corrupt. Shortly after Apellicon's death, the books were carried off to Rome in the wake of Sulla's conquest of Athens in 86 BCE. There, they came to the notice of Tyrannio the grammarian, who managed to gain access to the collection. Unfortunately, certain copyists employed by unscrupulous booksellers also enjoyed the same privilege; since their motives were financial, they were not concerned with accuracy and did not bother to collate the manuscripts they copied. Here, Strabo's account leaves off; he makes no mention of Andronicus.[8] While Plutarch omits the remark about the booksellers and their shoddy copyists, he adds that Tyrannio "prepared most" (not all, it seems) of the manuscripts, at which point he turned over copies of his work to Andronicus.[9]

While his exact role is disputed, Andronicus must have played a significant part in the preparation and circulation of Aristotle's works. At the very least, he must have assembled the available texts of Aristotle, formed discrete treatises out of disparate works, organized these treatises into a coherent system, and repaired difficulties in the text. Plutarch also states that Andronicus drew up a catalogue to accompany his new edition, the so-called *Pinakes* that was still in circulation in Plutarch's day. A similar volume for works in the Library at Alexandria was attributed to Callimachus.[10] Among other things, it apparently included a list of Aristotle's books that ran to a thousand separate titles and probably represented an attempt on the part of Andronicus to give a comprehensive list of all of Aristotle's writings.[11]

The final stage of Andronicus' editorial activity, according to Plutarch, was to make his edition public. Ushering a writing into the public domain might have implied nothing more than allowing it to be read publicly. He may also have allowed his students, friends, or other interested parties to copy some or all of the works, or he may have taken steps to reach a wider audience, for example, by lodging a copy with a bookseller.[12] Apparently a commercial market for such books did exist, given Plutarch's remark about the unscrupulous booksellers and their scribes. But if this new collection of Aristotle's works enjoyed a wide circulation, it is most strange that highly literate and philosophically inclined individuals such as Seneca, Philo of Alexandria, Quintilian, and Lucian show very little if any

sign of acquaintance with it.[13] Even Plutarch, who tells the story of
Aristotle's books and mentions Andronicus' *Pinakes*, never gives a
direct quote from Andronicus' edition.[14] Pliny the Elder claims to
have made extracts from fifty volumes of Aristotle's zoological works
while Varro is called a "reader of Aristotle" by his friend Vaccius,
but neither of them seems to know Aristotle's works in their new
form.[15] Andronicus is never mentioned by either author. Scholars
who might have reasonably sought out Aristotle's texts, such as the
Stoic Areius Didymus, who produced a lengthy epitome of Aristotle, Atticus (the second-century Platonist), Diogenes Laertius, and
Stobaeus seem entirely ignorant of Andronicus' person and his editorial efforts.[16] One can only assume that at the very least, Andronicus' edition of Aristotle's work was not widely circulated.

We may also wonder, along with Barnes, whether Andronicus'
contribution was quite as foundational and systematic as the story
implies. There is no reason to doubt that the *Pinakes* existed, and
that it presupposes significant editorial work on the part of
Andronicus and Tyrannio. What is most intriguing, however, is the
need for a myth of the loss and recovery of the library. The circulation and acceptance of this explanatory story, true or not, suggests a
widely held belief that Aristotelians were crucially dependent on
written texts for their philosophical investigations. Without their
texts, Aristotelians were at a loss, like archeologists without a site in
which to dig. In this way, Peripatetics seem quite different to the
other groups examined thus far.

Jots and tittles: pseudepigraphy, textual criticism, and corpus organization

Andronicus devoted himself to determining the genuineness of Aristotle's work, to some (perhaps fairly minor) involvement with the
text, and finally to the ordering of the corpus as a whole. Peripatetics
of the first and second centuries continued to work on these
problems, and we shall briefly pass these activities under review,
treating questions of authenticity, text-critical problems, and corpus
organization. While most of the literature from this period has not
survived, later commentators on Aristotle – Simplicius, Olympiodorus, Ammonius, Philoponus, Elias, and others – often include the
opinions of earlier commentators. Much of this work is preserved
and presented in the Berlin Edition of the *Commentaria in Aristotelem
Graeca* (CAG).[17]

Aristotelians of the first and second centuries CE never explicitly stated a set of philological criteria for judgments about pseud-epigraphic texts; at least, no such remarks survive. But arguments for and against the authenticity of certain texts reveal five basic criteria for such judgments. The first is consistency of content with other generally accepted works.[18] The second is stylistic: an overly congenial style raised suspicions, since Aristotle had a reputation for writing terse and difficult prose.[19] A third criterion was attestation by other ancient authors. For example, in order to demonstrate the antiquity of *De Interpretatione*, Alexander tried to show that Theophrastus had utilized the text.[20] A work might also be mentioned or imitated by later individuals, establishing a *terminus ad quem*. Theophrastus and Eudemus, for example, both wrote *Analytica Priora* of their own.[21] A fourth criterion was intertextual reference between genuine works.[22] Andronicus, for example, dismissed *De Interpretatione* from the list of Aristotle's works based on a seemingly erroneous reference to *De Anima*. A fifth criterion concerns the placement of the text in question within Aristotle's corpus of writing. A perceived problem of placement within the mutually reinforcing lattice of Aristotle's work raised the question of authenticity. Judging from Alexander's remarks, we may infer that the origins of the book that goes under the title "Alpha Elatton" or "Little a" of the *Metaphysics* was much disputed in antiquity.[23] Alexander takes it for a genuine work of Aristotle and insists that this is its proper location, though he admits that the latter parts of the book seem more characteristic of an introduction to a treatise on physics.[24]

So when it came to determining whether a work derived from its putative author, it appears that Aristotelians shared several critical methods with members of other philosophical schools. We have seen that discussions of content and external attestation were important to Epicureans when considering the authenticity of Epicurus' works. Aristotelians, however, had additional criteria at hand when deciding this question because of the systematic character of Aristotle's *oeuvre*. Intertextual reference and neatness of fit among the various works in the corpus as a whole provided Peripatetic scholars with extra leverage when making judgments about the pedigree of an Aristotelian text.

Textual problems large and small were a pervasive fact of life for Aristotelian scholars. Given the mechanics of writing and copying, all users of texts in antiquity encountered such difficulties, but students of Aristotle's texts may have been even more accustomed than philosophers of other Schools to dealing with textual problems.[25] We have seen that Strabo and Plutarch both describe a profound mismanagement of Peripatetic literature. While these authors may have given oversimplified accounts, the facts which their accounts explain – namely, that Aristotle's books were hard to obtain and riddled with errors – are probably solid, even if their explanations for these facts are not plausible in all their details. The texts themselves were often obscure under the best of circumstances, and the proper sense of a given passage might easily have eluded even a diligent copyist. Mindful of these difficulties, a reader/copyist encountering a corrupt text would have been quick to consider how a mistake or an ill-advised textual emendation on the part of a previous copyist could have resulted in a difficulty and how yet another textual emendation might solve the problem. We can see this process at work in the following example preserved in Simplicius' commentary on the *Topics*, in which he quotes a string of earlier commentators. One commentator frequently mentioned is Aspasius, active in the second century CE.[26] The text under discussion is *Phys.* 219b7–8: "Time is the thing being measured and not the thing by which we measure." Simplicius knows of some commentators who have changed the text. Given the fact that

> we seem to measure by time (for we speak of there being some quantity of years and of a feast lasting so many days), some people have changed the text, as Aspasius says: Time is *not* that which is being measured, but the thing by which we measure.[27]

In other words, an anonymous reader, not understanding the sense of the passage and perhaps assuming a scribal mistake had been made, has turned the statement on its head by introducing a negation. Aspasius goes on to explain how the original text does in fact make sense.

This is only one of many cases in which we find Aristotelian scholars dealing with textual problems both large and small. Alexander of Aphrodisias, a Peripatetic philosopher who flourished at the end of the second and the beginning of the third century CE, comments on several different types of textual difficulties he encountered in the course of his reading.[28] The first concerns minor additions or deletions that would have clarified the meaning of a difficult text. A confusing piece of syntax tended to invite the reader to make a change, and many probably obliged.[29] A second kind of error involves confusion in letter recognition on the part of the copyist.[30] The most important type of textual problem, however, is that in which sizable pieces of text are at issue or where a difference in syntax is important for interpretation. Examples include problems with case, substitution of different words, or the addition (or deletion) of material ranging in length from a few words up to several lines of text.[31] Some of these may be explanatory glosses that have found their way into the text, and in such cases Alexander offers no objections as long as the meaning is made clearer: "in some copies, the expression 'complete' appears, and the meaning is more clear . . ."[32]

In certain cases, textual problems involve additions or deletions of substantial portions of text to the point where it is possible to speak of two separate versions of the same work. In his treatment of the order of Aristotle's books, Adrastus mentions two different versions of the *Categories* which were found in ancient libraries, each with a different opening, adding that one version was brief and concise in its expression, and made fewer distinctions.[33] Another instance of major textual confusion occurs with Aristotle's ethical treatises. Aspasius, in his commentary on the *Nichomachean Ethics*, deals with a text where Aristotle seems to equate "the good" and "pleasure" in an unfortunate way, and this gives rise to a difficulty:

> For in the *Nichomachean Ethics* it is discussed, and there Aristotle says clearly about pleasure that it is not the same thing as happiness but accompanies it like the bloom on the cheek of youth. It is a sign that the present passage is not by Aristotle but by Eudemus . . .[34]

This commentary by Aspasius, which bears no title, covers Books 1–4 and 7–8 of the present-day version of the *Nichomachean Ethics*. It seems that in this section of his commentary, which is ostensibly on Book 7 of the *Nichomachean Ethics*, Aspasius considers himself to be discussing the *Eudemian Ethics*. It is a well-known fact that Books 5–7 of *NE* are identical to Books 4–6 of *EE*. If Aspasius' remark is to be trusted, this shared material should be regarded as originally belonging to the *Eudemian Ethics*, at least in some versions of this work.[35] Finally, it appears that parts of the *Physics* also circulated in different versions.[36]

In all likelihood, these irregularities resulted from the vicissitudes to which manuscripts were naturally subject. Ancient readers did think it possible, however, that textual irregularities could be traced to members of rival schools. Aspasius, for example, believed that the Platonist Eudorus had insinuated his doctrine of the Forms into some versions of Aristotle's text.[37] True or not, the fact that Aspasius proposed such an explanation is striking: apparently, even the texts within one's own canon were widely perceived to be vulnerable to this sort of intrusion.

Finally, Aristotelian scholars continued to argue over the organization of Aristotle's work. It seems that Andronicus' way of organizing the corpus was well received: nearly all Peripatetics after him approved of or at least acquiesced to the pre-eminent position given to the study of logic. One exception, however, was Andronicus' own student, Boethus of Sidon.[38] Boethus believed that the best approach to philosophy began with the study of physics. This did not reflect a devaluation of the logical treatises on Boethus' part; it was Boethus who was responsible for a commentary on the *Categories* which Simplicius praises as the most sophisticated work of its kind.[39] His conviction about the importance of physics may have been based on philosophical principles.[40] He may also have been motivated by pedagogical concerns: one should commence the study of unknown and unfamiliar subjects by beginning with known and familiar subjects – namely, the objects of the physical world.[41] The intimidating array of logical terms and conventions that would have greeted the neophyte reader of Aristotle may have convinced Boethus that it was better to start elsewhere. In any case, there is no evidence that he actually attempted to overhaul Andronicus' editorial work, or that he proposed some other way of ordering the corpus.

Further discontents with the sequence of Aristotle's works gathered around localized problems, for example, the relationship between the *Categories* and the *Topics*. Disagreement over this and other issues prompted Adrastus of Aphrodisias, who was active some time before the middle of the second century CE, to write a work entitled *Concerning the Order of Aristotle's Treatises*, in which he discussed both the arrangement of Aristotle's books and their titles.[42] The work does not survive and its contents can only be inferred from passing remarks by later commentators, but the proper arrangement of the logical treatises was among the subjects covered. Simplicius also reports that Adrastus concerned himself with the proper title for the *Physics*, which went under a variety of names.[43] Adrastus argues for the latter, once again staking out the same position as Andronicus.[44] His work testifies to the presence of a continuing discussion and lively disagreement about the organization of Aristotle's works.

In the final analysis, it is likely that the majority of textual difficulties examined here did not stem solely from the bibliographic blunder described by Plutarch and Strabo, or from sinister third parties sowing tares in their neighbor's texts, but to scholastic practices within the Peripatos itself. It has been suggested that Aristotelian School literature was a cooperative enterprise, with later contributors making additions and amplifications to an existing body of literature, just as a modern researcher might add to a database.[45] Aristotle even alludes to the cooperative nature of the philosophical enterprise:

> The study of Truth is in one sense difficult, in another easy. This is shown by the fact that whereas no one person can obtain an adequate grasp of it [the truth], we cannot *all* fail in the attempt; each thinker makes some statement about the natural world, and as an individual contributes little or nothing to the inquiry; but a combination of all conjectures results in something considerable.[46]

There is also evidence that Aristotle himself introduced many changes in his own work, based on glosses and detours that treated specific problems. Werner Jaeger has drawn attention to material of this nature in the *Metaphysics*: "We must always bear in mind the fact that the *Metaphysics* is not a literary work edited by its author but a text that gradually changed under his hands as he used it for his lectures (*scholai*) in the Peripatus [*sic*]."[47] As we shall see below, it is not unlikely that the commentaries of Alexander of Aphrodisias were similarly compiled over a long teaching career. In any case, such literary practices would certainly have contributed to the confusion that characterizes the Aristotelian textual tradition. It is not at all surprising that a myth of bibliographic catastrophe was required to explain such disorder.

It is fitting to end this necessarily detailed treatment of philological practices by stressing a crucial fact that differentiates Aristotelians from other groups studied thus far. From Andronicus on through the second century, many Aristotelian teachers devoted themselves to the task of polishing and refining Aristotle's literary corpus. At the very least, it gave Aristotelians something to do. Perhaps there are two kinds of truth in Strabo's remark, that without books, Aristotelians were unable to philosophize. Without books, they were cut off from the intellectual traditions of their School. And without books, they were also deprived of one of their *raisons d'être*; namely, to organize the corpus of knowledge bequeathed to successive generations of Aristotelians in the form of written texts.[48]

Commentaries simple and complex

Unlike the Stoics and Epicureans, Peripatetics demonstrate a special attachment to the genre of commentary, a fact which conveys an important difference of emphasis among these Schools, and, I will argue, different classroom practices. At a glance, it seems that most Peripatetic teachers of note from the first and second centuries wrote commentaries on some part of Aristotle's work.[49] Certainly there were teachers who chose not to write or had no students to act as their literary executors, as Porphyry did for Plotinus.[50] But even with these qualifications, it seems that pedagogical practices in Aristotelian groups generated a plentiful amount of explanatory literature.

The definition of "commentary" may appear self-evident, but it is not always easy to distinguish a commentary from a collection of glosses or notes on the one hand, and a monograph on the other. In the present study, the term is employed whenever the lemmata to be explained are explicitly stated in the text itself.[51] In some cases, the entire text to be discussed may appear in the lemmata; at times, only the beginning of the section of text to be explained is quoted. A user of a commentary with such partial lemmata would thus require a text of the work being studied at his or her disposal. In what follows, I shall be attentive to just such questions of usage: would a reader have used a commentary in conjunction with the text being studied, or would it have stood on its own? Does the commentary in question seem to be a transcript of classroom sessions? Would it have been suited for use by an individual or in a class?

Commentaries in general, whether they deal with poetry, history, or philosophy, may be divided into two basic types.[52] The first (Type I) is the continuous variety, where the author discusses the whole (or a significant portion) of a given work in its original order, using the structure of the base text as a spine for the commentary. The second (Type II) treats only selected passages of one or more works. These works are not accountable to the contours of a base text, but follow instead an underlying question or topic of interest, perhaps the explanation of historical, geographical, or scientific material, or matters of strictly philological interest, such as unusual words or word order. Type II commentaries, then, may consist of extracts on any number of topics even from separate works, with attached comments or other "literary mortar" from the excerptor/collector. The single formal feature that characterizes both types I and II is the lemma-comment form. Either of these might be described as *hypomnēmata*, although Type I documents, which may appear most commentary-like to moderns, are not always called such by the ancients. Alexander of Aphrodisias refers to his works as *hypomnēmata*, while Philo does not use the term of his continuous commentaries on the Greek Bible.

Taking a cue from Simplicius, I will examine a few commentaries on Aristotle that range from the simple to the complex.[53] A rudimentary and seemingly introductory example is *PFay*. 3, which dates from the time of Domitian or Trajan.[54] It is a particularly precious piece of evidence, since it is the earliest known commentary on the *Topics*, predating those hitherto known by perhaps seventy-five years.[55] Furthermore, all the other commentaries and fragments of commentaries on Aristotle still extant have passed through many stages of copying, in which their original form has been altered. In spite of its poor state of preservation, *PFay*. 3 shows us the actual form of a philosophical commentary as it would have appeared during the late first or early second century.

Only three fragmentary columns containing excerpts of *Top*. 109a34–5, b4–9, b9–12, b13–15 are preserved, and unfortunately the best-preserved section is largely taken up by a lemma from the *Topics*. Each selection from the *Topics* is followed by a brief paraphrase. The neatly written, medium-size uncial characters and the correction in a second hand suggest that *PFay*. 3 was produced for and enjoyed circulation; it is somewhat more formal and carefully written than a set of private notes, though it is by no means de luxe. *PFay*. 3 does not define problematic terms in great detail, mention other writers or writings, or discuss problems of interpretation. Instead, the author is content simply to paraphrase the *Topics*. The paraphrase appears to have been rather terse: in the few surviving portions, comment is roughly equal in length to the lemmata. It seems that the text of the *Topics* was quoted continuously, although it is impossible to say how much of the text was treated.

As for formal characteristics, the lemmata are set off from the following paraphrase by *ekthesis* (projection into the left margin) of roughly two spaces, a graphic gesture that would have allowed a reader to distinguish text from lemma. A column of text would have looked something like this:

LEMMALEMMALEMMALEM
MALEMMALEMMALEMMAL
EMMALEMMA PARAPHRAS
EPARAPHRASEPARAPHR

ASEPARAPHRASEPARAP
HRASEPARAPHRASE LEM
MALEMMALEMMALEMMAL
EMMALEMMALEMMALEMM
ALEMMALEMMALEMMALE
MMA PARAPHRASEPARAPH
RASE . . .

Lemma follows the commentary immediately on the same line and commentary follows lemma; the divisions between them are marked by small *vacats* that are not particularly obvious to the eye.[56] Grammatically, the lemmata stand clear from the surrounding text: they are not introduced with "he says" or "it says" with the following clause placed in the infinitive, nor are there any other expressions that mark the boundary between lemma and comment.[57]

At the end of col. 2 line 14, in the midst of a quote from the *Topics*, we find a faint mark (">"), which the editors call "the common angular mark used for filling up space at the end of a line."[58] Written in uncials without word division, lines 12–16 appear somewhat as follows:

RASEPARAPHRASEPARAPH
RASEPARAPHRASEPARA
PHRASEPARAPHRASEEI >   14
PASPARAPHRASEPARAPH
RASEPARAPHRASE . . .

The mark does more, however, than simply fill up space in a short line. In fact, the line immediately preceding is also short relative to other lines in the column, but no such mark appears there. Rather, it is a clue to the reader that the word at the end of line 14 ("*ei*") is continued on the next line ("*pas*"). Without such a mark, a reader might conceivably have mistaken this for the conjunction *ei*, "if," rather than *eipas*, the aorist second-person singular of *eipon* "to say." This mark was added by a reader who must have found the small space at the end of line and the dangling *ei* to be somewhat misleading; the character is lightly drawn, and thus does not derive from the original scribe. This might suggest a context in which a properly phrased reading was important; namely, a venue that was not entirely private. Still, since the text would almost certainly have been read out loud, it is possible that even a solitary reader would have added such a performance cue.

To what uses would a text in this form have been suited? Would this have helped a reader working through the *Topics* without the benefit of a teacher? Would it have served a teacher who was reading through the *Topics* with a class and who wanted a text of Aristotle with exegetical trimmings? Or would it have served as the script for a reading of Aristotle's *Topics* by a philosopher to a wealthy patron? In fact, any one of these scenarios is possible, though I consider the first to be the most likely. The relatively short lemmata and their clear offsetting from the comment would have allowed a reader to dispense with the original text. Indeed, *PFay.* 3 might almost be termed an interlinear version of the *Topics*.[59] As such, the reader who needed to make frequent reference to commentary for explanation would be relieved of the need to handle two rolls simultaneously, a very difficult task. A reader who needed the continuous text of Aristotle along with interpretive supports would have found this text to be a handy script. One could read only the lemma and make reference to paraphrase when confusion arose; one could also read only the comment, making only casual reference to the lemma. Still, given the *ekthesis* of the lemmata, the text of Aristotle is graphically privileged; in this case, the commentary stands in a subordinate role. If paraphrase is the simplest variety of commentary, then *PFay.* 3 is best suited for inexperienced readers of Aristotle, rather than scholars.

Later authors also wrote commentaries that offered more than simple paraphrase, but which may still be termed introductory. Aspasius and Adrastus (*fl.* early second century) both wrote "exegetica" on the *Categories*. In the only surviving testimony to these works, Galen remarks that his commentary on the *Categories* will be of use only to someone who has already read the book with the help of a teacher, or who has read the book with the aid of the exegetica of Adrastus or Aspasius.[60] This is an interesting remark: it presumes that individuals will be reading by themselves or perhaps in small groups without the benefit of a teacher. The demand for documents that would help solve problems suggests that not all interested readers could find capable teachers, or it may reflect adult readers who felt too old for sitting in classrooms.[61] It also confirms the hierarchy of commentaries mentioned by Simplicius: some commentaries were meant for expert readers. Both commentators also discussed the *Nichomachean Ethics* (*NE*), and we will devote some attention to these texts, since portions of each are still extant.

Aspasius' commentary covers Books 1, 2, 3, 4, 7, and 8 of the *Nichomachean Ethics*, and qualifies as Type I, according to our definition.[62] Short lemmata are followed by a mixture of commentary and paraphrase. Unlike *PFay.* 3, the lemmata are often introduced by "he says" or "it says," a device which serves to mark off Aristotle's text from the surrounding comment. This practice, however, is not always followed: an auditor without a text of the *Ethics* in hand might occasionally be at a loss to distinguish lemma from comment or paraphrase. Presumably, a teacher/reader would have offered cues to readers that would have made such transitions obvious. On occasion, the paraphrase alters the original in significant ways, as for example in the commentary on *NE* 1095b14ff., where Aristotle discusses modes of life devoted to pleasure, the public arena, and contemplation:

Arist., *NE* 1095b14–19	Aspas., in *Eth. Nic.* 10.13–14
For there are three especially eminent vocations, the one just mentioned [the life of enjoyment; *apolaustikos*], the political (*politikos*) and third, the contemplative (*theoretikos*).	... there being three careers, the contemplative (*theoretikos*), the one devoted to pleasure (*apolaustikos*), and the life oriented towards wealth (*chrēmatistikos*).[63]

Aspasius has substituted the life oriented to wealth for the public life and changed the order of the list. He omits Aristotle's remarks about the life given to pleasure and, although the following comment clearly shows that Aspasius is reading and paraphrasing Aristotle's remarks about the political life, he chooses to avoid the appellation *politikos*. At times, Aristotle's text is almost completely effaced behind paraphrase, and on certain occasions, Aspasius can simply ignore portions of text.[64] As a result, this particular commentary would not have met the needs of a reader who wanted Aristotle's exact language. Given the attention to detail and to textual issues seen in the first part of this chapter, such readers did exist. But in accord with Galen's suggestion, a book such as this would have been useful for someone approaching the *Nichomachean Ethics* without the benefit of a teacher. A newcomer to Aristotelian philosophy might have read straight through such a commentary without making reference to the original text.[65] Indeed, it is entirely possible that a person who had read only this text might legitimately say, "I have read the *Nichomachean Ethics*."

Aspasius also takes up other issues of particular interest to commentators. As noted above, he often discusses textual problems.[66] Topics of special interest are often treated in short excursuses.[67]

There is scant reference to other Aristotelian interpreters; he refers to other Aristotelian treatises that touch on the point being discussed and he mentions "early" Peripatetics such as Theophrastus, but he cites the "later" Peripatetics such as Andronicus and Boethus only once.[68] Engagement with the doctrines of other philosophical schools is often didactic, rather than polemical.[69] In accordance with Simplicius' categorization, it is easy to visualize this text as falling somewhere between "easy" and "intermediate" in the spectrum of different commentaries. Its task is to facilitate a basic grasp of the text, not to engage in polemic, nor to address difficult questions.

Adrastus' work on the *Nichomachean Ethics* may be considered a commentary of the Type I variety: though it deals only with selected portions of text, it follows the contours of the base text.[70] It offers an interesting contrast to Aspasius' commentary, since it focuses on issues that Aspasius overlooks – namely, the literary and historical allusions in the *Nichomachean Ethics*. Not only does Adrastus explain such allusions, he adds extra illustrative material drawn from poetry and drama that bears on the point being made. For example, in a discussion of voluntary and involuntary actions (*NE* 1110a28), Aristotle mentions Alcmaeon, who seeks to exculpate himself of matricide by claiming to have acted under compulsion. Aspasius omits any mention of Alcmaeon; in general, he does not even mention Aristotle's illustrative material. Adrastus, however, cites a line from the play, offers alternative reasons for the act, and adds examples of other figures from literature who performed difficult acts to attain some good.[71] At *NE* 1116a24–6 and 34–5, Aristotle mentions Diomedes and Hector as examples of courage. Aspasius skips over this, but Adrastus extends the quotation.[72] Adrastus also gives attention to details of Attic usage.[73] There is no evidence that Adrastus' work was intended to serve as a companion volume to Aspasius' commentary, but their different points of emphasis would have made such a pairing quite natural.

Still other authors, among them Alexander of Aphrodisias and Herminus, devoted themselves in roughly equal measure to basic explanation and to the solution of problems. As such, their works may have been suitable for more advanced students.[74] Almost nothing is known of Herminus, and very little about Alexander.[75] Fortunately, though much of Alexander's work is lost, even that which remains is voluminous, being far too large to characterize here in any but the most general way. He often treats special problems or topics and devotes attention to textual problems. In similar fashion to Adrastus, his commentaries generally proceed line by line, but paraphrastically so: lemmata often lose their distinctiveness and succumb to paraphrase. Like Aspasius, Alexander often marks the beginning of a lemma with "he says," "it says," or its equivalent. Alexander's commentary is generally more fulsome than that of Aspasius and often meanders.[76] The highly discursive nature of the commentary calls to mind a rather windy pedagogue in a particularly expansive mood.[77] The detour involving Theophrastus' distinction between commonplace and precept is irrelevant to the point under discussion, i.e., how a mistaken predication can disqualify an argument; that, as well as the pedantic introduction, "it is necessary not to be ignorant of the fact that Theophrastus . . . " etc., raises the possibility that these commentaries derive from Alexander's lectures: it would not be strange for a detour-prone lecturer to make further distinctions or qualifications whenever the opportunity arose.

Boethus' work on the *Categories* represents the most technical type of commentary. Simplicius cites it often, referring to its author as "the amazing Boethus." Apparently it was notable for its thoroughness, even compared to Alexander's. Boethus dealt with the work on a phrase-by-phrase basis and seems to have dedicated an entire book to the category of Relation.[78] His was certainly not a commentary aimed at the student who was approaching the *Categories* for the first time. Often, he sought to break new ground in the discussion of problematic areas.[79] In other cases, he defended Aristotle against certain critics, both from within the Peripatetic school (e.g., Andronicus), and from outside opponents such as the Stoics.[80] His sophisticated commentary is a reminder that complexity in explication does not necessarily increase over time, for his is one of the earliest commentaries, predating the very elementary *PFay. 3* by at least one hundred years.

The great variety of such commentaries shows students and scholars working at different levels in their attempts to understand and to develop Aristotle's ideas as expressed in his writings. This level of commitment to the explication of Aristotle's books is quite striking, especially when compared to the literary practices of the Epicureans and Stoics who produced very little in the way of commentaries. The way in which such commentaries are "from lectures" or "for lectures" is difficult to discern. Most of the commentaries described here could have fulfilled both functions. Analogies from Galen are once again instructive. There is one case in which a student of Galen has asked for transcripts from a class. Galen replies,

Since you wish to have also in note form the answers I was

giving to the question which you proposed to us from the book written by Antonius the Epicurean, *Watchfulness Against Symptoms of Disease*, I will do as you ask, and herewith, I make my beginning.[81]

We do not know what changes Galen made in his notes before passing them on to his student, or if he used notes at all. It is conceivable that he spoke *ex tempore*, and has merely written up or, rather, dictated his responses. In either case, the text we have arises from and reflects the substance of class discussion. It also shows, incidentally, that a student might have brought a book to class, from which questions could be posed for discussion, and that the teacher would devote substantial amounts of class-time to answering them.

Still, we cannot automatically assume that commentaries that are filled with oral features necessarily proceed from the classroom. It may be the case that a writer has deliberately adopted this style in order to create the feel of the classroom. Cicero, for example, created fictional philosophical dialogues. But though these must have been somewhat idealized, the literary conceit turns on the plausibility of a similar discussion taking place in an actual teaching situation. According to Aristotle (*Rhet.* 1413b), certain individuals wrote plays meant specifically for consumption by readers, where the implied audience (theatergoers) is not the real audience (readers). And of course, standard Greco-Roman education stressed the technique of *prosōpopoiia*, "writing in character." It is possible that the least elaborated texts, those without any elements of conversation, direct speech, etc., are freshest from the classroom. Such texts were embedded in a situation where all the surrounding context was already provided. It is the solitary reader, who reads a text abstracted from its original setting, who needs this classroom furniture.

Pseudo-Aristotelians at work: epitomes and paraphrases

Apart from Andronicus, there is no clear-cut instance of a Peripatetic teacher writing or using a simplified or altered version of Aristotle's work.[82] There are, however, a few writers whose works fall naturally under this heading, even though their status as Peripatetic teachers is unclear. Nicolaus of Damascus, court philosopher to Herod the Great, is one such individual. He is of interest to the present study in light of his work, *On the Philosophy of Aristotle*, generally referred to as the *Compendium*.[83] Two documents falsely attributed to Archytas, the Pythagorean mathematician and contemporary of Plato, also date from our period of interest and qualify as "rewritten Aristotle." Finally, *De Mundo*, a treatise on cosmology falsely attributed to Aristotle himself, also invites examination.

Andronicus may have been the first Peripatetic in our period of interest to paraphrase Aristotle's work. Simplicius calls him one of "the ancient interpreters of the *Categories*," and twice describes him as "the one paraphrasing the book of the Categories."[84] On occasion, Simplicius relates one of Andronicus' paraphrastic renderings.[85] Andronicus also seems to have had no qualms about disagreeing with Aristotle: he apparently suggested that the ten categories might be derived from the two basic principles, Being and Relation.[86] He placed Relation at the end of the list of Categories, and also proposed that "when" and "where," which Aristotle had treated as subordinate to extension, should stand on their own, renaming them "Time" and "Place."[87] In his willingness to part ways with Aristotle, Andronicus' attitude differs noticeably from the pious veneration of later commentators.[88]

Nicolaus' status as a Peripatetic is somewhat ambiguous. He is called "the Peripatetic" once by Plutarch (*Mor.* 723D), and often referred to as such by Athenaeus (e.g., 4.153f., 6.249a). Josephus mentions him frequently as a familiar of Herod, where he appears as a court orator, but Josephus never describes him as a Peripatetic or even as a philosopher. His written *oeuvre* was large and eclectic, including works of dramatic poetry, a *Universal History* in 144 books, a life of Augustus, a book on strange customs, an autobiography, as well as other titles bearing on Aristotelian subjects.[89] There is no mention anywhere of students or of his own teachers, a fact which raises some doubt about his formal credentials as a Peripatetic philosopher. Furthermore, his *Compendium* treated only Aristotle's works on natural science; there are no indications that he dealt with the logical works at all, a remarkable omission when compared with other Aristotelian philosophers.[90] In all probability, Nicolaus earned his Peripatetic sobriquet on the strength of his *Compendium*, not from his membership in an actual Peripatetic school.[91]

As for his treatment of Aristotle's works, Nicolaus' intent was to clear up omissions or inconsistencies in definitions and also to fill in gaps in the argument. As such, his document would fill the needs of readers or hearers who were not deeply involved in a Peripatetic teaching circle. In the context of a class, a student could always seek clarification from an experienced reader of Aristotle. But a reader making his or her way through *de Caelo* or any other Aristotelian text without some interpretive aids would soon encounter difficulties. It is reasonable to assume that the *Compendium* was produced in Nicolaus' capacity as a philosophical expert in the service of a wealthy patron interested in natural science, not as a teaching document for use within a Peripatetic school.[92] It was a well-established role: Elizabeth Rawson observes,

> one of the main functions of scholars dependent on great men was simply to help their patrons study literature, especially Greek literature, in a world where there were not yet any Greek–Latin or Latin–Greek dictionaries, and not all glossaries of obscure, dialect or technical words were sufficiently well-arranged to be easily consulted.[93]

So while Nicolaus does not serve as primary evidence for a formal Aristotelian teaching circle, he is still worth noting in his role as a text-broker.

Archytas, the Pythagorean mathematician and contemporary of Plato, is falsely credited with two paraphrasing documents based on Aristotelian texts. In reality, both works probably date to the last half of the first century BCE. The first, *On the General Proposition*, is a summarizing document whose contents are described by a modern editor as "similar, but not identical" to the first nine chapters of Aristotle's *Categories*.[94] The second text (which I leave aside for the present), *On Antitheses*, deals with chapters 10–15, the *Postpraedicamenta*.[95] The division between these two texts seems to reflect concerns about the placement of the *Postpraedicamenta*, a fact which persuades its most recent editor to date *On Antitheses* to the last half of the first century BCE, when discussion about this issue was most lively. Given the fact that Archytas was known to be a contemporary of Plato, the attribution to Archytas of both writings probably represents an attempt to take the credit for originating the Categories from Aristotle. It also features noticeable Pythagorean flourishes: the author ends by asserting that the ten categories correspond to the ten fingers. As such, it is unlikely that this piece of literature derives from a Peripatetic.

In the process of systematizing Aristotle's discussion, the author of *On the General Proposition* introduces certain changes to the text. Besides omitting Aristotle's opening discussion about equivocal and univocal names and compound terms, the author also changes the order of the Categories. Quality and Quantity are interchanged; Relation (*pros ti*) is rendered more fully by *pros ti pōs echon*; the pair Active/Passive is moved forward; Where and When are moved to the end; Possession stands before Disposition.[96] Furthermore, the author expressly states that the Categories are applied to things themselves, not just language about the things, which was a long-standing interpretive crux. He also appropriates many of the examples which Aristotle used to illustrate the various categories: Aristotle gives "man" and "horse" as examples of Substance; Ps.-Archytas uses these and adds "fire" and "water." Furthermore, in both texts, each Category is examined individually and divided into sub-types. In some cases, the number and names of the subdivisions are the same, but certain changes are introduced by the author. Half the treatise (26.16–30.16 Thesleff) is given over to an examination of the various Categories under the terms "general" and "particular", i.e., whether and how the categories in question apply to individual subjects or to the species or genera in which individuals are included, a schema that Aristotle did not employ systematically in the *Categories*. Ps.-Archytas is therefore a more radical paraphrase than that of Nicolaus. The author also draws on material in other Aristotelian treatises when necessary, for example, in his discussion of Place (29.5–10 Thesleff; cf. Arist. *Phys.* 209a23–5, 212a), which demonstrates his familiarity with the Aristotelian corpus. On occasion, however, the document shows the accretion of elements foreign to Aristotle.[97]

Unlike Nicolaus' *Compendium* or Ps.-Archytas' *On the General Proposition*, Ps.-Aristotle's *De Mundo* is not, strictly speaking, a paraphrase, since it is not tied to the text of any one Aristotelian work. The work itself makes an implicit claim to Aristotelian authorship, based on the dedication to Alexander (presumably, Alexander the Great), but scholars are generally united in presuming the pseudepigraphic nature of *De Mundo*, differing only over the details of date and authorship.[98] *De Mundo* would answer to the definition of a paraphrase, however, if one allows that a body of thought can be paraphrased or restated. Its closest neighbor in the Aristotelian corpus would be *De Caelo*: both deal with cosmology. But *De Mundo* presents the subject in a popularizing format that is decidedly unlike *De Caelo* or any of the technical treatises. In view of its lively style, it resists classification with other introductory works on cosmology.[99] Consider the following extract of *De Caelo*:

The activity of a god is immortality, that is, eternal life.

Necessarily, therefore, the divine must be in eternal motion. And since the heaven is of this nature (i.e., is a divine body), that is why it has its circular body, which by nature moves forever in a circle. Why, then, is not the whole body of the world like this? Because when a body revolves in a circle some part of it must remain still, namely that which is at the centre, but of the body which we have described no part can remain still, whether it be at the center or wherever it be.[100]

Here is a selection from *De Mundo* on the same subject:

The center of the cosmos, which is unmoved and fixed, is occupied by "life-bearing earth," the home and mother of living beings of all kinds. The region above it, a single whole with a finite upper limit everywhere, the dwelling of the gods, is called heaven. It is full of divine bodies which we call stars; it moves eternally, and revolves in solemn choral dance with all the stars in the same circular orbit unceasingly for all time. The whole of the heaven, the whole cosmos, is spherical, and moves continuously, as I have said . . .[101]

Here we find no derivation of facts about the universe by deduction from first principles, no rhetorical questions, no worries about the center of a revolving object remaining at rest; the author of *De Mundo* is content to make declarative statements about heavenly geography, together with some literary flourishes ("like a solemn choral dance") and poetic allusions. But in spite of its simple form, its conclusions are generally in line with the doctrines stated in the technical treatises.[102] Based on its diffusion, it must have been a popular work, and probably enjoyed a wider circulation than the technical treatises.[103] Like Nicolaus' *Compendium*, it was probably directed at a group of readers who were not professional students of Aristotle.[104]

"It was discussed": texts in use

We know that the commentaries of Aspasius, Adrastus, and Alexander were read in at least one ancient philosophical school:

In meetings of the school he [Plotinus] used to have the commentaries read, perhaps of Severus, perhaps of Cronius or Numenius or Gaius or Atticus, and among the Peripatetics of Aspasius, Alexander, Adrastus, and others that were available.[105]

It is a statement to which we will return in the next chapter. Unfortunately, there is no comparable piece of evidence that shows the role played by books within Peripatetic teaching circles. Indeed, most of the Peripatetic literature of this period has not survived. The exception is the work of Alexander of Aphrodisias. By a further examination of his extant literature with an eye towards audience echoes and school procedures, I shall attempt to show that his commentaries still carry traces of their classroom origins. In particular, I propose that philosophical teaching in Alexander's circle took the form of textual exegesis: a reading of an Aristotelian text with explication by the teacher (*exēgēsis*), perhaps followed by questions and a period of discussion on selected topics (*koinologia*). Written texts of Aristotle and Theophrastus, and perhaps commentaries thereon, were crucial for this type of teaching and would have been present and available for consultation.

In spite of the relatively large quantity of Alexander's surviving literature, very little of it informs us about his person or his teaching activity. Based on the introduction to his treatise *On Fate*, it is clear that Septimius Severus had granted him some sort of formal appointment, but nothing is known about the location of his school, nor do we know the names of any of his students.[106] Explicit echoes of the classroom are relatively faint in Alexander's commentaries, but this is not surprising, given the number of stages through which this material has passed.[107] If the commentaries were based on student notes (or on those of the teacher), many of these classroom echoes would have been stripped away when the lectures were formally written up for distribution. Such literary polishing, in fact, was probably expected of someone editing his own notes or those of his teacher. Arrian, for example, felt it necessary to apologize for the rough quality of his *Discourses of Epictetus*, claiming that the work had "escaped" before it was ready.[108] On the other hand, the *Diatribes* of Musonius Rufus have passed through the hands of an editor who has pruned away most of their classroom echoes, along with the edge of Musonius' personality.

The most telling evidence of a classroom origin for Alexander's texts is found in those remarks that seem to presume a group discussion.[109] Such hints are provided by the presence of "to inquire" (*zētein*) or "to say" (*legein*) in the past tense, as in the following examples: "there was an inquiry as to how Aristotle said, in the first book *On the Soul*, 'the living creature that is universal is either nothing or posterior.'"[110] "There was an inquiry as to how it is not disease, rather than lack of physical fitness, that is opposed to physical fitness."[111] Or, in reply to a hypothetical question posed for discussion, the response begins with "it was said first of all . . . "[112] Once, in response to a question about the human will, the text begins, "someone also stated the following opinion," and after a preliminary assertion, continues, "and this too seemed so to everyone," before a solution is offered.[113] Such remarks are familiar from Epictetus and Musonius Rufus.[114]

Apart from these explicit linguistic clues, certain other features of Alexander's work suggest classroom origins. His digressive and rather pedantic style, which may signal oral delivery, has been noted above. His habit of posing problems and then proposing alternative solutions also suggests a pedagogical context.[115] Nothing would have prevented a solitary scholar from writing this way, but posing problems and investigating the strengths and weaknesses of various solutions would be very typical of a classroom environment. Points where alternative solutions are proposed may also represent places where new material was added, based on interesting class discussions. These kinds of accretions would follow naturally from the process of teaching and discussion.

A classroom origin for the short works (e.g., the *Quaestiones*) also seems especially plausible in light of their different literary genres. These have been divided by their modern editor into five categories: (1) problems along with their solutions, (2) exegeses of difficult Aristotelian texts, (3) short treatments of assorted topics, (4) paraphrases (*epidromai*) and (5) collections of stock arguments on subjects of particular interest to Aristotelians.[116] This division is not entirely based on modern aesthetic judgments about literary genre; often, the individual sections are labeled as problems, interpretations (*exēgēseis*) and paraphrases.[117] Some of the material appears rather jejune and may represent student exercises. Other sections are certainly composite, representing a patchwork of disparate material combined by a later editor.[118]

All this is suggestive for Alexander's classroom procedure and the degree to which the extant treatises represent the teaching process. Further insight may be gained by considering how such works would have been written down. If it be granted, based on the foregoing arguments, that the commentaries are not just the product of a scholar working alone, then one can imagine two basic scenarios for how these writings should have been preserved and circulated.

Students may have taken detailed notes of all the proceedings in Alexander's class and written them up for distribution.[119] Or, the commentaries represent Alexander's own notes from which he lectured, notes which he augmented and changed throughout his teaching career. Plotinus' example is instructive: "From the first year of Gallienus Plotinus had begun to write on the subjects that came up in the meetings of the school . . . when I, Porphyry, first came to know him, I found that he had written twenty-one treatises" (*Life* 4.12). Additions probably reflected the subjects discussed in class: on two occasions, Porphyry remarks that Plotinus wrote on subjects that arose during meetings of the school (*Life* 5.5, 5.61). After a teacher's death, his papers and notebooks would have come into the hands of his pupils, who would have put them in some sort of order and perhaps added material from their own notes or those of other students; recall how Philodemus combined his notes with those of Bromius. In Porphyry's case, the basis for the *Enneads* were Plotinus' own treatises, which were inspired by the subjects discussed in the school. I would claim that as with Plotinus, Alexander's extant works were generated from his teaching activity, and that they incorporate his own notes *for* purposes of lecturing, rather than his student's notes *from* his lectures. One obvious reason for this is the first-person discourse: Alexander always employs "I" or "we": nowhere do we find, "Alexander said," or the like. By contrast, the *Discourses of Epictetus*, as well as those of Musonius Rufus, contain third-person remarks about things Epictetus or Musonius said or did. The exegetical nature of his work is simply a reflection of classroom discussion: whereas Plotinus spoke on assorted topics, Alexander explicated texts. As a result, his commentaries probably preserve the form and substance of his actual lectures.[120] This cannot be proved, but it is the most reasonable explanation for the shape of Alexander's extant writings.

Certain explicit statements testify to the use of books in Alexander's school. One illuminating remark occurs in his comments on *Top.* 101a25:

> But this class of arguments [dialectical arguments] was familiar to the ancients, and they used to conduct the majority of their classes in this manner, not from books as we do now (for at that time, these sorts of books did not yet exist), but when some thesis for discussion was proposed for this purpose, those who were being trained tried to establish a method for finding dialectical proofs, arguing for and

against the subject on the basis of generally held opinions. And there are books of such arguments from Aristotle and Theophrastus which contain proof for contrary assertions on the basis of generally held opinions.[121]

In this excerpt it is clear that books form the basis for teaching activity in Alexander's teaching circle. Presumably, this would allow us to infer the physical presence of texts in class. We might safely assume that at a minimum, the teacher has a copy of the text being discussed, or at least a commentary thereon in which the text was included; it is not unlikely that some students would have had copies of this text, or portions of it, as well. In fact, this may be the source of the different readings that Alexander often mentions in his commentaries. These may not derive from Alexander's collation of different manuscripts, but rather from the copies of books that other people have brought to class. It is possible that other Aristotelian texts would have been available for consultation. In fact, if we imagine a group that was meeting in the house of the teacher, presumably his entire library would have been present and available. On the other hand, the fact that students (or readers) are informed of the existence of books of Aristotle and Theophrastus containing theses for discussion indicates that these kinds of books were probably *not* a part of instruction, at least in Alexander's classroom: it would be superfluous to furnish this as new information if such books were a common part of class procedure. Given the implicit contrast between the way the ancients used to conduct classes and the way "we do it now, from books," it may be inferred that Alexander's class was devoted more to the exegesis of Aristotelian texts and less to the staging of mock arguments for and against sample propositions.

Another suggestive remark about classroom procedure occurs in *Quaest.* 3.2. After quoting a problematic section from Aristotle's *De Anima*, the text continues, "these things having been said by him [Aristotle], it was inquired more generally after (*apo*) the explanation (*exēgēsis*) whether the transition to actuality is a change."[122] It is possible that this alludes to the consultation of a commentary during class (i.e., "it was inquired from the written explanation"), a practice documented in the case of Plotinus.[123] It does not appear, however, that Alexander ever uses *exēgēsis* to refer to a piece of writing.[124] When he does refer to his commentaries, *hypomnēmata* is the term of choice.[125] Taking the preposition *apo* in a temporal sense, however, yields the translation, "after the exegesis," which would indicate that "exegesis" was a particular phase of classroom activity. I proposed in Chapter 1 that in the case of Epictetus' school, *exēgēsis* refers to a type of instruction distinct from a preliminary reading and from the analysis and the posing of hypothetical arguments. Perhaps the same was true in the school of Alexander.

Yet another term that refers to a particular phase of instruction in Alexander's class is *koinologia*, or "general discussion." In *Met.* 1008a30, Aristotle asserts the futility of conversing with a person who affirms and denies the same proposition: "Besides, it is clear that the examination (*skepsis*) of this is an examination of nothing."[126] Alexander's comment on the meaning of *skepsis* in this passage occurs at *in Met.* 296.23: "that is to say, *koinologia* and inquiry (*zētēsis*)."[127] *Koinologia* and inquiry are billed as a complementary pair of activities. A technical sense for *koinologia* is also evident in Alexander's commentary on the *Topics*, where it is used of logical arguments which are inaccessible to people without special training.[128]

Once again, Galen provides an interesting parallel. For Galen, *koinos logos* is explicitly linked to the activity of reading: it is the open discussion that follows the reading of a text.[129] This explicit tie with reading cannot be confirmed in the case of Alexander, but it is clear that *koinologia* carries some special connotation as a term describing one aspect of philosophical instruction in Alexander's class. The term finds a precedent in Aristotle's own writings, even though the usage may not be so pointedly technical:

> And a certain opinion on the soul has come down to us that is no less plausible than many others; it has, however, been the subject of critical remarks in school discussions.[130]

So in sum it is not at all unreasonable to suggest that *koinologia* corresponded to a period of discussion in Alexander's class that formed a complement to inquiry (*zētēsis*).

Conclusions

I have attempted to demonstrate that Alexander's commentaries show definite signs of classroom origins and that they are probably based on Alexander's own lecture notes. As such, they provide a rough transcript of the subject matter covered in his school on any given day. That subject matter seems to have been almost exclusively textual: certainly he would have treated special problems when the occasion arose, but it appears that the main vehicle for his teaching was the written text to be explicated. The fact that so many other Aristotelian teachers of the second century wrote commentaries suggests that this may have been the dominant mode of teaching in Peripatetic schools.[131] The commentaries of Adrastus and Aspasius may be aimed somewhat more at a reading audience. Dealing with the historical and literary allusions in the *Nichomachean Ethics*, Adrastus' commentary would be the best candidate for a reading audience. However, as we have seen, commentaries from all these individuals turned up in Plotinus' school, so works originally written for private use may eventually surface in a context remote from their point of origin.

In one sense, Aristotelians are the most "textual" of any of the groups encountered thus far. They lavished more philological attention on the written texts of their School, and classes, it seems, were largely devoted to continuous readings of Aristotelian treatises. The studious and bookish nature of Peripatetics would be consistent with the character of their founder: the following anecdote, drawn from the *Vita Marciana*, an anonymous life of Aristotle, serves as a fitting conclusion to the present chapter:

> And so diligent was he [Aristotle] that when he was a student of Plato, his house was called the "house of the reader." Quite often, Plato used to say, "let us go to the house of the reader," and coming within earshot, he would cry out, "The Intellect [i.e., Aristotle] is present: the lecture-room is silent."[132]

4

BOOKS BENEATH A PLANE
TREE: PLATONISTS

The "Plato-loving lady" addressed by Diogenes Laertius in his treatment of Plato was probably not the only person in antiquity who felt the need of assistance when addressing herself to the dialogues.[1] People with the means and inclination could have received such training within a school setting of some sort, where a teacher might have discussed the nature of the dialogue form, the different kinds of dialogues, and the way they should be organized. Moving beyond such introductory subjects, students would presumably have encountered the dialogues themselves. We know very little, however, about curricula in Platonist philosophical circles: would teachers and students have simply read through entire dialogues together as a way of learning Plato's thought? Or would a teacher have structured a course around themes in Platonic philosophy, illustrating topics of interest with selected passages?

Of course, philosophers were not the only people who read Plato. In this way, Platonic literature differs from the other bodies of literature we have examined thus far. Readers in search of literary gratification would hardly have turned to Chrysippus; nor to the writings of Epicurus.[2] And while the subject matter of Aristotle's philosophy would have been appealing to some, we would not expect to find *Prior Analytics* read as after-dinner entertainment.[3] The dialogues of Plato, however, offered both philosophical riches and literary gratification: "For everyone, even those who do not accept their teachings or are not enthusiastic disciples, reads Plato and the rest of the Socratic school . . . "[4] Indeed, we know of at least one teacher who worried that the literary excellencies of the dialogues could prove distracting to students.[5] In any event, there were many readers who would have approached the dialogues: serious students of philosophy as well as literary magpies. What helps and shortcuts would have been available? Did anyone actually sit down and read through entire dialogues?

In making our way towards answers to such questions, we shall follow the pattern established in previous chapters, dealing (briefly) with matters of authenticity and textual integrity, and with the various attempts to order Plato's literary corpus. We will consider commentaries, in particular the *Anonymous Commentary on Plato's Theaetetus*, as well as the surviving fragments of Harpocration. Some readers would also have consulted monographs on special subjects: Theon's *Mathematics Useful for Reading Plato* is one such book. Writers distilled dogmatic statements out of the dialogues and organized them in the form of epitomes and handbooks, such as Alcinous' *Didaskalikos*. Wholesale comparisons between Platonists and Peripatetics should be made with care, but mindful of the complexities I will suggest that readers of Plato's works relied on secondary materials to a somewhat greater degree than did their Peripatetic counterparts. The concluding section treats the elusive subject of actual usage: how texts were used in the schools of Taurus and Plotinus.

Arranging according to wisdom: strategies for reading

Introductory works attached to bodies of literature would have been a familiar literary genre to students of philosophy.[6] The *Pinakes* appended to Aristotle's works by Andronicus of Rhodes is one example of the type; another is the *Life of Plotinus*, written by Porphyry to serve as an introduction to the *Enneads*. Platonists also wrote introductions to Plato's literary corpus. Thrasyllus, a Platonist with a Pythagorizing streak and court philosopher to Tiberius, wrote a preliminary pamphlet to the works of Democritus entitled *Prolegomena to the Books of Democritus*, and given his extensive work on the Platonic corpus it is quite likely that he wrote a similar work for Plato's dialogues.[7] Theon of Smyrna, active under Hadrian, was responsible for a book entitled *Sequence of Reading Plato's Books and the Titles of His Compositions*,[8] while Alcinous, another second-century Middle Platonist, wrote an introduction to Plato's works called the *Didaskalikos* that was specifically addressed to readers about to encounter the dialogues.[9]

Authenticity and the proper order of works within a corpus are two of the major questions typically addressed in such introductions. As with most literary collections in antiquity, certain works attracted critical suspicion. Ancient critics raised doubts about several of the thirty-six dialogues typically included in both ancient and modern editions of Plato's work.[10] At least one ancient editor, however, did not expunge such works from the corpus on this account: Thrasyllus questioned whether Plato wrote the *Amatores*, but still included it in his fourth tetralogy (D.L. 9.37). Other pseudonymous dialogues sprang up at various times and places, but none of them attained a status approaching that of the dialogues assigned to the nine tetralogies.[11]

Related to the question of authenticity is the integrity and condition of the texts themselves.[12] Scholars have not reached a consensus about the existence of an early and authoritative edition of Plato's works. Some claim it was a project of the Early Academy,[13] and others argue for the existence of an Alexandrian edition.[14] Recently, it has been proposed that Thrasyllus (d. 36 CE) imported many significant changes into the dialogues.[15] Ultimately, all claims about authoritative editions issued at a particular time and place should be viewed with caution.[16] In any event, the text of Plato's dialogues during the Imperial period appears to be relatively stable, at least compared to the Aristotelian corpus. As literary pieces, Plato's dialogues more easily achieved a state of closure.

Organizing a collection of books is a complicated and subtle undertaking, one that conceals a multitude of presuppositions, assumptions, and cultural biases.[17] As an illustration, let readers consider the different ways the books on their shelves might be organized and the rationales for these different schemes. How, then, did ancient readers arrange Plato's books? Where should one begin? And where to go from there? It is a situation that requires no small imagination to appreciate in all its complexity: we must keep in mind all the constraints (availability of texts, manuscript paleography and orthography, social supports for reading, etc.) under which ancient readers labored, as well as the variety of aims and interests held by teachers and students. With modern presuppositions about reading, it seems hermeneutically responsible to start at the beginning of a dialogue and read to the end; we presume that the highest literary and philosophical yield is to be found by reading in a way that respects the literary integrity of the dialogue. Some ancient readers, however, favored a reading strategy best described as poaching. Calvisius Taurus, a Platonic teacher of the mid-second century CE, grumbled about such students: "One is eager to begin with the *Symposium* of Plato because of the revel of Alcibiades, another with the *Phaedrus* on account of the speech of Lysias."[18]

Students such as these were interested only in literary titillation, not in personal reform.

The *Symposium* and the *Phaedrus* were only two of many possible points of entry into the Platonic Corpus. According to Diogenes Laertius,

> Some begin from the *Republic*, some from the *Greater Alcibiades*, some from the *Theages*, some from the *Euthyphro*, others from *Clitophon*; some from the *Timaeus*, some from the *Phaedrus*, others from the *Theaetetus*, and many make their beginning from the *Apology*.[19]

Albinus mentions still other practices:

> Some begin from the *Letters*, others from the *Theages*; some, dividing them according to tetralogies, place first that which contains the *Euthyphro*, the *Apology*, the *Crito* and the *Phaedo*.[20]

Obviously, readers and teachers were not rigidly constrained by any one point of entry. And certainly, the availability of texts would have played a role in the decision. Presumably, some works were more difficult to locate than others.

Making a beginning was only the first task; a reader would still need a strategy for navigating through the rest of Plato's corpus. We know of at least five ways of arranging the dialogues. The first, a collection of four trilogies, is attributed by Diogenes Laertius to Aristophanes of Byzantium, a polymath of the third and early second century BCE, and head of the Alexandrian Library. The second arrangement, in nine "tetralogies," derives from Thrasyllus. The third is from Albinus, a second-century Platonist. The originator of the fourth scheme, extant only in a medieval Arabic source (al-Farabi) is unknown;[21] so too, with the fifth arrangement, attributed to a certain Theon, perhaps Theon of Smyrna.[22] Synoptically arranged, the schemes run as shown in Table 4.1. There is obviously a great deal of intricate structure and mutual influence evident in these schemes which cannot be discussed at present; interested readers are referred to the rich secondary literature on the subject.[23]

The sequences listed in Table 4.1 seem motivated by at least three distinct requirements presumably valued by the users behind the list. These may be termed "literary," "pedagogical" and "theoretical."

Table 4.1 Ways of arranging Plato's dialogues

Arist. Byz. D.L. 3.61–2	Thrasyllus D.L. 3.57–61	Albinus Prologue	Unknown (al-Farabi)	Theon (al-Nadîm)
1 Rep.	1 Euthph. (pei)	Euthph. (pei)	Alc. Ma.	Rep.
1 Tim.	1 Apol. (eth)	Meno (pei)	Tht.	Leg.
1 Criti.	1 Crito (eth)	Ion (pei)	Phileb.	Theag.
2 Leg.	1 Phd. (eth)	Charm. (pei)	Prot.	Lach.
2 Minos	2 Crat. (log)	Tht. (pei)	Men.	Amat.
2 Epin.	2 Tht. (pei)	Alc. (mai)	Euthph.	Charm.
3 Tht.	2 Soph. (log)	Theag. (mai)	Crat.	Alc. 1, 2
3 Euthph.	2 Pol. (log)	Lys. (mai)	Ion	Euthd.
3 Apol.	3 Parm. (log)	Lach. (mai)	Gorg.	Gorg.
4 Crito	3 Phileb. (log)	Tim. (phy)	Soph.	Hp. Ma.,
4 Phd.	3 Sym. (eth)	Apol. (eth)	Euthd.	Hp. Mi.
4 Epist.	3 Phdr. (eth)	Crito (eth)	Parm.	Ion
	4 Alc. 1 (mai)	Phd. (eth)	Alc. Mi.	Prot.
	4 Alc. 2 (mai)	Phdr. (eth)	Hipparch.	Euthph.
	4 Hipparch. (eth)	Sym. (eth)	Hp. Ma.	Crito
	4 Amat. (eth)	Epist. (eth)	Hp. Mi.	Phd.
	5 Theag. (mai)	Menex. (eth)	<Sym.>	Tht.
	5 Charm. (pei)	Cleit. (eth)	Theag.	Cleit.
	5 Lach. (mai)	Criti. (eth)	Amat.	Crat.
	5 Lys. (mai)	Phileb. (eth)	<Pol.>	Soph.
	6 Euthd. (ana)	Rep. (pol)	Charm.	
	6 Prot. (end)	Minos (pol)	Lach.	
	6 Gorg. (ana)	Leg. (pol)	<Lys.>	
	6 Meno (pei)	Epin. (pol)	Phdr.	
	7 Hp. Ma. (ana)	Crat. (log)	Crito	
	7 Hp. Mi. (ana)	Soph. (log)	<Apol.>	
	7 Ion (pei)	Pol. (log)	Phd.	
	7 Menex. (eth)	Parm. (log)	Rep.	
	8 Cleit. (eth)	Prot. (end)	Tim.	
	8 Rep. (pol)	Hp. Ma/Mi. (ana)	Leg.	
	8 Tim. (phy)	Euthd. (ana)	Criti.	
	8 Criti. (eth)	Gorg. (ana)	Epin.	
	9 Minos (pol)		<Cleit.>	
	9 Leg. (pol)		Menex.	
	9 Epin. (pol)		Epist.	
	9 Epist. (eth)			

"Literary" refers to schemes in which dialogues are linked in view of shared characters, setting, or incident. So, for example, there is an obvious connection between the *Euthyphro, Apology, Crito* and *Phaedo*, as they are all set within the narrative context of the trial and death of Socrates. So too with the *Theaetetus, Sophist,* and *Statesman*:

all feature the same characters. Thus, the trilogies of Aristophanes of Byzantium and the tetralogical scheme of Thrasyllus qualify as literary. The "pedagogical" arrangement of Albinus is explicitly geared to the needs of students, while the architect of the "theoretical" sequence behind al-Farabi arranges the dialogues in a sequence corresponding to a satisfying intellectual trajectory.[24] Theon's structuring principle is difficult to discern: al-Nadîm describes him as advocating tetralogies and his order has some slight points of commonality with that of Thrasyllus. This list may be confused, however, and no firm conclusions can be based upon it.[25]

In two cases (Thrasyllus and Albinus), the dialogues are "characterized" according to eight different types.[26] The following quote from Albinus serves as an exposition of these:

> Since it is necessary for us to become contemplators of our own soul and of divine things and of the gods themselves, and to attain to Intelligence, most beautiful of all, we must first purify our thinking from false opinions (peirastic dialogues). And after the purification we must awaken and call forth our natural intuitions, and purify these and make them shine out distinctly, to be our first principles (maieutic dialogues). After this, when the soul has been made ready, we must plant the appropriate doctrines in it, by which it is brought to perfection; and these are doctrines of physics and theology and ethics and politics (expository dialogues). And in order that these doctrines remain seated in the soul, they must be bound with a calculation of the cause, so that one may hold firm to the goal which has been fixed (logical dialogues). After this we must make ourselves proof against deception, so that we are not misled by some sophist, and do not turn our dispositions in the direction of the worse (anatreptic and endeictic/epideictic dialogues).[27]

Albinus has made the character of the individual dialogues the key to his organization: personal growth through a number of well-defined stages is the goal.[28] In fact, Albinus criticizes the tetralogical ordering:

> Of this opinion [i.e., in favor of tetralogies] are Dercyllides and Thrasyllus, but they seem to me to have wanted to make an arrangement based on persons in the dialogues and cir-

cumstances; which is perhaps useful for something else, but not indeed for what we now wish to do, which is to find a proper point of beginning and sequence of teaching in accordance with wisdom.[29]

Perhaps Thrasyllus' arrangement had bibliographic satisfactions; nine clumps of four books form a numerologically pleasing set. It is not, however, the best arrangement from a pedagogical standpoint.

Finally, only one of these arrangements, that of Thrasyllus, incorporates all the dialogues; certainly, there was much flexibility at this point. Iamblichus, in fact, reduced the canon of necessary dialogues to twelve.[30] Albinus also prescribes a "short course" for those who by age, ability, and academic training are already prepared to philosophize, and who are able to withdraw from the trammels of public life. Such readers may address themselves first to the *Alcibiades*, then to the *Phaedo*, the *Republic*, and finally the *Timaeus*.[31] The remark about age suggests that this short course was perhaps a prescription for older readers who might not normally be found sitting in classrooms, while a more complete cycle of readings may have been followed in a formal school setting.

A modern student of the different ordering schemes for the Platonic dialogues claims that "the tetralogies fail in several fundamental ways as a tool for the understanding of Plato," though the arrangement is "certainly superior" to the truncated canon of Iamblichus.[32] Whether these lists are "failures" or not can only be judged by whether they succeeded in the uses to which they were put. An ancient writer might claim with equal merit that modern approaches to the dialogues fail since they do not serve to purify the soul. If the goal is the most rational presentation of Platonic philosophy, then tetralogies are probably not the best sequence: the sequence given in the anonymous source quoted by al-Farabi may be more theoretically coherent than that of Thrasyllus. Albinus could argue that his list is superior for the moral development of students. And if the goal was apotheosis, a shortened list of dialogues such as that recommended by Iamblichus might prove superior. Different reading strategies reflect different patterns of use, and patterns of usage reflect the variety of aims pursued by Platonic teachers and students.

"Readers by themselves": commentary

Platonists devoted substantial energies to the writing of commentaries, though it appears that they did not match the devotion of Peripatetics in this regard.[33] Authors of commentaries to Platonic books in our period include:

Eudorus, *fl.* 25 BCE: *Timaeus* (perhaps),[34]
Gaius; early second century: *Republic* (perhaps just the Myth of Er),[35]
Theon of Smyrna, *fl.* 115–40: *Republic*,[36]
Calvisius Taurus, *fl.* 145: *Gorgias, Timaeus, Republic,*[37]
Albinus, *fl.* 150: *Republic* and *Phaedo,*[38]
Numenius, *fl.* 150: some treatment of the Myth of Er,[39]
Cronius, contemporary of Numenius: commentaries on unknown
    books,[40]
Atticus, *fl.* 176–80: *Timaeus* and *Phaedrus,*[41]
Author of *Anon. Tht.*: *Theaetetus, Symposium, Timaeus, Phaedo,*[42]
Harpocration, pupil of Atticus: *Alcibiades* 1, *Phaedo, Phaedrus,
    Timaeus,* and *Republic,*[43]
Severus, end of the second century: *Timaeus,*[44]
Democritus (date unknown; see Porphyry, *Life* 28): *Alcibiades* 1,
    Phaedo, and (perhaps) the *Timaeus.*[45]

In addition, we have the testimony of Plutarch and Galen,[46] who claim that many people have written commentaries on the *Timaeus*, as well as commentaries on papyrus not attributable to any known author.[47]

As we have seen, however, the term "commentary" (*hypomnēmata*) can mean many things, ranging from an informal collection of notes to formal treatises. Here, it will be my task to illustrate the different types of commentaries on Platonic texts, to observe any characteristic differences among them and the other commentaries examined thus far, and, most important, to consider the most plausible context for their origin and use. Unfortunately, the shortage of surviving evidence severely limits the range of such inquiries. A happy exception is the *Anonymous Commentary on the Theaetetus*, which I will treat in some detail. Some scanty remains from Harpocration's commentaries yield a few clues about his exegetical methods, and these offer an interesting point of comparison to *Anon. Tht.*

Discovered in the ruins of a house in Hermopolis, Egypt, *Anon. Tht.* consists of seventy-four lengthy columns as well as many fragments.[48] The author is unknown, but the text has been dated by paleographic criteria to the first or second century CE, and perhaps earlier.[49] It is a Type I commentary; though it does not treat the whole content of the text, the *Theaetetus* serves as its structural backbone. By beginning with a discussion of the aim of the dialogue as a whole and the integrity of the text, it acknowledges the dialogue as a literary entity. The author alludes to the introductory elements of the dialogues, and even mentions a corrupt version of the *Theaetetus* which omitted the opening (3.27); however, the narrative elements are not considered worthy of commentary. Roughly half of the text appears in the lemmata: the commentator includes most (though not all) of Socrates' comments while omitting those of his conversation partners, keeping only those remarks on which Socrates expresses approval. On occasion, the text of the *Theaetetus* that falls between two successive lemmata is summed up by a paraphrase.[50]

Plate 2 shows the formal layout of *Anon. Tht.*[51] The standard format is the full quotation of the lemmata followed by paraphrase and explanation, though there are many cases in which the paraphrase is omitted and explanation begins immediately.[52] With few exceptions, each line of the lemmata is set off from the surrounding comment by the *diple* sign (>), as in lines 14–16 and 25–34 in col. 21 of Plate 2.[53] Furthermore, the beginning and end of the lemmata are generally marked with a *paragraphos*, a short horizontal line.[54] Most of the lemmata begin and end in the middle of a line; the copyist does not begin a new line when the text changes from text to commentary or vice versa. Quite often, a short space of one or two letter-widths is left before the lemma begins or after it ends.[55] In addition to the space, a small raised dot is used on occasion; an example is visible in line 24 of col. 22, following YOIC. Unlike some of the Peripatetic commentaries we have seen, the lemmata are strongly marked, and never altered to conform to the grammar of surrounding commentary. In this sense, *Anon. Tht.* appears most similar to *PFay.* 3, where *ekthesis* is used to mark off the lemmata.[56] Second-person utterance is used occasionally but not frequently.[57]

The commentator addresses several different kinds of problems: difficulties in word order and archaic expressions draw comment, often on subjects that do not appear particularly difficult.[58] Obscure pieces of local color are elucidated.[59] Problems in the logic of the narrative attract the commentator's eye and apparent inconsistencies with Socratic statements made elsewhere are discussed.[60] So, for example, at *Tht.* 151b2–3, Socrates says that not all people seem to him to be pregnant, while at *Sym.* (206c1–3) he claims that "all people are pregnant both in spirit and in body." The commentator

Plate 2 Anonymous Commentary to Plato's Theaetetus, cols 21–2, *PBerol.*
9782, courtesy of the Ägyptisches Museum und Papyrussammlung of
the Staatliche Museen zu Berlin Preussischer Kulturbesitz.

resolves this apparent inconsistency by stating that Socrates means
not everyone "in this life," i.e., in this particular incarnation, is
pregnant, but taken as a general statement everyone may be said to
be pregnant (57.11–42). It is significant that while problems raised
by the text may receive more than one possible answer (e.g., at
34.9–36.35), such difficulties usually receive a definitive solution.
The author of *Anon. Tht.* is more determined to achieve closure in
such matters than, for example, Alexander of Aphrodisias. The

102

commentator is especially thorough in his explanation of mathematical concepts: nearly nine columns of text, including a diagram, are devoted to *Tht.* 147d3–5, and the mathematical remarks that occur elsewhere in the dialogue provoke lengthy comment. Finally, the author peppers the text with polemical remarks directed against Stoics, Epicureans, and other (unidentified) opponents.[61]

What, then, do these formal features imply about the setting from which *Anon. Tht.* originated and the venue for which it was designed? More succinctly, *"from* where and *to* whom?" As for "from," these characteristics suggest a literary work that does not spring directly from class proceedings, i.e., it does not represent notes taken in class by a student or the papers of a teacher. We find no traces of what might be described as "other voices," by which I do not necessarily mean real retorts or questions (as one hears in the *Discourses* of Epictetus), but even rhetorical "others," either in the form of questions or opponents. There is nothing of the sort encountered in Alexander of Aphrodisias, such as, "it was said," or "there was a question about . . ." or any other such oral residue. Nor do we encounter any detours that sound like professorial rambles. Finally, alternative solutions to problems of the sort that might be generated in a class discussion are also lacking.[62] We may contrast this with Alexander's commentaries once again, or, more pertinently, with the remarks on the *Timaeus* by the second-century Platonist Calvisius Taurus, where several positions on the generation of the world are reviewed.[63]

As for its destination ("to whom"), *Anon. Tht.* creates the impression of a literary work tailored for isolated readers looking for help in approaching the *Theaetetus* on their own. The full quotation of the lemmata and the paraphrasing that stands in place of omitted text suggest that the commentary might even have been used in lieu of a text of the *Theaetetus* itself.[64] Mathematics in the Platonic dialogues may have been a stumbling block for many readers, and the detailed treatment of mathematical portions of the *Theaetetus*, complete with graphic aids, suggests a reader without classroom supports. The first editors of the document observe that the quality of the papyrus and its orthography suggest it was produced specifically for commercial purposes.[65] Galen (or rather Ps.-Galen) seems to have such an audience in mind in the introduction to his *History of Philosophy*, when he claims to have written so that "lovers of learning on their first encounter with these subjects might not lack for explanations, but on their own, would be able to understand more clearly the things being said."[66]

Another instructive commentator to consider in company with the author of *Anon. Tht.* is Harpocration, a Platonist active in the latter part of the second century CE.[67] While the commentaries of Harpocration are lost, one of their characteristic features may be gleaned from allusions in later commentaries; namely, that Harpocration employed the aporetic method, or the posing of questions. This forms an interesting point of contrast with what we have seen in *Anon. Tht.* Olympiodorus preserves a remark of Harpocration's drawn from a commentary on the *Phaedo* :

> Then is it not, said Socrates, a sufficient indication, when you see a man troubled because he is going to die, that he was not a lover of wisdom but a lover of the body? And this same man is also a lover of money and of honor, one or both.
> Why has he [Plato] left aside the love of pleasure? Harpocration raised this difficulty, but did not provide a solution.[68]

An anonymous commentary on the *Phaedo*, does, however, preserve two answers attributed to Harpocration:

> Why did he leave aside the love of pleasure? Because a lover of the body would involve being a lover of pleasure; or that the lover of the body is just the same thing as a lover of pleasure. Other solutions: Plato censured this earlier in the dialogue, and now mentions those things he omitted earlier. This is how Harpocration explains it.[69]

Another remark from Harpocration on the *Phaedo* preserves a similar question on whether desire for material goods is the cause of wars.[70] It seems that Harpocration's exegetical work raised questions of a different nature than those encountered in *Anon. Tht.* The author of *Anon. Tht.* sought to explain difficulties that might block a basic understanding of the text, such as problems with strange vocabulary or mathematical concepts. The questions raised by Harpocration are of another order; they are problems suggested by the text, problems of a more general nature that would have been suitable for prolonged philosophical discussion, such as the causes of war. The absence of such material from *Anon. Tht.* is highlighted by the contrast; from this perspective, it appears that the commentaries of Harpocration more directly reflect classroom discussion, while *Anon.*

Tht. appears better suited to help solitary readers come to terms with the text as written.[71]

A first-cousin to the commentary is the monograph on a subject of particular interest (or difficulty). *Mathematics Useful for the Reading of Plato* by Theon of Smyrna, active under Hadrian, appears to be designed for readers anxious to apprehend this aspect of the dialogues.[72] I will not undertake a detailed description of the work here; I am interested rather in how such a text would have been used: would it have served as a resource for someone encountering a piece of mathematical argument in the dialogues (i.e., a sort of mathematical commentary), or does it represent an independent treatise on mathematics? Is this a book a teacher might have used as a resource in class, or does it represent the curriculum of a course in mathematics?

The author bills his work as one which will be of service to those who have not received a proper education but who nevertheless wish to approach the dialogues with understanding:

> Now when someone is trained in all aspects of geometry and music and astronomy, making the attempt to read the Platonic treatises is a most blessed undertaking, if indeed someone has the skill; but this is something neither simple nor easy [to acquire], requiring a great deal of labor from an early age. But for the sake of those who have deficits in their training, but who desire a complete knowledge of his treatises, we will treat summarily and quickly the necessary subjects and those things which are most important for the teachings concerning mathematical theory encountered in Plato.[73]

This being said, however, it becomes clear from the beginning that the text offers a relatively free-standing course in mathematics, making only occasional reference to the dialogues.[74] The clearest link with the text of the dialogues occurs when Theon quotes a fragment from the Myth of Er; but after a lengthy quote and a short paraphrase, we encounter: "So much for Plato. We provide an explanation of this in the *Commentary on the Republic*."[75] Apparently, treatment of specific problems is relegated to commentaries on individual books, commentaries which the author presumes the readers have in their possession or to which they have access.

It appears that not all of those for whom this document was intended were members of Theon's teaching circle, for in a discussion of astronomical principles, the author makes the following statement: "We have also prepared a model sphere in accordance with this description."[76] This has the sound of a remark directed at a readership one step removed from his actual class, as though a teacher were lecturing to students at a distance, students who must be introduced to classroom furnishings. As was the case with Galen, a well-respected teacher might often have been approached by friends or by people interested in his teaching who did not attend his class, and *Mathematics Useful for Reading Plato* seems tailored to such an audience. Of course, students who did attend the class but who also wanted a written version of subjects discussed in lecture – oral teaching "through *hypomnēmata*," as Galen says – would also be natural consumers for such a work.[77] As such, Theon's teaching activity probably took place on two fronts: in the classroom, and remotely by means of his writings.

Nearly all of the commentaries by Platonists in our period are lost, of course, so it would be rash to make blanket statements about what these must have looked like. Nevertheless, in the evidence that does survive, we do not find fully continuous commentaries comparable to those of the Peripatetics or the later Neoplatonists. Some of the commentaries by Platonists may have been structured topically: a fairly lengthy excerpt from Taurus' commentary on the *Timaeus* discusses the topic of whether the world is created or not. Even *Anon. Tht.* is not a fully continuous commentary: it extracts and comments only on Socrates' statements. The kinds of commentaries seen in the last chapter, where lemmata and comment begin to merge, are also lacking.[78] In the previous chapter, I suggested that commentaries with this formal feature reflect a continuous and sustained exegesis of a text by a teacher, where lemmata were altered and restated, embedded as they were within the surrounding comment. If an argument from silence counted as a good argument, the absence of this type of commentary among Platonist groups would suggest that teachers in Platonic schools were less likely to engage in this kind of continuous exegetical lecture. Perhaps they focused more on selected topics in the dialogues. In any case, the format of the extant commentaries such as *Anon. Tht.* suggests the existence of an audience of readers who were approaching Plato's works by themselves, outside of a school setting. Readers of this sort may have used a text such as *Anon. Tht.* in lieu of the actual dialogues.

Cliff notes meets the *Timaeus*: epitomes and handbooks

In addition to commentaries, we know of other texts designed to aid readers in gaining easy access to ideas contained within Platonic dialogues. The so-called *Timaeus Locrus* takes the form of a reordered and simplified version of the *Timaeus*.[79] In its present form it is cast into the Doric dialect and assigned to the Pythagorean philosopher Timaeus of Locri. It appears, however, to have existed first as an epitome of the *Timaeus* before it was tricked out in Pythagorean dress. Yet another type of distilled and homogenized treatment of Plato's work is Alcinous' *Didaskalikos*. In what follows, we shall examine both of these re-presentations of Plato's work.

The process of epitomizing is a more transgressive mode of literary appropriation than the act of commenting. The *Timaeus Locrus* is a parade example: there are noticeable differences in content, organization, and style between it and the *Timaeus*. Many sections of the dialogue are simply ignored while others are substantially reorganized.[80] All dialogical elements are omitted; there are no other speakers, and no dramatic staging. The *Timaeus* itself features three main sections: the first describes the origin of the universe according to Reason, the second according to Necessity, while the origin of the cosmos, of the gods, and of human beings receives an alternative explanation under each heading.[81] The third section blends the first two sections together as they pertain to the body and soul. This structural feature is collapsed in the *Timaeus Locrus*; cosmology comes first, followed by anthropology.[82] The author gives simplified (not expanded) treatments of mathematical and astronomical sections that might have proven difficult for his readers. Furthermore, the *Timaeus Locrus* is characterized by an earnest and didactic style of presentation, quite unlike the tentative and qualified manner in which Plato advanced his theories: "only if God concurred could we dare to affirm that our account is true."[83]

The following excerpt shows how the *Timaeus Locrus* achieves a fivefold reduction in the length of the original by removing layers of explanation and detail. Here is *Tim.* 80D–81B, on the subject of nourishment:

> And it is owing to this [the process of respiration] that in all living creatures the streams of nutriment course in this way through the whole body. And inasmuch as these nutritive particles are freshly divided and derived from kindred

substances, – some from fruits, and some from cereals, which God planted for us for the express purpose of serving as food, – they get all varieties of colors because of their commingling, but red is the color that runs through them most of all, it being a natural product of the action of the fire in dividing the liquid food and imprinting itself thereon. Wherefore the color of the stream which flows through the body acquired an appearance such as we have described; and this stream we call "blood," which is the nutriment of the flesh and of the whole body, each part drawing therefrom supplies of fluid and filling up the room of the evacuated matter. And the processes of filling and evacuating take place just as the motion of everything in the Universe takes place, namely, according to the law that every kindred substance moves towards its kind. For the bodies which surround us without are always dissolving us and sending off and distributing to each species of substance what is akin thereto; while the blood-particles, again being minced up within us and surrounded by the structure of each creature as by a Heaven, are compelled to copy the motion of the whole; hence, when each of the particles that are divided up inside moves towards its kin, it fills up again the emptied place. And when what passes out is more than the inflow every creature decays, but when less, it increases (tr. Bury, LCL).

Here is the same passage as rendered in the *Timaeus Locrus*:

All nourishment is supplied to the body from the heart as the root and from the abdomen as the source. Whenever the body is irrigated more than it is drained, it is known as growth; whenever less, it is known as decay.[84]

The author/editor has simply eliminated all the remarks about nutrition, attractive forces between like substances, and the color of blood. Examples of such truncation could be easily multiplied. Even at those points where essentially the same statement is made, the epitomizer simplifies Plato's syntax and vocabulary. Nowhere do we find an unaltered excerpt from the *Timaeus*.[85] So, while the author of the *Timaeus Locrus* may be accused of flattening out the richness of the original, the complete rephrasing of the dialogue represents a sizeable investment of editorial labor.

Based on the didactic tone of certain sections, it has been argued that the document springs from a school setting, combining an epitome and lecture notes deriving from a teacher's explanations of difficult passages.[86] Still, the *Timaeus Locrus* is marked less by explanation than it is by truncation and simplification: it eliminates problems, rather than explaining them.[87] So while some strata within the document may derive from lecture notes and therefore a classroom environment, the *Timaeus Locrus* is better described as a stripped down text of the *Timaeus*, not a transcript of class discussions.

From the standpoint of usage, the *Timaeus Locrus* might well have served as a surrogate for a reading of the *Timaeus*, a document known for its difficulty.[88] As noted, the style of the document is also comparatively simple. Readers anxious to mine the *Timaeus* for its basic cosmological doctrines and who wanted to avoid some complicated syntax might well have turned to the *Timaeus Locrus*.

Alcinous' *Didaskalikos*, which seems designed to summarize Plato's thought as a whole, differs noticeably from the *Timaeus Locrus*. The *Didaskalikos* is thematically structured, treating Plato's position on logical, physical, and ethical questions, drawing on several of the dialogues for support.[89] I will not give a detailed description of the text; that has been ably done by translators and commentators.[90] After a few introductory remarks, I will consider plausible contexts for its origin and use, and whether it would have supplemented or perhaps supplanted the Platonic texts themselves.

The *Didaskalikos* is at once closer to and farther away from the dialogues than the *Timaeus Locrus*; it is structured synthetically, and therefore conflates material from all the dialogues. On the other hand, it appropriates Platonic language more directly. Explicit borrowings of terms and phraseology are evident throughout; *Did.* 172.2–23 is one specific example.[91] One also finds explicit reference to places within the dialogues, though this habit seems to be restricted to just a few sections.[92] This stands in stark contrast to the *Timaeus Locrus*, which, because it seeks to supplant the *Timaeus*, could not in principle acknowledge it in this way.

The author does more, however, than slavishly reproduce phrases lifted from the dialogues. In many cases, he makes alterations in word choice or word order. So, at *Tim.* 30A4, the cosmos is described as being in a state of "discordant and disorderly motion." Alcinous renders this as "disorderly and discordant motion." At *Tim.* 74C7, the elements of water, fire, and earth are compounded with a mixture of "acid and salt"; Alcinous has "salt and acid" (172.28).[93] We also find simple additions and substitutions of single words. The reasons for this tendency are unclear; Whittaker argues convincingly that it is more than simply faulty memory or sloppy copying. For whatever reason, it appears that the author wished to leave his own mark on the material. Far from proving that the state of the text is still fluid and unsettled, it proves rather that the textual tradition is firm enough to invite such changes from an author who wants to brand the material as his own.

Careful comparison of the *Didaskalikos* with other doxographical works shows that Alcinous was quick to borrow material from other sources. Ch. 12, for example, is largely taken from Arius Didymus' handbook, *On the Doctrines of Plato*, and most of the *Didaskalikos* probably derives from the handbook of Arius and others like it.[94] But while the "bricks" may be borrowed, the mortar that holds them together is Alcinous' own. Procedural language is prevalent at such seams, and first-person discourse often crops up at these points. It also occurs in those sections where illustrative examples are provided.[95] Conversely, where there is much borrowing, there is little first-person discourse. So when Alcinous is simply passing on traditional material, his own voice recedes; when adding an explanation or describing the course of his discussion, it rises again to the surface. The use of first- and second-person discourse, however, is not a guarantee that we have a direct transcript of classroom utterance. This kind of language might be employed by an author who wants to create the feel of the classroom for the reader.

The ways in which such a document might have functioned are, of course, quite varied. It might have been used by other teachers as a convenient distillation of Platonic doctrines.[96] It is not impossible, however, that readers working on their own might also have begun with such a work. Indeed, in the final lines, the author calls the work an "introduction to the study of the doctrines of Plato" (§36). There is no doubt that a person who had been steeped in the dialogues would have been able to understand the *Didaskalikos* with greater ease, or that such a compendium could function as a document for review. Nevertheless, reading this digest of Platonic doctrines would certainly have been an easier proposition than picking up the *Timaeus* and perusing it unaided. During an age when the doctrines that lay behind the dialogue were of keen interest, it is not hard to imagine ancient readers who would have preferred to avoid the tricky business of extricating Platonic dogma from the dialogues.[97] The simplified language and thematic organization would certainly have been appealing to neophytes. Readers would also have been able to turn immediately to subjects of particular interest: say ethics or physics. And from an economic viewpoint, the *Didaskalikos* might have offered readers most of what they desired without the difficulty or expense of acquiring the dialogues themselves. The parting words of the author are significant: "what has been expounded here gives one the capability to examine and discover subsequently all the remainder of his doctrines."[98] As such, the author seems to conceive of his text as an introduction, not as a précis for review purposes. According to Seneca, it would qualify as a *breviarium*, not a *summarium*: "The former is more necessary to one who is learning a subject, the latter to one who knows it" (*Mor. Ep.* 39.1).

"For three days . . . ": texts in use

We are fortunate to have direct testimony about pedagogical procedures in two Platonic groups. Aulus Gellius makes several remarks about the teaching activity of L. Calvisius Taurus, a student of Plutarch and Aulus Gellius' own teacher. Porphyry gives an extended picture of Plotinus' teaching circle and its literary practices, and though this strains the chronological boundaries of this study, the value of the evidence is such that it would be unwise to ignore it. While the scarcity of the evidence allows only flickering glimpses of texts and teachers at work, it appears that the school of Taurus and that of Plotinus provide interesting points of contrast.

Aulus Gellius mentions that teaching took place in Taurus' own house.[99] This was probably the most common venue for philosophical teachers. Lucian places the Platonist philosopher Nigrinus in a similar setting:

> On entering [his house], I found him with a book in his hands and many busts of ancient philosophers standing round about. Beside him there had been placed a tablet filled with figures in geometry and a reed globe, made, I thought, to represent the universe.[100]

A similar situation may be presumed in the case of Taurus.

Gellius never provides us with a systematic account of Taurus' teaching practices.[101] Still, he relates several useful anecdotes in which teaching practices are obliquely represented. This is one of the most useful:

> I once asked Taurus in his lecture-room (*in diatriba*) whether

a wise man got angry. For after his daily readings (*cotidianae lectiones*), he often gave everyone the opportunity of asking whatever questions he wished. On this occasion he first discussed the disease or passion of anger seriously and at length, setting forth (*disseruisset*) what is to be found in the books of the ancients and in his own commentaries (*quae et in veterum libris et in ipsius commentariis exposita sunt*); then, turning to me who had asked the question, he said: "This is what I think about getting angry, but it will not be out of place for you to hear also the opinion of my master Plutarch (*Plutarchus noster*) . . . "[102]

Two types of instruction are evident here: the *lectio*, obviously the main course, and the question-and-answer session. Gellius never informs us about the substance of the *lectio*: was it arranged around a literary text, consisting of a reading and exegesis of continuous passages of one of Plato's dialogues?[103] Would students have read portions of the text or perhaps taken on roles of characters in the dialogues? Or is the class organized topically, invoking selections from various works on a given subject – say the topics found in Alcinous' *Didaskalikos*? Gellius does mention one occasion during which Plato's *Symposium* was being read before Taurus. It appears to take place in the classroom. After a section of Pausanius' speech on love was read (by someone other than Taurus, apparently) Taurus used the opportunity to needle Gellius about his affection for rhetoric:

> "Ho! you young rhetorician" – for so he used to call me in the beginning, when I was first admitted to his class, supposing that I had come to Athens only to work up eloquence – . . . I advise you to look upon this rhythm as an incidental feature; for one must penetrate to the inmost depths of Plato's mind and feel the weight and dignity of his subject matter, not be diverted to the charm of his diction or the grace of his expression (*NA* 17.20).

Apparently, this remark prefaced a lecture on the philosophical issues raised by the text. In any event, if the other students possessed Gellius' level of education, basic reading and exegesis would not have required much class-time.

The passage illuminates a crucial fact about Taurus' way of reading the dialogues. It seems he made a sharp separation between form and content on the assumption that these two components of a piece of writing could be separated, and that the gracious style might even distract a reader from matters of substance. If it is the substance, not the form, that counts, a reader might be well served by a document such as the *Didaskalikos*. One can imagine teachers who saw certain advantages to an unadorned presentation of Platonic doctrine, since the subject matter was not swathed in beguiling and distracting language. It was Taurus, after all, who chided students for picking out the naughty bits in the *Phaedrus* or the *Symposium*. Given his antipathy towards such reading strategies, Taurus probably would not have objected to bowdlerizing the text of these dialogues as long as the "thought" was preserved. In a very revealing remark, we find Porphyry editing a text about oracles:

> For I myself call the gods to witness, that I have neither added anything, nor taken away from the meaning of the responses, except where I have corrected an erroneous phrase, or made a change for greater clearness, or completed the meter when defective, or struck out anything that did not conduce to the purpose; so that I preserved the sense of what was spoken untouched, guarding against the impiety of such changes, rather than against the avenging justice that follows from the sacrilege.[104]

For Porphyry, it seems that the textual "vehicle" may undergo fairly profound alterations without affecting the payload. If other teachers in addition to Taurus stressed content at the expense of form, it is easy to see that documents such as the *Didaskalikos* would have had wide appeal.

As for the question-and-answer phase, Taurus begins by citing and discussing ancient authors on the subject followed by material drawn from his own commentaries. We can only speculate on the details of this procedure. We know that speakers often had books on hand when lecturing. In his essay *On Listening to Lectures*, Taurus' own teacher Plutarch criticizes students who think of philosophers as they would actors; i.e., respect them as they perform their particular task, but outside the classroom hold them in no special esteem:

> Now there is some reason that they should feel thus towards the popular lecturers (*sophistai*); for when these get up from the speaker's chair (*thronos*), and put away their books and

lecture notes (*biblia kai eisagōgai*), it is apparent that in the real pursuits of life they are small men and rank lower than the average; but towards philosophers of the real sort it is not right that they have such a feeling.[105]

Nothing in the language suggests that Plutarch believes books and notes are props only for sophists, though nowhere in this suggestively titled work does he show written texts functioning in a classroom situation. It does seem rather unlikely that Taurus would be rolling and unrolling books in order to read isolated passages. It would have far more efficient to utilize his own notes on anger, where, through a lifetime of reading and study, he had compiled excerpts from classical writers. If so, the "ancient texts" discussed were present only in the form of excerpts in his own personal commentaries. An example of this type of text is Plutarch's *On the Control of Anger*, which draws on poetic, dramatic, and philosophical texts bearing on the subject of anger and its treatment. Indeed, since students often inherited their teacher's writings, it is not impossible that some of the material in Plutarch's excerpts on the subject found its way into Taurus' own commentaries, the same commentaries that Aulus Gellius heard. Even then, though his *hypomnēmata* may have been physically present, Taurus probably would have been able to rely on his memory for most if not all of this material: Gellius prizes facile utterance that proceeds from an encyclopedic knowledge of literature, and it is difficult to account for his high opinion of Taurus if the latter could do no more than read out of prepared texts. Still, the practice was not unknown:

> A lecturer sometimes brings upon the platform a huge work of research, written in the tiniest hand and very closely folded; after reading off a large portion, he says: "I shall stop, if you wish"; and a shout arises: "Read on, read on!" from the lips of those who are anxious for the speaker to hold his peace then and there.[106]

Had Taurus' pedagogy been this clumsy, Gellius, erudite and quick to criticize, would surely have mentioned it.

Finally, in addition to formal lectures, Taurus often invited those students with whom he was on intimate terms (*iunctiores*) to dinners at his home. Each diner was obligated to bring a problem of a light and entertaining kind, suitable for a mind "enlivened with wine."[107]

Indeed, it appears that a significant fraction of studying under a given teacher involved trailing around after him and observing his behavior and conversation: "I often spent whole days in Rome with Favorinus. His delightful conversation held my mind enthralled, and I attended him wherever he went" (*NA* 16.3.1). Learned conversations in public places attracted the attention of intellectual idlers:

> Cornelius Fronto, Festus Postumius, and Sulpicius Apollinaris chanced to be standing and talking together in the vestibule of the Palace; and I being near with some companions, eagerly listened to their conversations on literary subjects.[108]

Obviously, having an entourage composed of well-heeled and sophisticated students could only enhance one's status. Students were also accustomed to travel with their teacher, and provocative subjects for conversation often arose in the course of the journey.[109] Taurus and his coterie once went to the trouble of visiting Gellius, who had fallen ill in the country (*NA* 18.10). All indications are that in this case, Taurus and his students formed a close-knit group for which the simple term "school" (if used in the modern sense) seems rather inadequate.

Another picture of texts and teachers at work may be gained from Porphyry's *Life*. Along with Arrian's *Discourses of Epictetus*, Porphyry's account of Plotinus' teaching circle is one of the most detailed portrayals of life in an ancient philosophical school.[110]

At the outset of a discussion of Eternity and Time, Plotinus gives a general sketch of the method he employs when dealing with difficult philosophical problems:

> We consider the statements of the ancient philosophers about them, who differ one from the other, and perhaps also different interpretations of the same statements, and we set our minds at rest about them and think it sufficient if we are able, when we are asked, to state the opinion of the ancients, and so we are satisfied to be freed from the need of further research about them. Some of the ancient and blessed philosophers have indeed discovered the truth; but some of them have done this more completely than others, and it is incumbent on us to examine how we too might come to an understanding of these things.[111]

This procedure would seem to involve the reading of philosophical texts. Indeed, Plotinus insinuates that some students of philosophy think their work is done when they have collected and recited the opinions of the ancients. For Plotinus, at least, this is a proper way to begin the task of philosophy, but it is not the way to end. Porphyry states explicitly that the writings of his teacher are "full of concealed Stoic and Peripatetic doctrines," Aristotle's *Metaphysics*, in particular; and concealed they are: the reader finds no explicit references to philosophical texts *per se* in the *Enneads*.[112] They are crowded with allusions and free paraphrases of Plato's works, but Plotinus never names and quotes a specific dialogue.[113] He refers to what characters in the dialogues say, but we never find an exact quote prefaced by "Plato says in the *Republic*," or the like.[114] As Porphyry says (*Life* 14.4), Plotinus has stated his own opinions rather than citing material handed down by tradition.

Still it is quite likely that before Plotinus stated his opinions, the texts of the ancients were cited and discussed, though Porphyry has not recorded this phase of instruction. Evidence for this claim is available though not plentiful. On one occasion, Porphyry overheard Amelius struggling to explain the phrase "the soul ceases (*lēgei*)," taken from *Tim.* 37a3–8, and realized that his difficulties arose from a corrupt text. In fact, the text should read "the soul says" (*legei*).[115] If we may assume that the incident occurred in Plotinus' class, where Amelius and Porphyry were both students, then we have confirmation that the text of the *Timaeus*, at least, was subjected to close analysis, and that students would have been expected to offer interpretations of the texts under discussion. This incidentally illustrates one way that text-critical problems came to light. When Alexander of Aphrodisias or Aspasius comment on textual problems, it may not be because they have collated manuscripts. Rather, problems might surface when students brought their own copies of written texts to class. One can imagine the following exchange happening on a regular basis: "What does your copy say? Mine has it this way . . . " Discussion could then ensue on which was the better reading. Modern teachers are able to assume that the texts in their students' hands have a much higher degree of uniformity.

We know, too, that commentaries played a role in the normal course of Plotinus' teaching, and this naturally presupposes that the texts on which the commentary is based are the subject of discussion:

In meetings of the school he [Plotinus] used to have the commentaries read to him, perhaps of Severus, perhaps of Cronius or Numenius or Gaius or Atticus, and among the Peripatetics of Aspasius, Alexander, Adrastus, and others that were available. He never let the commentators have the last word, but took an innovative and personal line in theoretical discussion, while bringing the mind of Ammonius to bear in matters of detail.[116]

This passage throws light on what the phrase "different interpretations of the same statements" might mean in the quotation from *Enn.* 3.7.1 mentioned just previously: different commentators would no doubt have given various interpretations of the same text. So in spite of the absence of explicit remarks or citations in the *Enneads*, we may safely presume that texts of Plato, Aristotle, and others were read in class sessions, and that commentaries on these texts were also consulted. It may be the case that only the commentaries with imbedded lemmata are present. While the kind of commentary offered by *Anon. Tht.* is probably rather elementary for a class such as Plotinus', a text featuring lemmata of interest, clearly marked by *ekthesis, diplai*, and *paragraphoi* would be well suited to such use.

As for the actual procedure of reading, Plotinus himself did not do the reading of the commentaries, if the passive voice of the verb "to read" in the above example may be taken at face value. Apparently, this task was performed by a student.[117] Perhaps Plotinus himself or another student read a relevant portion of Platonic dialogue or other work, while yet another student read the commentary on the text. The relatively advanced and well-off students in Plotinus' circle would certainly have had the means and motivation to acquire texts of the works being read or commentaries thereon.

Another important reference offers a tantalizing clue about the relationship between Plotinus' teaching and written texts:

Once I, Porphyry, went on asking him for three days about the soul's connection with the body. He extended the explanation to such an extent that when a certain man by the name of Thaumasius entered and said that he wanted to hear Plotinus make general remarks and also to speak on books but that he could not tolerate Porphyry's questions and answers, Plotinus said, "But if Porphyry asks questions and we do not solve his difficulties we shall not be able to say anything at all on the book [presently under discussion]."[118]

The passage contains several difficulties, and no one solution commands universal assent. Readers interested in the details are referred to the Appendix (see pp. 228–9). The translation I have given above presumes that Thaumasius expected to find himself in a classroom where the teacher went back and forth between remarks of general import and discussions of written texts. This was the case in Taurus' class: on any given subject, one would turn first to the ancients, and then add one's own synthetic and constructive comments based on or inspired by these texts. In principle, it was true for Plotinus' class as well (see *Enn.* 3.7.1, above), but Plotinus may have been prone to wander from the script. Porphyry tells this anecdote in order to show how solicitous Plotinus was in the question-and-answer portions of class, though at times this led to anarchy: "since he encouraged his students to ask questions, the course was lacking in order and there was a great deal of pointless chatter" (*Life* 3.36–7). Taurus kept a tighter grip on his students: questions were only allowed after lectures, and even then the opportunity to ask questions was not always offered. In this respect, he may be following in the steps of his teacher Plutarch: "Those persons who lead the speaker to digress to other topics, and interject questions, and raise new difficulties are not pleasant or agreeable company at a lecture."[119]

In spite of their different styles, Taurus and Plotinus seem to have run classrooms in which at least three different phases were traversed: (1) the reading and explanation of texts from the ancients, perhaps taken from commentaries or collections of excerpts, (2) general reflections by the teacher stimulated by these readings, and (3) periods during which questions from students were entertained. Using terms that appear in Porphyry's description of Plotinus' class, these three pedagogical moments might go under the rubrics of *exetasis*, *theōria* and *erōtēsis*.[120] It cannot be shown, however, that this pattern was always followed.[121] Plotinus' philosophical sessions do not seem to have been highly scripted affairs.

Conclusions

Would a person making a grand tour of ancient philosophical Schools have approached a Stoic, Epicurean, Aristotelian, or Platonist teacher expecting a distinctive kind of pedagogy? Did the various

Schools have different ways of appropriating their texts, or does this depend entirely on the individual teacher? In other words, would pedagogical procedures have varied according to "school" or according to "School"? A great deal depended on the individual teacher; witness, for example, Taurus' rather controlled lectures and the free-wheeling philosophical salon over which Plotinus presided, where a student might occupy a professor for three days with incessant questions. Certainly not every Aristotelian teacher left behind a corpus of commentaries; some of their written output can hardly be described as exegesis.[122] And ultimately, compared to Stoics and Epicureans, who wrote almost no commentaries at all, Academics and Platonists are much more similar than different.

Platonic teachers do not seem to have been as industrious as their Peripatetic counterparts in the production, use, and transmission of continuous commentaries. It might be objected that these texts are simply the victims of historical misfortune; however, if that was truly the case, it seems likely that the Neoplatonic commentators would have made more frequent mention of such works. Instead of continuous commentaries generated within and for the purposes of use in class, we find a text such as *Anon. Tht.*, which is essentially a commentary on an epitome of the *Theaetetus*, aimed at readers working without the benefit of a teacher. Digested, synthesized, and simplified works such as Alcinous' *Didaskalikos* and the *Timaeus Locrus*, texts whose aim was to increase the accessibility of Platonic doctrine on topics of special interest, played a large part in the promulgation of Platonic ideas. Allowing for exceptions to the general trend, Platonist teachers seem to have taken a selective approach to the dialogues, dealing with sections that treated subjects of interest, rather than reading continuously through a given dialogue. And it seems likely that literate individuals working on their own would have used these secondary works as a point of access to Platonic literature.

A little reflection shows why Platonist teaching circles generated and used secondary literature. Students and teachers interested in a given subject were required to come to terms with material scattered all over the dialogues, a situation that would encourage the process of gathering, grouping, and synthesizing. The shifting play of the dialogue form, the false opinions compellingly expressed, and Plato's penchant for irony would also have led students to concretize subjects of interest in a less ambiguous form. One might contrast this type of literature with Aristotle's works: students and teachers interested in logic, ethics, or physics, would know enough to begin with the *Categories*, the *Nicomachean Ethics*, or the *Physics*. But as we have seen, there were a multitude of inroads to the Platonic Corpus. In light of this, it is not surprising that readers interested in Platonic doctrine would have employed literature that aided in the systematizing process. In their full form, dialogues may not have functioned well as classroom texts. But qualifications are needed here too: we saw that Albinus recommended at least two different courses of reading in which individual dialogues are prescribed in set sequence.

Furthermore, the existence of synthesizing literature suggests a wider dissemination for Platonic writings, in spheres where teachers were not at hand to explain texts, and where readers would have been eager to assimilate Platonic ideas in simpler forms. Becoming superficially familiar with Plato's dialogues might have appealed to those wishing to acquire the trappings of Greek culture, or to people who wanted to associate in a familiar way with such people and presumably reap the benefits of such associations: guests at a dinner party might well have heard one of Plato's dialogues as after-dinner entertainment.[123] Such literary pretensions stood shoulder to shoulder with the visual language of the art and architecture of the day:

> Once the emperors themselves paid homage to Greek culture or, in the case of Hadrian or Marcus Aurelius, even actively placed it at the center of their own programs, many strata of society began to equate Greek myth, Classical art, and especially 'the philosophical way of life' with the most sought after lifestyle ... The result was men and women who had themselves depicted as philosophers or Muses, furnished their public and private rooms with copies or paraphrases of Classical masterpieces, and adorned their houses and tombs with representations of Greek myth.[124]

So, just as a modern businessperson might find it advantageous to learn golf, if not for love of the game then as a strategy for social maneuvering, an ancient person might have found reasons to acquire some familiarity with Plato. Literature that made this process easier would certainly have found consumers. So Whittaker's assurances notwithstanding, some readers might well have turned first to a document such as the *Didaskalikos* before or even instead of turning to the dialogues themselves, especially those readers who wanted a passing acquaintance with Plato, but who were either unwilling or unable to address his works at first hand.

At the end of Chapter 3 I concluded with a story drawn from the

Vita Marciana, that showed Aristotle hunched over his books while Plato reveled outside with his companions. The historical veracity of this picture need not be proven for the point to be made. Accurate or not, this view of the two founders probably reflects popular conceptions of the differences between Schools. The picture of Peripatetics as studious encyclopedists, and Platonists as rather more garrulous, public figures surfaces in Lucian's *Philosophies for Sale*: the Peripatetic knows about the lifetime of the gnat and the soul of the oyster, while love is the special expertise of the Platonist.[125]

5

JEWISH AND
CHRISTIAN GROUPS

General introduction

The attempt to treat "Jewish and Christian groups" within the same section runs the risk of flattening the diversity of late Second Temple Judaism. Still, all the groups treated here focused their attention in one way or another on the Hebrew Bible (or a Greek translation thereof), so I have opted to keep them together. As a nod to the differences, however, the chapter is divided into four distinct sections. The first of these sections deals with Philo as one of several different types of exegetes active in Alexandria. Ideally, it would be desirable to treat Hellenistic Jewish exegesis more generally by examining the other Jewish exegetes working in Alexandria, such as the "hyper-allegorizers" that Philo mentions on occasion. The problem, however, is one of evidence: Philo tells us very little about these individuals, and none of their writings appears to have survived. In the second section I will discuss a group, rather than an individual – namely, the Qumran Sectarians. The third section treats what I will provisionally call "scribal culture" in Palestine exclusive of Qumran. It is not possible to call this a "group" per se. Nevertheless, I will argue that the Judaism of Jesus and the religious authorities he clashed with is characterized by a distinctive way of dealing with texts relative to Qumran and Philo's group in Alexandria. The fourth and final section deals with the beginning of the Christian movement. For the present, we will treat only that phase of Christianity in which "scripture" still referred to the Greek Bible. Obviously, Christians in various places and at various times became quite attached to the writings that would eventually constitute the New Testament. Paul's letters were read in worship, Gospels were written, and commentaries were written on these letters and Gospels. Forays into this phase of Christian textual practice will be the subject of a future study.

At the outset of a rather long chapter that deals perforce with a wide spectrum of literature, I wish to reaffirm the basic principle behind my enterprise: this is a study about *people*; specifically, people using books. It is not about books or forms of literature as stand-alone objects. Such a study must begin with the remains of a literary interaction, namely the texts themselves; only then may we look to the people who used and produced them. Given the state of the evidence, the outline of the hands on the roll (or codex) and the hum of the classroom will be sometimes sharply, sometimes dimly, perceived. It is my goal to peer behind the forms of literature to the reading circumstance in which these texts were performed, and to do this in comparative perspective.

PART 1

LAWS TRANSCENDENT AND DAZZLING: PHILO OF ALEXANDRIA

Since all previous chapters have focused on groups, it would be consistent and desirable to speak here of "Hellenistic Jews" and their textual habits, rather than the literary practices of Philo, an isolated individual. Unfortunately, there is very little evidence about other Jews performing advanced exegesis of scripture. Scholars remain in disagreement about the proper social milieu of Philo's exegetical activities.[1] So while we would like to be able to speak about the group of which Philo was a member, there is simply not enough evidence for such a description. And it may be, as I will argue, that much of Philo's writing activity was an individual pursuit, not simply a transcript of or a script for school or synagogue activity. Philo's work is so rich, however, that it cannot be ignored, even if we cannot say how representative it was of Hellenistic Jewish exegesis.

Philo believed that just as a body houses a soul, so the biblical books harbored a teeming multitude of symbolic meanings accessible to those with the ability to read allegorically. His work as an allegorical commentator has intrigued generations of scholars; his debts to Hellenistic philosophy on the one hand and Jewish exegetical techniques on the other have been exhaustively described, and I will not undertake to duplicate that work here. Instead, we shall bring the same set of questions to Philo's work that we have brought to members of other book-centered groups. In comparison with Epicureans and Stoics, Philo shows no interest in text-critical

123

questions; his high view of the Septuagint seems to preclude errors in the text. We turn, therefore, immediately to commentary, and from there to use: based on the form of his commentaries, can we imagine the situation from which they emerged and in which they were subsequently used? Would they have been ancillary aids for a private reader working his or her way through a text? Can we imagine these texts as an exposition of a lectionary reading that Philo might have delivered in a synagogue or school setting? The detailed queries brought to Philo's commentaries are driven by these overarching questions about use.[2]

While it would be overly scrupulous to deny him the title of commentator, Philo never refers to any of his works as *hypomnēmata*; he prefers to call his literary creations simply "books" (*biblioi*), "treatises" (*syntaxeis*), or generically, "writings" (*graphai*).[3] Nor does he tend to use the various verbal forms of *hypomnēma* (e.g., *hypomnēmatizein*) to describe his authorial activity.[4] So while we may consider Philo as a writer of commentaries according to our definition of the term (lemma plus comment), Philo may not consider himself to be writing within that genre.

While Philo employs the technique of allegorical interpretation in nearly all of his works, not all of them qualify as commentaries even in our sense of the word. Traditionally, his exegetical works have been divided into three basic categories: the Allegorical Commentaries, which treat the first seventeen chapters of Genesis; the *Exposition of the Law*, a discussion of Mosaic Law, and the *Quaestiones*. We will first consider the form and style of the Allegorical Commentaries, and then turn to the *Quaestiones*.

Notwithstanding some significant detours, Philo follows the sequence of Genesis throughout the Allegorical Commentaries. The boundaries between the individual books marked by modern editors may not have been so marked by Philo himself,[5] nor is there any manuscript evidence indicating that the titles go back to Philo. At times, the commentary may give way to treatise: at the beginning of *De Plantatione*, Philo encounters a verse that mentions the drunkenness of Noah. This leads him to discuss the topic of drunkenness by adducing the opinions of other philosophers on the question. He then continues the treatment in the next treatise, *De Ebrietate*, and then takes up the thread of scripture once again in *De Sobrietate*.

Lemmata in the Allegorical Commentaries appear to have been quoted in full. They vary in length, from half of one verse to as many as six verses.[6] Quotations are often restated in the course of explanation.[7] Philo frequently cites other scripture in the course of explaining a verse, and often, he ends up commenting on these verses as well, which results in a series of nested comments. Texts invoked and cited in the course of the explication may be designated secondary (or tertiary).[8] In most of the commentary proper, the primary lemmata stand grammatically clear of the surrounding comment. Some treatises, however, show a definite tendency towards swaddling language.[9] In some cases, we find introductory remarks, e.g., "enough about x; let us turn to what follows."[10] But in most of the commentaries, the previous discussion simply ends with the presentation of a new verse without any transitional remarks. Philo does not deal with text-critical issues: unlike the author of *Anon. Tht.* or Alexander of Aphrodisias, he never makes any remarks about alternate readings in his text. Perhaps his concept of scripture and high estimation of the Septuagint precluded him from doing so.

Philo does not follow any set procedure for commenting on a verse. Indeed one of the distinguishing marks of Philo's commentaries is their apparently meandering quality, and students of Philo have found sometimes more, sometimes less method in his exegetical procedure.[11] On occasion, he deals with surface features in the text,[12] or with problems raised by the logic of the narrative,[13] but quite often he sees these as invitations to jump to the allegorical level, preferring to avoid too much trouble over difficulties in the text. In some cases, multiple interpretations are proposed and tolerated, without a definitive solution being offered.[14] And frequently, there is a hierarchy of interpretations; two interpretations may be valid, but one is for mature readers only: "There is another interpretation current of this matter, though not for vulgar knowledge. It may be entrusted to the hearing of the elders: younger ears may well be sealed against it" (*Sac.* 131). And while he does not shrink from asserting his opinion, he does at times confess to a certain tentativeness in interpretation. After commenting on Gen. 11:7, he remarks,

> This is our explanation, but those who merely follow the outward and obvious think that we have at this point a reference to the origin of the Greek and barbarian languages. I would not censure such persons, for perhaps the truth is with them also.[15]

Gen. 25:8 speaks of the death of Abraham "in a good old age, old and full of days," and Philo admits to be "greatly puzzled" by the addition of the remark, "full of days." Still, Philo always makes a proposal, even if he regards it as tenuous.

As for their style, the Allegorical Commentaries teem with rhetorical devices.[16] The posing of questions as a spur to discussion of a vexed point is very common: expressions such as "for what reason" (*dia ti*), "how" (*pōs*), or the slightly more removed "someone might ask" are ubiquitous. Philo uses a remarkable amount of first- and second-person speech, both singular and plural. He often employs apostrophe, personalizing or addressing some aspect of himself ("O my mind," etc.), and he likes to set up rhetorical questions posed by fictive opponents. There is a great deal of moral exhortation as well, and Philo's phrasing tends to become shorter and pithier in the hortatory sections that occur with increasing frequency at the end of many of the books. These elements are hallmarks of the diatribe style, and give the Allegorical Commentaries a distinctly schoolish character.[17] In the treatises proper, such as *Op.* or *Abr.*, *Jos.*, or *Mos.*, these elements are less in evidence.

Still, Philo's style cannot be described as diatribal in all respects; no one should confuse Arrian's notes from Epictetus' classes with Philo's commentaries: "Long stretches of his essays are in the florid style, richly decorated with metaphors and similes, but devoid of question figures, apostrophe, and the short kola and kommata that are characteristic of the diatribe."[18] This mixture of styles shows evidence, then, of extensive literary tooling. They are not stenographic records of speeches actually delivered, even though they are richly furnished with dramatic elements. As such, they bear comparison with Seneca's *Moral Epistles*, where Seneca constructs what I have called an inscribed classroom, a literarily constructed teaching theater.[19]

The *Quaestiones* make up another significant body of Philo's exegetical work. Like the Allegorical Commentaries, they proceed through scripture on a verse-by-verse basis. They appear to be continuous: gaps in the sequence may be traced to accidents of preservation.[20] As to their form, the individual questions often include sizeable fractions of the scripture lemma being discussed. Indeed, questions are often introduced by "why" (*dia ti*) followed by the entire verse, with no mention of the specific question at issue.[21] There is a somewhat greater emphasis placed on literal explanation in the *Quaestiones*; many of the solutions contain no allegorizing at all.[22] On some occasions, however, nothing in the verse seems to require explanation at the literal level, so Philo moves immediately to allegorical interpretation.[23] The answers to the questions posed are generally lengthy in comparison with many other question and answer commentaries, such as Porphyry's commentary on Aristotle's

Categories.[24] Question-and-answer commentaries deriving from the medical milieu also feature short answers, as does the *Homeric Questions*, a collection of pseudo-Aristotelian questions on contradictions and other problems in Homer.[25] The tenor of these texts is that of a catechetical examination; the questions are more focused and direct, treating matters of content and meaning, while those in *Quaestiones et solutiones ad Genesim* and *ad Exodum* are perhaps designed to spur discussion. These types of questions recall those posed by Harpocration in his commentaries on Plato.

There is much shared material between the Allegorical Commentaries and the *Quaestiones*, and scholars disagree on the precise nature of their relationship: specifically, whether one is based on the other.[26] It might seem natural to assume that the more complicated allegorical commentaries grew out of the more rudimentary *Quaestiones*, but quite often the material in the allegorical commentaries differs significantly from that in the *Quaestiones*. Conversely, there are subjects present in the *Quaestiones* but missing from the commentaries.[27] We need not subscribe to the either/or that is often posed.[28] Both could have developed simultaneously and independently: a basic core of exegetical work on traditional problems evolved over time in two different directions for two different audiences.[29] Nothing would have prevented Philo from adding or subtracting material from the Allegorical Commentaries throughout his life, and similarly with the *Quaestiones*. Indeed, some of the meandering quality of the Allegorical Commentaries may derive, not from different sources appropriated by Philo, or from sloppy thinking, but from the diachronic evolution of the work and the scholarly methods employed in its compilation.[30] There is no reason to assume that Philo would have written, completed and then circulated once-for-all, an entire tractate in finished form. Just as the Elder Pliny might have wished to augment his *Natural History*, just as Alexander of Aphrodisias might have added something new to his commentaries based on a school discussion, so too might Philo have often made additions to his commentaries.[31] In fact, it would be most unnatural if this were not the case.

"A continuous flood of instruction": Philo the teacher

Having observed some of the formal characteristics of Philo's exegetical writings, what can we infer about their origin and use? Are these the by-products of classroom/synagogue interactions? Do we imagine Philo striding into the school or synagogue with a prepared homily in the form of an allegorical exegesis? Are we to imagine him listening and partaking in discussion and debate, and then synthesizing these discussions in written form after the fact? I have argued in previous chapters that commentaries often spring from classroom teaching. Thus, the commentaries of Alexander of Aphrodisias may be based on Alexander's own notes or on those of students, and therefore reflect fairly closely how a class might go. Plotinus' works, though not scripts of classroom procedure, also seem substantively tied to discussions in the school. The situation is different with Philo. Bousset proposed that Philo was a member of a Jewish exegetical school operating in Alexandria and that he has appropriated large tracts of material from written works circulating in the school.[32] Bousset's detailed proposals have been criticized, but the basic instinct behind the work, that Philo is working within a wider exegetical tradition, must certainly be correct. Several recent studies have begun to illuminate the larger stage on which Philo's exegesis is set.[33] Others have claimed that Philo's work either represents or is based on homilies delivered on synagogue lectionary readings,[34] still others that his audience was not the general synagogue audience but a select group, interested in and trained to perform advanced exegesis of scripture.[35] Finally, it is also possible that like other wealthy Greco-Roman men of letters, Philo might have headed a kind of philosophical salon, quartered in his own home.[36]

Philo's own self-description and his use of teaching imagery and metaphors strongly suggest that he was engaged in teaching of some sort. In one passage he alludes to his generative role: "But we who are called begetters are used as instruments in the service of generation" (*QG* 3.48). A person with ability, says Philo,

> should be ranked among the teachers and instructors, and should provide as from a fountain to the young a plenteous stream of discourses and doctrines. And if some less courageous spirit hesitates through modesty and is slow to come near to learn, that teacher should go himself and pour into his ears as into a conduit a continuous flood of instruction until the cisterns of the soul are filled.[37]

Teaching benefits not only the student but the teacher as well: "the giving of instruction to others, constantly repeated, entails study and practice to the instructor and thus works the perfect consummation of knowledge" (*Gig.* 26).

Philo alludes at various points to places where teaching and scripture exegesis occur, though he does not place himself securely in any one of these venues. In a well-known passage, Philo refers to the "schools of virtue" that open on the Sabbath:

> So every seventh day there stand wide open in every city thousands of schools (*didaskaleiai*) of good sense, temperance, courage, justice and the other virtues in which those present sit in order quietly with ears alert and with full attention, so much do they thirst for the draught which the teacher's words supply, while one of special experience rises and sets forth what is the best and sure to be profitable and will make the whole of life grow to something better (*Spec.* 2.62).

It is not clear, however, whether this "school of virtue" denotes an actual building, or rather a "gathering" in a general sense. Philo rarely uses the term *synagōgē* or *proseuchē*, and the term *synagōgion* probably refers to the group, rather than a physical structure, for which his chosen word seems to be *proseuchē* or "house of prayer."[38] Philo's account of scripture exegesis among the Therapeutae is similar: in those cases too, one or two experienced members give an after-dinner lesson while the rest of the community listens in rapt attention:

> their leader ... inquires into some question arising in the Holy Scriptures or solves one that has been propounded by someone else ... His instruction proceeds in a leisurely manner; he lingers over it and spins it out with repetitions, thus permanently imprinting the thoughts in the souls of the hearers ... The explanation of the sacred writings treats the inner meaning conveyed in allegory. For to these people the whole law book seems to resemble a living creature with the literal ordinances for its body and for its soul the invisible mind laid up in its wording.[39]

While Philo describes the Therapeutae from an outsider's perspective, he clearly approves of their practices, and shares many of their ideas.[40] In fact, if someone had applied this description to Philo himself, no one would have taken it amiss. Instruction spun out in a leisurely manner with repetitions is a fair description of Philo's own style. Indeed, his own discursive style may be a deliberate attempt to imprint thoughts on the souls of his readers and hearers.

Both of these citations show a group listening to a speaker. Philo alludes indirectly to another sort of scholastic gathering. A detractor of Jewish customs is made to comment derisively on Sabbath practices in wartime:

> And will you sit in your gatherings (or "gathering places": *synagōgioi*) and assemble your regular company and read in security your holy books, expounding any obscure point and in leisurely comfort discussing at length your ancestral philosophy?[41]

This text seems to indicate a more dialogical session where extended discussion might have taken place. Interestingly, words implying a leisurely style of study abound in this quote as in the previous one. Nothing in the evidence prevents us from imagining Philo fitting naturally into either of these environments. We know, too, that he was aware of goings-on in public speaking venues (*akroatēria*) and the theaters, where philosophers of different stripes harangued, declaimed, and preached to sometimes indifferent audiences.[42] His negative appraisal of such environments, however, suggests that he had little sympathy for this style of teaching (*Abr.* 20).

Furthermore, the Allegorical Commentaries as we now have them are at once too rhetorically polished and also too circuitous to serve as texts for actual synagogue homilies or discussions.[43] On the other hand, it is equally difficult to imagine that these curious and complex works could have been conceived *ex tempore*, then committed to paper after the fact, either by Philo himself or by a note taker. In fact, the raw material and the rhetorical devices found in Philo's writings probably characterize his presentation, style, and method in teaching, but it seems unlikely that his commentaries are actual transcripts of oral discourses delivered in a synagogue.

One hint about Philo's working environment is obtained from a fascinating passage about a state of ecstasy achieved in the course of study:

> I feel no shame in recording my own experience, a thing I know from its having happened to me a thousand times. On some occasions, after making up my mind to follow the usual course of writing on philosophical tenets (*kata philosophian dogmata*) and knowing definitely the substance of what I was to set down, I have found my understanding incapable of giving birth to a single idea, and have given it

up without accomplishing anything, reviling my understanding for its self-conceit, and filled with amazement at
the might of Him that is, to Whom is due the opening and
closing of the soul-wombs. On other occasions, I have
approached my work empty and suddenly become full, the
ideas falling in a shower from above and being sown invis-
ibly, so that under the influence of Divine possession I have
been filled with corybantic frenzy and been unconscious of
anything, place, persons present, myself, words spoken,
lines written (*Migr.* 35).

It may be some consolation to those who have been puzzled by
the twists and turns of Philo's thought to be reminded that Philo
writes when he is out of his mind. The passage recalls the remark of
Socrates in Plato's *Phaedrus*:

And a third kind of possession and madness comes from the
Muses. This takes hold upon a gentle and pure soul, arouses
it and inspires it to songs and other poetry, and thus by
adorning countless deeds of the ancients educates later generations. But he who without the divine madness comes to
the doors of the Muses, confident that he will be a good poet
by art, meets with no success, and the poetry of the sane
man vanishes into nothingness before that of the inspired
madmen (*Phdr.* 245A).

In the same dialogue, Socrates warns Phaedrus, "do not be surprised
if I often seem to be in a frenzy as my discourse progresses, for I am
already almost uttering dithyrambics" (*Phdr.* 238C). Perhaps it is
not so surprising that Philo's written work often proceeds like
crazing on old porcelain.[44]

Philo's ecstatic writing sessions might have taken place in his
own home or in a school setting; recall the "inspired teacher" in
Plate 1 and the eager scribes (apparently) scribbling down every
word. It seems unlikely, however, that people would gather for
the purpose of repairing to their individual writing projects. More
probably, students, teachers, and interested onlookers met for the
kind of discussion mentioned above, where a speaker read and discussed a text, or where members of the group engaged in dialogue,
"expounding any obscure point and in leisurely comfort discussing
at length" philosophical subjects. So the kind of writing Philo has in
mind here is almost certainly a private affair, carried out by himself

in his own household. As Quintilian says, "Everyone, however, will agree that the absence of company and deep silence are most conducive to writing" (*I.O.* 10.3.22). We may, however, imagine the presence of one or more secretaries.[45] It is, moreover, an activity that he has obviously pursued frequently: in his own words on a "thousand occasions." Nothing at all would prevent a dedicated man of letters from devoting many hours each day to such an enterprise.[46]

So in this particular excerpt, the setting is most likely private, if we accept the statement that this session began with the intent of writing on philosophical subjects (or better, setting down concepts in an orderly way *kata philosophian*). Sitting down to write sounds like an individual, not a public, pursuit. Certainly, Philo craves privacy. "The man of worth," says Philo,

> withdraws from the public life and loves solitude . . . And therefore he mostly secludes himself at home and scarcely ever crosses his threshold, or else because of the frequency of visitors he leaves the town and spends his days in some lonely farm.[47]

In any case, a great deal of productive writing appears to take place during such euphoric moments.

We saw above that Philo recommends that a teacher should go out to the student and pour instruction into his ears (*Spec. Leg.* 4.140). He can hardly be recommending that teachers comb the highways and hedges, looking for shy students to indoctrinate. I suggest that Philo saw his writings as fulfilling this role, and that his written treatises would serve as teachers, filling the ears of readers with a "continuous flood of instruction." For Philo, a written text can serve this function; indeed, Philo himself testifies to this out of his own experience:

> But if you encounter (*entynchanein*) someone who has been initiated,[48] press him closely and cling inseparably to him, until you have seen everything clearly, lest knowing of some newer secret, he conceal it from you. I myself was initiated under Moses the God-beloved into his greater mysteries, yet when I saw the prophet Jeremiah and knew him to be not only himself enlightened, but a worthy minister of the holy secrets, I was not slow to become his disciple (*Cher.* 49).

In this striking passage, Philo speaks as though he chanced upon

Jeremiah on the street, as though he were a teacher whose school a person might attend. Obviously, such an encounter could only have been mediated by the written text of Jeremiah (Philo proceeds to quote from Jer. 3:4). To "go to school with Jeremiah" must in some sense mean "read and reflect on the written text of Jeremiah." This session between teacher and pupil happens in spite of the intervening gulf of time and location, and the written text is instrumental to this. For Philo, a text can be a teacher. Indeed, a particular kind of immediacy seems to be presupposed here in the act of reading, as though the text were a door through which one passed to "encounter" the person behind it.[49] Philo speaks elsewhere of a reading in which reader and hearer are unified. Commenting on Exodus 24:7, "he [Moses] read to the ears of all the people," Philo observes that this reading has a special quality:

> Some notice must be taken of [the words] "reading to the ears." Now this takes place without separation and interruption, for the air is not agitated from without as the sound reaches the hearers but [the voice of] the speaker resounds in them without separation or distance like some pure and lucid voice which is extended. And there is no third thing interposed, by the intervention of which the reception becomes less but the sound echoes more surely in an only purer form when the hearers and the word come together without any separation between them. That is the literal meaning. But as for the deeper meaning, since it was impossible for anyone to reach such a multitude of hearers or to come near and speak to their ears, it is necessary to hold the opinion that the teacher and the pupil were there. One of them [the teacher] speaks privately to his disciples without concealing anything, not even things not to be spoken of; the other is the recipient who offers himself as one worthy of voluntarily being a repository of the divine Law and a guardian of those things which it would not be proper to interpret to the many, whatever may happen (*QE* 2.34).[50]

The phrase "reading into the ears" has caught Philo's eye: why "read into the ears" when "read" might have been sufficient? Philo believes that a special kind of reading is indicated, one in which the sound does not fall on the ear from outside. It is as though the strings of the understanding were plucked directly, circumventing the act of hearing. And this is only the literal meaning. When the text of the commandments is read the teacher and the pupil are suddenly brought together: a classroom comes into existence in the act of reading. The teacher/text pours forth knowledge, concealing nothing, while the pupil becomes a repository to be filled in a perfectly efficient exchange of knowledge. A re-creation of the original teaching moment occurs, or at least, can occur, when God "opens the wombs of the soul." An interesting text that enriches our understanding of what Philo might have in mind is *POxy*. 1381.[51] Having written a book in praise of Asclepius, the writer makes the following claim:

> For every gift of a votive offering or sacrifice lasts only for the immediate moment, and presently perishes, while a written record is an undying meed of gratitude, from time to time renewing its youth in the memory.[52]

For this author, a text does more than convey information. When it is appropriated by a reader, its infancy, its point of creation is summoned up and re-staged; appropriated by a reader, it blossoms anew, like a dormant bulb in spring weather. Philo also connects the act of writing with birth: his remark about "wombs of the soul" in the passage quoted earlier is a striking image – wombs are both receptive and generative, receiving seed and giving birth. When a text is appropriated by a reader, we have a text reborn – returned to its infancy. In any case, the author of *POxy*. 1381, like Philo, appears to have a high estimation for the latent capacities of the written word.

In fact, we have evidence from Philo himself that all a person needs for initiation is a book and solitude. In his glowing description of the Therapeutae, he states that within the house of each member, there is a consecrated room,

> which is called chapel or cell (*semneion, monastērion*) and closeted in this [the Therapeutae] are initiated into the mysteries of the sanctified life. They take nothing into it, either drink or food or any other of the things necessary for the needs of the body, but laws and oracles delivered through the mouths of prophets, and psalms and anything else which fosters and perfects knowledge and piety. They keep the memory of God alive and never forget it . . . [53]

Six days out of seven are spent in this type of reflection, seeking wisdom by themselves in their private cells.[54] It is only one day a week that they attend group meetings. Whether or not this account reflects the actual practice of a group, Philo considers it an ideal.

We have already seen that Philo believes that the reading of a text can be described as a kind of initiation. The remark "keeping the memory of God alive" also recalls the speech of the Therapeutic preacher, which imprints itself on the memory in virtue of its repetition. But in addition to reading, the practice of writing also has its beneficial effects. Epictetus says that Socrates wrote as a means of conversing with himself when he was without dialogue partners (*Disc.* 2.1.32). Writing also helps the task of memorization. It is writing, not simply reading alone, that causes statutes to be "glued to the soul." Commenting on Deut. 17:18, where the king is enjoined to write out a copy of the laws in his own hand, Philo states:

> the lawgiver bids him write out with his own hand this sequel to the laws which embraces them all in the form of a summary. He wishes hereby to have the ordinances cemented to the soul. For thoughts swept away by the current ebb away from the mere reader, but are implanted and set fast in one who writes them out at leisure. For the mind can dwell at its ease on each point and fix itself upon it, and does not pass on to something else until it has securely grasped what goes before ... For prolonged associations produce a pure and sincere affection not only for men [*sic*] but for writings of such kinds as are worthy of our love. And this will be the case if the ruler studies not the writings and notes of another but the work of his own pen, for everyone is more familiar with his own writing and takes in its meaning more readily ... I write [the laws] in a book in order to rewrite them straightway in my soul, and receive in my mind the imprints of a script more divine and ineffaceable.[55]

Philo's activity as a writer may serve as an act of personal devotion, a kind of self-teaching and reflection as well as a means of teaching. This makes sense of the many passages in which Philo speaks of the perfect man as being self-taught, or when he addresses his own soul and mind.[56] The ideal student seeks silence and solitude, shunning public assemblies and every religious clique. Such a person finds

> pleasanter society in those noblest of the whole human race whose bodies time has turned into dust, but the flame of

their virtues is kept alive by the written records which have survived them in poetry or in prose and serve to promote the growth of goodness in the soul (*Abr.* 23).

A sense of yearning pervades the passage: the tone is autobiographical. Philo no doubt hopes that once his own body has returned to the dust his writings will carry the flame of his heart and mind to future generations. It may well be the case that Philo preached in the synagogue and held teaching sessions in his own home; it seems quite likely, however, that he preferred the company of books to the hubbub of the classroom. By writing, Philo served his own devotional needs, in so far as reading and reflecting on scripture placed him at the feet of Moses and Jeremiah. No doubt he hoped that his own writings would do the same for others. So when considering the possible milieux of Philo's written work, we should keep in mind that Philo's writing may be the product of solitary reflection, and that he sought to provide for his reader what Jeremiah and Moses had provided for him.

Conclusions

Several different points of origin have been suggested for Philo's work as a commentator. Clearly, he is not working in isolation from other students of scripture. His commentaries represent the approach to the scriptures which he might have employed in synagogue teaching or in other discussion settings. My results do not contradict the proposals of scholars such as Nikiprowetzky or Sterling, who seek to locate Philo's teaching activity in the synagogue or in his own residence. His written work and his activity as a teacher were obviously interwoven in a complex way, and this was the case, as we have seen, with Plotinus. Discussion in the school formed the subject matter for the treatises that he wrote.[57] Indeed, progress in writing may have been contingent on progress made in group discussion. In this sense, the books are derivative of the class material. The *Quaestiones* in particular may be the precipitate of, or scaffolding for, a teaching situation of some sort.

But I would argue that Philo's writing is generated first and foremost from the inner springs of his own intellectual and spiritual life: his treatises are not mere by-products of school sessions.[58] In this sense, he is unlike Alexander of Aphrodisias, or Plotinus, two figures whose writings stand in closer relation to school activity. Nevertheless, Philo hoped his writings would function as teachers.

The Elder Pliny was a man whose written work proceeded from a voracious desire to gather and control as much knowledge as possible. Whether his writings would benefit others did not appear to concern him. This is not the case with Philo. Philo writes for himself, but he also writes for others. He creates a "virtual classroom" by means of a written text. Where there is a text and a willing reader, there is a classroom. The rhetorical devices that are so plentiful in the commentaries all serve this purpose. It is a classroom where he has learned from Moses and Jeremiah; it is a classroom where he in turn would teach others.

PART 2

BOOKS AMONG THE SONS OF LIGHT: QUMRAN

The Qumran sectarians centered their lives around texts in a way that we have not seen with any of the groups studied thus far. Torah study was the *raison d'être* of the community:

> And every matter hidden from Israel but which has been found out by the Interpreter, he should not keep hidden from them [i.e., new members who have completed their two-year catechetical period] for fear of a spirit of desertion. And when these exist as a community in Israel in compliance with these arrangements they are to be segregated from within the dwelling of the men of sin to walk to the desert in order to open there His path. As it is written: «In the desert, prepare the way of ****, straighten in the steppe a roadway for our God». This is the study of the law which he commanded through the hand of Moses, in order to act in compliance with all that has been revealed from age to age, and according to what the prophets have revealed through his holy spirit.[1]

This striking passage in the *Community Rule* conveys the thrill of discovery that must have attended the study of scripture at Qumran. God's purposes in history were being laid bare, and some believed these findings should not be shared with new members of the community for fear they might apostasize and take this secret information along with them; members of the sect were prohibited from arguing with outsiders, lest some secret be disclosed to them.[2] According to the *Community Rule*, however, information was to be freely shared among those who had become full members of the community. Within the group, an egalitarian ethos reigned. A group with these commitments is a prime candidate for detailed study.

After a few preliminary remarks on the Qumran community itself, we begin with a study of commentary. The topic has been discussed often, but for the sake of completeness I will provide a brief introduction to the topic of pesher commentary. In previous chapters, we have examined the actual manuscripts of commentaries whenever possible for clues to their probable use, and our good fortune in possessing manuscripts used by the Qumran sectarians invites a similar approach. In this case, the treatment required is rather involved, and so I will elide some of the details and produce only the results of the study.[3] After examining scripture translation and targum at Qumran, I shall look at the ways in which the sectarians rewrote, excerpted, anthologized, and abbreviated the Bible. We also have explicit testimony about study practices at Qumran that may be compared with the results derived from our formal study of the literature. Finally, I turn to the book of *Jubilees* to account for the striking emphasis on writing and written texts at Qumran. I will argue that *Jubilees* is crucially significant for understanding the textual ethos of the Qumran sectarians, more important than has previously been recognized.

The community

Since one goal of the present study is to view ancient books and their readers in a performance context, I preface this chapter with a few remarks about the possible loci for private and public reading and teaching based on archeological excavations.[4] First, the complex of buildings was relatively small in scale, covering a space of 100×80 meters. The community itself may have consisted of only 150–200 members.[5] Most of these appear to have been men, although excavations in a smaller adjoining cemetery disclosed skeletons of women and children.[6] This has been taken as evidence that the rigorously celibate and male community at Qumran, thirteen miles distant from Jerusalem, was only one specialized group embedded within a larger movement with members in various towns and villages.[7]

A description of the physical layout of the community would lead us astray, and, of course, many of the identifications for individual sites are tenuous. Significant for our purposes are Room 30, which De Vaux designated the Scriptorium, based on the benches and inkwells found there, and Room 4, an adjoining room lined with benches, a room which could have served as a site for instruction or study in small groups.[8] It is interesting that these are located at the very center of the complex. Perhaps this way of organizing space is significant: it privileges the studying function of the community, placing it at the heart of the community, much as libraries tend to be placed at central locations on university campuses. Another site that might conceivably have been used for reading and teaching is Room 77, the Assembly Hall and Refectory. Large meetings of the entire community would have taken place here, the only room capable of housing the entire community.

"The interpretation concerns . . .":
pesher commentary

Until recently, "scriptural commentary at Qumran" meant "pesher commentary," the particular brand of ideologically driven, eschatological interpretation that was apparently practiced only by the Qumran sectarians. Recently, however, fragments of rather different commentaries have enriched and complicated our picture of biblical exegesis at Qumran. These fragments, which preserve portions of a running commentary to Genesis, or rather to selections from Genesis, have been called a "non-tendentious simple-sense expository biblical commentary."[9] Discussion continues, however, as to whether these fragments are best understood as commentary or as a kind of rewritten Bible.[10] Though we now turn to the pesharim proper, the existence of these texts may serve as a reminder that the pesher commentaries alone do not give a complete picture of scripture interpretation at Qumran.

Pesher commentaries merit the name "commentary" based on their formal structure, which features individual scripture lemmata followed by commentary. The name derives from the Semitic root *pshr*, meaning to "loosen" or "dissolve."[11] In works of this genre, a scripture lemma, varying in length from a single phrase up to five verses, is followed by the formulaic phrase, "the interpretation of it [the scripture lemma] concerns . . . " Slight variations of the formula occur, but the great majority are marked by the occurrence of *pshr*.[12] When a fragment of a scripture lemma is re-quoted in the body of pesher comment, it is often introduced by a "re-citation" formula, e.g., "as it is written," "as it says." The main scripture lemmata, however, are never introduced by such formulae.[13]

Pesher-style commentary seems to be largely restricted to the prophetic books. One commentary, covering the first two chapters of Habakkuk, is extant (*1QpHab*),[14] and there are remains of commentaries on Micah (*1QpMic*), and Nahum (*4QpNah*), Zephaniah (*4QpZeph*), Hosea (*4QpHos^a* and *4QpHos^b*), Isaiah (five distinct manuscripts: *4QpIsa^a*, *4QpIsa^b* . . . *4QpIsa^e*), and Psalms (*1QpPs*, *4QpPs^a*, *4QpPs^b*),[15] and finally, Malachi (*4Q Commentary on Malachi*).[16] The commentaries are written in different hands and exhibit different levels of formality in paleography and orthography. The oldest manuscript, *4QpIsaᶜ*, is written on papyrus, perhaps an indication that it was a private document; the other pesharim are written on leather.

The path from scripture to its interpretation is strongly molded by sectarian ideology. The author of the pesher commentary understands the prophetic writers to be referring proleptically to the people and events in the history of the Qumran community: to its past struggles with authorities in Jerusalem, its present situation, and its fortunes in the as-yet-to-be-consummated future:

> *Whither the lion goes, there is the lion's cub* [*with none to disturb it*. Interpreted, this concerns Deme]trius king of Greece who sought, on the counsel of those who seek smooth things, to enter Jerusalem. [But God did not permit the city to be delivered] into the hands of the kings of Greece, from the time of Antiochus until the coming of the rulers of the Kittim. But then she shall be trampled under their feet . . . [*vacat*] *The lion tears enough for its cubs and it chokes prey for its lionesses.* Interpreted, this concerns the furious young lion [who executes revenge] on those who seek smooth things and hangs men alive . . . [17]

This example highlights the specificity with which the text of prophecy was thought to refer to events in the life of the sect. There is general agreement that these remarks refer to the reign of Alexander Jannaeus, one of the Hasmonean kings who ruled Judea from 103–76 BCE: he is the "furious young lion" mentioned by the commentary.[18] Based on their collusion with Demetrius, the "seekers after smooth things" represent the Pharisees, the Jerusalem authorities at odds with the sect and its founders; the Kittim represent the Romans.

The precise method used in arriving at such interpretations is often difficult to discern. Sometimes, it is possible to observe certain exegetical techniques of a midrashic type at work in the commentary.[19] Occasionally, the commentator even goes so far as to alter the scripture lemma:

> *Why do you look on, O traitors, and are silent when the wicked swallows up one more righteous than he?* (Hab. 1:13). Its interpretation concerns the house of Absalom and the men of their council who were silent at the reproof of the teacher of righteousness and did not help him against

the liar who rejected the law in the midst of their whole con[gregation].[20]

In the Masoretic Text and the Septuagint, the prophet charges God with passivity in the face of evil: it is God, not a band of traitors, who looks on the treacherous and is silent. The author of the pesher commentary is known to employ different textual traditions when it suits his purpose; in this case, the change to the base text is probably deliberate, a striking instance of a text swept away by its interpretation.[21] Changes like this were carried out according to a hermeneutical principle that allowed the sectarians to read each phrase in isolation from the surrounding context.[22] But while certain exegetical moves reminiscent of rabbinic techniques seem to be present, the texts themselves highlight the importance of the divinely inspired interpreter, who knows the truth hidden in scripture, truths hidden even from the authors:

> *I will stand at my post and will take my place on my watch-tower;*
> *I will watch to see what he will say to me, and wh[at (answer) I*
> *will receive con]cerning my complaint. And the Lord answered me*
> *[and said, Write down the vision, make it plai]n on tablets, that*
> *[the one who reads it] may run with it.* [Its interpretation . . .]
> and God told Habakkuk to write down all the things that
> are to come on the last generation, but the end of the time
> he did not make known to him. And when it says: *That the*
> *one who reads it may run (with it).* Its interpretation concerns
> the teacher of righteousness to whom God made known all
> the mysteries of the words of his servants the prophets
> (*1QpHab* 6. 12–7.5).[23]

Texts such as these, which stress the role of the inspired interpreter, suggest a connection with mantic practices like dream interpretation.[24] Daniel's interpretation of the mysterious writing on the wall is introduced by a remark similar to that found in pesher commentary: "this is the interpretation of the matter."[25] In both cases, proper interpretation can only proceed from God's divinely favored interpreter. Another significant similarity between pesher-style commentary and dream interpretation is the final product: in both cases, information about past, present, and future events is disclosed. Here, affinities can be observed with oracular texts such as the Demotic Chronicle, in which obscure oracles are interpreted as referring to the re-establishment of the Egyptian monarchy.[26]

We also find a type of pesher commentary generally termed "discontinuous pesharim."[27] In this type of commentary, texts may be gathered from several different biblical books, juxtaposed, then interpreted, as in the following example, drawn from a text entitled *4QFlorilegium*:

> Explanation of *How blessed is the man who does not walk in the counsel of the wicked* (Ps. 1:1). The interpretation of the matter concerns those who turn aside from the way [of sinners concerning] whom it is written in the book of Isaiah the Prophet for the latter days, *And it will be that as with a strong [hand he will cause us to turn away from walking in the way] of this people* (Isa. 8:11); and they are those concerning whom it is written in the book of Ezekiel the prophet that they shall not [defile themselves any more] with their idols (Ezek. 37:23). They are the sons of Zadok and the m[e]n of their cou[nc]il who keep fa[r from evil . . .] and after them [. . .] a community (or together).[28]

4QFlorilegium is quite fragmentary, and the restorations are debated. In this case, paragraphing in the manuscript indicates that we possess the initial lines of the ancient manuscript, and as such have a self-contained "module" of interpretation. Another piece of interpretation of roughly equal length follows, which begins by quoting the first verse of Psalm 2, raising the possibility that these lemmata may function like *incipits*, summoning up the chapter as whole. These differ from the pesher-style commentary already seen by adducing supporting quotations.

Because of its affinities to oracular practices, and in terms of its strongly marked ideological perspective, pesher-style commentary appears to be remarkably different than the style of commentary treated in previous chapters.[29] By way of comparison, we do not observe multiple interpretations. These would compromise the univocal voice of the interpreter.[30] Nor is there any reference to other interpreters, named or unnamed. There is no explicit reflection on variants in the text, though the interpreter may capitalize on these when it is advantageous to do so. In fact, the interpreter may simply change the text when desired, although this is not carried out frequently or capriciously. The terse formulations do not suggest that these commentaries are transcripts of group discussion; they bear more resemblance to oracular utterance.

So much, then, for an introduction to the content and exegetical

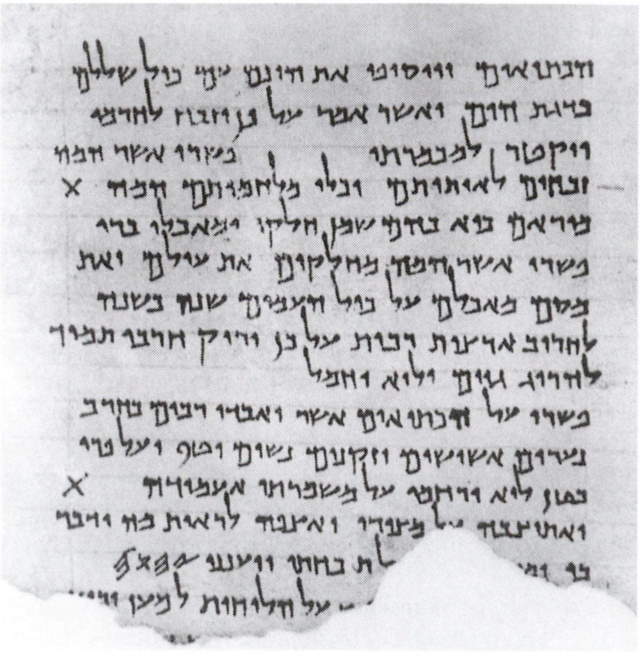

Plate 3 1Q*pHab* col. 6, courtesy of the Israel Museum.

method of the pesher commentaries. We must also exegete the formal dimension of the text – how knowledge was organized on the page. Plate 3 shows column 6 of the Habakkuk pesher. The spaciousness of the layout relative to *PFay. 3* and *Anon. Tht.* is immediately apparent. Another obvious difference in format between 1QpHab and the papyrus commentaries mentioned above is word spacing. This is typical of the Hebrew and Aramaic manuscripts from Qumran and stands in strong contrast with the Greco-Roman practice of writing *scriptio continua*.[31] The *vacat* – an open space of variable length – is another formatting device used in the Habakkuk pesher (see lines 3 and 9). The use of the *vacat* as a separative device is well attested from other Qumran manuscripts: *vacat*s of different lengths are frequently used in the Temple Scroll and the Isaiah Scroll, for example.

Within the pesher commentaries generally, a *vacat* of variable length (or an entire open line) may be used to mark the end of comment and the beginning of scripture, or it may be used to mark the end of scripture and the beginning of pesher comment. In some cases it may perform both functions. The pesher commentaries show different traits in the use of the *vacat*: in *4QpIs^a*, for example, both pesher commentary and scripture citation are marked by open lines and spaces. In contrast, the Psalms pesher shows a tendency to mark the beginning of scripture but not the beginning of commentary. The Nahum pesher swings in the other direction: it tends to mark pesher commentary, leaving scripture lemmata unmarked.[32] The Habakkuk pesher shows the most regular formatting of all the pesharim. An open space of some kind, either at the end of a line or in the middle of a line, almost always precedes the beginning of pesher commentary. A reader without any knowledge of Hebrew can immediately locate the beginning of commentary simply by scanning the column. Oddly, the place where pesher commentary ends and scripture begins is not marked in the Habakkuk pesher.

Another fascinating paleographic feature of the Habakkuk commentary is the "X" at the end of lines falling three or more spaces short of the left margin of a column (see the end of lines 4 and 12 of *4QpHab* col. 6 in Plate 3).[33] Marks answering to this same description are also found in *11QTemple^b*.[34] In the Habakkuk pesher, all of the crosses are drawn on or just within the vertically ruled mark that defines the left-hand margin. They are always followed by a word on the next line which would have extended significantly beyond the left margin.

What are the function of these two graphic gestures? Obviously, in nearly all cases, the *vacat*s mark a semantic division in the text. Beyond this, however, the space must surely represent a corresponding "mark" of some kind in the oral text produced by the reader.[35] Long spaces attract the eye, and warn the reader that a pause, or perhaps a change in the reading pace or intonation is required. The crosses stand in a complementary relationship to the spaces. Approaching the end of a line, a reader might have been misled by a long space, thinking that the end of a sentence or section had been reached, perhaps leading to an unwanted pause or change in intonation. The marks prompt the reader to continue on to the next line without any alteration in reading.

Careful examination of the manuscript leads to further insights. Based on certain errors, we know that the scribe responsible for the Habakkuk pesher was copying on a letter-by-letter basis; in other words, he was not taking in entire phrases at a time. As such, he may not have been a highly literate individual or a professional copyist. We can tell that the copying process was based on a written exemplar rather than dictation. Finally, it is also clear that the manuscript from which the scribe is copying is not furnished with *vacat*s – he is adding these himself.[36]

The way in which these formal characteristics are intertwined with textual performance are difficult to ascertain. It is possible that the texts were chanted or sung in some way, or that more than one reader assisted in the performance. According to Philo, two people may have participated in scripture reading and explication in Alexandrian synagogues:

> For that day has been set apart to be kept holy and on it they abstain from all other work and proceed to sacred spots which they call synagogues. There, arranged in rows according to their ages, the younger below the elder, they sit decorously as befits the occasion with attentive ears. Then one takes the books and reads aloud and another of special proficiency comes forward and expounds what is not understood.[37]

Whatever the significance of these formal features, they clearly indicate that it was important to the sectarians to inflect this "score" for proper performance, most probably in a public context. We know that a botched reading of scripture was a serious affair. An indistinct reading might have led a member to stumble:

> And anyone whose [speech] is too soft (?) or speaks with a staccato voice not dividing his words so that [his voice] may be heard, none of these shall read from the book of the Law, lest he cause error in a capital matter.[38]

In fact, the Hebrew allows for an alternative rendering: "And anyone who is too hasty in reading or reads in a continuous stream of language without making breaks between words in order that he may be understood ... "[39] A "blasphemous" slip, even an inadvertent one, committed in the act of reading or in the saying of prayers, could result in permanent expulsion from the community:

> If he blasphemed (*qll*) – either because of being terrified with affliction or because of any other reason, while he is reading the Book or saying benedictions – he shall be excluded and never again return to the Council of the Community.[40]

In contrast, a man who lay down in the middle of such a meeting and went to sleep would incur punishment for thirty days only (*1QS* 7.12). The severe penalty suggests that a great deal hung on a proper performance of the text.

Of course, these remarks refer to the reading of the Torah, and we should be cautious in making assumptions about the reading of other literature such as the pesher commentaries. Still, it is likely that the inspired interpretations of scripture deriving from a founder of the community would also be held in high esteem. In the Habakkuk pesher, at least, the interpretation is graphically privileged over the lemmata by the use of *vacat*s. So the formatting of the pesharim points to a performance context where much was at stake.

Targum: translating scripture

"Targum" is often used to refer to the Aramaic translations of the Hebrew scriptures preserved in written form, but in the rabbinic sources it refers to oral performance. The *practice* of Targum is the oral translation of a spoken Hebrew text, where a lector reads short portions of the Hebrew text, followed by an Aramaic translation performed by the so-called "meturgeman." The practice of targum, however, is most strongly attested for the third to the sixth centuries CE, and so I will not discuss it here.[41] We will, however, briefly discuss the written texts from Qumran that may be described as targums.

Two targums, one to Leviticus, the other to Job, have been discovered among the Qumran manuscripts.[42] The former has left very scant remains; the Targum to Job is more amenable to analysis. Targums found at Qumran, of course, come with a built-in *terminus ante quem*, namely 69 CE, when the settlement was destroyed. Linguistic criteria suggest an earlier date, perhaps during the second half of the second century BCE.[43] From an orthographic standpoint, the text is of good, albeit uneven quality. The roll is carefully lined and gives the impression of a scroll suitable for reading or public use, rather than a private copy. The Hebrew text type which lies behind this translation is not otherwise known, but it was certainly closer to the Masoretic Text than the Hebrew behind the Septuagint, which is about 15 percent shorter than present versions of Job. Ignorance of the *Vorlage* makes it difficult to speak of changes wrought by the translator. But even taking this into account, it appears that the translator has attempted to smooth out the text by resolving grammatical difficulties in the Hebrew and by adding or removing words, as for example, when he collapses two words of the Hebrew *parallelismus membrorum* into a single term.[44]

No external testimony about the reading of Job at Qumran has survived, so its actual use at Qumran is a matter for speculation. The Book of Job is not part of any known cycle of readings. Most likely, such a translation would have been used in lieu of the Hebrew text. However, when we consider the number of texts written in Hebrew which were certainly read publicly, such as the Isaiah Scroll, the Temple Scroll, the Pesher commentaries, the Thanksgiving Hymns, etc., it seems clear that passive understanding of Hebrew must have been relatively high within the Qumran community; and obviously, some members of the community knew enough Hebrew to copy and compose texts in Hebrew. Given the fact that the other Aramaic texts at Qumran appear to be non-sectarian in character, it may be that this document was written elsewhere and brought to the community library collection for reference purposes.[45]

Texts "at home and away": abbreviations and anthologies

Excerpting and abbreviating are similar activities in so far as they leave the language and phrasing of the text being operated on largely intact. As the name implies, excerpting involves lifting especially prized pieces of text from their literary surroundings. Excerpts are generally re-set in the context of an anthology. In principle, an anthology could consist of as little as two excerpts. Longer anthologies may reflect the organization of the texts they were taken from; in the case of fragments drawn from the Bible, the excerpter/compiler may observe canonical order. In most cases, however, excerpts within anthologies are reordered according to the needs dictated by some concrete circumstance of use, perhaps exegetical or liturgical in nature.

Abbreviated literature is attested at Qumran, though not richly: *4QCant*[a] and *4QCant*[b] are two sure examples. The former preserves a text of *Canticles* which omits chs. 4:8–6:10; the latter is very lightly abbreviated, omitting 3:6–8 and 4:4–7. It is possible that the text after 5:1 was also omitted.[46]

Excerpted and abbreviated literature from Qumran share several features as far as the physical manuscripts and orthography are concerned. Many of these texts are of small dimensions compared to other biblical manuscripts.[47] The columns of *4QEzek*[b] consist of only eleven lines, and the scroll itself measures only 11.2 cm. in height.[48]

The writing is also small compared to the larger scrolls. The *tefillin*, texts placed within phylacteries, are written on reused scraps of leather of irregular shape. The erasing is incomplete, rendering the writing nearly illegible. Very often, the text on one side is written perpendicular to that on the other; indeed, this appears to be a deliberate scribal practice.[49] While a few of these texts adhere fairly closely to the MT (e.g., the *tefillin*), many of these excerpted and abbreviated texts show harmonizing tendencies: for example, conflating the different versions of the Decalogue given in Exodus and Deuteronomy.

Anthologies, the literary end product of excerpting, range from simple to complex. An elementary example would be *4QDeut^n*, which contains only two excerpts, Deut. 8:5–10, followed by Deut. 5:1–6:1.[50] *4QDeut^j* includes two passages drawn from Exodus, followed by six selections from Deuteronomy. In some cases, texts from phylacteries and *mezuzot* have been recovered, and these too are types of the same genus.[51] *4QEzek^a* contains five fragments from the beginning of Ezekiel dealing with Ezekiel's vision of Jerusalem's destruction and the Heavenly Temple.[52] A text known as *4QTanhumin* ("Comforts") provides yet another instance of an excerpted text: it collects a series of passages drawn from the book of Isaiah chs 40–55.[53]

Anthologies are particularly suggestive pieces of literature from the standpoint of use, since a collection of excerpts can be assembled and sculpted by readers to fit the contours of a particular reading circumstance. Some of these texts have been termed "special use" manuscripts by their editors.[54] The forms of these rolls suggest several contexts for use: liturgy, study, private reading, and symbolic uses, where texts are used as talismans.[55] The targum to Leviticus, for example, may have been an anthology for ritual use.[56] We do not know precisely what rituals are in view, though later rabbinic tradition alludes to the recitation of Deut. 32 on the Sabbath, while Deut. 8:5–10 was connected with grace after meals in rabbinic tradition.[57] Deut. 32 is found in *4QDeut^j*, *4QDeut^k*, and *4QDeut^q*; Deut. 8:5–10 is found in *4QDeut^n*. All these texts are of small dimensions and would be easy to transport. *4QDeut^n*, for example, measures a mere 7 cm in height. A scroll of this size would reside easily in a pocket without being crushed. Such a scroll would also be convenient to handle, easy to roll and unroll.

A good example of a more complex type of anthology is *4QTestimonia*, in which five different excerpts with Messianic significance are gathered from Deuteronomy, Numbers, and also from the Psalms of Joshua, a non-canonical book otherwise unattested.[58] Two quotes comprise the first selection, Deut. 5:28 and Deut. 18:18. No *paragraphos* or open line separates these two, so they are apparently intended to stand together. The four groups are distinguished by open lines left at the end of quotes and by intervening *paragraphoi*.[59] The script is practiced but informal. Several characters are botched, and the single page features eight supralinear corrections. The leather shows no sign of stitching on its right or left edges, indicating that this was a stand-alone text.

The form of *4QTestimonia* invites questions about usage: was this document for public recitation or private study? Did it belong to an individual or to the group? Was it at home in a storage jar in a "library," in a private tent or cubicle, or in the pocket or purse of a community member? As a single leaf, it would have lain flat, and this format might have suited it for use as a lectionary or as a document for teaching.[60] On the other hand, people knew how to use a roll for public reading: presumably, the Isaiah scroll was used for such a purpose. A document that lay flat would be particularly useful for a person handling or comparing two texts at the same time. Rolling and unrolling one roll or several rolls to examine and compare disparate scriptures would have been difficult and time consuming. Copying a few significant texts onto a single sheet as an aid to synoptic comparison may have been the first step in close exegesis. Having the relevant scripture passages on one sheet or in a short roll would greatly aid an exegete who wished to make a careful comparison of several texts. *4QEzek^a*, an anthology of four passages from Ezekiel dealing with Ezekiel's vision and the temple, may represent such a collection. Indeed, we might reasonably imagine that an anthology of texts like *4QEzek^a* lies behind the exegesis contained in the *Songs of the Sabbath Sacrifice*, where different texts from Ezekiel are compared.[61]

In the case of a document like *4QTestimonia*, even beyond the usefulness of this format for textual comparison, it may also be that the simple juxtaposition of significant texts in close compass was felt to be significant, the assembled texts constituting a distilled eschatological proof. The congealed pattern has a semantic value in terms of its content to be sure; but we may also discern a symbolic value as a "proof object": the proof is discrete, compact, reducible to a single column of text, not distended or complex: "here it is, on a single sheet." As such, the text has iconic value apart from its semantic content.

Finally, anthological texts, particularly small ones, would be especially useful for personal meditation or reference.[62] We know

that the Qumran sectarians and other Jews in Palestine wore phylacteries and used *mezuzot* in accordance with Deut. 6:8. It is entirely
reasonable to assume that certain texts would be formatted in such a
way that they would be handy to use "when you are at home and
when you are away, when you lie down and when you rise" (Deut.
6:7).

"How lovely are her eyes": re-presented Bible

The Qumran cache of manuscripts has yielded several examples of
literature usually called "rewritten Bible." Three types of this literature may be distinguished.[63] The first consists of lightly reworked
versions of the Pentateuch such as *4QReworked Pentateuch* (*4QRP*).
Originally, this was considered to be a biblical manuscript. When
revisions are minor, it becomes difficult to discriminate between a
Bible manuscript based on a different text tradition and rewritten
Bible. When there is no fixed and agreed-upon entity commonly
accepted as Bible, "rewritten Bible" is a problematic concept.[64] The
second category includes more profoundly altered works such as the
Genesis Apocryphon and *Jubilees*. *Jubilees*, already known before the
finds at Qumran, was apparently very popular with the sectarians:
some twenty different copies have been found, and there is even
evidence of what might be called "rewritten *Jubilees*."[65] Finally,
books such as the *Temple Scroll* and the Hymns, or *Hodayot*, owe
substantial debts to biblical idiom, but are even more loosely related
to the sequence of biblical narrative.[66] For the present, I have
restricted myself to texts that retell and augment the biblical narratives, rather than those that use biblical language and phraseology as
lumber for entirely new structures.

4QRP is contained in five manuscripts representing at least four
or perhaps five copies of the same work or, at least, of a very similar
family of works.[67] The fragmentary nature of all these copies
obscures their extent, though it is believed that the original composition may well have included the entire Pentateuch.[68] The text
often departs from the MT and the LXX, reflecting what is probably
a pre-Samaritan text type. This affinity is reflected also in the formatting of the text, since in the majority of cases *4QRP* tends to
agree with the Samaritan Pentateuch in the way the document is
divided into paragraphs.[69]

Comparison of *4QRP* with the text of the MT, LXX, or SP is
not particularly illustrative for our purposes, since only minor variations are evident, some of which may represent different text

types rather than actual reworkings. Two types of reworking, however, are especially worthy of note. The first is a periodic reshuffling in the order of the text. For example, *4Q365* fr. 36, Numbers 27:11, is followed by Numbers 36:1–2. There is no way of knowing which text is the actual insertion; in other words, was 27:11 inserted in the midst of ch. 36, or was 36:1–2 inserted in the midst of ch. 27? Both texts touch on the same subject; namely, whether in the absence of sons, a daughter shall inherit her father's property at her father's death. Num. 27:1–11 treats the general case, in which Moses pronounces in favor of the daughters of a certain Zelophehad; 36:1–12 adds a codicil. Zelophehad's brothers successfully argue that if one of the daughters marries outside the ancestral tribe, then her inheritance is forfeited. No break between the two texts is observed: Num. 27:11 ends on the first word of line 3 of fr. 36, and Num. 36:1 begins immediately without any space or mark that would alert a reader.[70] Similar reshuffling is found in another copy of *4QRP*. In *4Q366* fr. 4 col. i, Num. 29:32–30:1 is followed immediately by Deut. 16:13–14. Both of these texts deal with the festival of Sukkot. The fact that col. ii of fr. 4 cannot be identified either with the text of Numbers ch. 30 or above, or with Deut. 16 or above, suggests that still more text from elsewhere was added.[71]

The second type of change concerns the addition of extra-biblical material. Four such additions have been found in the very fragmentary remains; presumably the scroll featured many more. One such addition occurs in *4Q364* fr. 3, col. ii. It consists of six lines added between Gen. 28:5 and 28:6, where Isaac sends Jacob out of the territory in order to find a non-Canaanite wife. The addition contains a personal address to Jacob, possibly from his mother Rebecca.[72] As such, this insertion would answer the question, "what was said on this poignant occasion of parting?" Fr. 15 features a two-line addition between Exod. 24:18 and 25:1–2. Only a few stray letters of the addition survive; its length is based on the size of the lacuna. It may have been a brief statement of what passed between God and Moses in the forty days and nights on Mount Sinai. Another addition occurs in *4Q365*, fr. 6a col. ii and 6c, where seven lines of text are added just prior to Exod. 15:22–6. Here, the writer has made further additions to the "Song of Miriam," performed after the deliverance of the people of Israel at the Red Sea. In fr. 23 of *4Q365*, eight lines of halakic material concerning the institution of two previously unknown festivals are inserted in the text of Leviticus; namely, that of fresh oil and the wood festival.[73] So on three occasions the additions supply material that might have been uttered on a momentous occasion.

4QRP thus appears to contain two distinct types of material: it adds minor expansions of a narrative variety, and it gathers texts on certain topics together in a way that would serve exegetical purposes. As such, this text could have served as a reference and as a source of slightly amplified biblical narratives. It probably functioned very much like a biblical text.

Another group of texts reflects a more profound reworking of the biblical material. The authors of these texts freely and radically paraphrased stories from the Pentateuch, and also added lengthy narratives of their own. The first of these is the book of *Jubilees*. Consider the account of Abram and Sarah given in Genesis 12:1–20 and the same tale as related by the author of *Jubilees*:

> When he was about to enter Egypt, he said to his wife Sarai, "I know well that you are a woman beautiful in appearance; and when the Egyptians see you, they will say, 'this is his wife'; then they will kill me, but they will let you live. Say you are my sister, so that it may go well with me because of you, and that my life may be spared on your account." When Abram entered Egypt the Egyptians saw that the woman was very beautiful. When the officials of Pharaoh saw her, they praised her to Pharaoh. And the woman was taken into Pharaoh's house. And for her sake he dealt well with Abram; and he had sheep, oxen, male and female slaves, female donkeys, and camels. But the Lord afflicted Pharaoh and his house with great plagues because of Sarai, Abram's wife. So Pharaoh called Abram, and said, "What is this you have done to me? Why did you not tell me that she was your wife? Why did you say, 'She is my sister,' so that I took her for my wife? Now then, here is your wife, take her, and be gone." And Pharaoh gave his men orders concerning him; and they set him on the way, with his wife and all that he had.

Here is the same story as it appears in *Jubilees* 13.10–15:

> And Abram went into Egypt in the third year of the week and he stayed in Egypt five years before his wife was taken from him. And Tanis of Egypt was built then, seven years after Hebron. And it came to pass when Pharaoh took Sarai,

the wife of Abram, that the Lord plagued Pharaoh and his house with great plagues on account of Sarai, the wife of Abram. And Abram was honored with many possessions: sheep and oxen and asses and horses and camels and male and female servants and silver and much gold. And Lot, his brother's son, also had possessions. And Pharaoh returned Sarai, the wife of Abram. And he sent him out from the land of Egypt.[74]

The writer of *Jubilees* has shortened the story, omitting all direct speech. As it stands the story is quite incomplete without knowledge drawn from the Genesis account: "before his wife was taken from him" presumes a reader familiar with the motivation for the whole incident, known from the Genesis story. This tendency to paraphrase and distill familiar stories from the biblical narratives is quite common throughout the book.[75] In a few cases, the narrative remains fairly close to the Genesis text, but this is less common.[76] The author also adds many large expansions, such as the battle between Jacob and Esau in chs 37–8, or the crows sent by the angel Mastema to despoil the earth (11:9–24).[77] As such, *Jubilees* is definitely styled as a supplement to the Torah, and in no way would have supplanted it.

Compare this epitomizing of the Abraham and Sarah story to the greatly expanded story as it appears in the *Genesis Apocryphon*, also discovered at Qumran. I include only the central portion of the lengthy story, beginning with the bedazzled advisors praising Sarah's attributes to Pharaoh:

[Col. 20] "how splen[did] and beautiful the form of her face, and how [. . .] soft the hair of her head; how lovely are her eyes and how pleasant is her nose and all the radiance of her face [. . .]; how lovely is her breast and how beautiful is all her whiteness? Her arms, how beautiful? And her hands, how perfect! And how attractive all the appearance of her hands! How lovely are her palms, and how long and dainty all the fingers of her hands. Her feet, how beautiful! How perfect are her legs! There are no virgins or brides who enter a bridal chamber more beautiful than she. Indeed, her beauty surpasses that of all women; her beauty is high above all of them. Yet with all this beauty there is much wisdom in her; and whatever she has is lovely." When the king heard the words of Hirqanos and the words of his two companions – for the three of them spoke as one man – he coveted her very much. He sent off in haste and had her brought to him. When he beheld her, he marveled at all her beauty and took her to himself as a wife. He sought to kill me, but Sarai said to the king, "He is my brother," so that I might be benefited by her. And I, *Abram*, was spared *because of her*. I was not killed. But I wept bitterly – I Abram, and Lot, my nephew, with me – on the night when Sarai was taken away from me by force. That night I prayed, I entreated, and I asked for mercy; in my sorrow I said, as my tears ran down my cheeks, "Blessed are you, O God Most High, my Lord, for all ages! For you are lord and Master over all, and have power to mete out justice to all the kings of the earth. Now I lodge my complaint with you, my Lord, against the Pharaoh Zoan, the king of Egypt, because my wife has been taken away from me by force. Mete out justice to him for me and show forth your great hand against him and against all his house. May he not be able to defile my wife tonight – that it may be known about you, my Lord, that you are the Lord of all the kings of the earth." And I wept and talked to no one. But that night God Most High sent him a pestilential spirit *to afflict him* and all the men of *his household*, an evil spirit, that kept afflicting him and all the men of his household. He was not able to approach her, nor did he have intercourse with her, though he was with her for two years.[78]

Even the English translation gives a good picture of the very different type of literature represented by the *Genesis Apocryphon*. The author heightens the narrative appeal of the story by casting it into the first person, as though narrated by Abram himself (recall that *Jubilees* removes all such material). A lengthy account of Sarah's beauty is added, as well as the anxious and devout prayer of the wronged husband, and a fuller account of how Pharaoh learns of Sarah's true identity from Lot. Some of the expansions may be exegetical in nature, prompted by a fissure in the text, but the extended rhapsody over Sarah's charms is hardly motivated by exegetical anxieties.[79] In fact, the *Genesis Apocryphon* seems to supply a great deal of material at just those points where episodes are sharply paraphrased in *Jubilees*.

In assessing how these works might have been used, we are somewhat hampered by their unknown provenance.[80] The *Genesis*

Apocryphon was first discovered at Qumran, but it shows no overt affinity with ideology current among Qumran sectarians. Indeed, the extensive fixation on Sarah's physical attributes is rather striking; it is difficult to imagine how this text, somewhat tumescent in places, would have functioned in public liturgy or study at Qumran, a community with definite encratitic tendencies; perhaps it was better suited to private study. This type of literature was probably aimed at an audience such as we might expect for Greek romances or for Jewish novels such as *Joseph and Aseneth*. This last text in particular goes to great lengths in its descriptions of physical beauty. It appears that we have to do with a work brought in from outside the community, not one generated within it.

Jubilees, on the other hand, was a great favorite at Qumran.[81] Given the book's emphasis on legal and ethical norms and especially on calendrical matters, it is hardly surprising that it should be a favorite of a rigorous group keenly interested in halaka and eschatological timetables. Although the excerpt adduced above does not feature this particular aspect of *Jubilees*, it may be said that *Jubilees* adds legal prescriptions while the *Genesis Apocryphon* supplies enticing details. The *Genesis Apocryphon* may have been appreciated for that reason by some readers. But the *Genesis Apocryphon* does mention the books of Enoch, and this may be significant, as I will discuss momentarily. This might explain, however, why only one copy of this text was found: at Qumran, at least, it was probably used as a reference, not for general reading consumption.

"All night long": study contexts at Qumran

Having examined the form and format of the manuscripts, can we find any external testimony about study practices at Qumran that would confirm or modify the picture of reading at Qumran? Two texts in particular, the *Damascus Document* (CD) and the *Community Rule* (1QS), provide useful material on this question.[82]

There is evidence that sectarians at Qumran studied individually or in small groups, and in corporate gatherings. The *Community Rule* describes a type of "Torah watch": "And where there are ten (members) there must not be lacking there a man who studies (*darash*) the Torah day and night continually, each man relieving another."[83] Whether this study consists of reading, chanting, or writing activity is unclear; *darash* is patient of several meanings.[84] Nor is it clear if this activity takes place in a space dedicated to the purpose; this is probably implicit if "relieving" is taken as a changing of the guard.

Perhaps study of this nature took place in or around the scriptorium (Room 30), or in the adjoining Rooms 1, 2, or 4; the last features benches around the walls.

The author of the *Community Rule* outlines procedures for a group meeting immediately following the reference to the Torah watch: "The Many shall spend the third part of every night of the year in unity, reading in the Book, studying judgment, and saying benedictions in unity."[85] "Book" probably refers to the Torah;[86] reading it appears to mean reading aloud to those assembled. Such a reading would have taken place in the refectory, the only place in the Qumran complex capable of containing all the members simultaneously. We saw earlier that the reading/performance of Torah at Qumran was taken very seriously; the careless reader was subject to stiff penalties.

The second activity mentioned is the "study of judgment" (*darash mishpat*). This "judgment" might refer to a text, such as *1QS*, or to material drawn from it.[87] In the latter case, we might imagine the repetition or chanting of short phrases. The study of *mishpat* may have been followed by a test: "And thus they shall be asked concerning judgment (*mishpat*), concerning any counsel, and (any)thing which is for the Many, each man presenting his knowledge to the Council of the Community" (*1QS* 6.9–10, tr. Charlesworth). The right of speaking went first to senior members of the community; the session was apparently moderated by "the Examiner."[88] Apparently, there was room for argument and debate, though not, perhaps, in this particular setting (*1QS* 9.16). In *CD* 14.6, a presiding priest is mentioned in addition to the Examiner.

In a third aspect of group study, members also participated in the joint utterance of benedictions, and during this activity also ran the risk of expulsion for "blasphemy" as noted above. It is not clear whether the sequence, Torah, *mishpat*, benedictions reflects an order of worship or simply a description of the contents of a study/worship session. Apparently, the entire gathered group was engaged in the same activity, either listening to a reading, hearing an explanation, or engaging in shared utterance: given the strict regulations for speaking in turn, we should not envision a setting with different groups pursuing different activities.[89]

The so-called *Messianic Rule* also alludes to a large-group gathering. Interestingly, it assumes that women and children will be present when scripture is read and interpreted:

When they come, they shall assemble all those who come, including children and women, and they shall read into

their ea[rs] all the regulations of the covenant, and shall
instruct them in all its precepts, so that they do not stray in
their [errors].[90]

The *Messianic Rule* is a prescriptive document for the community at
the end of days, and so this description may present an idealized
view of community polity. Even so, the inclusion of women and
children is significant, and may stand in contrast with Philo, who
claims that the Essenes avoid marriage. Women may have visited
the community, and of course the presence of women on certain
occasions need not imply that marriage was practiced. Different
Essene groups may have followed different practices in this regard.
While the center of the movement was located at the Qumran
settlement, Essenes elsewhere also met for fellowship and study. In
any case, both types of groups have rightly been called "studying
communities."[91]

A final text recommends the practice of close textual study of the
prophetic material and the writings of David, both of which are the
subject of the pesher commentaries. The text is *4QMMT*, the so-
called "halakic letter" from a leader of one branch of the Qumran
community to another. It was a popular document, it seems, as six
copies have been found.[92] The excerpt in question comes towards the
end of the letter:

"we have written to you so that you may study (carefully)
the book of Moses and the books of the Prophets and (the
writings of) David [and the] [events of] ages past."[93]

Elsewhere, the Books of the Prophets are considered, literally, foundational: in an interpretation of Amos 5:27, "the books of the Torah"
are the tabernacle of the king, the king represents the community,
and the prophetic books represent the pedestal of the images in the
tabernacle.[94] While the Torah is clearly normative for daily behavior,
and therefore of utmost importance, the prophetic books provide the
chart for the past, present, and the future of the community. Those
joining the sect, who were in the process of forming a sectarian
identity, would form a plausible audience for the prophetic books
and the commentaries thereon, which discover the sect along with
its protagonists and antagonists in the very pages of scripture. The
most literate members of the community would also have focused
their textual research on the prophetic materials, in search of these
discoveries.

Why so much writing at Qumran?

In the final analysis, however, these descriptions of public and private study cannot be taken as a comprehensive picture of study practices at Qumran. Nothing in these testimonies prepares us for the remarkable literary production and consumption that seems evident from the partial remains of the Qumran library. If only the *Damascus Document* and the *Rule of the Community* had survived, no one would have inferred the existence of commentaries on the prophetic books, for example, or books such as the *Temple Scroll* or the *War Scroll*. In fact, very few non-biblical books are mentioned by name, among them, the so-called *Book of Hagu*,[95] *Jubilees*, and a ledger inscribed with the names of community members.[96]

Strong evidence for the importance of writing at Qumran may be gathered from a favorite sectarian text in which books, writing, and the teaching of writing are strikingly valorized: the book of *Jubilees*.[97] *Jubilees* probably predates the founding of the Qumran Community, but this makes the text even more significant: reflection on *Jubilees* may have played a role in the community's formation. Certainly, the heavy emphasis in that book on calendrical matters and on books and writing were shared by the sectarians themselves. For the present, I wish to focus on the latter subject; namely, the fascination with writing and written texts that is evident in *Jubilees*. I will suggest that the Qumran sectarians may have understood *Jubilees* as programmatic for their own study practices.

Jubilees begins with a striking claim about its origins. Moses is on Mount Sinai, receiving a set of tablets written by God: this is the "first book of the Law" (6.22), which represents the Pentateuch. He is also commanded to write for himself "all of these words which I shall cause you to know today" (1.7, 26). The knowledge to be committed to writing concerns "what (was) in the beginning and what will occur (in the future), the account of the division of all of the days of the Law and the testimony."[98] The account of the "division of days" is nothing other than the book *Jubilees* itself. It is God's oral revelation at Sinai, spoken by the Angel of the Presence, and committed to writing by Moses.

The chief problem addressed by the book is the problem of forgetfulness. Forgetfulness leads to moral corruption; remembrance leads to right action. When Joseph was solicited by Potiphar's wife, he remembered "the words which Jacob, his father, used to read, which were from the words of Abraham" (39.6) and was able to resist her advances. To remember is to do; proper actions follow from right remembrance. Indeed, "to remember" and "to do" are essentially synonymous. *Jubilees* is intended by its author to function as a booster shot for memory. God gave laws on Sinai, but knew beforehand that they would be forgotten: "they will forget all of my commandments" (1.9); "they will forget all of my laws" (1.14). The function of *Jubilees* as a written text, and its stress on the writtenness of all things is for purposes of remembrance during a time when Hellenistic culture and social patterns threaten to corrode Torah-true behavior and observance:

> For I know and henceforth I shall make you know – but not from my own heart, because the book is written before me and is ordained in the heavenly tablets of the division of days – lest they forget the feasts of the covenant and walk in the feasts of the gentiles, after their errors and after their ignorance (6.35).

No doubt the author hopes that his readers will flee corrupt gentile practices with all the energy of Joseph bolting from Potiphar's house.

According to *Jubilees*, the thread of memory is kept alive by written texts. Biblical history is littered with secret books. Enoch was the first to learn the craft of writing:

> [Enoch] wrote in a book the signs of the heaven according to the order of their months, so that the sons of man might know the (appointed) times of the years according to their order, with respect to each of their months . . . and the Sabbaths of the years he recounted, just as we [the royal we of the Angel of the Presence] made it known to him. And he saw what was and what will be in a vision of his sleep as it will happen among the children of men in their generations until the day of judgment. He saw and knew everything and wrote his testimony and deposited the testimony upon the earth against all the children of men and their generations (4.17–19).

Nor was this all. He bore witness in writing against the Watchers, who mingled with human females. Having been translated alive to the Garden of Eden, he remains there perpetually, "writing condemnation and judgment of the world, and all of the evils of the children of men" (*Jub.* 4.21–3).[99] Writing and written texts figure prominently among later generations as well. The Angel of the Presence taught Noah the use of therapeutic herbs, and Noah committed this knowledge to a book which he passed on to his son Shem (10.12); he also taught the art of writing to his son Cainan. Unfortunately, Cainan misused his literacy. After he discovered a "writing which the ancestors engraved on stone," Cainan

> read what was in it. And he transcribed it. And he sinned because of what was in it, since there was in it the teaching of the Watchers by which they used to observe the omens of the sun and moon and stars and all the sins of heaven. And he copied it down, but he did not tell about it because he feared to tell Noah about it lest he be angry with him because of it.[100]

Seroh taught his son Nahor the researches of the Chaldeans for purposes of divination and astrology (11.8), and Terah taught Abraham how to write (11.16). Jacob learned the art of writing, but the ill-starred Esau, described as "fierce, rustic, and hairy," did not (19.14). In a dream, Jacob is allowed to read seven heavenly tablets, which he transcribed (32.21–6). When Jacob died, "he gave all of his books and his father's books to Levi, his son, so that he might preserve them and renew them for his sons until this day" (45.15). Every generation, it seems, bears responsibility for the transmission of written texts and for passing on the knowledge of writing. Based on the shape of Qumran literature and study practices, we may safely affirm that the Qumran sectarians have assumed the mantle of this responsibility as well.

Jubilees is crowded with still more references to writing and written texts. Heavenly tablets "engraved" with halakic prescriptions are frequently mentioned.[101] Indeed, earthly laws, events, and judgments are legitimated in so far as they are "written," "engraved," "ordained," "recorded," and "set down" on heavenly tablets. Patterns of language, nature, and history form a vast echo chamber. The Hebrew alphabet is implicit in the act of creation and in the history of Israel: there were twenty-two kinds of animals created in the six-day period of creation, and there were twenty-two generations from Adam until Jacob (2.16–23).

Abraham in particular received a special commission, being delegated by God to repristinate Hebrew as a spoken language:

And the Lord God said to me [the Angel of the Presence], "Open his [Abraham's] mouth and his ears so that he might hear and speak with his mouth in the language which is revealed because it ceased from the mouth of all of the sons of men from the day of the Fall." And I opened his mouth and his ears and his lips and I began to speak with him in Hebrew, in the tongue of creation. And he took his father's books – and they were written in Hebrew – and he copied them. And he began studying them thereafter. And I caused him to know everything which he was unable (to understand). And he studied them (in) six months of rain (12:25–7).

It is especially interesting for our purposes that copying the books precedes the act of study. We may recall that Philo recommended the practice of copying material to be closely studied as an aid to memorization. This practice would help to account for the quantity of biblical manuscripts found at Qumran.

In its capacity as a supplemental law, given to Moses on Sinai, the book of *Jubilees* may be in view in those texts at Qumran that refer to "another Law" or a "second Law":

The wicked watches [for] the righteous and seeks [to slay him. The Lo]rd {will not abandon him in his hand and will not] condemn him when he is judged. Its interpretation concerns the Wicked [Pri]est, who wa[tched the Tea]cher of Righteous[ness and sought] to slay him [. . .] and the Law which he sent to him.[102]

This "Law" sent by the Teacher of Righteousness cannot refer to the books of the Pentateuch: that would hardly merit death threats.[103] In an interpretation of Hos. 5:8, "Blow the horn in Gibeah, the trumpet in Ramah," the author writes, "the horn is the book of [. . . and the Trumpet is] the Book of the Second Law."[104] Pharisaic groups believed in a supplementary law given at Sinai but preserved only in oral form. The author of *Jubilees*, and perhaps the Qumran sectarians after him, believed that this revelation had been committed to writing. Indeed, the book of *Jubilees* is mentioned in the same breath with the Torah in *CD* (MS A) 16:1–4:

Therefore, a man shall take upon himself (an oath) to return to the Torah of Moses, for in it everything is specified. <And

the explication of their times, when Israel was blind to all these; behold, it is specified in the Book of the Divisions of the Times in their Jubilees and in their Weeks>.[105]

We might also have inferred that *Jubilees* could be considered as the Second Law based solely on the numbers of manuscripts discovered. Yadin has suggested that the *Temple Scroll* should be taken as the Book of the Second Law, and there are valid reasons for entertaining this possibility.[106] But based on the evidence just cited, *Jubilees* is also a likely candidate. Indeed, by telling of its own origins on Sinai, after the giving of the "book of the First Law," *Jubilees* implicitly names itself as the Second Law.

This difference over the writtenness of the Second law given at Sinai would have been a major point of distinction between the Qumran sectarians and groups such as the Pharisees, the "Seekers of Smooth Things" criticized in sectarian writings, who were committed to the (possibly oral) preservation of the "traditions of the elders." At this time, the doctrine of the Oral Torah, delivered to Moses at Mount Sinai, had probably not reached the form it would assume in the second century CE and after. The rabbinic gathering at Yavneh (ca. 100 CE) may have been a point in time where claims about "verbatim traditions framed by ancient authorities and handed down orally from then on" began to be made.[107] Caution should therefore attend any overly simplistic juxtaposition of "written" versus "oral" as a decisive axis of difference between the Qumran sectarians and the Judaism represented by the scribes, Pharisees, and Temple establishment. But the Qumran sectarians dedicated themselves to literary production in a way that the Pharisees did not, and this may flow from a heightened commitment to writing and written texts grounded in the book of *Jubilees*.

So in conclusion, we may imagine several reasons for the amount of scribal activity encountered at Qumran. The first reason is ideological. I believe that the Qumran sectarians considered themselves to be custodians of texts similar to the scribal characters in *Jubilees*. Maintaining and elaborating on this collection would have been one of the central tasks of community members. Josephus even states this explicitly: Essenes "display an extraordinary interest in the writings of the ancients," and upon joining the group, swear to "carefully preserve the books of the sect" (*BJ* 2.136, 142). Writing itself may have been seen as a religious obligation. Recall that the writing activity of Enoch and Jacob was in response to visions seen in dreams. It is quite possible that Qumran sectarians pursued a similar mode of authorship: pesher commentaries have been linked to oracular utterance on the basis of their literary form. The results obtained here show that *Jubilees* provided a warrant for the strikingly high level of involvement with written texts found in the Qumran community.

A second reason for the quantity of literary production at Qumran may have to do with study practices. According to *Jubilees*, Abraham copied his father's books before studying them. If sectarian study is modeled on this practice, where writing was employed as an aid to comprehension, this too would stimulate the production of written texts. We have seen that Philo recommends writing as an antidote to forgetting when he states that writing a text is a surer way to inscribe it on the soul than simply reading it (*Spec. Leg.* 4.160–4).

Writing may also have served as a tool for advancing literacy. Scribal errors in the Habakkuk manuscript show that the writer was copying on a letter-by-letter basis, perhaps not fully comprehending what he was writing. It is not unlikely that the literacy of some copyists in the Qumran community was marginal. On the basis of papyri from classrooms, it has been proposed that students in a typical Greco-Roman school may have learned to write before they could read.[108] If the same was true at Qumran, we could imagine that many of the surviving texts were written for pedagogical, as well as for devotional reasons. We know that minimal competency with texts was part of the price of admission to the Community. Boys were to be instructed in their youth from the *Book of Hagu*, and to be instructed in the "precepts of the covenant."[109] Of course, such training may well have taken place orally; literacy is not necessarily implied. But given the high premium placed on competence with texts, it would not be surprising to find that community resources would be allotted to the teaching of reading and writing.

PART 3

TEXTS AND TEXT-BROKERS: JUDAISM IN PALESTINE

We turn now to the types of Judaism reflected in the New Testament and in Josephus (exclusive of Qumran), prior to the destruction of the Temple in 70 CE. There is enough evidence to give this material a discernible center, if not a clearly definable boundary. It is a society in which the text of the law is ever-present, but one in which access to the text is controlled by a caste of interpreters. It is also a milieu which has produced much literature of interest to the present study.

Not surprisingly, the shape of the available evidence points to rather different patterns of textual usage than those seen at Qumran. Commentary from Jews in Palestine (again, exclusive of Qumran) is non-existent.[1] We do well to consider the social realities behind this surprising fact: were continuous commentaries generated by and used within particular kinds of school settings that existed only in Alexandria and at Qumran? Do they presume particular pedagogical strategies? While the practice of commentary is not well attested in the extant sources, other kinds of textual activities are quite evident. Certain groups are busily engaged in translating activity, rendering the Hebrew scriptures into Aramaic and into new Greek translations. We also find examples of "re-presented" Bible, such as Ps.-Philo's *Liber Antiquitatum Biblicarum* (hereafter, *LAB*).[2] Next, we turn to the available testimonia about the reading and explication of texts in the synagogue. Following this, we will consider the teachers who are doing the explicating by examining the role and function of the scribe as it appears in Ben Sira, the New Testament, Josephus, and in the inscriptional evidence. I will argue that "control of the means of interpretation" was a divisive issue in Palestine, and that this accounts for the idiosyncratic portrayal of scribes in the Gospels. Furthermore, I will propose that Jesus' activity as a non-authorized textual expert was one of the significant issues in his struggle with the religious authorities.

One limitation, already noted in the General Introduction, must be mentioned. I have not made any systematic use of the rabbinic evidence. Certainly, early traditions are to be found within the Mishnah and other rabbinic documents, relating to figures such as Johanan ben Zakkai, Hillel, Shammai, and others. This evidence, however, is difficult to assess, coming two or more centuries after the events it purports to describe. Certainly it was in the interest of the sages to ground and legitimize the forms of their community life by extending its roots backwards in time, and so all of this information must be carefully sifted.[3] Considerations of space and authorial expertise dissuade me from tackling this rich and complex body of literature.[4]

Of young girls and virgins: translating the Bible (Greek)

It is a striking fact that Jews translated their scriptures from Hebrew into Greek and also into Aramaic. This significant act of textual customization deserves careful study. Of the school groups studied thus far, only the Epicureans seem to have made the jump to a different language, namely Latin. Lucretius is the best example, of course, but we saw other Epicureans writing in Latin with the express intent of reaching greater numbers of people. Cicero was known to have translated Platonic dialogues into Latin, but this seems to have been more for his own benefit, as a way of attempting to take the measure of the best Greek literature in Latin, rather than a serious attempt to promulgate Plato's thought for a new reader-ship.[5] In some fields – medicine, for example – texts written in a language other than Greek were not taken seriously.[6] Among certain religious groups, translation was impossible in principle since the true significance of the text could only be experienced in its original language.[7] This may be seen as an attempt to preserve a certain national or religious identity from being dissolved amid a multitude of cultures and languages. Alternatively, literate elites may have insisted on the untranslatability of authoritative texts in order to maintain their own interpretational hegemony.[8] It is significant that many Jews were content to appropriate their scriptures in other languages, in spite of reservations voiced by certain individuals.[9]

The Septuagint (LXX) took its name from the seventy-two translators commissioned by Demetrius of Phalerum to render the Hebrew scriptures into Greek for the library at Alexandria. This, at least, is the account of the book's origins as portrayed in the *Letter of Aristeas*, which contains the many miraculous events that attended its nativity.[10] It was the Bible of choice for Greek-speaking Jews in the Western Diaspora, and it eventually became the Bible for Christians as well.[11] Originating in Alexandria sometime during the third and second centuries BCE, it met the needs of Diaspora Jews whose long residence in Alexandria fostered a community whose members, even members as cultured and sophisticated as Philo, could no longer read their own scriptures in Hebrew. While Philo thought the Septuagint was every bit as inspired as the Hebrew original, his opinion was not universally shared, for we encounter attempts to bring the Septuagint into greater conformity with the underlying Hebrew during the first and second centuries CE. Our story begins with these attempts.

Until recently, a thumbnail sketch of the various recensions of the Septuagint might have run as follows. In the first century CE, the text of the Hebrew Bible had achieved a state of relative stability and it was clear that existing Greek translations did not reflect this authoritative text. Furthermore, Christians were scoring theological points based on some of the loose renderings in the Septuagint.[12] In order to steal this Christian thunder, a proselyte from Christianity to Judaism by the name of Aquila executed a new version of the Hebrew Bible into Greek marked by a slavish fidelity to the original Hebrew. His version, completed around the year 128 CE, made for rough reading in Greek, and later scholars such as Theodotion (a contemporary of Irenaeus) and Symmachus (perhaps active under Marcus Aurelius, but at least prior to Origen) altered Aquila's version, striving to remain faithful to the Hebrew original while smoothing out the Greek.[13] Two other versions, dubbed Quinta and Sexta (based on their placement in Origen's *Hexapla*) show different degrees of the same tendency.

This traditional picture must now be discarded. First of all, the Septuagint was not completed by a single group of translators in a short span of time, as claimed in the *Letter of Aristeas*. The evolution of the Septuagint was more akin to the construction of a medieval cathedral: it took several centuries to reach its final form. It is, in fact "an ensemble of translations from different eras."[14] As such, each book of the Septuagint presents its own textual history.[15] Some of the supposedly literalistic renderings ascribed to later recensions may derive from the first translators.[16] It has also been firmly established that Aquila was not responsible for the first translation that conformed closely to the underlying Hebrew text. In fact, Aquila's work is not properly a translation *per se*; he only carried further the tendencies present in earlier modifications of the Septuagint. Earlier attempts featuring Hebraizing tendencies in translation have been gathered under the rubric of the so-called "*kaige* group." The name derives from the habit of rendering the Hebrew conjunction *gam* by the Greek term *kaige*. This feature, along with many others, distinguishes it from other versions.[17] Barthélemy treated the group as a recension because it did not appear to represent an entirely fresh translation directly from the Hebrew; it is rather a revision of the Greek towards a still-evolving Hebrew text. While opinions differ about the dates that mark the beginning of this work, there is general agreement that it was at least begun before the year 50 CE.[18] Barthélemy saw this revision as part of a comprehensive program instigated by the rabbis.[19] But in fact, like the Septuagint before it, this revision seems to have evolved over a period of time and may not spring so directly from a supposedly centralized rabbinate.[20] And while Aquila's dates are firm, it now appears that he owes much more to earlier versions than was hitherto believed. Theodotion, too, appears to have been working with an earlier text.[21] And besides the versions of Symmachus, Quinta, and Septa, other distinct recensions may also have existed.[22] Obviously, patterns of Jewish life, study, and worship led to a constantly evolving set of scriptures.

The detailed differences between these various recensions has been studied elsewhere in great detail.[23] For our purposes, it is enough to draw attention to the two basic directions these revisions took. The first was towards greater fidelity to the Hebrew text (*kaige* and Aquila).[24] Aquila goes to great lengths to show the form of the Hebrew text that lies behind the Greek; indeed, the Greek seems to function more as a pointer to the Hebrew, rather than as a stand-alone bearer of meaning. The second tendency was essentially a corrective to the first. Some translators who came after Aquila sought to balance literalistic tendencies with acceptable Greek style; Symmachus is an example of this tendency.[25] He was not averse, for example, to rendering the same Hebrew word by two different Greek words for the sake of stylistic variation. When he encountered an obscure word, he generally ventured a translation, whereas the *kaige* translator (or translators) and Aquila simply transliterated the Hebrew. In any case, these various attempts at revision highlight two interesting facts: Hebraizing translations such as Aquila's helped the reader up to the Hebrew original by means of a Greek stepladder; looser translations like that of Symmachus, while making reference to the Hebrew, were content to transmit the sense of the Hebrew in Greek terms.[26]

What information about the use and users of such texts follows from this? It is difficult to imagine that a translation such as Aquila's could have had a liturgical function. In fact, a school of some kind is almost certainly the most likely setting in which a translation like this might have been produced and used.[27] Here, it might have worked at two slightly different levels. For someone with a smattering of Hebrew, a literalistic translation would allow one to encounter the contours of the original text. A literalistic translation might also have worked for a person who had more acquaintance with Hebrew, but may at certain points have needed a way of checking the meaning of a difficult passage.[28] In either case, we could imagine that when a biblical text was under discussion in the study room of a synagogue, a student or teacher might have read the appropriate section from Aquila's translation. In other words, someone might have done dynamically what Origen did textually with his *Hexapla*: namely, arrange the text in parallel columns with other readings characterized by different strengths (and weaknesses) in order to approach the text from different angles.

We may also imagine the applicability of such a text outside of a school setting. Textual experts in Jewish society of this period were more than simply academic figures. In fact, to call them "academics" is somewhat misleading. Their status as legal experts places them in a much more important civic role. Their deliberations and disputes might have had ramifications for their legal judgments, and so for the lives of actual people. Such people would have been expected to provide legal pronouncements, and when difficult issues turned on shades of meaning, a reasonably but not consummately literate scribe might have found use for a Greek translation that was rigidly faithful to the underlying Hebrew. But we need not presume that Aquila's translation immediately (or ever) replaced the LXX. Origen found that a text with six columns was useful; perhaps other academic readers believed that more complete understanding could emerge from a text (or environment) in which there was a chorus of voices present. Recall that Plotinus characterized his method as follows: "we consider the statements of the ancient philosophers about them [philosophical concepts], who differ one from the other, and perhaps also different interpretations of the same statements" (*Enn.* 3.7.1). Either an academic or a forensic setting is a plausible venue for the different Greek translations of the Bible. Indeed, the two were closely related, if not synonymous in many cases.

"His eyes were not red":
translating the Bible (Aramaic)

Whether Aramaic targums and the Greek translations studied thus far are considered to be siblings or perhaps first cousins, they are clearly related phenomena. Certainly, they both qualify as translating activities, renderings of a text written in one language into another language, one presumably more familiar to the hearers.[29] And in so far as a highly literal translation such as Aquila's probably functioned in concert with a Hebrew text, the identification with targums is stronger still.[30] Still, there are some non-trivial differences between translations and targums: written targums typically add explanatory paraphrases, updated phraseology, and extra material not included in the base text. In this sense, they are something of a hybrid between translation and rewritten Bible.

It seems likely that written targums first arose as simple written translations from the Hebrew; certainly, the existence of the Septuagint would have provided a precedent for translation into other languages. It was only later that the *practice* of targum, i.e., performing the Aramaic and Hebrew text in concert, was developed. Aramaic translations have surfaced at Qumran, and these may be securely dated to a period pre-70 CE, but there is no evidence for the practice of targum during this period.[31] Rabbinic injunctions against committing targums to writing probably arose after proliferating Bible-like literature threatened to compromise the Hebrew text or the interpretive monopoly the rabbis wished to exert over their scriptures.

Two Aramaic targums that may be reasonably assigned to the second century CE are targums *Onkelos* and *Jonathan*,[32] the former being a targum to the Torah, the latter to the Prophets.[33] Other targums, such as *Ps.-Jonathan* and *Neofiti*, both to the Torah, certainly contain old material, but disagreements persist over the separation of such layers.[34] Assigning a definitive date to this type of literature is difficult, as it is notoriously subject to alteration and addition over time.

Onkelos (hereafter, *T.O.*) has been described as "simple and non-expansive,"[35] although "non-expansive" here is meant relative to the later targums, some of which feature lengthy additions. In fact, relative to the Greek translation of Aquila, *T.O.* and *Jonathan* both make noticeable changes to the base text.[36] For the sake of comparison, consider the following examples. First, the biblical text found in Gen. 28:13–17:

And the Lord stood over him and said, "I am the Lord, the God of Abraham your father and the God of Isaac; the land on which you lie I will give to you and to your offspring; and your offspring shall be like the dust of the earth, and you shall spread abroad to the west and to the east and to the north and to the south; and all the families of the earth shall be blessed in you and in your offspring. Know that I am with you wherever you go, and will bring you back to this land; for I will not leave you until I have done what I have promised you." Then Jacob woke from his sleep and said, "Surely the Lord is in this place – and I did not know it!" And he was afraid, and said, "How awesome is this place! This is none other than the house of God, and this is the gate of heaven."

And here is the text found in *T.O. Gen.* 28:13–17:

And behold, *the Glory of the Lord*[37] was standing over him, and He said, "I am the Lord, the God of your father Abraham and the God of Isaac: the land on which you are lying I will give to you and to your offspring. And your offspring shall be as abundant as the dust of the earth, and you shall *prevail*[38] to the west, and to the east, and to the north, and to the south; and all the families of the earth shall be blessed on account of you and on account of your offspring. And behold *my Memra* will assist you, and I will watch over you wherever you go, and I will bring you back to this land; for I will not leave you until I have done what I have spoken to you." Then Jacob awoke from his sleep and said, "In truth the *Glory of the Lord* dwells in this place, and I did not know it"; And he was afraid, and said, "How awesome is this place! *This is not an ordinary place, but a place which is the Lord's pleasure, and this is the gate facing heaven."*[39]

The italicized portions represent modest changes to the text. This level of intervention, or perhaps slightly less, is typical of *Onkelos*. The most extensive renovation occurs in *T.O.* to Gen. 49, Jacob's blessing to Judah:

The scepter shall not depart from Judah, nor the ruler's staff from between his feet, until tribute comes to him; and the obedience of the peoples is his. Binding his foal to the vine and his donkey's colt to the choice vine, he washes his garments in wine, and his robe in the blood of grapes; his eyes are darker than wine, and his teeth are whiter than milk (Gen. 49:9–12).

The *ruler*[40] shall never depart from the House of Judah, nor the *scribe/teacher* from his children's children for evermore – until the Messiah comes, whose is the kingdom, and him shall the nations obey. He shall lead Israel round about His city; the people shall build His Temple. The righteous shall be round about him, and they that carry out the Law shall be engaged in study with him. Let his raiment be of fine purple, and his garment all woolen, crimson and multicolored. *His mountains shall be red with his vineyards;*[41] his vats shall overflow with wine; his valleys shall be white with grain and with flocks of sheep (*T.O. Gen.* 49:9–12)

It would be inopportune to comment on the logic behind all the changes, some of which are based on intricate exegesis.[42] Throughout *T.O.* generally, the changes are as follows: a tendency to distance God from direct action or anthropomorphic behaviors,[43] collapsing of figurative language,[44] modernization of archaic names and terms,[45] fine-tuning of ambiguous language,[46] explanatory or interpretive glosses,[47] and finally, some mild censorship, varnishing indiscretions on the part of the patriarchs, matriarchs, or God.[48] And while it is true that the changes listed above are often, even typically, made, it does not mean that they are always and everywhere made. God still engages in anthropomorphic activity, some figurative language is allowed to stand, and grammatical ambiguities are sometimes reflected in the translation.[49]

In conclusion, we find that two types of movement are present within the Greek and Aramaic translations: the Greek translations move towards the Hebrew text; the Aramaic translations move away from it. Early Hebraizing translations were in circulation during the first century CE and possibly before. The process reaches its apex with Aquila in a translation which must have found its chief application in a scholastic or professional setting. Translations such as those by Theodotion and Symmachus, with their emphasis on readability, probably found a place in public performance. Even so, these translations strive to maintain fidelity to the Hebrew text. Aramaic translations, however, seem to move in the opposite direction, expanding, paraphrasing, and eliding to various degrees. The exegetical tooling evident in the targums indicates that these texts have also passed through scholarly hands, yet their freedom with respect to the base text is evident. Could the Greek and Aramaic translations, with their different commitments to the Hebrew text, have been executed by the same person or even the same school?[50] Or must we presume two different groups with different hermeneutical strategies, reflective, perhaps, of different audiences?[51] In any case, it appears that a great deal of this translating activity, both into Greek and into Aramaic, was taking place in Palestine.[52] Behind this exegetical and textual work there clearly lies a complex variety of popular and scholarly venues for textual performance that has yet to be fully understood.

"Dew from the ice of Paradise": re-presented Bible

Related to the translator's enterprise, but one step further removed, is the activity of retelling the biblical narratives, which results in a type of literature generally called rewritten Bible. I have favored the expression "re-presented Bible," since it suggests a process having a performance dimension, not one that is entirely scribal. We have already touched on *Jubilees* and the *Genesis Apocryphon*. Others have written excellent introductions to the topic of rewritten Bible, and it will not be necessary to cover that ground again, though some discussion of the literature will be required for the sake of completeness.[53] The focus here will fall on the social framework within which such activities might be plausibly located. We shall ask if this activity finds any precedent in the other school environments we have examined, and what particular type of reading or study situation provides a suitable frame for it. Was it written for performance or for reference? Would such literature have been used in conjunction with or instead of the narratives already present in the Hebrew Bible? Does it supplement scripture or supplant it?

From the standpoint of genre, rewritten Bible resists easy classification. At the level of formal description, *Jubilees* and Josephus' *Antiquities of the Jews* share many similarities. Episodes are shortened, and direct discourse is distilled and related in the third person. But *Jubilees* presents itself as the written version of the interview between Moses and the Angel of the Presence during Moses' forty-day sojourn on Mount Sinai. As such, it is sometimes classed as an apocalypse. In his *Antiquities*, Josephus strives to write a history that will be lively reading while pushing certain theological and ethical claims, so even though selected passages of the work may bear formal resemblance to *Jubilees*, these are two very different works.[54] In so far as he heightens psychological and erotic motifs, Josephus' work bears comparison with the Greek novels. So "rewritten Bible" may fall under several different genres.

A fine example of rewritten Bible is Pseudo-Philo's *LAB*, which is extant only in Latin, though it was originally written in Hebrew and has Palestine as its likely provenance.[55] Dating most probably from the first century CE, it falls directly in the midst of our period of interest.[56]

The author performs several types of editorial operations on and with the biblical materials, which may divided into four rough categories: (1) text is omitted entirely, (2) stories are retold in paraphrased and reduced form, (3) existing stories are interleaved with new material and thereby expanded, and (4) completely new stories about new characters are added.[57] As an instance of the first kind of editorial activity, the author bypasses much of the book of Genesis, omitting the first four chapters. The *LAB* begins with the genealogies in Gen. 5, adding the names of a great many sons and daughters omitted in the biblical account. All of the familiar biblical narratives about Abraham, Isaac, and Jacob and Esau are missing.

In some cases, scripture is followed rather closely, though paraphrased and shortened somewhat, as in ch. 3 where Noah's conversation with God after the flood is retold. The author employs much of the Genesis account, but trims redundant language, resulting in a story that is reduced by two-thirds. With the exception of a single stray phrase, the story in *LAB* consists entirely of reworked timber from Genesis. Also apparent is the tendency to reorder elements of the story slightly; this kind of local reordering is extremely commonplace. The author freely omits material as well: the story of Noah's drunkenness, which Philo treats in such detail, is missing from *LAB*. Apparently, it is behavior unbecoming to a patriarch.

On occasion, the author condenses or omits stories already known from scripture and adds new ones, sometimes with a summarizing remark as in the story of Samson:

> Now concerning the lion that he killed and concerning the jawbone of the ass by which he killed the Philistines and concerning the bonds that were broken off from his arms as it were spontaneously and the foxes that he caught, are not these written in the Book of Judges? (43:4)

New narrative modules may be added to old stories – Abraham in a fiery furnace is one example (ch. 6) – and places where scripture is tantalizingly silent are often filled out. The story of Jepthah's daughter is one such instance. Condemned by her father's rash oath to be sacrificed as a burnt offering, her story is especially poignant. The biblical account leaves her nameless, but the author of *LAB* gives her the name Seila, and furnishes her with more extensive dialogue (ch. 40). According to Judges 11:38, she bewailed her virginity; *LAB* fills this inviting lacuna with an actual hymn that puts words to her sad plight: " . . . O Mother, in vain you have borne your only daughter, because Sheol has become my bridal chamber . . . " Similarly, in the *LAB* versions of the David stories, we are supplied with a libretto of the songs that David sang to soothe Saul's troubled spirit (ch. 60).

Finally, the *LAB* includes lengthy narratives about figures barely mentioned or entirely absent in the biblical accounts. One such figure is the immensely capable Kenaz (Judg. 3:9), who once slew 45,000 Midianites single-handedly. Among other exploits, he managed to capture the seven magic stones of the Amorites, crystalline stones of extraordinary beauty that were capable of healing blindness. After obtaining the stones, Kenaz wrote the sins of the Amorites in a book and read it before the Lord. Both book and stones proved so adamantine that they could not be destroyed by human hands. Only when drenched by a cloud bearing "dew from the ice of Paradise" was the writing in the books expunged. As for the stones, an angel hurled them into the heart of the sea where they were swallowed up.

The author also takes the opportunity to retell and modify problematic biblical passages. Most people would agree that Judges 19 is such a passage. After a long day of travel, a man, his concubine and a servant enter Gibeah, a Benjamite village, and are taken in by an elderly gentleman. That evening, a band of licentious local riff-raff attacks the house. Ever hospitable, the host offers to send out his own virgin daughter and the man's concubine to sate the lusts of the mob. The visitor spares his host's daughter but sends out his concubine. Raped and abused through the night, she falls down dead at the door of the house. The man then cuts her body into twelve pieces and sends a piece to the Twelve Tribes accompanied by a note that blames the incident on the Benjamites. The story in *LAB* follows the same lines, but adds this remark: "they abused his concubine until she died, because she had transgressed against her man once when she committed sin with the Amalekites, and on account of this the Lord God delivered her into the hands of sinners" (45.3). The concubine's unfaithfulness may have been implicit in Judg. 19:2, where she leaves her husband for four months and returns to the home of her father. But apparently, the individual responsible for the *LAB* in its present form needed to make the guilt of the concubine more explicit for its new audience.[58]

It is easy to imagine these stories being performed: tales of miraculous and daring exploits would have had great performance appeal, even across the boundaries of social class. Certainly the *Odyssey* contains its share of exotic elements. On any given day in a Greco-Roman city, those with the requisite leisure might be found loitering in the agora, trolling about for stories of unusual people, places, and incidents. Acts 17:21 reports that the Epicurean and Stoic philosophers who frequented the marketplace "enjoyed nothing more than saying or hearing something new." Idling for the day in Brundisium, Aulus Gellius ran across a bookstall selling old books full of "marvelous tales," stories about dog-headed men and a people called the Arimaspi, who had eyes in the middle of their foreheads (*NA* 9.4). Even an individual as serious as Pliny the Elder would have been interested in remarkable tales: paradoxography was a well-established genre of literature. Furthermore, the addition of actual songs – of Jepthah's daughter, of Hannah, David, and others – is especially suggestive; this material would obviously lend itself to performance.

The lists and genealogies that occur early in the book might appear less suitable for public recitation; they seem to be chiefly documentary in nature, of interest only to people charged with keeping track of historical details. Nevertheless, the poems of Homer contain long stretches of such material – consider the recitation of Argive captains in Book 2 of the *Iliad* or the endless lists of battle casualties – and these poems are certainly products of oral performance. In fact, lists of names provided an opportunity for performers to impress an audience, accumulating detail to create an aura of facticity. This world of detail, deployed, mapped, and mastered, made for persuasive and effective performance. Similar superfetation of detail can also be observed in several fields of ancient knowledge, among them, medicine, astrology, and physiognomics.[59] So both these aspects of the *LAB*, the lists of names as well as the wondrous elements, are readily intelligible in texts designed for oral performance.

As for venue, the synagogue is probably the most likely candidate for the performance of such a text.[60] Colorful expansions, the poetic insets such as the lament of Jephthah's daughter, and explanations that resolve moral dilemmas (making the concubine in Judges 19

morally culpable), all these elements could find a home in a synagogue homily. We also know that many synagogues (e.g., at Ostia
and Dura, and now Jericho) show evidence of dining areas, and
edifying tales of wondrous and magical events inspired by biblical
narratives might have been performed after a synagogue meeting as
a form of entertainment.[61] Perhaps the stories about Kenaz and the
Magic Stones of the Amorites belong here, rather than in the formal
synagogue liturgy; however, too little is known about synagogue
practices at this time to support any hard and fast claims. We also
have evidence of extra-synagogal Jewish associations and dining
clubs.[62] It would certainly not be unprecedented for someone to read
from a text on such an occasion, or to stage a production of a story or
a dialogue; it was commonplace to hear a performance of some kind
during or after meals.[63] The *akroatēria* shunned by Philo, or other
public places where people gathered are other plausible venues for
the telling and trading of stories. We also know of the Homeridae,
traveling poets who performed Homer's poems before enthusiastic
crowds.[64] Stories about Judges such as Gideon, Samson, and Kenaz,
men who were essentially guerrilla fighters fantastically out-
numbered by corrupt gentiles, would have played well to an audience under the domination of the Roman Empire.

While there are a number of reasons someone might like to
rewrite, expand, distill, or otherwise alter biblical narratives, entertainment and edification both rank as important motivations. The
compiler of 2 Maccabees, for instance, states his reasons for condens-
ing the five volumes of Jason of Cyrene, which deal with the exploits
of Judas Maccabeus, into a single book.[65] "We wish," says the
author, "to take thought both for those wishing to read for edification, for those undertaking the task of memorizing the text, and for
the benefit of all those who pick up this text."[66] The epitomizer
attempts to enhance the readability and appeal of lengthy texts by
"seeking concise expression" and likens his task to that of a painter,
who makes the underlying structure beautiful and appealing. The
remark about memorizing is also very significant. Apparently, some
readers consulted books in order to memorize them, or at least,
portions of them, probably in order to reproduce the narratives
extemporaneously when the occasion called for it. Obviously, this
was an easier task with a written text to consult. Oral performance of
story and narrative, supposedly a feature of "oral culture," was often
aided and abetted by a written text. "Orality" may at times have had
a text under its cloak (*Phdr.* 228D–E).[67]

So we may imagine several cultural forces that would result in a work resembling *LAB*. The practice of re-presenting the Bible may be placed within the larger context of the Greco-Roman world, where Hellenized Jews sought to refashion their own history and culture into literary forms familiar to the culture at large. Ezekiel the Tragedian, the author of the *Exagōgē*, cast stories from the Greek version of the Pentateuch into iambic trimeters. The mixture of the wondrous and the antiquarian elements in the *LAB* point to a milieu of public performance and display. The synagogue appears to be the most plausible setting for the telling, trading, and embellishment of such stories, although it is probably not part of the lectionary proper. Instead, social gatherings in and around the synagogue were likely seed beds for such material.

"Find, open, read, observe": texts in use

Evidence for the reading of scripture in the third century CE is relatively plentiful. We know, for example, of the practice of targum discussed previously. But while the Mishnah contains many testimonia about practices in earlier times, the worth of this evidence is questionable for the time predating the destruction of the Temple in 70 CE and in the turmoil that followed. In our period, however, evidence for the reading of scripture in the Temple and synagogue is relatively scarce.

Prior to 70 CE, the Temple was almost certainly a center for the study of scripture. The young Jesus, for example, was reputed to have had his learned discussion with teachers in the Temple precincts (Luke 2:46). Apart from the Temple, however, the leading candidate for a "reading theater" is the synagogue.[68] Non-literary evidence confirms that the synagogue was a place for public reading. An inscription, presumably from a Jerusalem synagogue destroyed in 70 CE, honors a certain Theodotus Vettinus, priest and leader of the synagogue, who built the synagogue "for reading the law and for teaching commandments."[69] Many epitaphs from Jewish tombs bear the symbol of the ʿ*aron*, or Torah shrine, a peaked wooden cabinet for holding book rolls.[70] An inscription from Ostia mentions a certain Mindius Faustus, who "set up the cabinet for the holy law."[71] A pediment for such a chest has been discovered in excavations at Sardis, bearing the inscription, "Find, open, read, observe."[72]

In addition to the evidence for public reading from Philo and Qumran mentioned above, evidence from Luke–Acts may be invoked, especially Luke 4:16–21, where Jesus enters the synagogue in Nazareth and reads from Isaiah. While it is not necessary to assume that Luke's picture of Jesus' reading took place precisely as it is told, the author of Luke is presumably familiar with reading practices, if not in Palestinian synagogues then at least in meeting houses in the Diaspora. We may assume that for the purposes of verisimilitude, the author gives a plausible account of how such a reading might actually take place. As such, the story invites and repays close examination. Here is the story:

> When he came to Nazareth, where he had been brought up, he went to the synagogue on the sabbath day, as was his custom. He stood up to read, and the scroll of the prophet Isaiah was given to him. He unrolled the scroll and found the place where it was written: "The Spirit of the Lord is upon me, because he has anointed me to bring good news to the poor. He has sent me to proclaim release to the captives and recovery of sight to the blind, to let the oppressed go free, to proclaim the year of the Lord's favor." And he rolled up the scroll, gave it back to the attendant, and sat down. The eyes of all in the synagogue were fixed on him. Then he began to say to them, "Today this scripture has been fulfilled in your hearing."

These words elicit a positive reaction, but Jesus goes on to denounce the audience, and the story ends when they drive him out of the synagogue and try to send him over the edge of a cliff.

We are told first of all that "Jesus stood up to read": this may mean simply that he arose to go forward and then sat down again to read, or it may imply that he read while standing.[73] Certainly, handling a scroll while standing was a difficult task.[74] Most of the iconographic depictions of readers show them seated, using their lap as a support for the left arm and hand.[75] Furthermore, sitting is a typical teaching posture (Matt. 5:1). Matt. 23:2 speaks of "Moses' seat," from which the scribes and Pharisees are supposed to teach.[76] Jesus is then said to "spread out" or "unfold" (*anaptyssein*) the book (*biblion*).[77] It appears that the reader was responsible for locating the proper place within the roll ("he found the place where it was written"). The roll may well have had various formatting schemes in place to aid in this process: open spaces or *paragraphoi*, perhaps as in the Isaiah Scroll from Qumran, but these could change from roll to roll.[78] Nothing is actually said about the reading; indeed it is not even said that he read at all, just that "he found the place where it was written . . . "

After reading, he folded up (*ptyssein*) the book, gave it to the attendant, and sat down. This is odd; surely even an illiterate attendant is capable of rolling up a roll.[79] Would Jesus (or any reader in a synagogue) have stood in front of the audience for a full minute or two, uncoiling and coiling a roll? Perhaps the roll was merely closed rather than fully re-rolled. If a lectionary was followed, it would have been possible to open the roll at the point where the last reading left off. The next reader would then be fairly close to the beginning point of the next reading. One could give an unrolled roll back to the attendant, but Luke is quite explicit on the fact that Jesus unfolded and folded the book himself. Whatever may have been the case in actual practice, it seems likely that Luke is anxious to showcase Jesus' ease and familiarity with texts. The book is not unrolled for him; he unrolls it himself. Moreover, he locates the passage by himself: this was probably a more challenging operation than the actual reading, since it would involve the ability to skim text rather quickly and, presumably, in silence. Jesus opens, reads, and closes the roll, easily managing what for many would be a difficult feat of textual expertise. He is thereby shown to be an entirely self-sufficient handler and interpreter of texts.[80] The act also has a larger symbolic value for the author: it is Jesus who opens, i.e., explains, the scriptures (see Luke 24:45) and it is Jesus who represents their completion.

On this occasion, Jesus read from the prophet Isaiah. Was this preceded by a reading from the books of Moses? Based on internal and external evidence, we have seen that the Qumran sectarians read from the Torah during community worship, and that the Minor Prophets were probably also read in formal settings together with commentary. In Acts 13:15, Paul makes his way to the local synagogue in Pisidian Antioch on the Sabbath, and hears a reading of the "law and the prophets." Acts 15:21 states that Moses is read aloud every Sabbath in the synagogues. Synagogue lectionaries are known in Talmudic times, and differ from place to place. A group of reading cycles linked with Palestine featured a triennial structure with 154 *sedarim* (Torah selections), while the Babylonian cycle was completed in a single year.[81] During the time of our study, however, none of this can be proven.[82] We do not know if fixed passages of the prophets were always read with certain passages of the Torah, or if the reader might pick and choose. Perhaps Luke's emphasis on Jesus unrolling the scroll and rolling it up again may imply that he chose the passage himself.

In addition to the reading of texts, there is ample evidence for explication. After hearing Isaiah, it appears that the synagogue audience is expecting some comment on the reading from Jesus. In the surviving excerpts of the *Hypothetica*, Philo says that Jews gather on the Sabbath in certain habitual places for the reading of the law:

> And indeed they do always assemble and sit together, most of them in silence except when it is the practice to add something to signify approval of what is read. But some priest who is present or one of the elders reads holy laws to them and expounds them point by point (*kath' hekaston exēgeitai*) till [*sic*] about the late afternoon (*Hyp.* 7.13).

"Point by point" may rather mean "section by section," according to the method of division employed in the text being read. This literary evidence confirms the Theodotus inscription mentioned above, which links reading with instruction. Two possible methods can be imagined here, though it is not possible to decide between them. First, the whole reading takes place, after which the teacher recapitulates and explains portions of the text sequentially. Or, the reading itself may have been interspersed with commentary. Two or three verses may be read, followed by explanation, as with pesher commentary. In this case, Jesus' reading consisted of only two verses, read in full before comment was added. Customs probably differed from place to place and from speaker to speaker. Some speakers or readers were no doubt more loquacious than others or preferred a different style of explication.

Textual experts: scribes

Who was it that carried out the reading and explication of scripture? The Gospels attribute this function to the scribes (*grammateis*).[83] However, when one considers the different meanings attached to the term *grammateus*, it becomes clear that the New Testament picture of scribes is rather anomalous. One student of first-century Judaism has recently drawn attention to the fact that the New Testament portrays the scribe as a religious figure: "There is little evidence in other sources that there was such a thing."[84] In order to understand the reasons for this, it will be necessary to sample several different bodies of evidence, beginning with the biblical materials, the New Testament, Josephus, and the inscriptions. I will end the section by suggesting that the New Testament portrayal of scribes is informed (and deformed) by struggles over access to scripture and the right to interpret it.

A well-known description of the scribe and his vocation is found in Ben Sira 38:34–39:11. Much of his function revolves around study: he "devotes himself to the study of the law of the Most High." He seeks out ancient wisdom; he is concerned with prophecies; he "preserves the sayings of the famous and penetrates the subtleties of parables." However, the scribe of Ben Sira is no cringing scrivener. He is also a public figure: "He serves among the great and appears before rulers." With one foot in the past and one in the present, the scribe serves as a point of access to tradition and literature for people who do not have the leisure time or the skills for scholarly pursuits. The potter and smith, though crucial to the fabric of society,

> are not sought out for council, they do not attain eminence in the public assembly, they do not sit in the judge's seat, nor do they understand the decisions of the courts; they cannot expound discipline or judgment, and they are not found among the rulers (Sir. 38:33).

These are the prerogatives and duties of the scribe, according to Ben Sira. In a passage discussed previously, *Targum Onkelos* makes a striking interpretive move in the translation of Gen. 49:10: "The scepter shall not depart from Judah, nor the ruler's staff from between his feet." The targum to this passage renders the verse, "The ruler shall never depart from the House of Judah, nor the scribe/teacher from his children's children for evermore." The substitution has exegetical grounds,[85] but the equation of the scribe with the scepter, symbol of temporal power, is most significant. As the pen is the instrument for writing, so the scribe is the instrument for the articulation and expression of the law of the land.

The New Testament echoes some elements of Ben Sira's account. Scribes are teachers and textual experts; when judicial bodies are in session, they are found nearby, e.g., at the trial of Jesus (Mark 14:53). Significantly, none of what the scribe does requires explicit involvement with written texts. As portrayed in the New Testament, scribes are never found using or producing books, nor do they produce the various deeds, receipts, wills or certificates for which scribes were generally responsible. They were expected, it seems, to know very thoroughly the Law of Moses. Nowhere in any of the Gospels are Pharisees or Sadducees found quoting scripture nor is it implied that they do so; this function falls to the scribes. According to the author of Mark, it is the scribes who say that "Elijah must come first" (Mark 9:11), and that "the Messiah is the Son of David" (Mark 12:35). When the Sadducees put Jesus to the test over marriage in the resurrection he answers them by citing a passage in Exodus, and it is a scribe who appreciates the depth of the comment. More than just textual augurs, scribes are also responsible for teaching. This much is clear from Mark 1:22, where it is stated that Jesus' teaching carried authority, unlike that of the scribes. Finally, consistent with their textual expertise, scribes also function in judicial settings. When Jesus predicts his death in Jerusalem, it is at the hands of the scribes and high priests, not the Pharisees or Sadducees.[86]

The function of scribes as teachers is also carried over into Luke's account. In Luke 5:17,21 there is an implicit equation between scribes and the "teachers of the law" (*nomodidaskaloi*). And in Acts 5:34, Gamaliel, an elder and Pharisee, is described as a *nomodidaskalos*. Luke, in fact, is the only Gospel writer to employ this term. The author of Luke–Acts, however, also uses the term *grammateus* in a fashion that would have been more familiar to Greco-Roman readers in Acts 19:35, where "the *grammateus*," presumably the town clerk (so the NRSV), manages to calm the rioting townspeople of Ephesus. Apparently, this individual was recognized as an authority.

Compared to Mark, Matthew shows a glint of respect for the office of the scribe, although not for the particular office-holders. This may be a reflection of the schoolish nature of Matthew's readership.[87] Like Mark, he portrays them as experts in scripture and in prophetic interpretation. When Herod needs to know where the Messiah is to be born, he calls on the services of the high priests and scribes (Matt. 2:4). Matthew even arranges them in series with prophets and wise men: "I send you prophets and wise men and scribes" (Matt. 23:34). There may be a significance to the order: the prophets of the later biblical books, Daniel the sage and seer as a type of the wise man, and Ezra as the scribe.[88] Matthew even seems to allude to Christian scribes within his own community ("scribes trained for the kingdom of the heaven," in 13:52). A scribe presents himself to Jesus as a prospective student (Matt. 8:19).

Matthew also seems to have tightened the job description of the scribe relative to Mark. Mark lumps scribes and Pharisees together, while Matthew parses their respective tasks more closely: scribes quote scripture and judge incidents that fall under the strictures of Torah, while Pharisees take the lead when purity regulations are at issue. In Mark 2:16, the "scribes of the Pharisees" object to Jesus sharing food with ritually impure dining companions. In Matthew's version of this story, the Pharisees make this objection. A similar story is found in Matt. 15:1, where the "Pharisees and scribes" are mentioned with respect to the washing of hands; here the order "Pharisees–scribes" is significant: it is the only time this order appears in Matthew. Elsewhere (Matt. 5:20, 12:38, 23:2,13,14,15), the order is always "scribes and Pharisees." Mark speaks of "the scribes of the Pharisees" (Mark 2:16, 7:1), a problematic expression, since it is unclear how scribes would "belong" to the Pharisees; Matthew omits this expression, though he does, on occasion, speak of the "scribes of the people" (2:14). Thus, when Matthew speaks of the "scribes and Pharisees," it appears to be a circumlocution for "scribal interpretations of Torah and the traditions of the elders as purveyed by the Pharisees": these office-holders are proxies for their respective areas of expertise, and thus represent the weight of interpretive authority of Torah in its widest sense, both written and unwritten.

We saw that the scribe described by Ben Sira is a public figure who puts his expertise to work in the political arena: he "serves among the great and appears before rulers" (Sir. 39:4). Josephus reinforces this stress on the scribe as an office-holder. In his historical account of Israel, scribes are generally shown as servants of rulers and kings, or as attached to the Temple.[89] In *BJ* 5.532, Herod kills Aristeus, the "scribe of the council," i.e., the Sanhedrin, along with fifteen other eminent men. He also speaks of the "sacred scribes" (*hierogrammateis*), who correctly interpret an omen concerning the imminent destruction of the Temple (*BJ* 6.291). Josephus also alludes to the village scribe (*kōmogrammateus*, *AJ* 16.203), though in general, the scribes he mentions are of relatively high status. Most if not all of the people Josephus calls scribes are engaged in activities requiring fairly high literacy,[90] though they are called scribes because of their role or function within a larger structure, governmental or sacerdotal. He does mention two individuals named Judas and Matthias, whom he terms *sophistai*, describing them as

> the most learned of the Jews and unrivaled interpreters of the ancestral laws, and men especially dear to the people because they educated the youth, for all those who made an effort to acquire virtue used to spend time with them day after day (*AJ* 17.149).

In their function as teachers and as expert interpreters of the scriptures, such men might easily have gone under the name "scribe" in the parlance of the Gospel writers, but Josephus does not call them by this name, perhaps because they were not part of the Temple or government administration. Josephus uses the term *grammateus* rather differently than the Gospel writers because his Greco-Roman audience would have had a different understanding of the term.

Evidence drawn from other sources, especially epigraphic ones, shows that in Greco-Roman society generally, scribes were typically attached to institutions: in some cases temples, in others, political bodies.[91] Fraternities and *collegia* also list the *grammateis* as officers.[92] The reference in Acts 19:35 to the "town clerk" (*grammateus*) finds other epigraphic parallels.[93] Presumably, most of these individuals would have been literate to some degree, but often the post of *grammateus* was bestowed on a person in view of his status or patrimony.[94] *Grammateus* was often the equivalent of "secretary," and just as there is no guarantee that the secretary of the local Elks club must be highly erudite to hold the post, so it was in antiquity.[95] It is no wonder that Josephus describes Judas and Matthias as *sophistai* ("experts") not as *grammateis*. In fact, if the Greco-Roman audience for the Gospels assigned an air of officiousness to the word and thought it a description that one might apply to the Bob Cratchits of the ancient world, the Gospel writers may even have been making an implicit dig at Jewish scholars by using this term.[96]

Finally, a complete picture of scribal activity would be incomplete without reference to a body of evidence discussed earlier – namely, the work that was being done in the first centuries BCE and CE on literal Greek translations of the Hebrew Bible. It has not been possible to localize this activity. Barthélemy placed his "proto-Theodotion" in Palestine, *c.* 50 CE and identified him with Jonathan Ben Uzziel, a student of Hillel.[97] This aspect of his work has not convinced many.[98] But even if this particular identification fails, we have seen much evidence to suggest that Jewish students of the Bible were in the process of reworking parts of the Septuagint with reference to the Hebrew text. Not so much as a flicker of this activity is evident from Josephus or the New Testament. But obviously, these pursuits must be situated in some concrete social framework, either in a synagogue or school setting of some sort. So neither Josephus nor the New Testament yields a complete view of scribal activity in Palestine.

As noted above, there is an interesting contrast here between the portrayal of scribes in the New Testament, and that derived from Josephus and the inscriptional evidence. The Gospel writers characterize the scribes in a way that appears to be inconsistent with their real-world function known from other sources. This deformation in character rendition suggests an underlying tension over the office and role of the scribe. When we hear the Gospels say that "Jesus taught with authority, and not like the scribes," we see a literary portrayal tinctured with systematic resentment. When Jesus' disciples ask him, "why do the scribes say that Elijah must come first?" we sense a curiosity about a matter of scriptural interpretation that scribes are known to have discussed, but which has not (according to the author of Mark) been made plain to the people the scribes pretend to address. Scribes are caricatured, made to be something they probably were not, and we should ask why this was the case.

Here is one answer to that question. The ubiquitous presence of Mosaic law in Palestinian society, coupled with the restricted possibilities for actual access without the mediating presence of the scribe or other learned person, would have made these stewards and interpreters of the law into crucially important figures. Martin Goodman mentions the "large number" of biblical texts current in Palestine ("many thousands"), and states that "all adult male Jews had regular access to at least a Pentateuch scroll, since they could expect to hear it read aloud in synagogues at least once a week, on the Sabbath."[99] Even if true, we may wonder whether this constitutes true access: what percentage of Jewish males could read Aramaic, let alone Hebrew? And would they then have been empowered to interpret it on their own behalf? Would their decisions have been binding? In all likelihood, they would have received the response given to the blind man in John 9:34: " 'you were born completely in sins, and you are teaching us?' And they cast him out."

The social leverage of scribes would be further enhanced by the fact that they were (presumably) able to read Hebrew, though fluency in the language, even among relatively educated students, may not have been universal. The activity of highly literalistic translation of the Hebrew scriptures into Greek among some scholars is a sign that scribes sought to increase their mastery over the text by all means possible, including having highly literal translations at hand for reference and study. Language was a problem even for relatively educated people. David Sedley has proposed that Platonists began to write commentaries because people in the Hellenistic period who spoke only Koine needed help with Classical Greek.[100] Many students of philosophy were from a Latin-speaking background, and we have seen that Chrysippus's Greek may have been a problem for them. If this relatively literate constituency needed extra help to assimilate Classical Greek, it is easy to imagine that the difficulties posed by Hebrew would have rendered scripture even more inaccessible to the average Aramaic-speaking auditor.[101] Once again, it is probably not accidental that Luke portrays a Paul who declaims in Hebrew as well as in Greek (Acts 22:2). Paul, like Jesus, must be in firm control of the capacities needed to explain texts, and mastery of Hebrew is one such skill.

It would have been in the interest of such textual experts to control the dissemination of written texts of or about scripture and to restrict the prerogative of interpreting scripture to a select caste of individuals. Indeed, it is possible that issues of access and control lie behind the curious dearth of written commentary on scripture during this period.[102] Written texts escape control, and control of the text was of paramount importance to the power base of scribes and the people who employed them.

Of course, it was not simply the written text, but the traditions that grew up around it that were also closely guarded. Experts in "the traditions of the Fathers," those oral interpretations which grew up around the written law, would serve a similar function. They too were textual experts, though their text was not a written one.[103] In fact, as brokers of knowledge, those who control oral texts have, if anything, an even tighter grasp on power: oral teaching was not subject to the scrutiny of hostile critics, nor was it likely to "escape" as a written text might. Insistence on oral dissemination of knowledge suggests a pattern of authority tightly held by an authoritative teacher who has won or been given the role as the interpreter of text and tradition in a given teaching situation. The following midrash from *Tanhuma* dealing with control and access is worth quoting, even though it falls outside the chronological boundaries of this study:

> R. Judah b. Shalom [mid-fourth century] said: When the Holy one told Moses 'write down' (Exod. 34:27), the latter wanted the *Mishnah* also to be in writing. However, the Holy One blessed is He foresaw that a time would come when the nations of the world would translate the Torah and read it in Greek and then say: 'We are Israel', and now the scales are balanced! The Holy One blessed is He will then say to the nations: you contend that you are my children. That may be, but only those who possess my mysteries are my children, i.e., [those who have] the *Mishnah* which is given orally.[104]

Both groups of textual experts, then, were crucially situated in ancient Palestinian society. The expression "scribes and Pharisees" serves as a cipher for the power exercised by these interpreters of the text of scripture as it existed in its oral and written forms.

All this stands in striking contrast with the textual practices of the Qumran sectarians. The Qumran sectarians established a thick boundary around the community as a whole. But once inside this boundary, there seems to have been relatively free access to written materials. Indeed, study of these was mandatory. This form of textual polity worked well within the context of a small and self-contained splinter group. In society at large, a different mode of control emerged, one in which texts were tightly managed, even replaced by a caste of interpreters sequestered from the general populace not by geographical location but by skills such as literacy and social privilege.

While some have argued that scribes were of secondary importance, I believe that they performed a crucial service in their capacity as text-brokers and that such people might well have held a *de facto* monopoly on access to texts and traditions that governed people's behaviors.[105] It is important to add that they were not necessarily despised in this role, even though the New Testament suggests this. One should keep in mind Judas and Matthias, "unrivaled interpreters of the ancestral laws" (Josephus, *AJ* 17.149), who dedicated themselves to the education of young people. Gamaliel is described by the author of Luke–Acts as a "teacher of the law (*nomodidaskalos*) held in honor by all the people" (Acts 5:34).

The important fact for understanding the refracted view of the scribal office rendered in the New Testament is that the New Testament writers and their sources attributed to scribes an exaggerated and rather nefarious role because of anxiety over the issue of textual control. Thus, the deformation in the New Testament portrayal of scribes tells us something significant about one group's attitude towards text-brokers. It is this anxiety on the part of the New Testament writers and their sources that accounts for their warped portrayal of scribes.

One suggestive corollary follows from these results. As a person who employed an alternative hermeneutic or who simply offered another point of access to the Torah, Jesus would have posed a very real threat to the position of those ecclesiastical and governmental entities who "controlled the means of interpretation." It is commonplace among New Testament scholars to assume that Jesus stood in opposition to the Law, and that this was one of the things that set him at odds with the religious authorities.[106] However, it is not necessary to assume this in order to account for the institutional hostility triggered by Jesus. He may well have interpreted the Law differently at points, but it was the fact that he set himself up as an interpreter *at all* that was the basic affront. This represented a frontal assault on the interpretive monopoly held by textual experts and the institutional entities with which they were affiliated. Certainly, there were other reasons why Jesus aroused the hostility of powerful people in Palestinian society; his inflammatory language about the Temple is a case in point.[107] Nevertheless, it is reasonable to assume that Jesus' bid to provide an alternate point of access to the Law, or perhaps to "stand in for the law" in his capacity as its articulator and interpreter, was one significant strand in the cable that drew him towards his death.

PART 4

"UNLESS SOMEONE GUIDES ME": CHRISTIAN GROUPS

Bringing our set of questions about literary practices to the early Christian materials, we find a host of enticing leads that could be followed. The editorial work of Marcion and Tatian, for example, invites comparison with that of Zeno and Demetrius Lacon and Aristotelian commentators such as Aspasius and Adrastus. Knowledge of the literary practices of other book-centered groups promises to inform discussion about the nature of an entity such as Q. Indeed, better knowledge of patterns of textual use among Christians would enrich discussion of the Synoptic Problem generally.[1] We might consider Stephen's speech in Acts 7 as an instance of paraphrasing and epitomizing. Gnostic texts such as the *Reality of the Rulers* and the *Apocryphon of John* might be profitably examined under the rubric of re-presented Bible. As for commentary, the works of Basilides and Heracleon could be compared with those of Harpocration; the work of Origen looms on the horizon as a vast continent all its own, and his sophisticated engagement with texts is fully commensurable with that of the philosophers.[2] Connected with his work and that of Clement of Alexandria is the so-called Catechetical School at Alexandria. And finally, we might profitably ask of the papyri some of the same questions about public and private use that we brought to *PFay. 3, Anon. Tht.*, and *4QpHab*.[3]

189

This plentiful harvest of early Christian evidence has generated a forbidding amount of scholarship. Studies of early Christians and their literature have traditionally focused on issues of canon and canonization; recently, the material aspects of Christian book culture have come up for examination.[4] Anyone discussing books and their users in antiquity is deeply indebted to studies that explore ancient literacy.[5] Moving beyond the skill of reading (or the lack thereof), literacy as a catalyst for social change has been extensively studied from anthropological and from historical perspectives.[6] The study of orality and literacy in antiquity, pioneered by Parry, Lord, Havelock, Ong, and others is clearly related to the subject matter of the present study, and this body of theory has become increasingly sophisticated over the years, incorporating insights from anthropology, linguistics, media and folklore studies.[7] So there is a tremendous wealth of ancient and modern literature that could and should be considered in any study claiming to be a comprehensive treatment of Christian literary practices. It is neither feasible nor advisable to cover this entire literary landscape.

Mindful of the many roads that might have been taken, I have been highly selective both with the primary and with the secondary sources. Two subjects are proposed for examination. First, I will consider Paul as an example of a text-broker, and discuss what can be inferred about Paul's modes of teaching and the use of scripture in Paul's churches; this follows naturally on our discussion of scribes as text-brokers. Then, I will examine the *Epistle of Barnabas* as an instance of Christians anthologizing and commenting upon their central texts, and conclude with a reflection on Christian use of the codex form. But first, as a preface and foundation to these sections, we will consider teachers as textual performers within the agonal context of oral performance. As we shall see, textual expertise was one area in which would-be teachers proved their mettle. Jewish and Christian teachers, Paul among them, would have encountered in their audiences the expectation that their teacher was skilled in the literature of his or her tradition.

The demands of performance and the form of texts

In our discussion of textual practices among Jews in Palestine, we saw that the right to pronounce authoritatively on texts was the prerogative of a limited number of text-brokers. Some, but not all, of these figures would have gone under the name of "scribe." A person who commanded an oral text, a tradition not committed to writing, should also be considered a text-broker. A person might attain to this status in virtue of patrimony or proper connections. In other situations, the right to teach and interpret was won through public demonstration and debate. Writers of the period, especially the satirists, often remark on the contentious nature of the philo-sophical enterprise. The god Pan has described a discussion among philosophers as follows:

> They begin their discussions peaceably, but as the confer-ence proceeds they raise their voices to a high falsetto, so that, what with their excessive straining and their endeavour to talk at the same time, their faces get red, their necks get swollen, and their veins stand out like those of flute-players when they try to blow into a closed flute.[8]

The agonistic aspect of public speaking is evident in the athletic exertions that Lucian places in the mouth of Pan; even if it exag-gerates, the satire surely trades on scenes that would be familiar to his readers.

To speak publicly was to perform, and technical aspects of speak-ing, including both voice and posture, were measures by which an audience might judge a speaker. Pronunciation, correct word forma-tion, and a tone of voice appropriate to the subject matter, all were crucial to the speaker's success.[9] Quintilian devotes a lengthy discus-sion to proper hand gestures and bodily postures to be adopted by speakers.[10] These affectations were pervasive enough to draw forth yet another satirical thrust from Lucian in *A Professor of Public Speaking*, a treatise that richly documents the various aspects of the self-presentation of the orator.

Comprehensive control of one's subject matter was also of utmost importance. Orators of all kinds were very conscious of the public's appetite for conspicuous mastery and erudition – indeed, the term *sophistēs* simply means "expert" – and that the display of such erudi-tion would result in more pupils, more patrons, and higher status. Aulus Gellius' *Attic Nights* is filled with walking lexicons who gar-ner public admiration and social capital with their ability to settle arguments about arcane words and diction (e.g., *NA* 16.10). Con-versely, poor performance in such contests could result in an immediate tumble down the social (and financial) ladder. When Apollonius of Athens was bested by Heracleides in a rhetorical context, he was summarily deprived of his exemptions by the emperor, while Heracleides carried off gifts.[11]

The public appetite for display is evident not simply among rhetors but among philosophers as well.[12] The mutual loathing that often existed in principle between philosophers and orators was less evident in practice. In order to be effective as public speakers, both would have had to respond to the public appetite for display, and there are many figures of the first and second centuries that fit equally well in both categories: Euphrates, the Syrian Stoic, Maximus of Tyre, Dio Chrysostom, and many others. Dio's student Favorinus, for example, might be described alternately as a rhetor with philosophical interests or a philosopher with rhetorical interests. His work on exile has been vividly described by Paul Collart as "une légion d'exemples, une phalange d'arguments, un bataillon de héros mythiques et historiques . . . transformés en catapultes à citations." Scholars account for such material by claiming that it reflects the "Cult of the Past," manifest in "bibliomania, mimesis, compendia, *historiae omnigenae* and commonplace books."[13] Without disputing these claims, I would add that it also reflects a culture with an appetite for the public display of mastery, and the ability to cite and explain a wide variety of texts was one important skill which anyone who would command respect as a teacher had to demonstrate. Even if such rhetorical display was not central to a philosopher's sense of mission, many were probably required to advertise themselves in this way just to survive and thrive in the teaching enterprise. Ammonius the Peripatetic, highly esteemed as a philosopher, found it necessary to compose display speeches (*logoi epideiktikoi*). Porphyry, at least, believed that Ammonius would not wish to be represented to later generations by these works.[14]

The great value placed on publicly displayed erudition is evident in other fields as well: medicine is one example.[15] Galen performed public dissections of pigs, goats, and apes. He also performed public dissections of books:

> And when I came forward to display myself as having committed no falsehood in my anatomical treatises, I set up in public the books of all the anatomists, thereby giving each of those present the means to propose whatever part he wished to be dissected.[16]

The degree of difficulty is raised by the extemporaneous nature of the challenge. Galen boasts of being able to cite and interpret any

passage in these books at the drop of a hat. Some prominent physicians in the front row remarked that only the books of Lycus of
Macedon were worthy of examination, all the rest being out of date,
and so Galen proceeded to engage in a detailed comparison of
their respective works that lasted at least two days: "It was, then,
in accordance with their request that I proceeded, with respect to
every proof that was demanded of me from one day to the next."[17]
On yet another occasion, Galen engaged in a public discussion of
the "books of the ancient physicians," and "according to custom,"
a stylus was planted in the text at the point under discussion.[18]
Facility with texts is crucial not only in the theater of public
disputation but in the treatment of patients as well. In a guide
book designed to help people find a good doctor, Galen recommends that the client test prospective doctors on the thoroughness of their book learning.[19] Practitioners in other fields such as
astrology, physiognomy, and magic were also quick to display
their erudition.[20] The highly elaborated scheme of gnostic myth
may be one area in which a teacher/speaker would have had an
opportunity to display his or her knowledge and powers of cre-
ative innovation. As such, it may be profitable to view these
schemes from a rhetorical, as well as a theological standpoint. By
relentlessly heaping up names of divinities in magical spells,
magical practitioners no doubt sought to invoke and enlist as
many powers as possible; in addition, this practice would also
serve to persuade the client of the magician's professional abilities
and of the worth of the spell.

These facts about teaching illuminate the use of and appeal to
texts within all the groups we have studied. Literary works that
feature a parade of quotations are responding to expectations that
people had of teachers. Starting at the beginning of Philodemus'
work *On Piety*, for example, one finds the following concatenation of
names:

> Ariston reproaches Metrodorus . . . ; And with these Polyae-
> nus engages in his books *Against Ariston* . . . and in his book
> *Against* . . . ; and Metrodorus makes such a distinction in *On
> Change* . . . ; But Epicurus teaches in his work . . . ; Metro-
> dorus too finds a defense in saying in *On Gods* and further
> in *On Change* that that which has no share of the void en-
> dures . . . ; And according to Epicurus in *On Gods* . . . ; And
> having written another book *On Holiness* . . . and in Book
> 12 of *On Nature* he says . . . , etc.

We have seen that when a thinker such as Taurus the Platonist is queried about anger, he begins by citing the opinions of other ancient philosophers, ending with his own teacher Plutarch. Plotinus remarks that a teacher must do more than simply cite the opinions of the ancients, thereby suggesting that many philosophers were content having done this much. To be sure, when Philodemus reels off a litany of names and quotations from Epicurean founder-figures and others he is at one level making his case with the resources of his intellectual tradition. He is also fulfilling public expectations that teachers be able to produce these kinds of references. By doing this, philosophers are engaging in a similar enterprise to the magician who heaps up the names of gods and demigods or the doctor who makes superfine distinctions in the kinds of pulse.[21] So this bibliographic habit functions at two levels: the quotes adduced by a Taurus or a Philodemus may well be germane philosophically; but from a rhetorical standpoint, the easy and fluent citation of such material shows the teacher to be a masterful guide to the body of knowledge in question. It is easy to imagine that on certain occasions, activity is taking place on one level more than the other.

With this background information about the importance of texts in the presentation of those who would be teachers, we turn to Paul and then to the *Epistle of Barnabas*.

"As when present, so when absent": Paul as teacher and text-broker

It is generally assumed that since Christianity evolved out of Judaism, habits of reading and study in Christian assemblies would have continued in the trails blazed by Jews in the synagogues, and this must certainly have been true in many cases. Indeed, I will argue that Paul, like the textual experts in Palestine, served as a text-broker for his congregations. Like them, he was reluctant to share this prerogative with others. Paul would certainly not have described himself as a scribe; indeed, he sharply differentiates his own approach from that of the wise man (*sophos*) and the scribe (*grammateus*; 1 Cor. 1:20). Nevertheless, Paul's way of employing and explaining scripture suggests that this "Hebrew born of Hebrews" has not renounced the patterns of textual usage imbibed in the course of his upbringing and education.[22] Paul brings a conversion experience to the Hebrew scriptures and with that experience a new set of eyes that cause him to refer them to Christ, but while Paul might have argued a set of different points, it would be surprising if his scholarly habits had radically changed. They were simply placed in the service of different arguments.

That being said, however, there is precious little information about Paul's use of scripture in his teaching.[23] We have many questions: When Paul made his initial overtures to a new audience, did he employ scripture in his exposition, even with non-Jewish listeners who may have been strangers to the Septuagint? When he taught more serious students in his stall in the market-place, in a synagogue, or in a private home, did he read and explain texts, and if so, what was the nature of this explication? Did Paul enter the room clutching bundles of rolls to which he might make reference? Is his manner of textual explanation at all analogous to anything we have seen in the other school-groups examined thus far?

For the sake of clarity, we may think of three different audiences which Paul would have addressed: (1) initial contact either with Jews or with pagans unfamiliar with his gospel, (2) audiences that stand in a liminal relationship to Paul: this might include seriously interested individuals who have yet to join his group, Christians personally unknown to him, i.e., audiences to whom he must prove himself, or members of Paul's own communities that are in danger of slipping away, and (3) full-fledged members of Paul's own assemblies. In all three cases, exposition of scripture would have played a role, and we shall address each in turn. We should also allow for a differentiation that cuts across these three categories, that of social class. Paul's initial approach to relatively high-status individuals such as Stephanus, Gaius and Erastus, this last the city treasurer of Corinth, probably would have differed significantly from his presentation to leather-workers and tradespeople. "Not many of you," says Paul, "were powerful, not many of noble birth" (1 Cor. 1:26), but some were, apparently, and these individuals were important for the support and maintenance of Paul's gospel. Such auditors might have had greater expectations for their teacher where learning was concerned. This, in fact, may account for the attachment of some of the Corinthians to Apollos, as will be shown in what follows.[24]

Based on what we have seen thus far, it is not unlikely that Paul would have made known his familiarity with the scriptures in his initial overtures both to Jewish and to non-Jewish audiences. With Jewish audiences, scripture represents shared territory. Paul is, after all, a Jew, and in his attempts to reach such an audience, it is only natural that he would capitalize on the fact that Jews would have respected their own sacred writings. Even though teacher and student are strangers to each other initially, the text that both recognize as authoritative provides a convenient meeting ground. This is all the more true if what I have argued in previous chapters is correct; namely, that access to Jewish scripture was brokered by a relatively restricted number of literate individuals. Therefore, under conditions characterized by low literacy, scarcity of texts, and restricted access, an individual who could provide access would have found an eager audience.[25] We need not naively take Acts at face value and imagine that Paul spent all his time haggling over scripture in synagogues. As part of its systematic attempt to show that the gospel was preached and rejected by Jews, Acts shows Paul seeking out synagogue audiences in order to "argue/discuss with them from the scriptures, explaining (*dianoigein*) and demonstrating that it was necessary for the Messiah to suffer and to rise from the dead" (17:2–3).[26] In fact, Paul may have preferred to teach in private, rather than in public.[27] Still, it is not necessary to swing to the other extreme and believe that Paul never darkened the door of a synagogue. As a Jew and as a seasoned controversialist, he would not have been averse to carrying his mission through the doors of a local synagogue when the situation required it. After all, for the sake of the gospel, Paul was prepared to become "all things to all people" (1 Cor. 9:22), and this would surely have included adaptation when necessary to prevailing modes and manners of teaching, in private or in public.

With non-Jewish audiences, is it likely that Paul would have made reference to the Septuagint even though this book might have been unfamiliar to his pagan audience? In light of the hoary antiquity of these texts, even pagans would have conceived a respect for the books of Moses; at least, those pagans who were interested enough in Jewish religion to give an ear to Paul's message. According to Numenius, the second-century Platonist, Plato was simply Moses speaking Attic Greek.[28] Josephus records an encounter between a traveling Jewish "teacher" and a Roman noblewoman:

> There was a certain Jew, a complete scoundrel, who had fled his own country because he was accused of transgressing certain laws and feared punishment on this account. Just at this time he was resident in Rome and played the part of an interpreter of the Mosaic law and its wisdom.[29] He enlisted three confederates not a whit better in character than him-

self; and when Fulvia, a woman of high rank who had become a Jewish proselyte, began to meet with them regularly (*epiphoitān*), they urged her to send purple and gold to the temple in Jerusalem. They, however, took the gifts and used them for their own personal expenses.[30]

Apparently, curiosity about the laws of Moses could be found even among the Roman nobility. Beyond this example, ancient occult literature of mysterious and forgotten origins would have impressed many, the older the better.[31] So even if Paul's audience was not intimately familiar with the Books of Moses and the Prophets, this would not necessarily have stopped him from invoking them, since manipulation of texts is one of the ways that teachers proved their mettle. Whether or not they knew the references or followed the arguments, at least some first-time auditors would have been watching to see if Paul was an able spokesperson for the traditions he represented, and part of this would have involved readily evident command of scripture.

We can only infer how Paul would have addressed a circle of serious but as-yet-unattached auditors. Based on Gal. 3:1, it appears that a "display of Christ crucified" was of decisive effect in precipitating the conversion of the Galatians: "O foolish Galatians, who has bewitched you? It was before your eyes that Jesus Christ was publicly exhibited (*prographein*) as crucified!" So runs the NRSV rendering of this enigmatic passage.[32] Paul uses the term *prographein* on one other occasion, at Rom. 15:4: "For whatever was written in former days (*prographein*) was written for our instruction, so that by steadfastness and by the encouragement of the scriptures we might have hope."[33] Here the sense is what one might expect from the morphology of the word, "to write beforehand" or "write ahead of time."[34] In this case, however, the addition of "before your eyes" (*kat' ophthalmous*) seems to complicate this understanding of the word, and so most commentators agree that the term has the well-attested sense of "clearly posted," "plainly portrayed," or "placarded," as one might speak of a public advertisement.[35] As such, Paul's preaching of the gospel had the effect of making Christ crucified so lively as to be almost visible.[36] On this account of things, we must imagine Paul giving a graphic description of the crucifixion as a way of moving his audience. The use of *prographein* in this sense does indeed find support in Greek usage.[37] Still, if we allow that *kat' ophthalmous* means "before your face," or "in your presence,"[38] and that Paul's exegesis of scripture before the Galatians might be described as a public display of the sort that teachers and speakers were wont to give, then understanding *prographein* in the sense of "written before-hand" yields an intelligible sentence: "O foolish Galatians, who has bewitched you, you to whom Christ crucified was shown before your very faces to be already written in scripture." In fact, this is how Jerome read the passage: the Vulgate uses *praescribere*, "to write first" for *prographein*.[39] *Praescribere* can refer to the act of writing a preface at the beginning of a document; it can also mean "write earlier." A letter traced out for children to follow when learning to write goes by the name of *praescriptum*.[40] Taking *prographein* in the sense of "written beforehand," we might suppose that Paul demonstrated to the Galatians that the story of scripture and the story of Christ's shameful death and vindication are in reality the same story; it had all been written beforehand. What had happened in Christ was not a new innovation on God's part or on Paul's part:

> For I handed on to you what I in turn had received: that Christ died for our sins in accordance with the scriptures, and that he was buried, and that he was raised on the third day in accordance with the scriptures (1 Cor. 15:3).

In the course of proving and expanding on this point, Paul would no doubt have adduced and explained passages where early Christians found allusions to Christ and his affliction, texts such as Isaiah 53:7–8 or Psalms 22:6–8, among others. The scene portrayed in Acts 13:32–43 gives an example of how such a presentation might go, even if it is not literally true of Paul. A similar strategy of reading is evident in Paul's understanding of 1 Cor. 10:4, where the "spiritual rock" that followed the Israelites is identified with Christ.

These two construals of the passage are not necessarily incompatible. Perhaps Paul did engage in graphic descriptions of the crucifixion. Certainly the same individual who wished that his opponents might castrate themselves (Gal. 5:12) was not above expressing himself in colorful language. Additionally, he may well have demonstrated to the Galatians in the course of his teaching that his gospel, which has Christ's death as its centerpiece, was already inscribed in the pages of scripture. This reading has the advantage of chiming well with the other *pro-* words that follow a few verses later: "scripture, foreknowing (*proeidenai*) that God would justify the Gentiles on the basis of faith, proclaimed the gospel beforehand (*proeuangelizein*) to Abraham" (Gal. 3:8). Furthermore, this understanding of 3:1 makes it a fitting preface to a chapter in which Paul begins an exegetical contest with opponents who are themselves using scripture to draw the Galatians out of Paul's orbit and into their own. In effect, Paul begins by saying, "my gospel is just that which has already been written in scripture; this is something you have seen proven and something you have accepted."

If this "enrichment" of the term *prographein* be granted, then we may conclude that Paul would indeed have employed scripture in his appeals to his as-yet-unconverted hearers. He also makes ample use of scripture when addressing himself to other audiences with whom he stands in a liminal relationship – namely, groups that were escaping from his sphere of authority, and groups that have yet to come under it. It is not surprising to find that Galatians and Romans feature generous amounts of scripture quotation. Paul's opponents, who have been preaching the necessity of circumcision, have been citing a great deal of scripture in their overtures to the Galatian Christians. Martyn argues plausibly that Paul's opponents made frequent reference to scripture in order to make their case for circumcision and that Paul is therefore compelled to discuss passages he might prefer to leave alone. Indeed a person trying to argue against circumcision might prefer to leave Abraham, the patriarch to whom the covenant of circumcision was given, out of the picture.[41] Paul is simply trying to wrest them away from the opposition, flipping the texts on their backs, as Hays remarks.[42] In chs 3 and 4 of Galatians, Paul conducts a rather intricate argument, which may have convinced some exegetically acute listeners among the Galatians. For those who could not or did not follow the argument, it would have been important at least that Paul shows himself capable of answering his opponents from the pages of scripture. This contest between rival interpreters takes place before an audience that will cast their lot with the teacher who best meets their expectations for what teachers should provide. The case is not necessarily decided by who makes the better argument; at least, it is not decided only by this; it was important to make a good show, and part of this required an obvious facility with scripture. Paul himself may have had doubts about the strength of his arguments, since, in a parting remark, he seems to cast a shadow over the whole enterprise of learned disputation: "See the large letters I make when I write in my own hand." Large letters were a mark of a clumsy and unpracticed writer; by saying this, Paul may be contrasting himself with those making claims to philological expertise.[43] With his remark about clumsy penmanship, he backhands the literary pretensions of his opponents by claiming that his gospel is not based on philology or clever displays of textual artistry. This would accord well with Paul's strategy elsewhere of playing his opponent's game and then changing the rules or dispensing with the game altogether if necessary.[44]

The situation with his letter to the Romans is rather different. Here, Paul is not locked in a contentious dispute. Rather, he is writing a letter that will, among other things, present himself as a capable teacher to readers who have no direct experience of his teaching. As I have argued, one aspect of a teacher's self-presentation is facility with the texts and traditions of his school. Therefore, it comes as no surprise that of all Paul's letters, Romans features the most citations, both in terms of sheer numbers (fifty-one of the eighty-nine total), and in terms of frequency per unit of text. Different proposals have been offered to explain this curious fact. The extensive use of scripture in the argument, as well as the direct address in 2:17–29, has convinced many interpreters that Jews were at least a part of Paul's Roman audience.[45] Without negating any of the theological or audience proposals that presume certain problems or constituencies in the several communities Paul addresses, I suggest that pedagogical tactics play a significant role in Paul's use of scripture. Paul needs to quote scripture often and easily in order to make his reputation as a competent and captivating teacher. Romans is the only one of Paul's letters written to a community which he did not found and which he has not visited. Where the need to establish (Romans) or re-establish (Galatians) one's teaching authority is keenly felt, frequent citation of scripture is to be expected.

Finally, what role would scripture reading and explication have played within groups who were confirmed and securely tied to Paul's apron strings? Strange to say, it is here that we have the least information. Philippians is the letter which gives evidence of the best relationship between Paul and a church, and here we find no citation of scripture at all. It is also somewhat surprising that we never find Paul urging his congregants to read and study scripture. In Corinthian gatherings, "one has a hymn, a teaching, a revelation, an ecstatic utterance, or an interpretation of such an utterance" (1 Cor. 14:26); perhaps the reading of scripture is simply presupposed, but nothing is said about it, either in the Corinthian correspondence or in the other genuinely Pauline letters.[46] A verse such as 1 Tim. 4:13 ("until I come, give attention to *anagnōsis*", which the NRSV takes as "the public reading of scripture") is conspicuous by its absence from the genuine letters. No one would have considered it strange had a verse like this occurred at the end of 1 Thessalonians or in 1 Corinthians, a letter much concerned with worship practices, or any other of Paul's letters. It may be that most of the scriptural interpretation taking place in Pauline groups was what Paul (or one of his delegates) provided, either in person, or by his letters which were read during meetings (1 Thess. 5:27). If scripture reading was accompanied by explanation, and if those capable of explaining scripture tended to acquire authority whether they sought it or not, then it stands to reason that Paul might wish to keep this privilege to himself and his designated co-workers. As a result, in Paul's absence scripture may have been read and explained somewhat less than we would have expected.

This suggests that one fault line between Paul and his problem parishioners occurred along the lines of literacy and competing interpretations of scripture. In 1 Corinthians and then in Galatians, we encounter a situation where rival interpreters are at work. In the first case, the dispute is intra-mural in character.[47] To hear Paul begin 1 Corinthians with a denunciation of "the wisdom of this world," and the knowledge of "the scribe" is suggestive; so too, to observe the apparent partisanship in the community between Paul and Apollos (1:12ff.). If the account in Acts may be trusted on this point, Apollos was a Jew from Alexandria, a man from the same intellectual milieu as Philo. "An eloquent man who was powerful in the scriptures," he was "speaking and teaching accurately the things concerning Jesus."[48] Not accurately enough, however, for when he encountered Priscilla and Aquila, who were disciples of Paul, they "took him aside and explained the Way of God to him more accurately." Apollos' abilities with the scriptures are stressed, but doubts are immediately raised about the accuracy of his teaching; he needs a bit of trueing from Paul's subordinates. This learned Alexandrian Jew would have naturally attracted a coterie of followers who found his presentation as an interpreter of scripture to be particularly compelling. Even without the evidence of Acts, we know that Apollos attracted a following, since there were those in the Corinthian congregation who said, "I belong to Apollos" (1 Cor. 1:12). It is significant that just after mentioning Apollos, Paul asks, "Where is the wise man? Where is the scribe?" By so doing, Paul waves aside displays of erudition and literary ability and, perhaps, Apollos' particular area of expertise.

All of this implies that Paul would have drawn on scripture with new audiences, with seriously interested parties, and with confirmed members of his groups (at least, when present), though it does not materially advance our understanding of the details of Paul's textual teaching. To return to the question posed at the beginning of this section: how would Paul have read and explicated scripture? In order to make progress on this front, we must canvass the letters for clues about how Paul might have explained texts. Some caution must be exercised here; we cannot take it as given that Paul's letters represent styles of teaching and exhortation that he employed when he stood before an audience.[49] We have seen in previous chapters that the explanation of written texts was a centerpiece of classroom instruction in several different schools – Epictetus is one example – and that in differing degrees, commentaries reflect classroom procedure. This was true among the Peripatetics such as Alexander of Aphrodisias, where we found evidence of classroom echoes. While we saw that Philo was writing his Allegorical Commentaries chiefly for readers, nevertheless the highly rhetorical features of his writings certainly reflect the kind of teaching he would have offered in person. Indeed, he uses such features to imitate and therefore create an inscribed classroom.

This leads us to ask if there are any places in Paul's letters where we find him explaining texts and employing the same type of language that we have found in commentaries springing from classroom utterance. Of the eighty-nine times he cites scripture, there are very few places where he engages in line-by-line explication; generally, Paul invokes scripture as a support for a point already made, rather than drawing his points out of scripture.[50] The clearest instance of the lemma-comment form is found at Rom. 10:5–8:

> For Moses writes concerning the righteousness based on law that *the person who does these things will live by them* (Lev. 18:5). And the righteousness based on faith says *do not say in your heart* (Deut. 9:4) *'who will go up to heaven?'* (Deut. 30:12) that is (*tout' estin*), to bring Christ down, or *who will go down to the abyss'* (Deut. 30:13), that is (*tout' estin*), to bring Christ up from the dead. But what does it say? (*ti legei*) *Near you is the word, in your mouth and in your heart* (Deut. 30:14) that is (*tout' estin*), the word of the faith which we preach.[51]

Students of Paul's hermeneutic have long been fascinated with this passage.[52] I will not discuss Paul's complex interpretational moves here, but merely draw attention to certain formal aspects of the passage. The remark, "what does it say?" by which Paul goes from Deut. 30:13 to 30:14, occurs frequently in Philo. *Tout' estin* is also a remark frequently encountered in commentaries as an introduction to explanation or paraphrase.[53] Why does Paul suddenly engage in this type of line-by-line explanation? It is difficult to say; we should take note of the fact that this is very unusual in the letters.[54] Perhaps it is because he is turning a rather sharp corner hermeneutically speaking (at least for modern readers – the author of the pesher commentaries would not have been alarmed). In the original context of this passage, it is the Law that is accessible: it is not in heaven, it is not across the sea, it is "in your hands, so that you might perform it." It may be that he is twisting a piece of scripture out of the hands of his opponents: one can easily imagine a law-observant Jew adducing this scripture as part of an argument that the Law can and should be followed: "This commandment which I command you this day is not too hard for you, neither is it too far away," etc.[55] In accord with this type of argumentation, Paul could be adopting the idiom of a teacher explaining a text to students. In any case, as we saw with Philo, "that is" and "what does it say?" are the kinds of remarks with which an author furnishes an inscribed classroom, and this in turn reflects the kind of language that would in fact be encountered in a school where a text is being explained. Paul may be doing something similar to Philo, constructing an epistolary classroom for his audience.

On two other occasions, Paul interprets a scripture narrative, not a specific passage of scripture *per se*. This occurs at Gal. 4:21–31 and 1 Cor. 10:1–13. In the former, he finds the Gospel prefigured in the story of Hagar and Sarah, whose offspring are the children of the slave woman (representing the coercion of the Law) and of the free woman, who represents the freedom of the Gospel preached by Paul.[56] He follows a similar strategy in 1 Cor. 10:1–13, where the Rock from which the Israelites drank in the Wilderness is understood as a figure for the Messiah.[57] Based on these examples, where scripture narratives are subordinate to the career of the crucified and resurrected Christ, it appears that, strictly speaking, scripture was of secondary importance for Paul: his central "text" is the master narrative of Christ's descent, death, resurrection, and ascent as summed up in Phil. 2:5–11.[58]

Scripture would have been of crucial importance for Paul in confirming and fleshing out this master narrative, but ultimately it is Christ, not scripture, that is the axle on which all else rides. Paul is making a theological remark when he says that he preaches Christ and him crucified, but he is also describing his pedagogical strategy. As such, Paul's manner of teaching where written texts are concerned would certainly have been topically, not literarily structured. It seems unlikely that Paul would have treated his congregations to an extended reading of Deuteronomy or Isaiah with continuous explication. In other words, meetings of Paul's congregations probably did not feature the sort of reading and commentary that Philo says typified the group meetings of the Therapeutae. Indeed, this may not have been Paul's habit, even with his close associates. Scripture modules on subjects of interest to Christians, such as the Law, the place of Israel in God's new covenant, the nature of faith, etc., accreted over time, passing from teacher to student, surfacing in the evidence as discrete, homily-like passages such as 1 Cor. 10:1–13.[59] So ultimately, certain qualifications should be made when talking about Pauline communities as "book-centered."

In the service of this topical mode of teaching, it is highly likely that Paul had at some point in his career prepared written notes on these subjects, derived from his own teachers or from his private reading, and it is not unreasonable to assume that portions of these notes would have been incorporated into his letters or into his teaching. In fact, this is an attractive explanation for the eclectic nature of Paul's scripture quotations:

> The diversity of text-types that appear in Paul's quotations could now be traced to the fact that Paul copied his excerpts from a variety of manuscripts housed at sites all around the eastern Mediterranean world, where he was a constant traveler.[60]

One might add that material heard orally could also be in view; we saw that in Epictetus' classroom, the texts of Chrysippus under discussion may have simply been transcribed by students. A recently published papyrus, dating from the third century CE, provides an example of the form such private notes might have taken. *PMich.* inv. 3689 is concerned with the subject of judgment, and contains quotes or paraphrases of Matt. 3:12 (or Luke 3.17), Col. 3.10, Jer. 18:3–6, and 1 Cor. 3:13.[61] Punctuation suggests that the text may also have served as a script within a performance context: places where a reader might pause for a breath are marked.[62] It does not seem likely, however, that Paul would have stood before a group only to read a collection of excerpts from a tightly wadded piece of papyrus (as did Seneca's tiresome lecturer in *Ep. Mor.* 95.2), or that he would have worked his way continuously through a long text such as the Isaiah Scroll.

While the evidence of Acts is suspect where Paul is concerned, it reflects widespread Greco-Roman assumptions about the image of an effective teacher and preacher. The writer of Acts places Paul in a variety of agonal situations. His public disputation with Tertullus the rhetor (Acts 24) and before King Agrippa (ch. 26) are two examples; so too are his other public speeches before detractors and his "arguments" (*dialexeis*) in the synagogues (17:2,17, 18:4, 24:12). By appealing to Caesar, Paul earns himself a berth in the World Series of agonal declamation. Finally, by teaching "in public and in private" (Acts 20:20), Paul is following a well-established pedagogical pattern: public display of competence results in a bustling private teaching load.[63] Apollos also engages in scriptural duels with Jewish opponents: "for he powerfully refuted the Jews in public (*dēmosia*) showing (*epideiknymi*) by the scriptures that the Messiah is Jesus" (Acts. 18:28). The vocabulary of public display is familiar from the field of oratorical performance.[64] We do not know the details of how such a public display of exegesis would have developed, e.g., whether actual texts would have been present, or what level of interchange there would have been between speaker and audience. Some sessions were no doubt characterized by more conflict than others.

This portrait of Paul Agonistes may be something of a Lucan construction; as we have seen, Paul alludes to a rather different view of his skill in public disputation in 2 Cor. 10:10. At least, he reports what his opponents in Corinth have been saying about him in his absence: "His letters are weighty and strong, but his bodily presentation is weak and his speech (*logos*) despicable."[65] We have seen that Paul's opponents in Galatia are presenting themselves as interpreters of scripture; perhaps the same is true of "super apostles" mentioned in 2 Corinthians.[66] In any case, even if Paul was not forceful in public debate, his presentation, even in private settings, would have had to conform to a significant degree to the kind of teaching that his auditors would have found persuasive.

Some of Paul's auditors are portrayed as skilled enough to access scripture for themselves. Having heard Paul's preaching, the Jews of Beroea "cross-examined" (*anakrinein*) the scriptures every day to see if his claims about Jesus were grounded in scripture (Acts 17:11). As a result of such study, many believed. Obviously, Paul's preaching would have made appeals to texts that critical listeners would want to check. Or at least, the writer of Acts would have us believe that Paul's scriptural claims made in the context of his missionary preaching would withstand scrutiny from people familiar with the Jewish scripture.

"Not as a teacher": the *Epistle of Barnabas* as anthology and commentary

The pattern followed in earlier chapters requires that we also inquire after the practice of textual commentary among Christians. But while Christians made use of the Greek Bible, it was a long time before they began to write continuous commentaries on any of its constituent books. It was not until late in the second century that commentaries by Christians on books of the Greek Bible first appeared.[67] A few Christians did, however, begin to write commentaries on books contained in the New Testament at a fairly early date. Basilides, an Alexandrian intellectual active in the first half of the second century, was responsible for (at least) twenty-three "*hypomnēmata*," though we cannot say what form these took, whether they were miscellaneous notes after the fashion of Plutarch's excerpts on anger, or continuous commentaries on individual books.[68] In any case, material from 1 Peter is under discussion. Somewhat later, Heracleon (*c.* 160–80), a student of Valentinus, wrote what appears to have been a continuous commentary on the Gospel of John.[69]

While we do not find examples of Type I commentaries, some early Christian literature, by quoting and explaining scripture, could have functioned as a commentary. The *Epistle of Barnabas* answers in part to this description, though formally speaking it is more anthology than commentary.[70] The author strings together excerpts from the Greek Bible at a rather breathless pace. At the same time, it qualifies as a commentary in virtue of its explicit citation of scriptural lemmata followed by explanation. Specifically, it is a Type II commentary according to the definition put forward earlier, in which the author is using scriptures drawn from many separate books and arranging them around an organizing idea or theme, rather than around a base text.

Consider the following "interpretive module" (*Barn.* 6.8–19), which we may profitably consider in its entirety as an example of anthologizing and commentary. Here is the first section:

> What does the other Prophet, Moses, say to them? "*Lo, thus says the Lord God, enter into the good land (gē) which the Lord sware that he would give to Abraham, Isaac, and Jacob, and inherit it, a land flowing with milk and honey.*" What does knowledge say? Attend! Hope, it says, on that Jesus (i.e., Joshua) who will be manifested to you in the flesh. For the human person is earth (*gē*) which suffers, for the creation of Adam was from the face of the earth (*gē*).

In the first place, the scripture lemma as presented is a conflation of Exodus 33:3 (which includes the imperative "go up") and Lev. 20:24, which speaks of inheriting the land.[71] Both passages describe the land as flowing with milk and honey, and so gravitate together. The section is rich in dialogical elements: here and in what follows, questions, exclamations, and imperatives abound. Joshua, though not explicitly mentioned in these texts, is a fixture in the conquest narratives and his name is taken as a figure for Jesus (Jeshua).[72] The author is also drawn to the expression *gē*, which stands behind "land" and "earth" in the translation. In what follows, we find the author elaborating on the term, rather like a jazz musician might improvise on a musical theme:

> What then is the meaning of "*into the good land, a land flowing with milk and honey*"? Blessed be our Lord, brethren, who has placed in us wisdom and understanding of his secrets. For the prophet says: "*Who will understand a parable of the Lord save he who is wise, and learned, and a lover of his Lord?*" Since then he made us new by the remission of sins he made us another type, that we should have the soul of children, as though he were creating us afresh.

After establishing the Christological significance of the whole complex of conquest material in virtue of the doubly valent name Joshua and placing the term *gē* on the table, the author returns to the lemma. But after citing it, he detours briefly to engage the audience in a brief tête-à-tête ("Blessed be our Lord, brethren . . . "), celebrating the ability given to insiders to understand divine secrets. It is a preface to the rather striking hermeneutical move that follows, a deep breath before a long jump:

> For it is concerning us that the scripture says that he says to the Son, "Let us make man after our image and likeness, and let them rule the beasts of the earth, and the birds of heaven, and the fishes of the sea." And the Lord said, when he saw our fair creation, "Increase and multiply and fill the earth"; these things were spoken to the Son. (tr. Lake, LCL)

The author makes the surprising point that the Genesis narrative is speaking not about the creation of the world in past time, but about the creation of the "new person," i.e., the newly baptized Christian, based on the equivalence between human being and earth, asserted previously. It is an interpretive move that the author of the pesher commentaries would have understood.

> Again I will show (*epideixein*) you how he speaks to us. In the last days he made a second creation; and the Lord says, "See, I make the last things as the first." To this then the Prophet referred when he proclaimed, *"Enter into a land flowing with milk and honey, and rule over it."*

To establish his point in another way, the author employs an allusion, it seems, to Matt. 20:16, "the last will be first and the first last," as well as several texts from Isaiah, among them 43:19 ("I am about to do a new thing") and 65:17 ("I am about to create new heavens and a new earth").[73] He then rejoins the lemma under explanation. In what follows, he continues to improvise on the motif of creation:

> See then, we have been created afresh, as he says again in another Prophet, "See," says the Lord, "I will take out from them" (that is those whom the Spirit of the Lord foresaw) "the hearts of stone and I will put in hearts of flesh." Because he himself was going to be manifest in the flesh and to dwell among us. For, my brethren, the habitation of our hearts is a shrine holy to the Lord. For the Lord says again, "And by what means shall I appear before the Lord my God and be glorified?" He says, "I will confess to thee in the assembly of my brethren, and will sing to thee in the midst of the assembly of saints" (Pss. 43:4, 22:5). Therefore (*oukoun*), it is we ourselves whom he led into the good land.

The presence of the risen Lord in the community of Christians is taken to be the fulfillment of both texts from the Psalms: Jesus is glorified through his incarnation; he appears within the assembly of the saints. The author comes full circle, proving to his satisfaction that it is the Christians who are to be led into the good land. He then continues with the second half of the initial scripture lemma:

> What then is the milk and the honey? Because a child is first nourished with honey, and afterwards with milk. So then we also, being nourished on the faith of the promise and by the word, shall live and possess the earth. And we have said above, "And let them increase and multiply and rule over

the fishes." Who then is it who is now able to rule over beasts or fishes or the birds of heaven? For we ought to understand that to rule implies authority, so that one may give commandments and have domination. If then this does not happen at present he has told us the time when it will; – when we ourselves also have been made perfect as heirs of the covenant of the Lord.

The brisk pace at which the author of *Barnabas* adduces lemmata from different parts of scripture suggests that anthologies of scripture quotations hover in the background.[74] *Barnabas*, therefore, may serve as evidence for the use of so-called Testimony Books by Christians.[75] We need not (and cannot) make claims about the exact form of this literature, other than that it probably consisted of excerpts drawn from the Bible on various topics of specific interest. Every literate Christian teacher and preacher might have possessed such notes which could have been passed on to students or other Christians. As we have seen, this type of literature has surfaced at Qumran; *4QTestimonia* is a case in point. No less germane is *4QEzek^b*, which contains excerpts from Ezekiel on the Temple, or *4QRP*, which gathers together texts on the subject of inheritance. In a discussion of *4QEzek^b* in Part 2 of this chapter, I suggested that gathering texts on a given subject would have greatly facilitated the process of textual comparison and exploration. So the idea that the author of *Barnabas* might make use of one or more anthologies of texts has precedent and reason on its side.

We might ask whether the point of origin of the *Epistle of Barnabas* as we have it is to be found on the scholar's desk or the speaker's podium. I consider the latter to be more likely. The origin of this text can be visualized with the help of Plate 1, where the words of an inspired speaker are uttered and committed to paper. In that portrait, the speaker clutches in his left hand a closed roll; similarly, no doubt, there is a text somewhere in the background of the *Epistle of Barnabas* too – private notes analogous to those of the Platonist Calvisius Taurus. Such works could be augmented through private study and reflection, and gradually accrete more material over time. And when they were delivered orally and perhaps transcribed, the process began anew.

In any case, by its free and easy association and interpretation of scripture, this text mimics the actual performance of a teacher. As such, it would have been experienced most profoundly in actual performance: it was to be heard, rather than read. I think it unlikely that hearers or even readers would have followed all the threads of argument. Its effects are experienced in the rhetorical, as well as the rational register. It is a Christian declamation, a piece of textual display, a fact confirmed by the presence of the term *epideixis*, "I will display." As such, the impact of a text such as this is best appreciated when it is understood not simply as a text whose every thread is to be traced by the exegete, but as an example of a textual performance whose overall effect is to amaze and gratify an audience. In virtue of his easy facility with texts, this speaker/author is acting as a text-broker *par excellence*, juggling with a number of seemingly disparate lemmata, yet returning to tie up a dangling thread deftly.

In fact, the author betrays that he is assuming the role of a teacher by his assertion of the contrary. Rather unexpectedly, the author blurts out, "And though I wish to write much, I hasten to write in devotion to you, not as a teacher, but as it becomes one who loves to leave out nothing of that which we have" (4.9). The letter also begins with a similar remark: "But I will show you a few things, not as a teacher (*didaskalos*) but as one of yourselves" (1.8). This surprising disavowal of the teacher's role may be nothing more than false modesty.[76] But in spite of the author's protestations to the contrary, he is in fact writing exactly in the capacity of a teacher: collecting texts on topics of interest, explaining the significance of such texts, and following with ethical exhortation. No doubt this reticence is inspired in part by Matt. 23:8: "You are not to be called 'Rabbi'; for there is only one teacher for you."[77] It is my claim that the disavowal of the teaching role indicates a level of anxiety about the text-broker role, felt, resented, and reflected in the New Testament account of the scribes. The remark, "I am not a teacher; I am one of you," presupposes a situation in which the role of a teacher is or has been experienced as problematic.

It may also reflect a situation in which the activities of teachers have led to division. In all probability, groups of Christians gathered around individual teachers in such a way that rivalries resulted. When Ignatius, a stout defender of ecclesiastical apparatus, states that "Jesus Christ is our only teacher" (*Magn.* 9.1, *Eph.* 15.1), he is manifesting a concern about the fissiparous forces generated by individual teachers. Such forces threatened the unity of congregations at an early date, probably even before Paul wrote 1 Cor. 1:10–17. Teachers may have held formal posts in local Christian congregations, but this is not necessarily the case.[78] To the degree that scripture was important to Christians, any literate person who could read and explain it to others would have occupied an important place.

When literacy was low and texts were scarce, people who possessed these texts and the skills to interpret them would naturally have attracted a coterie of followers. This is especially true in a movement such as Judaism or Christianity, both of which had a set of written texts at their core. Even though Christians were not drawn from the bilges of society as was once believed, the rate of literacy among the average group of Christians would have been significantly lower than the literacy rate within a group of Stoics, Peripatetics, or Platonists. Some Epicurean groups may have included illiterate members, but for the most part students in such schools would have already completed many years of study. No such requirement was in place for Judaism and Christianity. So within these movements, people who could provide a point of access to the scriptures of these book-centered movements would have become *de facto* authorities, whether they sought this power or not. Perhaps it is this social dynamic that helps account for the "bewitching" of the Galatians that so puzzled Paul.

Lucian provides an example of the power conferred by literacy in his tirade against Peregrinus:

> It was then that he learned the wondrous lore of the Christians, by associating with their priests and scribes in Palestine. And – how else could it be? – in a trice he made them all look like children; for he was a prophet, cult-leader, head of the synagogue, and everything, all by himself. He interpreted and explained some of their books and even composed many, and they revered him as a god (*Peregrinus* 11).

Even after Peregrinus found himself in prison, Christians continued to visit him and to supply him with food. Eventually he fell afoul of the movement, but before that point, he was revered as "the new Socrates." Certainly Peregrinus' personal charisma had a great deal to do with his meteoric rise among the Christians. Still, the one outstanding aspect of his abilities that Lucian brings to the fore is his ability to interpret, to explain, and even to compose texts.

I began this discussion of the *Epistle of Barnabas* by treating it under the heading both of commentary and of anthology. It features a great deal of scripture citation, as we have seen. *1 Clement*, written from the church in Rome to Christians in Corinth, around or slightly before 100 CE, is quite similar to *Barnabas* in this regard. As with *Barnabas*, it is highly likely that *1 Clement* is also based on collections of scripture texts.[79] In any case, whether there are

211

collections of excerpts behind these texts or not, *Barnabas* and *1 Clement* may both have functioned as anthologies themselves. The texts cited are crucial ones for Christians, and the authors have abstracted them from their literary context in the Jewish scriptures (or from other anthologies or letters), gathered them together in a coherent sequence, provided supporting material, and quoted passages at length. This "re-framed" Bible may well have been the script for many a Christian performance of scripture. In a context where scripture is being appropriated in new ways by groups forging new and distinct identities, extensive interpretive framing is to be expected. Later, when Jewish and Christian groups were entirely separate, when Christians laid full claim to the Greek Bible as a Christian document, it would have been possible for the entire work to re-enter Christian circles as the Old Testament.

Of course, we need not presume that Christians were the only ones to fracture the Jewish scriptures into pieces to meet their particular needs, both practical and exegetical. Jews themselves produced collections of excerpts, as was clear from the Qumran materials. Furthermore, this way of making reference to texts of the ancients was common in the Hellenistic schools as well. Collecting excerpts on subjects of interest, organizing them, and setting them in a frame tailored to the question at hand was what students expected of their teachers. By producing and using anthologies, Christian teachers were working within established patterns of school practice.

Christians and the codex

This understanding of the process of textual appropriation prompts a parting observation on the Christian preference for the codex form.[80] I have proposed that access to authoritative texts and the right to interpret them is a vexed issue in Judaism and nascent Christianity. I have also argued that pieces of Jewish scripture were re-set in Christian frames as one way of establishing interpretive hegemony over the text. In light of this fact, it is possible that Christian use of the codex may have been accelerated by the desire to distinguish their version of the scriptures physically and formally from those of Jews. The idea is not new.[81] But if what I have argued is correct, this claim may be seen in a new light. Christians, or at least some Christians, appropriated the Hebrew scriptures shivered into fragments and placed them in new frames. This was convenient, of course, for several reasons, but it also served to erect a formal distinction between "their writings" and "our writings." It would not be at all surprising if Christians sought to inscribe these re-set scriptures in a medium that would have distinguished them from the Jewish scriptures. The process was probably not entirely conscious; rather, it was a matter of "feel." The use of a new or altered form of media that corresponds to new patterns of life and study comes as no surprise. We have seen that the early Christians employed anthologies, and there is a certain commensurability of form between the anthology and the codex. The roll is continuous and unbroken; the codex, on the other hand, is discontinuous, interrupted from page to page. It is hard to know what "feel" early readers and writers would have had about the form of their written media. But it may not be an accident that Martial, who alone among literary figures favored the codex, wrote epigrams.

In addition, the change may have arisen partly from patterns of textual use. If, as I have argued, Christians favored anthologized and excerpted literature, they would have become familiarized with the papyrus notebooks or wax tablets that typically accepted such informal writing. Over time, the convenience of this medium would have made itself felt, and soon continuous texts were being committed to codices.[82] It has often been argued that the "startling break" with the Jewish tradition of committing scripture to rolls required a "big cause." As one authority on the subject has observed,

> It is not surprising that some of our earliest Christian manuscripts should be of the Old Testament. What is surprising is that the format in which they are written should be the codex and not the roll; this startling break with Jewish tradition, implies, I think, that these early manuscripts of the Old Testament had been preceded by specifically Christian works with which the new format originated.[83]

Without attempting to gainsay these theories, I favor a gradualist explanation that relies on many "little causes." In this case, the little causes are the notes and excerpts that Christians committed to tablets or leaves of papyrus, excerpts which were augmented over time, used in study, teaching, and preaching. Adding new excerpts to books in roll form was difficult, and when habits of textual use favored the collection of excerpts on subjects such as the Messiah, the Temple, cult observance, etc., tablets and papyrus notebooks would have certainly been employed. Perhaps it became clear that these papyrus notebooks were adequate for most situations in which texts were used, either in study or in teaching.

Conclusions

A number of concrete results have emerged from this treatment of the way Jewish groups handled their written texts. Several different proposals have been made regarding the social context for Philo's exegetical work. I have not simplified this picture but made it more complex by arguing that Philo's work as a commentator springs first and foremost from his own spiritual and intellectual discipline. While he has incorporated into his commentaries materials that he himself has heard and also taught, what we have in the commentaries is not simply the transcript of (or for) this activity. Philo hoped that his writings would themselves serve as teachers. The rhetoric of the Allegorical Commentaries is an attempt on Philo's part to create a virtual classroom, where students will read and encounter texts as Philo himself has read and encountered texts.

The form and format of the pesher manuscripts shows that the Qumran sectarians performed the pesher commentaries in settings where it was important not to stumble in reading, which I take to mean formal sessions of study or worship. After examining individual and group study practices at Qumran, we sought an explanation for the remarkable emphasis on writing and written texts at Qumran, and proposed that one part of the picture was a high esteem for the *Book of Jubilees* and for the attitudes towards texts and study that it exemplifies. With its frequent remarks about lost books, its stress on writing and study, and most of all, with its status as a Second Law given on Sinai, *Jubilees* forms a blueprint for the intense commitment to writing and written texts found at Qumran.

With respect to scribalism in Palestine, the practice of Greek and Aramaic translation illustrates two complementary movements in scribal scholarship, a move towards the Hebrew text, and a move away from it. In the first, the reader is brought to the text; in the latter, the text is brought to the reader. Perhaps these different writings are the products of different schools. We have seen such alternatives portrayed in other school groups: in the case of the Aristotelians, for example, students are brought to the originals by means of exegetical teaching that becomes written commentary; among Epicureans, the texts were generally adapted to the consumers. I think it more likely, however, that both types of translations could have been used by members of the same group without unbearable friction. If these individuals are better described as "civic professionals," rather than "academics" (in modern terms, they would possess a law degree, rather than a Ph.D.), their interests may have been multivalent. Texts that carried the reader towards the original could be useful in research, in close argument, or in decision-making in difficult cases. Texts that accommodated themselves to the hearers would have been useful in preliminary stages of study, as alternate voices, or in public venues where non-specialists were present. As for rewritten Bible, I have argued that the synagogue is the most likely setting for its performance, though not perhaps in formal preaching or reading. Instead, fanciful tales such as Kenaz and the Magic Stones, and even the lists and genealogies of that work, are most likely located in performances of the sort one might hear during or after a group meal.

Until the advent of the Internet, most people did not buy and sell stocks themselves; they used the services of a broker. The same is true for legal materials. Most people would not and could not access relevant legal texts for themselves; they require the services of a professional. In Palestine, most people did not, indeed, could not, read and interpret the texts that governed the details of their religious, economic, and private life. That task fell to the scribes and teachers of the law. The rather deformed picture of scribes offered in the New Testament may be traced to anxiety about the use of and access to authoritative texts. In ancient society, access to texts and the ability to interpret them translated into significant social clout. It was not through education, reading, word lists, commentary, and paraphrase that people gained access to texts; that could be had only through expert interpreters. Parabiblical literature such as the *LAB* was popular and edifying, but knowledge of such literature would not empower a person from a legal standpoint. It would be too cynical to assume that there was a conspiracy to substitute the fanciful and the frivolous for more substantive literature that would have been useful in gaining access to the Torah. But even without proposing a "bread and circuses" rationale for the existence of rewritten Bible literature, it is still possible to see how such literature might have been diverting in both senses of the term.

In considering the role of the scribes as text-brokers, I have also proposed that interpretation of texts formed one of the flashpoints of conflict between Jesus and other interpreters. The conflict need not have arisen over radically different interpretations of scripture, though Jesus and the scribes certainly interpreted the scriptures differently in certain respects. The difficulty arose simply because Jesus set himself up as an interpreter of texts in the first place. As such, he threatened those whose power and prestige within society were based on their control of the means of interpretation. It is common to assert that Jesus' charismatic teaching and popularity with the people aroused the jealousy of the religious authorities and the notice of the Romans. All this is certainly true. My particular point is more specific. It was Jesus' threat to the interpretive monopoly held by the scribes that led, in part, to his death. Even if, as is quite certain, the Gospels do not give an accurate portrayal of the scribes and their social functions, the very fact that the Gospel writers characterize scribes as they do indicates that control of texts and their interpretation was a vexed issue in first-century Judaism.

Several claims about Christian uses of texts have been advanced in the present chapter. I have suggested that Paul's pattern of scripture use owes a significant debt to his upbringing and education in Judaism, especially his desire to remain a text-broker for his congregations. The ability to cite and explain scripture with easy facility, to bring disparate texts into fruitful conversation, is one of the abilities that an audience would have expected from a teacher. Becoming acquainted with a text – not, perhaps, the actual LXX, but rather Paul's interpretation of selected portions of it – was a rite of passage and initiation that should be considered along with rituals such as baptism as a significant form of socialization into Pauline groups. Once people were inducted into the group, teaching became a matter of making appeals to concepts that had already been accepted, sealing and confirming these ideas with scriptural warrant. In any case, Paul may have preferred to keep the prerogative of scriptural interpretation to himself, and this explains why we do not observe any remarks about the reading of scripture in Paul's churches. It would be foolish to claim that scripture was never read in Pauline churches. It may, however, have been read rather less than we might have expected.

Finally, I have also argued that many Christian performances of scripture would have had as their libretto the notes of a teacher or preacher consisting of an anthology of excerpts; the *Epistle of Barnabas* is one example. Others have examined the exegetical intricacies of the *Epistle of Barnabas*; I have viewed it from a rhetorical perspective as a piece of virtuoso textual interpretation, a demonstration of interpretive mastery that people would have expected from religious or philosophical teachers. Finally, I have suggested that Christian use of anthologies behind or even identical to texts such as *Barnabas* and *1 Clement* was a response to the constraints and restrictions of the scribal culture within which Christianity was born. The scripture that Christians sought to claim was deeply imbedded within an interpretive tradition administered by a restricted caste of experts. Prying these texts away from that tradition and those interpreters required an act of textual aggression. The use of anthologies and even the switch from roll to codex were strategies, perhaps not entirely conscious, that served to liberate the scriptures for use by a movement in the midst of forging a new and distinct identity.

GENERAL CONCLUSIONS

The nature of this project has required that eight distinct areas of evidence be treated with a fair degree of thoroughness. At each stop along the way, useful results both of a specific and of a general nature were obtained, and I will restate those briefly now that all the comparative material is in view. Following this, I will describe a provisional taxonomy that describes the different patterns of authority that obtain between texts and teachers in ancient school groups.

Arrian's notes provided us with an exceptionally clear window on procedures in Epictetus' class. The notes themselves focus on Epictetus' colorful and memorable utterance at the expense of technical matters; nevertheless, it is clear that a large portion of class time was spent in the exegesis of written texts, especially those by Chrysippus. Taking a cue from *Disc.* 4.4.14, we found that four stages were typically traversed in the explanation of texts in Epictetus' class: reading, exegesis proper, analysis, and argument. The first stage involved a simple reading of the text. Elaboration of the different senses of technical terms went by the name of "exegesis." "Analysis" entailed critical appraisal of the logical coherence of statements, and gave students the chance to employ the armory of logical tools so beloved by Stoics. Finally, "argument" was a time in which students might extend the arguments in a given text or propose their own. In all these stages, reference to written texts present in the classroom is presumed, and the systematic investigation of these texts would have been the principal structuring element in class.

In virtue of the admonitions given to his correspondent Lucilius, I have treated Seneca as a Stoic teacher, although he did not, as far as we know, ever function as a teacher in a philosophical class.[1] Nevertheless, he constructs an epistolary classroom in which he attempts to guide Lucilius' reading and moral development as surely as if they were present together in the classroom. Indeed, the relationship is similar to the personal mentoring that Persius received from Cornutus. We examined the books and the reading practices that Seneca recommended, and explored two metaphors that he used for books; namely, that books are good friends, and that books are good medicine. While Seneca saw the virtues in such "book therapy," he was also quick to point out the need for the ministrations of a teacher. In all this, Seneca demonstrates a remarkable freedom with respect to Stoic texts. He casually ridicules Stoic founders, including Chrysippus, who formed the backbone of Epictetus' curriculum.

Coming to the Epicureans we encountered a rather different attitude towards the founders and their books. Although commentary was noticeably absent, we found that most Epicureans were great users of texts in all forms. The shape of these texts, however, was rather amorphous. Among most Epicureans, it appears that writing was tailored to the reader, rather than tailoring the reader to the writing, and this resulted in a riot of literature, much of it (according to Philodemus) of middling quality. Furthermore, "most Epicureans" did not exercise themselves sufficiently in the texts of the School.[2] These sentiments probably reflect social diversity within the Epicurean movement. Philodemus remarks on the obligation that less learned members of the school have to educate themselves, and on the complementary obligation on more learned members to aid them in this task. The diversity of the movement is also confirmed by Cicero, who upbraids Rabirius and C. Amafinius for their poor style and inaccurate translation of philosophical terms into Latin. The jump to Latin is highly significant: most people who enjoyed the leisure necessary to pursue philosophy were probably skilled enough in Greek to read their philosophy in the original tongue.[3] Coupled with the use of simplified reading materials, this suggests that Epicureans may have been extending their appeals to less literate members of society; namely, readers who were more comfortable with Latin. We need not, however, turn immediately to the "ill-bred" to find less literate members of society who would benefit from having philosophy cast into their native tongue or into simplified forms. Given the relatively gender-balanced nature of the Epicurean School as a whole, it may be that part of the audience for such literature consisted of women, who were routinely denied the benefits of education offered to men.

In contrast with Epicureans, Peripatetics were notable for the striking amount of continuous commentary they generated, more than any other School group examined. Even allowing for the vicissitudes of preservation, Aristotelians seem remarkable for their extensive efforts as commentary writers. After examining different commentaries ranging from simple to complex, I proposed that education in many Aristotelian classes was structured around the continuous exegesis of Aristotle's treatises. Based on Galen's comments, we also saw that some commentaries, such as those of Adrastus and Aspasius, would have serviced readers working on their own. Obviously, there was a market for exegetical aids among people who were not members of formal philosophical schools. With some tangible success, we explored the commentaries of Alexander of Aphrodisias for classroom echoes, and I argued that Alexander's commentaries give good evidence of activity in his class. It did not prove possible to describe stages in the discussion of texts as we did in the case of Epictetus. However, *koinologia* surfaced as a technical term for open discussion of a technical nature, paired with "inquiry" (*zētēsis*).

Platonists and Academics (for the purposes of this study, it is not necessary to distinguish them) show themselves to be writers of commentaries, though not to the degree found among Aristotelians. We encountered two varieties of commentary that reflect different points of origin and different destinations. *Anon. Tht.* may well have sprung from a classroom setting, but it has been tailored to meet the needs of a reader working on his or her own. Harpocration's commentaries, on the other hand, ask and answer questions of a different variety, questions which seem to reflect a somewhat more immediate relationship to classroom pedagogy. We also saw that there was a tendency to deal with Platonic material abstracted from its dialogical frame. The difficulties of approaching a large and complex body of written work, full of Socratic feints and false opinions, would have encouraged this process. Furthermore, the literary pleasures of the dialogues apparently caused some readers to luxuriate in these elements alone, at the expense of their moral and philosophical content. Alcinous would probably not have wished for readers to slight the dialogues in favor of his *Didaskalikos*; even so, it would not be surprising if this happened in some cases. The popularity of Plato's work created a large audience for his writings, and many of these would-be readers may not have had recourse to a philosophical school with its interpretive supports.[4] Finally, we saw examples of texts at work in two different teaching environments, the school of Taurus, and that of Plotinus.

In Chapter 5, we examined four different Jewish groups: Philo, Qumran, scribal culture in Palestine, and the first Christians. Each area yielded concrete results. Philo's allegorical hermeneutic has received extensive treatment in the modern secondary literature; the social context for his scholarly work has also been studied in detail. Nevertheless, the proposal that I made is somewhat new. Without arguing against other scholarly claims about Philo's *Sitz im Leben* (synagogue, School of Wisdom, private dwelling), I tried to show that while Philo's writings reproduce the rhetoric of the classroom, they spring first and foremost from his own devotional activity. Philo considered himself a teacher, and it would be most surprising if he did not serve in this capacity in one or all of the above-mentioned venues. Nevertheless, Philo gives evidence that his teaching activity, perhaps like that of Seneca, took place by means of writing. The rhetorical aspects of his commentaries, I argued, were part of his attempt to create an inscribed classroom. Philo believed this was possible because he himself was a student of Moses and Jeremiah, in a relationship that can only have been mediated by written texts.

In the section on literary practices at Qumran, we observed the importance accorded to textual performance as evidenced by the paleography of texts such as the Habakkuk pesher, and by regulations on the reading of scripture. A strikingly egalitarian textual polity obtained within the community; all members, it seems, were required to participate in study and all members were afforded access to the exegetical findings of other members. Reflecting on the many forms of literature that circulated among the sectarians, I argued that a programmatic attachment to *Jubilees* would account for the diversity of literature observed at Qumran, and the striking emphasis on writing observed there.

Turning to what I have termed "scribal culture" elsewhere in Palestine, we found a very different manner of dealing with texts. The evidence suggests that in Palestine, scribes (by which I mean textual experts generally) served as text-brokers. A situation in which the Torah governed many aspects of religious and civil life (no division here, really) coupled with low literacy in Greek and Aramaic and even lower literacy in Hebrew, would have made people who were in a position to read and to offer binding interpretations of the Law into powerful individuals. This state of affairs created certain resentments that manifest themselves in the New Testament portrayal of scribes. The gospel writers sound noticeably cross when discussing the scribes: scribes are portrayed as a religious group, parallel to the Pharisees, and this conflicts with the picture of scribes gained from other sources. I argued that this stems from the problem of restricted access to texts – not just to texts *per se*, but to the rights and privileges that went along with the power to interpret them. It is common for a person or a group deprived of something to organize this frustration by assigning blame for the deprivation to an agent or group of agents, even if this entails constructing an entity where none exists, or enhancing an inchoate entity into a more clearly defined and targetable adversary. It makes sense to assume that just this sort of frustration lies behind the characterization of scribes by the Gospel writers. We saw that Luke's account of Jesus reading in the synagogue, as well as his early sojourn in the Temple, are part of an attempt to show Jesus as a competent interpreter of texts. For Luke, of course, Jesus not only provides the key to the scriptures, he *is* the key to the scriptures. Whether this is true of Jesus' own self-understanding is open to question. In any case, Jesus probably did present himself as a text-broker, and it was this interpretive activity on Jesus' part, I claimed, that contributed to his troubled relationship with the established guild of interpreters. We need not presume that Jesus offered radically different interpretations of scripture, though he may have done so at points. But the simple fact that Jesus set himself up as an alternative point of access to authoritative texts would have been alarming to those who controlled the means of interpretation.

And finally, the Christians. While some Christians may have objected to the scribal hegemony exerted by textual experts, it is not obvious that all Christian teachers immediately promoted free access to scripture. Indeed, it would be more accurate to say that the Qumran community is the counterpoint to the textual polity of scribal culture. There, it seems, members were encouraged to read and pursue textual study. Once admission to the community was achieved, access to texts was free and open. I began by proposing that Paul shared certain patterns of textual usage with the textual experts at whose hands he received his education, and this hypothesis was confirmed by the pattern of scriptural quotation in his letters. Paul, it seems, preferred to arrogate scripture and its interpretation to himself and to his designated co-workers. Allowing this office to fall to anyone outside of Paul's immediate orbit was liable to lead not simply to variant interpretations but to increased status on the part of the interpreter and, consequently, to the dissipation of Paul's teaching authority. Finally, considering the form of Christian writings such as *Barnabas* and *1 Clement*, I proposed that these texts reflect the need for teachers to exhibit conspicuous mastery of the texts and traditions of the School they represent. I also suggested that anthologized collections of Bible texts lay at the base of many Christian performances of scripture; this aggressive re-framing of scripture texts helped Christians establish their own interpretive traditions.

Teachers and texts: a model

The material gathered has given us a perspective from which to address several topics that have occupied scholars of Hellenistic philosophy. For the present, I will concentrate on one of these – namely, the relationship between teachers and texts as vessels or conduits for school traditions. Pierre Hadot argues that after the destruction of Athens, the traditional institutional locus of the Schools, in 88 BCE, texts of founder-figures became the central axis of authority, and that students and teachers of philosophy from the first century BCE up through the third century CE essentially confined themselves to the exegesis of these authoritative texts.[5] According to this view, the center of authority in these groups is found in the texts of the school, and it was the chief business of teachers and students to explore, explain, and elaborate these meanings. Texts replaced institutions as the linchpin that held these groups together.

A rather different view has also been put forward – namely, that it was the individual teacher, not the texts of the school, that served as the mediator for a school's traditions. One statement of this view runs as follows:

> The chief vehicle for the transmission of Platonic doctrine during all this time is not so much a series of written and published treatises as the oral tradition of the schools, embodied, perhaps, in notes written up by either teacher or pupil . . . but only rarely taking a public form even theoretically observable to us. To talk of the 'influence', then, of Antiochus, Posidonius or Arius Didymus on the scholasticism of the mid-second century AD [sic] is grossly to oversimplify the situation. They are indeed there, as remote influences, but the chief influence upon a philosopher is that of his own teacher, and the works of Plato and Aristotle as seen through his eyes, and his chief influence in turn was his teacher, and so on . . . [6]

Even with the inevitable qualifications that their proponents might wish to offer, it is difficult to see how these two perspectives might be reconciled. In fact, both views are right with respect to certain bodies of evidence but wrong with respect to others. On balance, the second position, that authority accrues to teachers rather than texts, is probably to be preferred. However, it does not do justice to a teacher such as Philo. We saw that for Philo, texts are teachers: Philo's teachers are Moses and Jeremiah, and Philo too intends to teach by means of texts. Similarly, Aristotle's texts served as the tree which was dressed and ornamented by the comments of Peripatetic teachers. Taurus the Platonist allowed texts to do the talking when questioned about philosophical subjects, and even a teacher as unfettered as Plotinus used texts as his starting point. And presumably, Diogenes of Oenoanda believed that his exorbitant investment in a public inscription would prove effective. Similarly, the first position, that school traditions were exclusively vested in texts, understates the role of the teacher, who is responsible for help-ing students to approach difficult texts in the first place. While we have seen that careful exegesis was practiced in Epictetus' class, Epictetus was quick to relativize the worth of written texts as ends in themselves. Given their potential to mislead, any claim that pre-tends to be true of the philosophical Schools as a whole should be viewed with a jaundiced eye.

In light of the evidence we have gathered, I would like to propose a model for thinking about the different relationships that obtained between teachers and the written texts of their School. Three basic types may be distinguished: (1) text functions as teacher, (2) text and teacher act in concert, and (3) teacher as text. In fact, these are not categories or pigeon holes but rather points on a line; not all the teachers and teaching situations will fit neatly under one heading. Ultimately, my proposal is a provisional scaffolding: an aid to thought. Still, a richer scheme of classification holds forth the pro-spect of following the contours of the ancient world more closely than the either/or mentioned above.

First, under text as teacher, we encounter a situation where the text (or texts) of a given school are the central axis of authority. Diogenes of Oenoanda is the best example of this kind of teacher/text configuration. His "text" is not imbedded in any kind of peda-gogical frame. It is committed to the stones and placed before the public eye in the hope that by its unaided presentation it will impress its message on passers-by. Philo may also be placed in this category. We saw that his ideal philosophers, the Therapeutae, retreat to their *monastēria* for six days out of seven. Only on the seventh day do they engage in group study. Of course, this report need not be true at all for it to be revealing about Philo. Taking a cue from *POxy.* 1381, I suggested that Philo understood reading as a matter of re-creation rather than simple remembrance. Reading Moses and Jeremiah conjured their presence and staged a pedagogical moment that stretched across time, threading author and reader together by means of a text. It goes without saying that this type of study is suitable only for highly educated people who have access to books and a great deal of leisure at their disposal.

The second category features teachers and texts operating in a more or less balanced relationship. Most of the teachers we have examined belong somewhere in this rather broad category. Here, we have to do with a situation where, in most cases, the text being interpreted is actually present and available to the interpreters – if not in the original version, perhaps in a distilled or epitomized form. A minor division within this category can be made; namely, between teachers who structured their pedagogy around the structure of the text being examined, and those who invoked texts in a more topical fashion. An example of the first would be the teaching circles of Alexander and the other Peripatetics, who, it seems, devoted themselves to a systematic reading of Aristotle's treatises. This did not prevent Alexander from pursuing his own line of inquiry: recall that Aristotelian lemmata are set within Alexander's own discourse. As such, they are obviously manipulated by an interpreter, not set off by themselves, as in *PFay.* 3 or *Anon. Tht.*; still, the structure of the class was based on the text under investigation.

An example of the second division within category two would be the classes of Taurus the Platonist and Plotinus. Based on his aversion to seemingly frivolous aspects of the dialogues, Taurus may have focused on certain parts of the dialogues at the expense of others (as did the author of *Anon. Tht.*). Certainly, during the question and answer portion of class, he operates in this fashion. And even though Taurus gives the impression of a weighty pedagogical presence that seems ill-suited to subordination to another authority in the class, even if that authority is the text of Plato, he still answers questions by arranging citations from books. This is true both in Aulus Gellius' report of him, and in the extant portions of his commentary on the *Timaeus*, where he is content to simply list the opinions of the ancients. Plotinus, too, may be ranked here. He began by discussing the texts of Plato and Aristotle, but strove to go beyond simply citing and understanding the ancient texts. Other teachers, less innovative or adventuresome than Plotinus, were probably content to cease their labors after citation and explanation.

Still under the second main category, I would rank those teachers who would defer noticeably to the authority of the texts they treat.

Zeno of Sidon, the teacher of Philodemus, should probably be located here. Zeno practiced what I called "pre-emptive editing" of Epicurus' works, and this would seem to indicate a degree of freedom with respect to the writings of the School. But I would argue that even though the texts *qua* texts of the school may have been seen as needing correction and maintenance, Zeno saw himself and his editing as being in the service of the traditions behind the text. Recall, too, that the corpus of texts in the Epicurean School was rather amorphous. Epicurus' *On Nature* does not appear to have been a completely integral entity. Epicurus himself distilled and epitomized it, so what we have in the case of the Epicureans are various textual manifestations of a body of thought. The texts, though imperfect vessels, contain this, and so while Zeno might tinker with the text, he would probably have deferred to the authority of the tradition behind it.

Moving towards the fringe of the category, farther along in the direction of increased authority on the part of the teacher, one might also locate Epictetus. Serious exegesis was the daily bread of his class, but Epictetus was always careful to observe that books stand in the service of life, not vice versa. Seneca too should be ranked in this category, though as with Epictetus authority flows more from teacher than from text. Certainly he values the writings of the members of other Stoics (especially Roman Stoics). However, it was Seneca who said, " 'Thus said Zeno, thus said Cleanthes, indeed!' Let there be a difference between yourself and your book! How long shall you be a learner? From now on be a teacher as well!" [7]

The third category is that of teacher as text. Here, the teacher stands, as it were, in front of the text, acting as its spokesperson, articulator, and even its proxy. In this configuration, the interpreter of the text arrogates, consciously or unconsciously, the authority of the text of which he or she is the authorized interpreter. The text itself may not even be available to the students; indeed, these students may not even be literate. I am inclined to place Musonius Rufus here, but very close to the edge bordering on category two. Information on his pedagogical procedures is sketchy; it seems very likely that texts or excerpts thereof were employed in his class. Still, the anecdote told of him, that the farm is the most desirable classroom, where students could watch their teacher at work, suggests that attention in Musonius' class was focused chiefly on the teacher, not on any other source of authority. Many of the Jewish teachers whom I have termed generically as scribes, and to a certain degree, Paul, are best located in this category. I would also place the author of the pesher commentaries among this company, chiefly because of the oracular status the author assumes. The interpreter who finds meaning in a text not known to its prophetic authors is making a striking claim to interpretive authority.

Ultimately, there is a complex symbiosis that obtains between texts and teachers. Texts are in need of teachers to be understood and transmitted. But in the period of our study, it seems that teachers are also in need of texts, to formulate their ideas, to structure their activity, and as a field in which to prove their erudition. As articulators and explicators, teachers tap into the authority that courses through the revered text. So ultimately, the either/or often posed is reductive. Teacher and text actuate each other.

Of course, the teacher who has absorbed and synthesized the texts of the ancients and fully harnessed their wisdom to his own personal charisma, an individual who stands in place of texts, this person can himself become a text. Ending at the point we began, we may think again of the philosophical speaker grasping his closed roll, eyes ahead and hand upraised in a gesture of authority and inspiration (Plate 1). His words are committed to texts by the scribes in the foreground. We have come full circle: text has become teacher, and now teacher has become text.

APPENDIX: WHAT DID
THAUMASIUS WANT?

The translation given in the main text (pp. 116–7) incorporates my interpretive judgments on a number of difficult points. Other readings are possible. The section in question is taken from *VP* 13.10–17:

Τριῶν γοῦν ἡμερῶν ἐμοῦ Πορφυρίου ἐρωτήσαντος, πῶς ἡ ψυχὴ σύνεστι τῷ σώματι, παρέτεινεν ἀποδεικνύς, ὥστε καὶ Θαυμασίου τινὸς τοὔνομα ἐπεισελθόντος τοὺς καθόλου λόγους πράττοντος καὶ εἰς βιβλία ἀκοῦσαι αὐτοῦ λέγοντος θέλειν, Πορφυρίου δὲ ἀποκρινομένου καὶ ἐρωτῶντος μὴ ἀνασχέσθαι, ὁ δὲ ἔφη, "ἀλλὰ ἂν μὴ Πορθυρίου ἐρωτῶντος λύσωμεν τὰς ἀπορίας, εἰπεῖν τι καθάπαξ εἰς τὸ βιβλίον οὐ δυνησόμεθα."

Armstrong's translation runs as follows:

A man called Thaumasius came in who was interested in general statements and said that he wanted to hear Plotinus speaking in the manner of a set treatise, but could not stand Porphyry's questions and answers. Plotinus said, "But if when Porphyry asks questions we do not solve his difficulties we shall not be able to say anything at all to put into the treatise."

The first difficulty concerns the meaning of οἱ καθόλου λόγοι. The phrase has typically been understood to mean "general statements," but it is difficult to make sense of this if Thaumasius is taken as the subject of πράττοντος, which has οἱ καθόλου λόγοι as its object: is it likely that Thaumasius would have entered while making general remarks? One might perhaps read, "making a study of" (e.g., Lim 1993: 160). This rendering of πράσσειν as "study" is

228

not entirely satisfactory. The most relevant parallel (Epictetus, *Disc.* 2.17.27) has "syllogisms" as its object, and one could translate πράσσειν there as "make" or "construct" syllogisms. We have seen, in fact, that the making of syllogisms and arguments was one phase of classroom instruction. My translation presumes that Plotinus is the subject of πράσσειν. Lim claims that Thaumasius is a student of general propositions in the narrowly Aristotelian sense of *An Pr.* 29b, and (tentatively) speculates that Thaumasius may even be studying Ps.-Archytas' Περὶ τῶν καθόλου λόγων.

It has recently been proposed (Jones *et al.* 1971: 1:889), that οἱ καθόλου λόγοι refers to "Imperial accounts," and that ὁ καθόλου λόγους πράσσων actually refers to a Roman financial official, the procurator *a rationibus*; the claim is accepted by Brisson and Goulet-Cazé (Brisson *et al.* 1982: 1:86, 268). "Managing the Imperial accounts" eases syntactical strain. However, this piece of information seems gratuitous; furthermore, as Lim observes, this is an unusual construction for a Greek writer to use when referring to this office. As Lim notes, mention of this official almost always involves ἐπί in some form (see also Mason 1974: 58).

A second difficulty concerns εἰς βιβλία and what it could mean to εἰς βιβλίον λεγεῖν: did Thaumasius expect to hear (1) a lecture consisting of general theoretical statements coherently arranged (Armstrong: "speaking in the manner of a set treatise"), (2) something he could write down in book form (Bréhier 1924–38: 15: "[il] dit qu'il voulait l'entendre faire une conférence suivie et propre à être écrite"; Harder 1958: 5:3:31: "er wolle etwas hören zum Nachschreiben") or (3) did he simply want to hear Plotinus explaining books? (Schissel 1926: 269: "er wolle ihn allgemeine Lektionen erteilen und Texte interpretieren hören"; so also Goulet-Cazé 1982: 1:268: "qui dit qu'il voulait l'entendre parler sur des textes," and Lim 1993: 160: "he wished to hear Plotinus lecture with reference to written [philosophical] texts"). Lim's otherwise helpful article does not comment on the meaning of εἰς in the next clause; his translation ends with "Plotinus said . . ." Goulet-Cazé's "sur des textes" is not materially different from Lim's "with reference to," and has the benefit of doing the same work a few lines later. The most straightforward rendering of εἰς βιβλίον λεγεῖν is simply to speak on or about a book. The precise phrase εἰς βιβλία λεγεῖν does not seem to be attested in Porphyry or elsewhere, though Galen (*in Hp. Prorrh.* [16.793K]) mentions πολλοὶ τῶν γεγραφότων εἰς τὸ βιβλίον ὑπομνήματα, i.e., exegetes who have written commentaries "to" or "on" the treatise in question.

NOTES

GENERAL INTRODUCTION

1 See Lucian, *Double Indictment* 6, on beard and book as part of the philosopher's self-presentation. On the iconography of intellectuals in antiquity, see Zanker 1995 (pp. 260–1 on this particular portrait).

2 See Philostratus, *Lives of the Sophists* 579.

3 Visual representation of readers nearly always shows them seated. See also Plutarch, *On Listening to Lectures* 12 (*Mor.* 43F).

4 *Disc.* 1.4.14. The implicit equation between reading and understanding is presumed in Oldfather's translation (LCL), where the phrase, Λάβε τὴν περὶ ὁρμῆς σύνταξιν καὶ γνῶθι πῶς ἀνέγνωκα is rendered as "see how I have mastered it."

5 *N.A.* 13.31: ita et sententias intercidebat et verba corrupte pronuntiabat. "Murder" is from the translation of J.C. Rolfe (LCL).

6 *De libr. propr.* 2 (19.22K = *Scr. Min.* 2:101 ed. Müller).

7 *Conf.* 4.16, tr. Pine-Coffin 1961.

8 McKenzie 1986: 10.

9 Dagenais 1994: xviii.

10 On the relationship between the form and content of printed texts, see, in addition to McKenzie 1986, Chartier 1994 and Said 1979.

11 Brian Stock (1983: 88ff.) proposed the term "textual community" in his study of eleventh-century dissident groups. In a later work, he describes them as "microsocieties organized around a common understanding of a script" (Stock 1990: 23). He suggests the applicability of the concept to Jewish and Christian groups, but operates at a very high level of generality (1990: 156–8). Fox (1994: 126) adopts the term "textual community" in his treatment of Christian literacy.

12 On the concept of scripture among Christians, Jews, and Greeks, see Stroumsa 1998: 9–10.

13 While noting points of commonality, Meeks (1983: 81–4) points to the absence of cultic or ritual practices in the Schools; see Ascough 1998: 29–49 for a review of various proposals.

14 *De puls. diff.* 3.3 (8.657K), quoted in Walzer 1949: 14.

15 Galen's remarks on Jews and Christians may be found in Walzer 1949, along with texts and commentary.

16 Galen, *De Propr. Lib.* 2 (= *Scr. Min.* 2: 99 ed. Müller).

17 E.g., Lucius Crassicius, a successful teacher who suddenly left his students to become the disciple of the Stoic philosopher Quintus Sextius (Suetonius, *Gramm.* 18); for further discussion with more examples, see Nock 1933: 164–86.

18 Τὸ δι᾽ ἀλλήλων σώζεσθαι, *Lib. Dic.* fr. 36.1–2 ed. Olivieri (1914): 17.

19 *Epidr.* ch. 35 (76.6–16 ed. Lang); the translation is from Hays 1983: 121.

20 Wilken 1984: 77: "the philosophical schools were not simply intellectual schools of thought but ways of life . . . similar to what we today would call religious movements."

21 *Ep. Mor.* 108.22; see also Epictetus *Disc.* 1.11.39 on the ridicule directed at the σχολαστικός, or "frequenter of schools," and Frischer 1982: 55–60 on the generally low esteem in which philosophers were held.

22 Alexander 1995: 62.

23 *1 Apol.* 60. Pagan charges directed specifically at Christian illiteracy are gathered in Hilton 1997; see also Benko 1980.

24 *PHerc.* 1005 col. 16.1–19, and 17.5–11 ed. Angeli (1988). These texts will be treated in Chapter 2.

25 On Christians and their social status, see Meeks 1983: 51–73 and the literature cited there.

26 On the concept of eclecticism in our period, see Dillon and Long 1988.

27 Trypho is mentioned at *Life of Plotinus* 17.3; concealed doctrines at *Life* 14.5.

28 Sedley (1989: 100) claims, "the Peripatos' fall from prominence under Strato only serves to re-emphasize the indispensable cohesive force exerted by a school's commitment to its scriptures. Without them, there was no school."

29 Alexander (1990: 233) emphasizes the influence of the teacher: "books are of secondary importance in the passing on of a school tradition." So also Thomas 1992: 162, citing Alexander: "written texts . . . might be seen as subordinate to the oral methods of teaching."

30 Gamble 1995: 141.

31 E.g., for abbreviated literature: ἀνακεφαλαίωσις, ἀποφθέγματα, εἰσαγωγή, ἐπιτομή, ἐπιδρομή, ἐκλογαί, ἐγχειρίδιον, κεφαλαιώδης, περιοχή, συναγωγή, σύνοψις, τὰ ἐξ, ὑποθέσις, breviarum, compendiarium, summarium, etc. Galen mentions the different terminology used by writers in his day to refer to the same kind of literature: "some of those who wrote before me have called such writings sketches, just as some have called them outlines, while others call them introductions, synopses, or guidebooks" (ὑποτυπώσεις γοῦν ἐπέγραψαν ἔνιοι τῶν πρὸ ἐμοῦ τὰ τοιαῦτα βιβλία, καθάπερ τινὲς ὑπογραφάς, ἕτεροι δ᾽ εἰσαγωγὰς ἢ συνόψεις ἢ ὑφηγήσεις, in *De libr. propr.* Proem = *Scr. Min.* 2:93.8–11 ed. Müller). For modern treatments, see Untersteiner 1980 and the review of Untersteiner by Capasso (1981); also Moraux 1970, and Puglia 1982.

1 "NOT SUBJECTS OF A DESPOT": STOICS

1 *De Fin.* 3.2.7, tr. H. Rackham (LCL).
2 *Mor.* 1047B; *Herm.* 2.
3 Sedley (1997: 114) observes, "no commentary can be shown to have been written on a Stoic text before the sixth century AD."
4 Critical editions are those of Osann 1844 and Lang 1881. Modern critical scholarship employs the chapter, page, and line numbers of Lang's edition.
5 See Nock 1931 (col. 1004 on his possible acquaintance with Seneca), Most 1989, and Dawson 1992: 23–38. Reppe (1906) gathers testimonia and adds extensive comments on Cornutus' literary corpus; see Hays 1983 for a translation of the *Epidrome* with introduction, notes, and English translations of testimonia.
6 *POxy.* 3649 has the title (but nothing else) of Book II of a work called περὶ Ἑκτῶν, on which, see Turner 1975: 1–4. For the rest, see Reppe 1906.
7 Nock 1931: col. 995.
8 *Epidr.* ch. 35 (76.6–16 ed. Lang); the translation is from Hays 1983: 121, as are the other translations from the *Epidrome* that follow.
9 *Epidr.* ch. 1 (1.1–2.4 ed. Lang).
10 See Nock 1931 and Hays 1983 for details on literary debts.
11 *Ep.* 33.4, tr. Gummere (LCL).
12 *Epidr.* 31 (64.15–17 ed. Lang); tr. by Hays, with alterations.
13 Lutz 1947: 12. All subsequent references from Musonius employ the page and line of Lutz's edition.
14 *Diss.* 18A (114.30–1): "The words spoken on that occasion concerning food and nourishment seemed to us more unusual than the customary discourses day by day."
15 Zeno of Citium (114.19–26, 128.11); Cleanthes (34.23–8).
16 *Diss.* 8 (62.37–40).
17 Fr. 44.
18 *Diss.* 11 (82.31–3).
19 For biographical matters and literary questions about the *Discourses*, see Souilhé 1948: i–lxxxiv and Hershbell 1989. Schenkl 1916, with its invaluable lexical aids, is the critical edition of choice. In the following references, I have used the translation of Oldfather in the LCL edition; all three-digit references are to the book, chapter, and section of the *Discourses*.
20 For the purposes of this chapter, I shall assume that the *Discourses* give a reasonably accurate picture of life in Epictetus's classroom. On the accuracy of Arrian's representation of Epictetus and his teaching, see Hershbell 1989: 2152–3. Oldfather (p. xiii) considers the *Discourses* to be "a stenographic record of the *ipsissima verba*" of Epictetus. For an alternative view, see Wirth 1967.
21 Ὁ ἐξηγητὴς τῆς φύσεως (1.17.16).
22 Epictetus sometimes offers high praise with tongue in cheek, but here the sentiment appears to be genuine.
23 On the Liar, 2.17.34; *Concerning Things Possible*, 2.19.9 (cf. D.L. 7.191); "Introductions" (εἰσαγωγαί) of Chrysippus, Antipater, and Arche-

demus are mentioned in 2.17.40 (cf. D.L. 7.193–6). See also Sextus Empiricus *Adv. Math.* 2.159, Athenaeus *Deipn.* 4.159d, and Origen, *Cels.* 4.63. On Chrysippus's "type" of εἰσαγωγή, see Untersteiner 1980: 93. On introductions in general, see Schäfer 1959.

24 The title does not appear in Diogenes Laertius' list of 705 books. "Concerning choice" may be a description of the contents, not a proper name, and could represent other texts on the subject of choice. Zeno and Cleanthes, however, did write books under this title (Zeno: D.L. 7.4; Cleanthes: D.L. 7.174).

25 D.L. 7.190–202.

26 Λάβε τὴν περὶ ὁρμῆς σύνταξιν καὶ γνῶθι πῶς ἀνέγνωκα.

27 2.23.42, 3.22.95, 4.1.131, 4.4.34 (only here with explicit attribution to Cleanthes), *Ench.* ch. 53.

28 3.2.13,16; see also 2.17.40, 2.19.9, and 3.21.7. Antipater was the successor of Diogenes of Babylon and the teacher of Panaetius. Sextus Empiricus calls him "one of the most distinguished men in the Stoic sect" (*Adv. Math.* 8.443). Seneca mentions "Archidemus" with approval in *Ep.* 121.1, along with Posidonius.

29 An amusing anecdote, but probably apocryphal. See 3.2.15, with Old-father's note. According to D.L. 7.71, Crinus was a Stoic logician and the author of a dialectical handbook.

30 Most often the Epicureans: 2.19.20, 22; 2.20 ("Against the Epicureans and the Academics"), 3.7; Peripatetics: 2.19.20, 22 (Aristotle is never mentioned); Academics: 1.5, 1.27.2,15, 2.20.

31 Marrou 1956: 156.

32 1.17.12, 3.22.63, 24.67, 4.1.114, 6.20. This last reference is a piece of bold speech to King Cyrus, of which Epictetus approves.

33 There are seventy-one allusions or quotations in Schenkl's *Index Locorum* to Platonic texts; thirty-three of these are in reference to Socrates's final days as reported in the *Apology* and *Crito*. Epictetus does draw on Xenophon for his picture of Socrates (e.g., 1.12.3, 2.12.7,15, where he refers the reader to Xenophon's *Symposium*), but his reminiscences of Socrates are for the most part drawn from Platonic texts.

34 E.g., 3.23.21; cf. *Crito*, 46B. See also 2.18.20 and *Leg.* IX 854b. An extra variable in these considerations is Arrian's faithfulness in transcribing Epictetus' remarks, as well as the vicissitudes of manuscript transmission.

35 1.8.11,13 (generic reference to Plato as a philosopher), 1.28.4 and 2.22.36 (paraphrase of *Soph.* 228C, spoken by the Stranger), 2.17.5 (Plato on the definition of terms), 2.18.20 (Athenian in *Leg.* 9.854b). Only once do we find "as Plato says" when Socrates is speaking (4.1.172, an echo of *Phd.* 64D).

36 On Homer as a "strong" allegorist, deliberately cloaking a morality tale in poetic garb, see Long 1992: 43.

37 On the neglect of Panaetius and Posidonius by Stoics in the Imperial period, see Pohlenz 1964: 291–2.

38 Although the *Suda* claims that Epictetus "wrote many things." Based on this, Stellwag (1933) maintains that the *Discourses* were edited by Epictetus himself. Souilhé (1948: xv–xvii) finds little evidence other than that of the *Suda* to commend this suggestion.

39 Lutz (1947: 9, n. 22) assumes that the five reasonably long fragments, entitled by Stobaeus Ῥούφου ἐκ τῶν Ἐπικτήτου Περὶ φιλίας, derive from a written treatise of Musonius; they are printed in Vol. 2 of the LCL edition of Epictetus, pp. 444–8 and Lutz 1947: 136–9. It is possible, however, that they are based on Epictetus' private notes, just as the *Discourses* are based on Arrian's notes. The title, "Remarks of Epictetus on Friendship" does not appear to refer to a separate treatise on friendship by Epictetus, but may be a description of material from Books 5–8 of the *Discourses*, which are no longer extant; so Souilhé 1948: xii–xiv.

40 2.1.32. This may be an ironic statement after the fashion of Socrates. But see also 3.23.20 and 4.4.22.

41 Stoics of the second century used Arrian's notes from Epictetus' class as inspirational reading. See Aulus Gellius *NA* 19.14.

42 For treatments of Epictetus' pedagogy, see Hijmans 1959: 41–6; Souilhé 1948: xxiii–xxxvi; Bruns 1897; Colardeau 1903: 71–170.

43 4.4.14: ἀλλ' αὐτοῦ καταλήγομεν ἐν τῷ μαθεῖν, τί λέγεται, καὶ ἄλλῳ δύνασθαι ἐξηγήσασθαι, τὸν συλλογισμὸν ἀναλῦσαι καὶ τὸν ὑποθετικὸν ἐφοδεῦσαι.

44 Regarding the last two stages of analysis, see also 4.6.15–16: "I am not satisfied with mere learning, but I turn over and over the arguments presented to me, and fashion new ones, and do the same with equivocal premises."

45 "The functions of grammar consist of four parts, as Varro claims: reading, exposition, correction, judgment. Reading involves bringing out different parts of the text and pronouncing with dignity the style of the characters involved. Exposition is the explanation or testing of the meaning of obscure parts of the text. Correction is the correction of errors in diction in the text or its expression; judgment is the estimation of what other poems and writings we consider valuable" (Varro, fr. 236 in Funaioli 1964: 266–7).

46 The ambiguity between public and private in the use of ἀναγιγνώσκειν specifically in Epictetus is noted by Chantraine 1950: 2:120.

47 The term appears only twice in Epictetus, at 1.10.8 and at *Ench.* 49. Elsewhere, see Sextus Empiricus, *Adv. Phys.* 2.19 (= *Adv. Math.* 10.19). In Porphyry, *Adv. Chr.* §58, it refers to the public reading of scripture, as also in John Chrysostom, *PG* 55.594 and 59.711. See also *PMich.* 55, r25 (3rd century BCE), where it refers to a public pronouncement by a king, exonerating an individual from certain legal charges.

48 1.10.8: ὅταν ἡμέρα γένηται, μικρὰ ὑπομιμνῄσκομαι, τίνα ἐπαναγνῶμαί με δεῖ. Oldfather describes the passage as "somewhat obscure." His interpretation follows that of Bruns 1897 and Schweighäuser 1799–1800, vol. 2.1: 147–8; namely, that a student would first recite and interpret a text, whereupon the teacher would follow with a rereading (ἐπαναγίνωσις) and exposition of his own. Simplicius, in his commentary on *Ench.* 49 (67.28 ed. Hadot 1996), uses the term παραναγινώσκειν, "read alongside with," as an equivalent.

49 Souilhé (1948: xxxiii–xxxiv) claims that ἐπαναγιγνώσκειν includes interpretation, commentary, and personal reflections by the teacher.

50 See also Quintilian *I.O.* 1.4.3: "correct reading precedes interpretation."

51 Lucian, *Ignorant Book Collector* 19 (tr. Harmon, LCL)
52 1.17.17 implies that Chrysippus would be easier to understand had he
   written in Latin. Many of Epictetus' students were of Roman origin (so
   Souilhé 1948: xxxii, who cites 1.4.22, 1.21.13–14, 2.16.24, 29–30,
   3.5.1, 3.21.8, 3.24.4ff.), and had probably acquired Greek as a second
   language. On the question of bilingualism and the teaching of Greek in
   Rome, see Marrou 1956: 258–64.
53 1.4.14. On students reading to one another, see 2.17.35.
54 *I.O.* 2.5. This type of teaching, says Quintilian, "is quite below the
   teacher of rhetoric."
55 Following, perhaps, the model of Socrates. See 1.17.12, where Epictetus
   invokes Socrates' example on the definition of terms, and 2.12.7ff.
   See also 2.17.6,13 and Lucian, *Vit. Auct.* 21, where the Stoic remarks
   to his confused buyer, "you are not familiar with our vocabulary
   (*onomata*)".
56 2.21.11, regarding the student who criticizes his teacher.
57 Lucian, *Herm.* 1.
58 See Plutarch, for example, who devoted several treatises to Stoic "contradictions," especially in Chrysippus. This raises an interesting question: how much time would have been devoted to the study of works
   from rival Schools?
59 Hershbell 1989: 2158. All of 1.7 and 1.8 stress the need for skill in
   argumentation for the aspiring philosopher. 1.17 is entitled, "That
   Reasoned Arguments are Necessary"; see also 2.25 and 26. In 2.19, the
   Master Argument is not deemed irrelevant; on the contrary, it is
   important to form one's own judgments on such questions. Logic stands
   in the service of ethics, but ethics cannot dispense with logic. See Hijmans 1959: 39–41 and De Lacy 1943: 112–13 on the importance of
   logical analysis in Epictetus' thought.
60 See also 1.29.34, 2.3.4, 2.21.17, and 3.6.3; cf. 3.26.19 and 4.16.13.
61 See Oldfather's remark in his note to 1.7.1. See 2.21.17 and 3.21.10 on
   μεταπίπτοντες λόγοι; Simplicius, *in Ar. Phys.* 1299.36–1300.10 (=
   Hülser 1987–8: 1025, Long and Sedley 1987: 2:228–9). Treatises dealing with equivocal premises were circulating under Chrysippus' name,
   though Diogenes Laertius held them to be spurious (D.L. 7.195–6).
62 1.7.1ff., tr. Long and Sedley (1987: 2:226).
63 In addition to 1.7.1ff., see also 1.25.11, 1.26.1,9,13, 2.21.17, 3.2.17,
   3.24.78, 4.4.15.
64 On such statements, see *SVF* 2.62.4 (= Ammonius, *in Aristot. de interpret.* 2.26 ed. Busse); on Stoic classifications of arguments, premises and
   syllogisms, see Long and Sedley 1987: 1:212–30.
65 1.26.1. This may have been composed by the student though it might
   also have been derived from an author such as Chrysippus, who wrote
   several treatises on hypothetical syllogisms (D.L. 7.196).
66 2.17.35–6 (Xenophon, Plato, Antisthenes); 3.21.7 (Archedemus,
   Antipater).
67 3.24.103; see also 2.18.2, 4.5.36, 4.6.13,15.
68 1.4.13, 3.26.19.
69 In Epictetus' case, "slave" (ἀνδράποδον) might also mean "slave to
   external impressions." See 1.4.14, 1.6.30, 1.7.31, 1.9.20 *et passim*. His

habit of addressing students this way was apparently a practice Epictetus learned from Musonius (1.7.32).

70 The question is prompted by a remark of Bonhöffer ([1894] 1968: 2), who claims that Chrysippus was for Epictetus a "heiliger Kodex" (quoted by Souilhé 1948: xxxiv).

71 E.g., John Chrysostom, who complains about the low level of interest in scripture among the members of his congregation (PG 59.78).

72 *Ep.* 6.3–5. For the most part, I use Gummere's translation in the Loeb series. I have also consulted Scarpat 1975, which is extensively annotated.

73 It is not necessary for my purposes to decide whether the letters are real pieces of correspondence or moral essays in an epistolary form. See Mazzoli 1989: 1846–50, for a review of the literature on this problem.

74 See Balogh 1927, Hendrickson 1929 (for important examples not cited by Balogh), Knox 1968 (for critical and cautionary remarks about overstatements by Balogh), Starr 1991, and Gavrilov 1997, with the accompanying postscript by Miles Burnyeat.

75 *Ep.* 78.5, 15.7–8. See also Pliny, *Ep.* 9.36.

76 On the slaves trained for this purpose, see Forbes 1955: 348.

77 *Ep.* 46.3. Cf. Dio Chr. *Or.* 18.6–7: with comedy and tragedy, "the effect is enhanced when one is relieved of the preoccupation of reading."

78 See Pliny, *Ep.* 3.5.15. Plutarch also compiled an extensive collection of excerpts: see *Tranq. An.* 1 (*Mor.* 464E–F) and *Cohib. Ir.* 9 (*Mor.* 457D–E). On the practice generally, see Skydsgaard 1968: 101–16, who discusses the practice in Varro, Cicero, Pliny, Plutarch, and others. He does not mention Seneca.

79 *Ep.* 87.3; similarly with Pliny, who took his writing materials on hunting trips (*Ep.* 1.6, 9.36).

80 In the Preface to his *Noctes Atticae*, Aulus Gellius calls his individual essays "*commentarii.*"

81 *Ep.* 2.2. See also 45.1: "A limited list of reading benefits; a varied assortment serves only for delight"; cf. 84.5.

82 But cf. *Ep.* 6.5, cited earlier.

83 See also *Ep.* 10.5, 12.10.

84 See *Ep.* 108.32ff. A certain Quintus Octavius Avitus wrote eight volumes entitled "Resemblances" ('Ομοιοτήτων) in which he documented borrowings by Virgil and their sources (Suetonius, *Vita Vergili* 45). For a comprehensive treatment of the *grammatici* in a slightly later period, see Kaster 1988.

85 Suetonius, *De Gramm.* 10.

86 *Ep.* 88.39: "And shall I study the absurd writings of Aristarchus, wherein he branded (*compunxit*) the text of other men's verses . . . ?"

87 *Ep.* 104.21–2 (the Catos, Laelius, Tubero, Socrates, Zeno, Chrysippus, Posidonius); 108.38 (Plato, Zeno, Chrysippus, Posidonius); 22.11 (Zeno and Chrysippus); 33.4 (Zeno, Cleanthes, Chrysippus, Panaetius, Posidonius); *De Ben.* 7.8.2 (Socrates, Chrysippus, Zeno).

88 *Ep.* 82.9 and 83.9, where he ridicules Zeno for making absurd syllogisms about serious topics in moral philosophy.

89 *De Ben.* 1.3.8: "Chrysippus, too, whose famous acumen is so keen and pierces to the very core of truth, who speaks in order to accomplish

results, and uses no more words than are necessary to make himself intelligible – he fills the whole of his book with these puerilities . . . "

90 Far more than he quotes any Stoic philosopher: *Ep.* 2.5, 4.10, 7.11, 8.7, 9.1,8,20, 11.8, 12.10, 13.16, 14.17 (perhaps Metrodorus), 15.9, 16.7, 18.9,14–15, 19.10, 20.9, 21.3–4, 22.5,14–15, 23.9–10, 24.22,23 (three separate quotes), 25.5,6, 26.8, 27.9, 28.9, 29.11, 30.14. At this point, quotations from Epicurus suddenly become relatively infrequent, appearing only in 52.3, 66.47, 79.15, 92.25, and 97.13.

91 *Ep.* 46.1. See Cicero, *De Fin.* 1.26, 2.15.

92 *Ep.* 76.4. This is apparently somewhat unusual for a man his age: he feels it necessary to defend himself against the charge that he is too old for sitting in classrooms.

93 *Ep.* 7.1–2, 94.40.

94 *Ep.* 104.21–2. See also 25.6: "set as a guard over yourself the authority of some man, whether your choice be the great Cato, or Scipio, or Laelius"; 52.7–8: "you may go to the ancients; for they have the time to help you."

95 *Cher.* 49.

96 *Ep.* 8.6: "When I commune in such terms with myself and with future generations"; 22.2: "such advice may be given, not only to our absent friends, but also to succeeding generations."

97 In *Ep.* 94 and 95, Seneca discusses the need for a special division of philosophy to deal with precepts and their relation to speculative philosophy. He argues that general principles and practical maxims are a necessary complement to one another.

98 See also Lucian, *Nigr.* 37.

99 *Tim.* 86E–87A, tr. Bury (LCL). For a broad treatment of ancient views of the body–soul relationship, see Pigeaud 1981.

100 *Ep.* 6.6. Gummere takes *oratio* as "written word." Scarpat 1975: 123 has "discorso scritto." Any kind of fixed utterance, written or read as a prepared lecture appears to be in view.

101 *Ep.* 64.2–4. Sextius was a Roman Stoic, active under Julius Caesar. "Though he writes in Greek, he has the Roman standard of ethics." On "animated" writings, see 24.22, where precepts are described as "*dicti animosi.*"

102 On the dialogical and diatribal aspects of Seneca's letters, see Stowers 1981: 69–75.

103 On Hierocles, see von Arnim *RE* 9.2, col. 1479, Parente 1989, Inwood 1984: 151–3.

104 Porphyry, *Ep. ad Aneb.* 2.8; Eusebius, *Praep. Evang.* 5.10; Tzetzes, *in Hom. Il.* 123.11,28, and 146.16. Van der Horst (1984) compiles testimonia and fragments. A recent study is Frede 1989.

105 *HE* 6.19.8.

106 Two sources only: Persius' Fifth Satire and Suetonius' *De Poetis.*

107 Galen, 12.879K, describes Aristocrates as a γραμματικός (see *RE* 2, col. 941). Wellmann (1895: 9, quoted in Pohlenz 1964: 2:144) believes he is identical with the Pneumatic physician Claudius Agathinus.

108 "Seed of Cleanthes" may refer to that philosopher's reputation for hard work, a quality that Persius also attributes to Cornutus.

109 Persius, 5.21–9, tr. Ramsay (LCL).
110 Persius, 5.41–4, tr. Ramsay (LCL).
111 Suetonius, *Life of Persius*.
112 It is interesting that physicians are also well represented in Plotinus' school. This indicates the presence of significant links between the practitioners of philosophy and medicine.
113 Galen, *De venae sect*. 5 (11.221K).
114 Sedley 1989: 97–8. The bulk of his article, however, is devoted to an analysis of Epicurean evidence.
115 Socrates, Diogenes, Zeno (*Disc*. 3.21.19); Socrates, Zeno, Cleanthes (3.23.32); Zeno and Socrates (3.24.38); Socrates and Zeno (*Ench*. 33.12); Chrysippus, Zeno, Cleanthes (1.17.11–12).
116 Diogenes and Socrates together (9×); Diogenes only (10×); Socrates only (43×); Zeno only (3×).
117 Dillon 1996: 338. See also Alexander 1990: 233–4.

2 "SALVATION THROUGH EACH OTHER": EPICUREANS

1 Philodemus, *Rhet*. 1 col. 7.18–29 (ed. Longo Auricchio 1977: 21 = *Rhet*. 1:12.18–29 ed. Sudhaus).
2 Eusebius, *Praep. Ev*. 14.5.3.
3 I note at the outset of this chapter that most of the translations of Epicurean texts are my own, though I have been greatly helped by the Italian translations of Angeli, Indelli, and others.
4 For the volumes and their contents, see Gigante 1979 and Capasso 1989; updates to this list may be found in the annual issues of *CErc*.
5 *PHerc*. 229, 437/452, 247/242, 1428, 1610, 1788, 1077, and 1098. On the history and the mechanics of unrolling the Herculaneum papyri, see Obbink 1996: 37–62; see also Dorandi 1990: 65, and Fosse *et al*. 1984.
6 Longo Auricchio and Capasso 1987: 43–4.
7 Fosse *et al*. 1984: 9.
8 One roll by Metrodorus, one by Carneiscus, two by Colotes, four rolls by unknown Epicurean authors, and four rolls of Chrysippus. The count is based on the table in Gigante 1979: 53–7, augmented slightly by later discoveries.
9 See Kleve 1996 and Capasso 1994: 200–4.
10 So Dorandi 1990: 64. Many of these fragments may derive from the same rolls, separated during the unrolling process. Longo Auricchio (1970: 127–8) assigns *PHerc*. 1674, 1086, 425, 1079, and 1580 to the same roll; so also *PHerc*. 1672, 1117, 1573, 409, and 408, based on orthography.
11 *PHerc*. 998 fr. 11 (ed. Arrighetti 1973: 321): Σύντομον δέ τινα καὶ κεφαλαιώδ[η] καὶ ἐπιτομικὸν τῶν διὰ πλε[ι]όνων τε θεωρημένων ὅρον τινὰ προφέρεται ἐν τῶι Β καὶ Λ.
12 Cavallo 1983: 28–46.
13 Cavallo 1983: 60, based on the apparent provenance of the manuscripts, described as "mediterraneo greco-orientale," and Philodemus' origins in Palestine and sojourns in Athens.

14 For an overview of the different phases of Philodemus' literary output, see Gigante 1995: 20–47.

15 Cavallo 1983: 65.

16 Kleve 1989.

17 Dorandi 1980.

18 *PHerc.* 155 and 339 both have the same text of Philodemus' *On Stoics* but *PHerc.* 339 is written in an untidy and semicursive style, with lines of different length and irregular columns, while *PHerc.* 155 is "refined in every aspect" (Cavallo 1983: 62).

19 Crönert [1906] 1965: 183–4. Against this idea, see Cavallo 1984: 13–17 and Cavallo 1983: 61–2. For a review of the issues, see Tarán 1981a: 200–3.

20 Textual variants between different manuscripts of *On Nature* are discussed by Arrighetti (1973: 625) who describes them as "not very numerous." For the most part, they consist of the addition (or omission) of single words. Arrighetti does, however, note the great quantity of punctuation in *PHerc.* 697 relative to 1056, and alludes to the "critical labor exercised by scholars on writings of the Master" (625). See also Puglia 1987: 81–3.

21 See Longo Auricchio 1970: 122, on the relationship between *PHerc.* 1672 and 1674, two editions of Bk. 2 of Philodemus' *On Rhetoric.*

22 Dorandi 1988. But Obbink claims that 247/242 and 1610 are not a second edition of *De pietate* (Obbink 1996: 53, n. 3).

23 Cantarella and Arrighetti (1972: 7) note the absence of the *Greater Epitome.*

24 Some sayings collections must have been circulating among Epicurean groups. Later, Diogenes of Oenoanda includes maxims of Epicurus not found in the Κύριαι Δόξαι in his inscription. In *PHerc.* 1005, col. 10.17 (ed. Angeli 1988: 176), Zeno is said to have written a book entitled Περὶ παροιμιῶν καὶ τῶν ὁμοίων, so presumably literary works in this genre were not unknown. In col. 11.11–12 of the same work, Philodemus mentions the (possibly spurious) "Instructions" (Ὑποθηκαί) attributed to Metrodorus.

25 *PHerc.* 176 (ed. Angeli 1988: 27–51) comes closest. Dorandi (1983: 77) speculates that *PHerc.* 176 represented Philonides' epitome of letters, but describes the conjecture as "hazardous." While the treatise is filled with extracts from letters, it is not a source book of letters *per se,* but rather an apologetic for the lives and characters of the first members of the Epicurean school. The nature of *PHerc.* 1418, Philodemus' Περὶ τῶν Ἐπικούρου τε καί τινων ἄλλων πραγματεῖαι μνημάτων (ed. Spina 1977) seems to require that Philodemus had access to collections of letters in which the contents were dated. In the *Vita Philonides* fr. 14 (ed. Gallo 1975: 2:68) the author (probably Philodemus) mentions epitomes of such letters, so they were apparently in circulation; a perusal of *Epistularum fragmenta* in Arrighetti (1973: 421–76) highlights the amount of epistolary material in the Herculaneum documents.

26 D.L. 10.25. Crönert ([1906] 1965: 114) suggested that Apollodorus was the author of a text called the *Encheiridion,* although later scholarship has assigned it to Demetrius Lacon.

27 See Delattre 1996.

28 Cavallo 1984: 25–6.

29 *Vita. Philon.* fr. 66.6–8 (ed. Gallo 1975: 2:75): σπουδ[ὴν ἔχων τῆς] συ[να]γωγῆς τῶν Ἐπ[ι]κού[ρο]υ βυβλίων. General facts on Philonides may be found in Gallo's introduction to the fragments; see also Puglia 1982: 19, and Philippson 1941: cols. 63–73.

30 According to Gallo 1975: fr. 11.1–5, he spent eighteen months in Athens. Because of Philonides' close ties with the Seleucids, Usener (1901: 148) supposed that he was collecting works for the Seleucid library. It is (at least) equally likely that he was assembling books for his own school; so Gallo 1975: 1:141.

31 Clay 1982: 17–26. Gigante (1995: 22) considers the notion "unlikely."

32 D.L. 10.26. On the grounds of the school and books left under the care of Hermarchus, see D.L. 10.20–1.

33 In one instance, a certain Hermodorus, a student of Plato, brought school writings to Sicily, where he sold them. See Zenobius 5.6 in von Leutsch and Schneidewin 1958: 116. The incident is also mentioned by Cicero, *ad Att.* 13 21.4.

34 Starr 1987; see also Irigoin 1994: 39–82.

35 Having been reared in Syria, Philodemus may have been exposed early in his career to Epicurean groups once patronized by Philonides.

36 Keenan 1977: 93: "greetings . . . books of (?) Metrodorus . . . Epicurus' (book) 'On Justice' . . . best 'On Pleasure' . . . For the 2nd book 'On . . .' . . . (to?) another friend."

37 Fr. 16 col. 1.4–6 (ed. Chilton 1967 = Fr. 63 col. 2.4–6 ed. Smith 1993: 263).

38 *Vita Philon.* (*PHerc.* 1044) fr. 30.3–8 (ed. Gallo 1975: 86): Φιλωνίδης . . . συντάγματα ἑκατὸν εἴκοσι πέντε ἐκδεδω[κώς, καὶ ἐνί]ους ὑπομνημ-[ατισμ]οὺς [τοῖ]ς γνωρίμο[ις ἀπέλι]πε. Crönert ([1906] 1965: 181–2) expressed skepticism about the number 125; perhaps Philonides was not the author but rather the "literary agent" for the works of others (on which, see Usener 1901: 147–8). In the ancient context, of course, the idea of "publishing" is misleading. To publish was to make a work "available for copying by others." See Starr 1987: 216.

39 *Vita Philon.* fr. 7.1–14 (ed. Gallo 1975: 60): [ἐν μέν]τοι βυβλίοις ὑπ[ο]-μν[ήμα]τα φέρει δύ' ἀρχαῖα, τῶν παρ' Εὐδήμωι καὶ τῶν πρὸς τὸ ἕκτον, καὶ πε[ρὶ τ]ῶν ἐπιστημονικῶν δ[ι]ανοήσεων καὶ τῶν παρ' Ἀρτέμωνι ἀπὸ τοῦ πρὸς τὸ πρῶτον μέχρι πρὸς τὸ τρίτ[ον] καὶ <τρι>[α]κοστόν, ἐκλ[ι]πόν[των τ]ινῶν, καὶ σ[χολ]ῶν τῶν [π]αρὰ Διονυ[σοδ]ώρωι. φέρε[ι δὲ] καὶ σύντ[αγμα] π[ρὸς τὸ]ν Παταρέ[α].

40 Pfeiffer 1968: 213, n. 5.

41 *PHerc.* 862 col. 3.10–12 (ed. Capasso 1988: 140): διακούῳν καὶ ἀναγι-νώσκων τὰ τἀνδρὸς ὑπεμνηματισάμην ("whenever I heard or read things from Zeno, I noted them down").

42 *PHerc.* 1389 (ed. Crönert 1975: 88): Φιλοδήμου Κατ[α τῆς] ἀ[πο]-δεί[ξ]εως ἐκ τῶν Ζήνωνος σχολῶν γ ', also *PHerc.* 1003 (ed. Crönert 1975: 92), where a piece of the remaining *subscriptio* reads Φιλοδήμου περ[ὶ τ]ῶν Ζ[ήνων]ος.

43 For Bromius, see *De Signis* col. 19.4–11 (ed. De Lacy and De Lacy 1978: 54 = §27); for Demetrius, col. 28.13–14 (p. 69 = §45).

44 *De lib. dic.* (ed. Olivieri 1914): Φιλοδήμου τῶν κατ᾽ ἐπιτομὴν ἐξειργασμένων περὶ ἠθῶν καὶ βίων ἐκ Ζήνωνος σχολῶν.

45 "In the vast philosophical production of Philodemus of Gadara, there is no allusion to strictly philological work on the texts of the founders of the school" (Puglia 1982: 33).

46 For Zeno's *vita* and extant fragments, see Angeli and Colaizzo 1979; on Zeno's philological activity, Puglia 1982: 21–9.

47 *PHerc.* 1005 col. 11.1–20 (ed. Angeli 1988: 176–7): . . . [ἐρχόμενον ἀκριβεί]αι πρὸ[ς τὰ τῶν ἀνδρῶν, πε]ρὶ πολλῶν ἡγ[εῖσ]θαι [τὰ]κε[ί]νοις ἀρέ[σ]κοντ᾽, [ἐκ] τῆς ἀ[ρ]χῆς ὑποψί[α]ν τινὰ [λ]αμβάν[ει]ν, ὡς περὶ τινων ἐπιστολ γ καὶ τῆς [Πρὸς Πυ]θοκλέα περὶ μ[ε]τεώρων ἐπιτομῆς καὶ τοῦ Περὶ ἀρ[ετ]ῷ[ν], καὶ τῶν εἰς Μητρόδωρον ἀναφερομένων ῾Υποθηκῶν καὶ τῶν Μαρτυριῶν καὶ μᾶλλον [δ]ὲ τοῦ Πρὸς τὸν Πλάτωνος Γοργίαν δευτέρου, καὶ τῶν εἰς Πολύαινον τοῦ Πρὸς τοὺς ῥήτορας καὶ τοῦ Περὶ σελήνης καὶ τῶν εἰς ῞Ερμαρχον· ἐξέλεξεν δὲ καὶ [– – –] γραμμένῳ[ν] . . . ῾Υποψία was a technical term used by Alexandrian textual critics sniffing out falsely attributed books. On ὑποπτεύειν, see Untersteiner 1980: 115, and Angeli 1988: 296.

48 D.L. 10.3; see also Athenaeus, *Deipn.* 13 611B.

49 Puglia 1982: 22. List of works in D.L. 10.24–5. The origin of the *Epistle to Pythocles*, accepted as genuine by Diogenes Laertius, is debated, with scholars such as Usener, Schmid, and Philippson arguing against authenticity, while von Arnim, Bignone, and Arrighetti argue in its favor. For full discussion, see Angeli 1988: 289–91.

50 *De Dinarcho* 6 304.21–305.4 (stylistic); 9 305.18–22 (artistic); 7 306.8–16, 307.7–21 (chronological). So Untersteiner 1980: 112; in addition, see Bühler 1977: 51–2.

51 *Rhet.* 2 col. 23.7–11 (ed. Longo Aurrichio 1977: 93 = 1:49.7–14 ed. Sudhaus): τὸ δὲ Πολυαίνο[υ] λεγόμεγο[ν] Περὶ ῥητορικῆς, ᾠὺ[χ ὑπ]άρχον Πολυαίγου, καθάπερ ἐνεφανίσαμεν . . .

52 *PHerc.* 339 (*On Stoics*). The text is in Dorandi 1982.

53 Lists and catalogues: col. 13.19–20 (ed. Crönert [1906] 1965: 60): ὡς αἱ τ᾽ ἀναγραφαὶ τῶν π[ι]νάκων [α]ἵ τε βυβλιοθῆκαι σημαίνουσιν. References to *Politeia* by Diogenes, Chrysippus, and Cleanthes: col. 13.21–8 (ed. Cröner [1906] 1965: 60–1); discussion by Longo Auricchio 1971.

54 *PHerc.* 1012 (ed. Puglia 1988) appears to be a collection of remarks on difficult points of Epicurean doctrine. On the range of Demetrius' activities as a critic and literary figure, see Romeo 1988: 33–40.

55 *PHerc.* 1012 col. 39.1–4 (ed. Puglia 1988: 167): [ἄλ]λων ἀ[ντιγρ]-άφων οὕτως ἐχόντ[ων ἢ] τῶν μεταγραψάντων ἀπὸ τῆς ἰδίας ἀπαιδευσί[ας] τοῦτο ποιησάντων; col. 41, where a copyist has made an attempt to restore a lost piece of text, but ends up making matters worse; carping about copyists in col. 21.3–4 ([Δι]όρθωσις δὲ κακὴ γραφι[κὰς ἁ]μαρτίας ποιεῖ) and col. 25.1–3: [διορ]θώσαντες εἰς ἁμαρτη[θέντ] ἀντίγραφα.

56 *PHerc.* 1012 col. 34.2–8 (ed. Puglia 1988: 164): Καὶ κ[α]θ᾽ ὑπόβασιν δὲ τῶν παρ[α]γεγραμμένων εἰς τὰ ἐδ[άφ]η τῶν ἀντιγράφων ἔστιν εὑρε[ῖν] [[ευρειγ]] γραφι[κ]ὰς ἁμαρ[τί]ας κειμένας, κτλ. ("And on the basis of remarks written in the margins of the copies, it is possible to find the presence of scribal errors").

57 *PHerc.* 1012 col. 44.6–8 (ed. Puglia 1988: 171): Νεύει δ' ἐπὶ τὸ τοῦτ' εἰσ[ά]γειν τὸ ἁμάρτημα [τοῦ γρα]φέ[ω]ς: "But he [Zeno] inclines towards the introduction of error on the part of the copyist."

58 *PHerc.* 1012 col. 38.1–13 (ed. Puglia 1988: 166): ... ἡ παν]τὸς τοῦ ἀλγοῦντος ὑπεξαίρεσις». Τὸ μὲν γὰρ "παντὸς" διέλκεται κατὰ τὰ ἀντίγραφα, προστιθεμένου τοῦ «παντὸς» ἔν τισιν, ἐν δέ τισιν μὴ προστιθεμένου. Κατὰ πάντα δὲ τὰ κα[κ]ῶς ἔχοντα ἀντ[ί]γραφα [γέ]γραπται «ἡ τοῦ ἀλγοῦντος ἐξαίρεσις» οὐχ «[ὑ]πεξαίρεσις», [ὡς δηλο]ῖ τ[ὸ κα]κένφατον τ[ὸ] τῆ[ς] ἐξ[αιρέ]σεως, ὑποπτε[ύο]με[ν . . . . .] τ[ὰ γ]ραφέγτα . . . For the merits of restoring κακῶς vs. καλῶς, see Puglia 1988: 166. Ἐξαίρεσις can be used to mean "defecation," which might account for the adjective κακένφατος.

59 *PHerc.* 1012 col. 41.1–9 (ed. Puglia 1988: 169): καὶ Ἐπικούρου διαπορίαν νομίσει]εν ἄν τις: «Εἰ σοφὸς ἀνὴρ [τρ]οφῆς φροντιεῖ», καίτοι [δ'] ο[ὕ]τως ἔχουσαν: «Εἰ σοφὸς ἀνὴρ ταφῆς φροντιεῖ», τάχα περιπεσὼν ἀν[τιγ]ράφοις ἐν οἷς, ἐκτετρωγμέν[ο]υ τοῦ ἄλφα, τε[λέσ]αι τὸ ῥ[ῆμα] θέλων, τὸ [ρ]ω [καὶ τὸ ὃ γ]ραφεὺς ἐνέω[σ]ε[ν].

60 See, for example, Epicurus' remark preserved in the inscription of Diogenes of Oenoanda, "If a person has these (food, drink, shelter) and can expect to have them (satisfied) in the future, he could challenge even Zeus in a contest over happiness." See Clay 1990: 2537.

61 D.L. 10.82, 85, 138–9. In addition to the *Large Epitome* and the *Small Epitome* (the latter being probably the *Epistle to Herodotus*; see D.L. 10.85), we know of an Ἐπιτομὴ τῶν πρὸς τοὺς φυσικούς, the Κύριαι Δόξαι, a collection of maxims summarizing his philosophy, a work entitled τὰ δώδεκα στοιχεῖα (fr. 56 Usener 1887), as well as αἱ Ἀναφωνήσαι, or "Utterances," mentioned by Philodemus in *De Ira* col. 45.6 (ed. Indelli 1988: 100).

62 So De Lacy 1948: 20.

63 *De Fin.* 2.7.20.

64 *Vita Philon.* col. 14.3–10 (ed. Gallo 1975: 68): Πεπόηκεν [sc. Φιλόνιδες] δὲ νέοις ἀργοῖς ὠφελίμους καὶ [τ]ὰς ἐπιτομὰς τ[ῶν] ἐπιστολῶν τῶν Ἐπικούρ[ου], Μητροδώρου, Πολυαίνου, Ἑρμάρχου καὶ τῶν σ[υνηγ]μέ[νω]ν κατὰ γένος ἐπ[ι]στο[λῶν] . . .

65 D.L. 10.35. Usener (1887: liv–lvii) believes that Seneca's many quotations from Epicurus were taken from one of Philonides' epitomes. For a study of Seneca's use of Epicurus, see Setaioli 1988: 171–248.

66 D.L. 10.26, 97, 118, 120, 136, 138. Diogenes Laertius quotes from the first, fifth, seventeenth, and twentieth books of the Ἐπιλέκτοι Σχολαί; he does not give its total extent.

67 For the argument that Demetrius Lacon is the author of the Ἐγχειρίδιον, see Puglia 1986.

68 *PHerc.* 1013 col. 17.7–11 (ed. Romeo 1979: 19): ἐν τῶι αὐτ[ῶ]ι βυβλειδ[ί]ωι καὶ ἐ[πιγ]ραφομ[έν]ωι Ἐγχειριδίωι. Romeo takes these as referring to the same work.

69 *PHerc.* 1012 col. 52.1–4 (ed. Puglia 1988: 176): ἦν ἐπὶ τοῦ προχειροτάτου βυβλειδίου στῶμεν, ταῖς ἐπιγραφομέναις Κυρίαις δόξαις. Remarks on content in Puglia 1986: 50 and Angeli 1988: 42. According to Broccia (1979: 17–18), Ἐγχειρίδιον designated a type of literature, not necessarily a small or "handy" book.

70 Philodemus may allude to this in *De Signis* col. 28.13–14 (ed. De Lacy and De Lacy 1978: 69), when he remarks that "in Demetrius' account the errors are stated very briefly" (Ἐν μὲν τῶι Δημητριακῶι σ[φ]όδρ᾽ ἐπιτόμως ἔκκε[ι]ται).

71 *PHerc.* 1012 col. 51.1–21 (ed. Puglia 1988: 175): Συντομί[ας γὰρ στο]-χαζόμενοι καὶ κα[τὰ τὴν τῶ]ν ἀκουόντων δι[δαχὴν ἁρ]μοζόμενοι πολ[λάκις καὶ] τὴν παράδοσιν [τῶν δοκο]ύντων – ὅσον [δ] οὐ [καὶ τὴν εἰ]σαγωγὴν ἐνα[λλάττοντε]ς ταύτηι τῆ[ι διδαχῆι – δει]κνύουσ[ιν] καὶ [.............] ἀρέσκοντε[ς τοῖς πολλο]ῖς τοῦτο ποιοῦ[ντες . . .] Ν τις ΕΙΚΑ[......]Ρ[......]Ο σύντομον [......] ΕΙ[.......]. Διόπερ ο[ὐδενὶ] μὲν ἔξεστιν ΣΥΝΕΚ[....]ΚΑ[...κ]ακρῦν καὶ τὴν [τού]τω[ν παράδο]σιν καὶ τὴν [εἰσαγωγήν, σ]υντομίας [γὰρ χάριν εἴωθε]ν ἄμφω π[οιεῖν, ἀκόλου]θα δὲ διὰ μ[ε]ικ[ρῶν πᾶς καθηγ]ητὴς ἀπο[δείξει . . . Παράδοσις . . . may have meant "written tradition"; so Puglia 1986: 46, n. 10.

72 *PHerc.* 1005 col. 4.2–18 (ed. Angeli 1988: 172–3): ὁ μὲν γὰρ ἐγνωσμένος ἢ καὶ διιστορημένος ὑφ᾽ ἡμῶν, ὃς καί φησι εἶν[α]ι ὁ γνήσιος ἀναγνώ[σ]της ἐπὶ γραφὰς [ἐγλεκ]τὰς κα[ὶ πλ]ήθη συγγρα[μμ]άτων, κἂν βάληι [γ]ε [κα]λῶς, ἀνείληφε πολ[λὰ]ς ἐγλογὰς καὶ τῶν μ[ὲ]γ ἐπὶ μέρους διανο[η]μάτων ἀπειρότατός ἐστιν. ἃ δὲ προστάττεται ποιεῖν, ἐπὶ κεφάλαι[α βλέ]πει, καθάπερ ὂν λ[έγου]σιν ἐκ βυβλίου κυβ[ερνήτ]ην καὶ διὰ παντ[ός – – – . Somewhat later, Galen will use this same proverb to criticize those who think they can learn medicine from books without the assistance of a teacher. See *Temp. Med.* 6 Pref., 11.796–7K, and *De libr. propr.* 5 (*Scr. Min.* ed. Müller 1884–93: 2:110.25 = 19.33K), where Galen speaks disparagingly of those who, "according to the proverb, navigate out of books." In *Loc. Aff.*, 8.144K, he takes pride in the fact that he did not learn from ὑπομνήματα, but from the pre-eminent teachers in each sect.

73 *PHerc.* 1389 (ed. Crönert 1975: 90 = Angeli and Colaizzo 1979: 103): κε[φα]λαιώδης [τινὰ] μνήμην [συλλογισ]μῶν τῶν διὰ πλειό[ν]ων εἰρημένων. Crönert claims that this refers to poorly done extracts of the writings of Epicurus which must have led to false conclusions (p. 92).

74 *PHerc.* 1005 col. 6.3–8 (ed. Angeli 1988: 174): "[if he maintains that] it is possible to explain these obvious things, and he thinks the same way about everything, how can we possibly discuss more subtle issues from books with such a person?" (ὡς ἐν[δέ]χεται φανότατα πέφρασ[θαι, κα]ὶ νοεῖ ταὐτὸ παν[ταχη]ι, ὧδε πού δυνησό[μεθ᾽ ἐκ βυβλί]ων σοφώ[τατ᾽ ἐ]ξενεγκεῖν; note the extensive reconstruction).

75 *De lib. dic.* col. 7b 3–11 (ed. Olivieri 1914: 47): ἐφαρμόσαι γὰρ μόνον δεῖ τὰ πλεῖστα τῶν εἰρημένων ταῖς τοιαύ[τ]αις παρρησίαις, ἔργον δὲ τοὺς ἐπιτομικῶς ἐξεργαζομένους πᾶν εἶδος ἀκριβοῦν ὡς τοὺς ἀνελλιπῶ[ς] ἕκαστον ἐξοικονο[μ]οῦντας. The text is from Angeli 1988: 42.

76 *PHerc.* 1005 fr. 86 (ed. Angeli 1988: 158): ὥστε καὶ π[ροτ]ίθ[ε]σθαι με[τρί]ω[ς] πάντα κ[αὶ μ]ηδὲν ἐλλείπειν τῶν ἁ[ν]η[κ]όντων ἔω[ς] πρὸς [τἄπ]αντα, μέ[ντ]οι [δὲ καὶ τ]ὸ κατὰ μέρος ἂν [οὔποτ᾽ ἀπολελείφθαι. Because of the highly fragmentary state of this part of the roll, however, the subject about which the author makes this comment is not preserved.

77 *Tusc. Disp.* 4.3.7, tr. Rackham. See also *Tusc. Disp.* 1.3.6, 2.3.7, 4.3.6; *Acad.* 1.2.5, and below.

78 *Ep. ad fam.* 15.19.2.

79 The title does not survive. Based on its contents, Puglia (1988), the editor of the text, has titled it *Textual and Exegetical Problems in Epicurus*. Romeo (1988: 39) says that "it is not a continuous commentary on a single work of Epicurus."

80 *PHerc*. 862/1485 (ed. Capasso 1988: 146 = col. 14.5–7 ed. Scott 1885): τῶν παρὰ τοῖς ἀνδράσιν ἐξηγήσεις.

81 All that remains of the title is Πρὸς τοὺς . . . Vogliano (1926: 37, n. 1) suggested σοφιστάς; he is followed by Sbordone (1947). Diels 1917: 62 proposed Στωικούς. Angeli (1988) takes πρὸς in the sense of "to" rather than "against," and suggests ἑταίρους, "To the Friends." For a fuller account of the discussion see Asmis 1990: 2378, n. 27 and Angeli 1988: 71–81.

82 *PHerc*. 1005 col. 14.13–18 (ed. Angeli 1988: 180): ἀλλὰ τὸ σχετλιώτατο[ν] ἐκεῖν᾽ ἐστὶγ [ἐ]πὶ τοῖς πλείοσιν τῶν Ἐπικουρείων ὃ τὴν ἐν τοῖς βυβλί[ο]ις ἀ[νε]γεργησίαν ἀπαραίτητο[ν ποιεῖ . . .

83 *De Ira (PHerc*. 182) col. 45.16–23 (ed. Indelli 1988: 96): [ὥστε θαυμάζειν ἐπ[ὶ τοῖς] βυβλιακοῖς εἶναι θέλουσιν, ὅτι ταῦτα καὶ τὰ πρότερον ἐπισημανθέντα παραλιπόντες ἐξ ἀκολουθίας τὸ θυμωθήσεσθαι κατὰ τοὺς ἄνδρας τὸν σοφὸν ἀπεδείκνυον].

84 Cicero, *Tusc* 4.3.6: Cum interim illis [Peripatetics, Stoics, and Academics] silentibus, C. Amafinius exstitit dicens cuius libris editis commota moltitudo contulit se ad eam potissimum disciplinam . . . Post Amafinium autem multi eiusdem aemuli rationis multa cum scripsissent, Italiam totam occupaverunt, quodque maximum argumentum est non dici illa subtiliter, quod et tam facile ediscantur et ab indoctis probentur, id illi firmamentum esse disciplinae putant. The text and translation are Castner's (1988: 7). See also *Tusc*. 1.6, 3.7 on Amafinius and his co-workers.

85 Cicero, *Tusc*. 2.7–8.

86 *Acad*. 1.5 (tr. Rackham, LCL).

87 Farrington (1939) argued for the existence of a large movement among the lower classes towards Epicureanism; Momigliano (1941) disputes his claims. The diffusion of Epicureanism, however, may have been rather wide. See Gigante 1983b: 26, n. 2 and Gemelli 1983.

88 *PHerc*. 1005 col. 16.1–19 (ed. Angeli 1988: 181): δ[ύ]ναγ[ται] μ[ὲν] τοῖς [β]υβλίοις παρακολουθεῖν οἳ καὶ τετυ[χ]ότες ἀγωγῆς Ἕλλησι καὶ [ο]ὐ [Πέρσαις] πρεπούσης καὶ παι[δευθέ]γτες ἐν μ[α]θήμασι, δι[δά]σκουσι καὶ [τ]ὰ τῶν ἐπιτετηδευκότων ἀσάφειαν ἐξευρίσκειν καὶ ὁμοειδῆ γ, εἰ μηδὲν ἕτερον, ἐκ παιδίου μέχρι γήρως φ[ι]λοσοφήσαντες καὶ τοσαῦτα καὶ τοιαῦτα ταῖς ἀκριβείαις συντεθεικότες· ο[ἳ] δὲ δουλεύσαντες ἐργατικῶς ἢ ἀνάγ[ω]γοι καὶ γράμματα μὴ μ[α]θόντες [– – –.

89 Epicurus refers to εἰς ἀσχολίας βαθυτέρας τῶν ἐγκυκλίων τινὸς ἐμπεπλεγμένοι, "those involved too deeply in the business of some regular occupation" as a distinct class of people within the School (D.L. 10.85, trans. Bailey 1926: 57).

90 *PHerc*. 1005 col. 20.2–15 (ed. Angeli 1988: 183–4): . . . καὶ ἐπ[ὶ] τῆς ἀναγνώσεως καὶ γ[ραφῆς] τῶν βυβλίων [τούτοις δύ]ναται παρα[κ]-ολου[θεῖν] καὶ τὸ γένος [ο]ὐκ ἔχει πο[νη]ρὸν ὑπὲρ οὗ ἄ[λλα] συνδιασ-[τελ]οῦμεν ὥσθ᾽ ὁ τὴν συμμετρίαν ὑπερβαίνων ἢ κολούων κἂν τοῖς

ἱκανοῖς οὐ προσηκόντως ἀναστρεφόμενος [ἐξ]ετασθήσεται κατὰ τὴν ὅλην ἀγωγὴν οὐκ ἐγκα[θή]μενος.

91 The only other instance known to me in which members of a "school" undergo training in order to appropriate school writings is the Catechetical School in Alexandria, where Origen assigned responsibility for introductory studies to Heraclas. See Eusebius *HE* 6.15.

92 *PHerc.* 1065 col. 19.4–12 (ed. De Lacy and De Lacy 1978: 54). The translation is the De Lacys'.

93 Compare the conversational tone of Epicurus' *On Nature* Bk. 28, fr. 13 col. 5 and col. 13 (ed. Sedley 1973: 48). The "lecture" is billed as a conversation between Epicurus and Metrodorus, and shows evidence of much personal address, similar to Arrian's *Discourses of Epictetus*. Arrighetti (1973: 727) maintains that *On Nature* was a somewhat haphazard document that reflected "the daily work of thinking, research, and polemic in the school," not an organic series of systematic lectures.

94 See *PHerc.* 1389 (in Crönert 1975: 88–92), which contains material from Zeno's lectures. In the dispute over the nature of sophistic rhetoric, Zeno was at pains to justify his position based on the writings of Epicurus: *Rhet.* ch. 2, cols. 43.36–44.2 (ed. Longo Auricchio 1977: 133–5 = 1:77–8 ed. Sudhaus).

95 De Lacy and De Lacy (1978: 14–21) reproduce but do not discuss these marks.

96 The critical edition is that of Olivieri 1914. For a recent English translation based largely on Olivieri's text, see Konstan *et al.* 1998.

97 In fr. 6, there is a remark about the so-called "famous letter" (ἡ λαμπρὰ καλουμένη ἐπιστολή) of Epicurus; in fr. 20 there is mention of Epicurus' books against Democritus and Heraclides, and in fr. 72 mention of a letter from Epicurus to Idomeneus; Angeli (1983: 626) maintains that Tab. II fr. 6: (περὶ [– – –] τῶν βυβλίων μὴ κ̣[– – –] θεῖν, πρὸς ο̣ἷς τε γὰρ εὐ[– – –]ως εἰ κ[αὶ] μ[ά]λιστα ταύτ[ηι] κέχρηνται, Λεοντέα καὶ Ἰδομενέα καὶ Πυθοκλέα καὶ Ἑρμαρχον) refers to examples drawn from books in which the practice of frank criticism built character.

98 *De lib. dic.* fr. 20 (ed. Olivieri 1914: 10): νομίζουσιν ἐν τοῖς κατὰ πρόβλημα λόγοις ὑπερέχεσθαι μόνον.

99 *De Ira* col. 19.25–7 (ed. Indelli 1988: 77): μήτε [τ]οῦ διὰ συζητήσεως μετέχειν ἀγαθοῦ.

100 See Purcell 1983; also Meeks 1983: 191 for remarks on "status inconsistency," a concept that may have utility for Epicurean communities as well.

101 See Howe 1948: 341.

102 So Fantham 1996: 10.

103 Fr. 3 cols. 5.12–6.2 (ed. Smith 1993: 152): ἠθέλησα τῇ στοᾷ ταύτῃ καταχρησάμενος ἐν κοινῷ τὰ τῆς σωτηρίας προθεῖν[αι φάρμα]κα (tr. on p. 368). Earlier translation and commentary by Chilton 1971, based on his critical edition of 1967. I have favored Chilton's translations in places where new fragments or readings discovered by Smith do not change the sense. For a general review, see Clay 1990.

104 Smith 1993: 83, 86, 93.
105 For a recent discussion, see Clay 1990: 2460–2.
106 On Trajan's Column, see Brilliant 1984: 90–123.
107 The translation of Chilton (1971: 3).
108 Also fr. 116 (ed. Smith 1993: 410): "[both to you and] to those who [will come] after you . . . For the means of salvation is there. It is in case you have not yet [attained any] knowledge of these matters that we turned so many letters (γράμματα) to stone for you."
109 Cols. 4–5 (ed. Smith 1993: 368). The pharmacological metaphor occurs also in Philodemus, *PHerc.* 1005 fr. 81 (ed. Angeli 1988: 156–7): "with regard, however, to the books, these I have for the attainment of ὑγίεια" [punctuated as a quote by Angeli: «περὶ μέντοι γε [βυβλίων] τάδ᾽ ἐς ὑγίε[ιαν] ἧκα [δι᾽ ἐ]κείνω[ν]»].
110 *Ep.* 94.28–9. See also 104.47.
111 Frischer 1982.
112 On anthological and mass-produced literature in pre-revolutionary France, see Chartier 1995: 83–97. On popularizing literature in more contemporary settings, see Radaway 1991.
113 Sedley 1989: 105–6.

3 A LIBRARY LOST AND FOUND: PERIPATETICS

1 Strabo, 13.1.54, tr. Barnes 1997: 2. See also Plutarch, *Sulla* 26.
2 Donini (1994: 5094) remarks, "it is not very easy to find precise indications of the eventual destination, nor the actual origin of this production [commentaries by Alexander of Aphrodisias] within the exegetical activity of the school as it unfolded in lessons. Perhaps it is reasonable, then, to deny for the time being, that we see in the commentaries and in the treatises, long or short, of Alexander and of other Aristotelians and Platonists, the end result, or the instrument, or both together, of teaching, if this term is understood in a restricted and technical sense; that is, as the activity of a teacher who works in a school setting, giving lectures or directing exercises by a circle of disciples." Moraux (1970: 31) takes a contrary view: "In most cases, we do not have to do with works written to be read and consulted in libraries but rather with the fruits of the oral teaching of the commentator in question."
3 A detailed discussion of the misadventures of Aristotle's books is given in Barnes 1997; see also Gottschalk 1987: 1083–8 and Lynch 1972: 146–9, 200–7.
4 Two basic positions have found supporters: the first places Andronicus in Athens during the first half of the first century BCE, the second locates him in Rome and dates his edition between 40 and 20 BCE. Gottschalk (1987: 1093) favors the earlier date; Düring 1950: 65–8 prefers a late date. Moraux (1973: 45–58) leans towards the early date, but thinks the "Andronicus problem" is probably insoluble.
5 Barnes (1997) argues that Andronicus' work did not result in the revolution in Aristotelian studies that is often proclaimed.
6 Strabo, 13.1.54
7 So Gottschalk 1987: 1083.

8 This is an interesting omission, since Strabo knew Tyrannio personally, as well as Boethus of Sidon, who was Andronicus' student. Strabo's comments on the subject, however, are part of a digression and not an attempt on his part to give a complete account of the fate of Aristotle's library.

9 *Sulla* 26: Τυραννίωνα τὸν γραμματικὸν ἐνσκευάσασθαι τὰ πολλά, καὶ παρ' αὐτοῦ τὸν Ῥόδιον Ἀνδρόνικον εὐπορήσαντα τῶν ἀντιγράφων εἰς μέσον θεῖναι καὶ ἀναγράψαι τοὺς νῦν φερομένους πίνακας.

10 On Πίνακες in general, see Moraux 1951: 221–33, and Pfeiffer 1968: 126–34.

11 Elias, *In Cat.* 113.17–19 (*CAG* 18,1).

12 See D.L. 5.73, where Aristotle in his will juxtaposes τὰ βιβλία ἀνεγνωσμένα ("uncirculated works") to τὰ ἀνέκδοτα ("published" or "circulated") works. For appropriate cautions about editing, publishing, and the commercial book trade in antiquity, see van Groningen 1963, Irigoin 1994, and Starr 1987.

13 For a treatment of Lucian's reference at *Philops.* 14 to a work entitled ἡ φυσικὴ ἀκρόασις, see Düring 1950: 40–1. The title is fairly generic and could represent a description, not an actual title.

14 Düring (1950: 40, n. 4) believes he can show that in Plutarch, "no passage with certainty can be said to emanate from direct study of a text similar to our text in the Corpus Aristotelicum."

15 *HN* 8.44; *Rust.* 2.5.13.

16 See Moraux 1986b: 288–9; on Areius Didymus, see Moraux 1973: 436–7; on Stobaeus, Gottschalk 1987: 1129.

17 For an introduction to the literature as a whole, see Praechter 1990 and the series of review articles on *CAG* volumes, also by Praechter. When referring to the works contained in the *CAG* collection (Ammonius, Porphyry, Dexippus, Simplicius, Elias, Philoponus, Olympiodorus), I include the author and the name of the commentary, e.g., Simpl. and the name of the commentary, *in Cat.*, for Simplicius' commentary, *On the Categories.*

18 Olympiodorus reports that some doubted the genuineness of the *Categories* since it seemed to propose a definition of "synonym" that differed from that offered in the *Poetics*; see Olymp., *in Cat.* 23.1–4 and Moraux 1974: 268. Certain critics also questioned whether the ideas of vision articulated in *Meteorology* were consistent with Aristotle's views expressed elsewhere; see Olymp., *in Mete.* 4.16–5.23, discussed by Moraux 1974: 279. Aristotle's account of pleasure in what is now *NE* 1153b7–13 led Aspasius to assign the text to Eudemus; see *Anon. in NE* 151.18–27 (*CAG* 19,1).

19 Alexander found in *De Interpretatione*, for example, the terse and difficult style typical of Aristotle; see Boethus, *In libri de interpretatione ed. sec. (de int. lib. ed. sec.)* ed. Meiser 1880, 11.22–12.3. The Neoplatonic commentators assumed that Aristotle's dense style was a deliberate technique. See Ammon., *in Cat.* 7.7–14, Simpl., *in Cat.* 7.1–22, Philop., *in Cat.* 6.17–28, Olymp., *in Cat.* 11.21–12.17, Elias, *in Cat.* 124.25–127.2; references from Moraux 1974: 278.

20 Quoted by Boethus, *de int. lib. ed. sec.* 12.3–12 (ed. Meiser 1880). Adrastus tried to prove the antiquity of the *Categories* when

he mentioned that copies of this work were found in ancient libraries.

21 See comment on *POxy.* 3320 by Barnes 1980: 19. The papyrus preserves some comments on a text similar to Aristotle's *APr.* 47b29ff.

22 In Bk. 3 of his commentary on the *Metaphysics*, Alexander cites an allusion to Bk. 1: "From this it is clear . . . that the book is Aristotle's work and belongs to this treatise" (*in Met.* 187.6–8 and 196.20–3). Similarly, while Alexander admits that Bk. 4 of the *Meteorology* does not logically follow on Bk. 3, concerns about its authenticity are allayed by the implicit references to *Generation and Corruption* (*in Mete.* 179.1ff.).

23 *In Met.* 137.1: "Bk. 2 of the *Metaphysics*, Alpha Elatton, is the work of Aristotle"; also 143.23–144.5. For an introduction to the question, see Dooley and Madigan 1992: 3–5; also, the articles in Moraux and Wiesner 1983.

24 *In Met.* 169.20ff.

25 Von Wilamowitz-Möllendorf (1881: 286) claims that relative to the Platonic corpus, the Aristotelian textual tradition is in a state of "chaotic confusion."

26 On Aspasius, see Becchi 1994: 5365–96. On intellectual criteria, Donini has questioned whether Aspasius should be considered a Peripatetic. See the discussion in Becchi 1994: 5371; he and Moraux still assign Aspasius to the Peripatetics.

27 Simpl., *in Phys.* 714.31–4.

28 Sharples 1987 gives a full account of Alexander and his literary activity. His commentaries on *Metaphysics, Prior Analytics I, Topics, De Sensu, Meteorologica*, and *De Sophisticis Elenchis* are still extant (in *CAG*), as are several short works.

29 See *in Met.* 37.20–1: "the reading would be more consistent if γάρ was used instead of δέ"; *in Met.* 339.3: "what is meant is said unclearly"; also *in Met.* 68.3–4, 114.22, 273.34–6.

30 ἀνικίαν for ἀδικίαν (*in Met.* 75.26), or εἴθ᾽ αἱ αὐταί for εἴθ᾽ αὗται (*in Met.* 194.3–4).

31 Case: ἐπιστήμης ἀποδεικτικῆς for ἐπιστήμην ἀποδεικτικήν at *in An. Pr.* 9.10–11; substitution: τρία γένη for τέτταρα γένη, *in SE* 18.24; addition and deletion: the addition of γένη ἔχον, *in Met.* 251.21; extra material at *in Met.* 58.31–59.2, 91.5–6, 145.21–2, 273.37–274.1, 356.34–5; *in An. Pr.* 304.13–17; deletions: *in Met.* 104.20–1, 341.30, *in Sens.* 101.4; three different readings of *Phys.* 214a6 (Simpl., *in Phys.* 655.22ff.); some copies of *Phys.* missing 214b28–215a1 (Simpl., *in Phys.* 667.4); *in Phys.* 247b10, a μέν lacks for an expected δέ clause (Simpl., *in Phys.* 1078.7).

32 *In An. Pr.* 304.13–17: φέρεται δὲ ἔν τισιν ἀντιγράφοις ἡ λέξις ὁλόκληρον καὶ σαφέστερον οὕτως ἔχουσα.

33 Simpl., *in Cat.* 18.16.

34 This is the translation of Kenny 1978: 30.

35 Scholars of the nineteenth century generally regarded the *EE* as spurious. Jaeger believed it to be the work of Aristotle while he was still under the influence of the Academy and it is this view that Kenny criticizes.

36 Book 7 of Aristotle's *Physics* seems to have been transmitted in two different versions. See Hagen 1994: 102–3.

37 At *in Met.* 58.31ff. Moraux (1969: 492–504) exonerates Eudorus of the charge of tendentious editing leveled by Aspasius.

38 Boethus' dates are as uncertain as those of Andronicus. According to Philoponus, *in Cat.* 5.18, he was a student of Andronicus. The evidence is late but not disputed; see Moraux 1973: 53.

39 Simpl., *in Cat.* 1.17.

40 So Tarán 1981b: 743.

41 Philop., *in Cat.* 5.16–18; Elias, *in Cat.* 117.21–2.

42 Adrastus wrote a commentary on Plato's *Timaeus* used by Theon of Smyrna, in a work datable to 147 CE. Moraux 1984: 294 tentatively places him in the first third of the second century. For the title of his work, see Simpl., *in Phys.* 4.12, *in Cat.* 18.16; Simplicius refers to it as Περὶ τῆς τάξεως τῆς Ἀριστοτέλους φιλοσοφίας at *in Cat.* 16.12.

43 "Περὶ ἀρχῶν," according to some, or "Φυσικῆς ἀκροάσεως," while others called the first five books "Περὶ ἀρχῶν" and the last three "Περὶ κινήσεως."

44 Simpl., *in Phys.* 4.11–15, 6.4–9; for Andronicus, Simpl., *in Phys.* 923.7.

45 Jaeger 1912. Lynch 1972 has shown that the Lyceum did not enjoy the continuous and untroubled existence previously believed.

46 *Met.* 993a30–b3, tr. Tredennick (LCL). See also *NE* 1098a20–5.

47 See Jaeger 1956: 152. Jaeger's critical edition of this text (OCT, 1957) encloses such material in double brackets. For a discussion of Jaeger's edition, see Renehan 1990: 153–8.

48 Donini (1994: 5092) suggests that Stoicism went into decline while Platonists and Aristotelians survived, precisely because Platonists and Aristotelians were charged with the maintenance and upkeep of a defined corpus of literature that could be continually mined for new meanings as new questions presented themselves.

49 Authors from the first century BCE (Boethus) up to the second century CE and their commentaries include: Boethus, *Cat.*, *APr.*, *Ph.*; Ariston, *Cat.* (perhaps a monograph on the category Relation); Sotion, *Cat.*, *Top.*; Apollonius, *Cat.*; Achaius, *Cat.*; Alexander of Aigai, *Cat.*, *Cael.*; Adrastus, *Cat.* (?), *Ph.* (?), *NE*; Aspasius, *Cat.*, *Int.*, *Ph.*, *Cael.*, *Sens.*, *Metaph.*, *NE*; Herminus, *Cat.*, *Int.*, *APr.*, *Top.*, *Cael.*, *Metaph.*; Alexander of Aphrodisias, *Cat.*, *Int.*, *Top.*, *APr.*, *PoAn.*, *SE*, *Sens.*, *Ph.*, *Cael.*, *GC*, *Mete.*, *de An.*, *Mem.*, *Metaph.*

50 Longinus, quoted by Porphyry, *Life* 20, mentions that the Peripatetics Ammonius and Ptolemaeus, "both the greatest scholars of their time . . . did not write any work of professional philosophy . . ."

51 Turner 1968: 113.

52 This division is based on del Fabbro 1979: 70.

53 Simplicius, *in Cat.* 1.1ff., ranks the works written on the *Categories* according to their degree of complexity, beginning with Themistius' paraphrase as the simplest and ending with Boethus' commentary as the most sophisticated.

54 Grenfell and Hunt 1900: 87–9; recently re-edited by Serena Funghi and Cavini (*Corpus* 3:14–18).

55 Sotion (first half of the second century) and Herminus (second half of

the second century) were the first known authors to comment on the *Topics*.

56 In columns 1 and 3, comment and lemma are separated by a single letter-width space, which, according to Del Fabbro 1979: 73, 77, is characteristic of other continuous commentaries such as *PLille* and *POxy*. 2221. Other diacritical marks, such as the *diple* or *paragraphos* often used to separate lemmata and commentary, are entirely lacking in *PFay*. 3.

57 The commentaries of Alexander of Aphrodisias, for example, swaddle the lemmata from Aristotle's works within Alexander's own discourse.

58 Grenfell and Hunt 1900: 88. Serena Funghi and Cavini do not reproduce or comment on the mark. A similar mark, very furtive, also appears at the end of line 16, which is also rather short.

59 Del Fabbro's description of some Type I commentaries as "edizioni commentati" (Del Fabbro 1979: 71) is an apt description of *PFay*. 3.

60 Galen, *De libr. prop.* 11 (19.42K = *Scr. Min.* 2.118.22–119.2 ed. Müller): κοινωνεῖν ἐκέλευσα τῶν ὑπομνημάτων ἐκείνοις μόνοις τοῖς ἀνεγνωκόσι παρὰ διδασκάλῳ τὸ βιβλίον ἢ πάντως γε προεισηγμένοις δι' ἑτέρων ἐξηγητικῶν, ὁποῖα τά τ' Ἀδράστου καὶ Ἀσπασίου ἐστίν.

61 See Seneca, *Mor. Ep.* 76.1–2.

62 In *CAG* 19,1, ed. Heylbut.

63 The text runs as follows in the two versions: Aristotle: τρεῖς γάρ εἰσι μάλιστα οἱ προύχοντες, ὅ τε νῦν εἰρημένος (*sc.* ὁ ἀπολαυστικός) καὶ ὁ πολιτικὸς καὶ τρίτος ὁ θεωρητικός. Aspasius: τριῶν γὰρ ὄντων βίων τοῦ τε θεωρητικοῦ καὶ τοῦ ἀπολαυστικοῦ καὶ τοῦ χρηματιστικοῦ.

64 E.g., the paraphrased lemmata at *in NE* 15.2–14 (on *NE* 1097a15–24). At 14.13ff., Aspasius omits any treatment or quotation of *NE* 1096b19–1097a1. He also tends to ignore Aristotle's literary asides, though he does offer additional illustrative material at 133.7ff.

65 Becchi (1994: 5371, n. 38) believes this commentary represents a unified composition for readers, rather than notes from lectures collected by a student.

66 Like Alexander, he does not always choose between readings but offers interpretations of both variants, e.g., at 166.27: γράφεται δὲ καὶ οὕτως· ... αὕτη δὲ ἡ γραφὴ δηλοῖ, κτλ.

67 E.g., 2.15–3.29 on the terms τεχνή, μεθόδος, πρᾶξις, προαιρέσις; 42.27–47.2, on the passions; 67.26–68.3, on προαιρέσις; 163.27–164.32, on friendship.

68 He mentions *An. Pr.* at 7.21; *Phys.* at 7.21; *An. Po.* at 49.1, and *Top.* at 124.13. Andronicus and Boethus appear in his discussion of the passions at 44.21–33; see Gottschalk 1987: 1156–7.

69 At 13.4–18 the occasion arises for a didactic excursus on Pythagorean doctrine, and at 150.3–18, Aspasius elucidates but does not attack the position of Speusippus on pleasure. But at 24.24, he defends Aristotle against "some people" who questioned the claim made at *NE* 1099b3ff., where Aristotle says that those who are of low birth, solitary, or childless cannot be happy.

70 The work does not survive in its entirety. It has served as a source for the compiler of a patchwork commentary on the *Nichomachean Ethics* (in *CAG* 20, 122–255). It may have been simply a collection of scholia on

selected texts. Athenaeus, *Deipn.* 15 673 E–F, mentions a book by Adrastus entitled περὶ καθ᾽ ἱστορίαν καὶ λέξιν ζητουμένων, and since many of the scholia in the anonymous commentary answer to this description, the commentary has traditionally been ascribed to Adrastus. This is hardly conclusive, but the attribution to Adrastus of at least some of its content is *communis opinio*. The Aldine edition of 1536 carries the title, ἀνωνύμου, ἢ ὥστινες ὑπολαμβάνουσιν, Ἀσπασίου σχόλια εἰς τὸ Β τῶν Ἀριστοτέλους ἠθικῶν Νικομαχείων. Its original form is unclear: Moraux (1984: 323) considers it a monograph, not a continuous commentary.

71 At *Anon. in NE* 142.4–143.5, Adrastus mentions Zopyrus, who cut off his own nose and ears as part of a plan to secure Babylon for Darius (*Herod.* 3 153–60), on which see Mercken 1990: 424.

72 *Anon. in NE* 164.9.

73 *Anon. in NE* 155.1–17, on πόνερος vs. πονερός; similarly on οὐδὲν πρὸ ἔργου, 156.1–14; noted by Mercken (1990: 425).

74 Simpl. *in Cat.* 1.13: ζητημάτων ἐφήψαντο μετρίως, ὡς ὁ Ἀφροδισιεὺς Ἀλέξανδρος καὶ Ἑρμῖνος καὶ ὅσοι τοιοῦτοι ("They touch on questions to a degree, as do Alexander and Herminus"). This may include developing lines of thought that Aristotle does not pursue. Of Alexander's commentary on *Prior Analytics*, Barnes *et al.* (1991: 11) say: "Alexander will often elaborate on issues toward which Aristotle merely gestures."

75 Herminus was Alexander's teacher, but whenever Alexander mentions him, it is for the purposes of disagreement. See Sharples 1990: 86.

76 In his comment on *Top.* 109a27–8 (found at *in Top.* 135), the discussion begins with a quote and then darts away to Theophrastus' distinction between παράγγελμα and τόπος, language which Aristotle does not use. Aristotle's τόπος is declared to be in fact a παράγγελμα, and the lemma is quoted again at 135.14, this time with more fidelity to the received text. But the discussion of παράγγελμα continues until 135.24, when Alexander reaches back to the previous section. He then weaves this together with a third citation of Aristotle's text. He cites it yet again for a fourth and final time at 136.12ff. Only at this point does the discussion move forward to the material following, and here, he quotes 109b4–6 (at 139.19), but omits 109b6–8.

77 Reflecting on another type of oral literature, Shinan (1983: 47) lists certain aspects of oral discourse that also characterize Alexander's style, among them, "repetitions and recurrent formulas; direct addresses to the audience; parallelisms and symmetries; anaphora and short dialogues and monologues."

78 Simplicius, *in Cat.* 30.2, describes him as ὁ ἐξηγούμενος καθ᾽ ἑκάστην λέξιν. For the book on Relation, see Simpl., *in Cat.* 163.6. This may have circulated separately under the title Περὶ τοῦ πρός τι καὶ πρὸς τί πως ἔχοντος.

79 See Gottschalk 1987: 1108–9 for a discussion of Boethus' subtle treatment of time, preserved in Simpl., *in Cat.* 432.24ff.

80 Andronicus turned ποῦ and πότε into χρόνος and τόπος. Boethus sided with Aristotle in subordinating χρόνος and τόπος under Quantity (see Simpl., *in Cat.* 347.6 for Andronicus, 348.2ff. for Boethus).

81 *De affect. et pecc.* 1 (*Scr. Min.* 1 ed. Marquardt), 1.1–5: Ἐπειδὴ καὶ δι'
ὑπομνημάτων ἔχειν βούλει, ἃ πρὸς τὴν ἐρώτησιν ἀπεκρινάμην, ἣν
ἐνεστήσω πρὸς ἡμᾶς ὑπὲρ τοῦ γραφέντος Ἀντωνίῳ τῷ Ἐπικουρείῳ
βιβλίου περὶ τῆς ἐπὶ τοῖς ἰδίοις πάθεσιν ἐφεδρείας, ἤδη πράξω τοῦτο, καὶ
τήνδε τίθεμαι τὴν ἀρχήν. Plutarch's essay *On Listening to Lectures* was first
delivered orally and then put into written form: "The discourse which I
gave on the subject of listening to lectures I have written out and sent to
you" (*Mor.* 37C, tr. Babbitt, LCL).

82 Themistius, active during the mid-fourth century, claims to be the
first to paraphrase Aristotle. At the beginning of his paraphrase of
Posterior Analytics, he remarks that it would be superfluous to produce
another commentary, since so many already exist. But an attempt "to
extract the intentions of the things written in the books, to set
things forth briefly, and to conform to the brevity of the Philosopher
seemed to me something new and worthwhile." See Blumenthal
1979: 175.

83 For biography, testimonia, and fragments, see Drossaart Lulofs 1965.
The original text of Nicolaus' compendium is no longer extant and
exists only in a Syriac compilation of extracts.

84 Simpl., *in Cat.*159.32, 26.17, 30.3.

85 E.g., at *in Cat.* 21.22–4. Another case where Andronicus offers a
rewording of Aristotle is recorded by Simpl., *in Cat.* 201.34–202.5,
treated in Gottschalk 1987: 1106.

86 Simpl., *in Cat.* 63.22, although he elsewhere remarks that Andronicus
"maintained the tenfold number of genera" (*in Cat.* 342.24). See
Gottschalk 1987: 1105.

87 On Relation, Simpl., *in Cat.* 157.18.

88 See Moraux 1973: 103–4.

89 There is also mention of a work entitled Περὶ τοῦ παντός, quoted by
Simplicius at *in Cael.* 3.25, and a Περὶ θεῶν, which Simplicius cites at
in Phys. 23.14, 25.1, and 151.21.

90 The Syriac compiler has left out large portions of the original, but it can
be inferred that the *Compendium* contained treatments of Aristotelian
treatises in the following order: *Physics, Metaphysics, De Caelo, De
Generatione et Corruptione, Meteorologia, Historia Animalium, De Partibus
Animalium, De Anima, De Sensu, De Insomniis, De Generatione Animalium,
De Longaevitate,* and (probably) *De Plantis.*

91 Drossaart Lulofs 1965: 20: "it seems doubtful whether Nic. had any
connexion [*sic*] with the schoolmen of his time, and was not rather a
kind of freelance." In the manuscript containing the Syriac epitome of
the *Compendium*, the text being copied is ascribed to "Nicolaus the
Rhetor," which fits his function as described by Josephus, e.g., *BJ*
1.637–8.

92 Of course, nothing would have prevented this document from
being used in this way. Simplicius, for example, uses it as a
resource.

93 Rawson 1985: 51.

94 The Περὶ τοῦ καθόλου λόγου was first known from Doric fragments
quoted by Simplicius. A complete Koine text (eight pages) is also preserved in Codex Ambrosianus. The text, a German translation, and

commentary may be found in Szlezak 1972. This edition continues to employ the pagination of Thesleff's earlier critical edition, which is followed here.

95 Περὶ ἀντικειμένων survives only in Simplicius' commentary on the *Categories*. The most recent critical text is Thesleff 1965.

96 The order of the Categories was apparently fluid. Porphyry, *in Cat. Proem.* 111.9ff., places Relation third after Quantity, arguing that Quality presupposes Relation. Philo, *Dec.* 30 has the same order as Ps.-Archytas, with the exception of Where and When, for which he substitutes Time and Place. Eudorus of Alexandria (a Platonist, first century CE) argued for the order Substance, Quality, Quantity, Time, and Place.

97 This is most evident in the discussion of time. Compare Aristotle, *Phys.* 219b2, Ps.-Archytas, 24.15–16 (ed. Thesleff), and Simpl., *in Cat.* 350.10ff. On the issue, see Szlezak 1972: 117.

98 G. Reale (1974) is an exception: he believes the text may be assigned to an early stage in Aristotle's career, while he was tutor to Alexander the Great. Against this, see Gottschalk 1987: 1135–7.

99 E.g., the Εἰσαγωγὴ εἰς τὰ φαινόμενα of Geminus (*c.* 70 BCE) and the Κυκλικὴ θεωρία μετεώρων of Cleomedes, which Festugière (1949: 2:479–92) distinguishes from *De Mundo* on stylistic and rhetorical grounds.

100 *De Caelo* 286a, tr. Guthrie (LCL).

101 *De Mundo* 391b, tr. Furley (LCL).

102 Gottschalk (1987: 1134) describes *De Mundo* as "Aristotelian in all essentials," but "Aristotelianism with a difference." He notes, among other things, the unusually personalistic qualities of the Unmoved Mover, which *De Mundo* 397b20 describes as "creator and savior of the world."

103 Stobaeus quotes a large section of the text; it was also translated into Latin, Armenian, and Syriac.

104 Moraux 1984: 58–9.

105 Porphyry, *Life* 14.10 tr. Harmon (LCL). The fact that Plotinus "had the commentaries read" may indicate that students were responsible for this task.

106 *De Fato*, 164.3ff., in the edition of Bruns 1892, reprinted with translation and commentary in Sharples 1983.

107 Classroom residue is more distinct in some of the later commentators, especially Olympiodorus, Proclus, David, and Stephanus, where πρᾶξις refers to the daily lesson as a whole, θεωρία to the general discussion, while λέξις refers specifically to the exegetical analysis of a text. See Praechter 1990: 47–9; 1904: 382–5; 1905: 532–3; 1906: 898–9; 1908: 222–5.

108 *Discourses*, I proem. They are said "not to have been composed" (συγγράφειν).

109 The following discussion owes much to Sharples 1990: 103–11.

110 *Quaest.* 1.11 (Bruns 1892: 21.15); tr. Sharples 1992: 50; also *in Top.* 133.24: "There was an inquiry as to how a problem could be false" (noted by Sharples 1990: 105) and *Eth. Prob.* 148.12: "we inquired what happiness was. . . ." This use of ζητέω and λέγω seems

NOTES

particularly common in the short works; these may be somewhat closer to their oral origins than the commentaries.

111 *Quaest.* 1.9 (ed. Bruns 1892: 19.17). The translation is that of Sharples 1992: 46. Not all instances of ἐζήτησε or ἐλέγετο are significant; in most cases, they are intertextual references, harking back to subjects discussed earlier in the writing. Of course, if the commentaries reflect actual teaching (even if they are not always verbatim transcripts), then these intertextual references may also carry the echo of the classroom.

112 *In An. Pr.* 218.13; similarly at *in An. Pr.* 191.24 and 192.13, all noted by Sharples 1990: 104. Also *Eth. Prob.* 127.20: "some such thing was also said . . . (ἐλέγετο δέ τι καὶ τοιοῦτον, ὅτι κτλ.).

113 *Mantissa* (ed. Bruns 1892: 169.34 and 170.3): καὶ αὐτὸ ἁπασῖν ἔδοκει; noted by Sharples 1990: 109.

114 In the latter, for example, at *Diss.* 3 (ed. Lutz 1947: 38.25), "Someone once asked him," *Diss.* 4 (42.34), "once, when a discussion arose," etc. A great many of Musonius' Discourses are introduced in this way.

115 E.g., in his commentary on the *Physics*, quoted by Simpl., *in Phys.* 941.23–942.25. Moraux (1967: 169, n. 1) lists fourteen instances of this in fragments from Alexander's commentaries on the *Physics* and *De Caelo*. See Dooley 1989: 25, n. 41 for many examples of this practice in the commentary on the *Metaphysics*. The technique is common in the short works as well, as in *Quaest.* 2.3. Gottschalk (1987: 1160) remarks that posing alternative solutions could be "a deliberate didactic technique."

116 Bruns 1892: v–xiv; Sharples 1990: 97.

117 In all probability, it was a student of Alexander, and not Alexander himself, who edited these writings and provided them with titles. Scholiasts also attempted to classify the material into these categories at an early stage. See Bruns 1892: ix.

118 E.g., *Quaest.* 1.11 (ed. Bruns 1892: 21.14ff.). The inept editing of some of the short works leads Bruns to suppose that they have been edited by someone who was not an immediate student of Alexander.

119 E.g., Amelius (*Life* 3), who wrote up 100 notebooks-worth of material taken from Plotinus' lectures, or Arrian, whose *Discourses of Epictetus* is based on his class notes.

120 Of course, we should not assume that they represent *all* the material discussed. In the course of transmission, extraneous material may have been left aside.

121 *In Top.* 27.12–16: ἦν δὲ σύνηθες τὸ τοιοῦτον εἶδος τῶν λόγων τοῖς ἀρχαίοις, καὶ τὰς συνουσίας τὰς πλείστας τοῦτον ἐποιοῦντο τὸν τρόπον, οὐκ ἐπὶ βιβλίων ὥσπερ νῦν (οὐ γὰρ ἦν πω τότε τοιαῦτα βιβλία), ἀλλὰ θέσεώς τινος τεθείσης εἰς ταύτην γυμνάζοντες αὐτῶν τὸ πρὸς τὰς ἐπιχειρήσεις εὑρετικὸν ἐπεχείρουν, κατασκευάζοντές τε καὶ ἀνασκευάζοντες δι' ἐνδόξων τὸ κείμενον. καὶ ἔστι δὲ βιβλία τοιαῦτα Ἀριστοτέλους τε καὶ Θεοφράστου γεγραμμένα ἔχοντα τὴν εἰς τὰ ἀντικείμενα δι' ἐνδόξων ἐπιχείρησιν.

122 Ταῦτ' εἰπόντος αὐτοῦ ἐζητήθη καθόλου ἀπὸ τῆς ἐξηγήσεως, εἰ <ἡ> εἰς τὴν ἐνέργειαν μεταβολὴ κίνησίς ἐστιν (ed. Bruns 1892: 81.17). Perhaps because of the odd sense of the passage, Bruns replaces ἀπὸ with ὑπὸ, without manuscript support. Sharples (1994: 39) translates:

"These things having been said by him [Aristotle], it was enquired in general from the commentary, whether the transition to actuality is a change."

123 So Sharples 1990: 105, n. 153.

124 Several of the *Quaestiones* go under the title ἐξήγησις, but these are probably added by later editors. The term always refers to an explanation of a text and not a written document.

125 *Quaest.* 1.11 (ed. Bruns 1892: 21.18, 22.26) makes reference to ὑπομνήματα on *De Anima*; *in Top.* 7.11 mentions ὑπομνήματα on *Prior Analytics*. On ὑπόμνημα and ὑπομνηματίζειν, by which Alexander means "to comment on a text," see Sharples 1985: 113.

126 Ἄμα δὲ φανερὸν ὅτι μηδενὸς πρὸς τοῦτον ἡ σκέψις.

127 Τουτέστιν κοινολογία τε καὶ ζήτησις.

128 See *In Top.* 28.4: διὰ μὲν οὖν ἀληθῶν τε καὶ ἀποδεικτικῶν οὐχ οἷόν τε κοινολογεῖσθαι πρὸς αὐτούς (sc. οἱ πολλοί). At *in Top.* 531.22, 548.27 and 549.3, κοινολογεῖν is used of technical philosophical conversation of the dialectic and contentious varieties, not suitable for those beginning the study of philosophy. Plutarch, *Mor.* 462B uses κοινολογεῖν in the general sense of learned discussion, perhaps among equals, rather than between teachers and students.

129 Galen, *In Hipp. de natura hominis*, Introduction to Bk. I (ed. Mewaldt 1914: 3.4ff.): "I did not demonstrate at the beginning of the treatise those things that I knew he already understood accurately, nor did I recapitulate as it is customary to do whenever the common discussion is about to take place among all those having read it" (ὅταν κοινὸς ὁ λόγος ἅπασι τοῖς ἀναγνωσομένοις αὐτὸν ἔσεσθαι μέλλῃ).

130 καὶ ἄλλη δέ τις δόξα παραδέδοται περὶ ψυχῆς, πιθανὴ μὲν πολλοῖς οὐδεμίας ἧττον τῶν λεγομένων, λόγους δ᾽ ὥσπερ εὐθύνας δεδωκυῖα καὶ τοῖς ἐν κοινῷ γινομένοις (v.1. λεγομένοις) λόγοις. My translation, "in school discussions" is, perhaps, slightly tendentious. It does, however, work well as a contrast to *ta legomena*, the things generally or commonly said. Allan (1980: 249), who draws attention to this passage, says that the view in question "has been submitted to scrutiny in discussions which are occurring ἐν κοινῷ," and considers this to be the type of informal discussion that might arise after the reading of a text. W.S. Hett's translation (LCL) ignores the force of the μέν–δέ clause: "There is another traditional theory about the soul, which many find the most credible of all current theories, and which has been approved by the verdict of public opinion."

131 At the end of the day, I find myself in disagreement with P. Donini's claim that we should not presume to find "the end result, or the instrument, or both together, of teaching, if this term is understood in a restricted and technical sense" (see above, n. 2).

132 The text is from Düring [1957] 1987: 98: καὶ οὕτω φιλοπόνως συνὴν Πλάτωνι ὡς τὴν Πλάτων αὐτοῦ ἀναγνώστου οἰκίαν προσ αγορευθῆναι. θαμὰ γὰρ Πλάτων ἔλεγεν, Ἀπίωμεν εἰς τὴν τοῦ ἀναγνώστου οἰκίαν, καὶ ἀπόντος τῆς ἀκροάσεως ἀνεβόα· Ὁ Νοῦς ἄπεστι, κωφὸν τὸ ἀκροατήριον.

4 BOOKS BENEATH A PLANE TREE: PLATONISTS

1 D.L. 3.47. Nor was she the only woman to have been interested in Plato: Epictetus observes that many women in Rome are reading the *Republic*, supposedly on account of its egalitarian view of marriage (fr. 15, ed. Oldfather, LCL).

2 Cicero, *Tusc.* 2.2.7.

3 Barnes and Griffin 1997: vi: "Consuls and chefs, we are told, read Plato's dialogues; but it is unlikely that Aristotle's *Physics* or his *De anima* was perused in the Senate or in the kitchen."

4 Cicero, *Tusc.* 2.2.8. Trapp (1990) finds many echoes of the *Phaedrus* in the literature of the second century CE.

5 Aulus Gellius, *NA* 17.20.

6 On such introductions, see Mansfeld 1994, and for a later period, Westerink 1962.

7 Dunn 1974: 61. He also wrote treatises on astronomy and the "music of the spheres." See Tarrant 1993: 7–11 for details and testimonia.

8 Theon's book is no longer extant. It is mentioned by the tenth-century bibliographer al-Nadîm in *The Fihrist of al-Nadîm* (tr. Dodge 1970: 614).

9 Critical edition by Whittaker 1990; English translation with commentary in Dillon 1993.

10 See Athenaeus, *Deipn.* 11.506c and D.L. 3.62 on *Alc. 2*, and D.L. 3.37 on *Epin.* For modern studies, see Tarán 1975. On Plato's *Letters*, see Edelstein 1966 and Rist 1965.

11 *De justo, De virtute, Demodocus, Sisyphus, Eryxias, Axiochus*, and *Definitiones*. On these, see D.L. 3.62 and for modern treatments, Müller 1975 and Oswiecimski 1978.

12 Discussion of the early history of the Platonic corpus has focused chiefly on the Flinders Petrie papyrus. Dating to the third century BCE, it contains sizeable pieces of the *Phaedo* and *Laches*. Solmsen 1981: 110, n. 14, describes its readings as "wild," an adjective borrowed from Von Wilamowitz-Möllendorf. Usener (1892: 3:129) describes it as "corrupt in every respect." John Mahaffy, the original editor of the text, is more restrained, and describes the papyrus as preserving "a tradition distinct from that afterwards current," though not so different as to affect the argument; see Mahaffy 1891–3: 34. In fact, there are no substantial pieces of text either added or missing; for the most part, differences concern word choice, word order and the addition of single words. See Alline 1915: 69 for an account of (early) scholarly disagreements on the subject.

13 Von Wilamowitz-Möllendorf 1962: 324, Alline 1915, Bickel 1944, Solmsen 1981, and Tarán 1976: 767.

14 The argument for an Alexandrian edition generally departs from D.L. 3.65–6, where Antigonus of Carystus alludes to an edition of Plato's work furnished with critical signs to help the reader. Jachmann (1941) and Carlini (1972) argue for an Alexandrian edition.

15 Tarrant 1993. The detailed arguments that Tarrant advances for his thesis would require equally detailed engagement that would lead us astray.

16 Barnes 1991: 127, dismisses all such "authoritative" editions: "nothing speaks for an authoritative ancient text of Plato, whether Academic or Aristophanic or Thrasyllan."

17 See, for example, Chartier 1994.

18 Aulus Gellius, *NA* 1.9.9.

19 D.L. 3.62.

20 *Prol.* §4, 149.4–8 ed. Hermann. The most recent critical edition of Albinus' *Introduction* is Nüsser 1991. I have quoted from this text, but employed Hermann's line numbers, following Nüsser.

21 Arabic text and Latin translation in Rosenthal and Walzer 1943; English translation in Mahdi 1962: 53–67. Tarrant (1993: 35) tentatively suggests Galen as the author. Rosenthal and Walzer (1943: xv) suggest Theon of Smyrna; they also mention Themistius as a possible candidate. Dunn (1974: 147) inclines towards Themistius as well. Dialogues in brackets do not appear under their proper name: the epitomizer, through whom the text has been filtered, seems to have misconstrued the proper name as a description; on this see Mahdi 1962: 60 and Rosenthal and Walzer 1943: 10.

22 Dodge 1970: 592–3.

23 Thrasyllus, quoted by Diogenes Laertius, claimed that Plato himself organized the dialogues into tetralogies (D.L. 3.56); this is doubted by most scholars. Some argue that the tetralogies date back to the Early Academy, e.g., Bickel 1944: 129–30, Von Wilamowitz-Möllendorf 1962: 324, Chroust 1965: 46, and Philip 1976: 307. Points of evidence adduced to prove these contentions are threefold: (1) there is a hint of a tetralogical order within the dialogues themselves (*Pol.* 257A and *Criti.* 108A, C); (2) Diogenes Laertius remarks that Aristophanes of Byzantium and those like him have "wrenched" (ἕλκειγ) the dialogues into the form of trilogies (D.L. 3.61), a statement that may imply a pre-existing order; (3) Varro refers to the *Phaedo* as "IIII" at *Ling. Lat.* 7.37, which seems to imply that the *Phaedo* was "fourth" in some arrangement, presumably the first tetralogy. Others dispute these pieces of evidence and claim that the tetralogies derive from the first century BCE, perhaps stemming from Dercyllides, Thrasyllus, or some unknown figure. For arguments in favor of a later (i.e., first century BCE or later) date for the origin of the tetralogies see Usener 1965: 3:104–62, Alline 1915: 112–14, and Dunn 1974: 102. Pasquali (1988: 265) thinks it cannot be proven that the tetralogies preceded the trilogies of Aristophanes. Tarrant (1993) argues that it is Thrasyllus who has organized the dialogues into tetralogies. On the problem generally, see Dunn 1974 and Mansfeld 1994: 58–107.

24 See Mahdi 1962: 53–67. The sequence begins with the nature of humankind (*Alc.* 1) and proceeds to the problem of knowledge (*Tht.*), and so forth. Porphyry's organization of Plotinus's works would qualify as theoretical since it commences with moral behavior in the human sphere and after rising through the hierarchy of Being, culminates at the One (*Enn.* 6).

25 Al-Nadîm's transcription of Theon's list is introduced by the phrase "among these [books] were the following," which suggests that al-Nadîm may not be giving a comprehensive listing.

26 There is no agreement on the origin and date of the character classification. Philip (1976) presumes that such diaeresis was only practiced in the Early Academy, never afterwards, and that this suffices to anchor it chronologically; similarly Chroust 1965: 42. Tarrant (1993: 46–57) attempts to show that "the full details of the character classification do not antedate Thrasyllus." Dunn (1974: 20–1) believes the character classification predates Thrasyllus, and places it in the first half of the first century BCE. Nüsser (1991: 140–1) locates its origin between 84 BCE, the date Aristotle's esoteric works were brought to Rome, and the death of Thrasyllus in 36 CE; Mansfeld (1994: 5, 95) dates the classification after Thrasyllus but before Albinus.

27 *Prol.* 150.15–30, tr. Dunn 1974: 182.

28 Albinus does not actually give a list of dialogues shown above. He begins his *Prologue* by classifying the dialogues according to type; towards the end, he states that peirastic dialogues should be read first, followed by maieutic dialogues, etc. It is possible that the sequence of dialogues *within* each type could vary, for example, that the *Meno* should come before, not after, *Euthyphro*.

29 Albinus, *Prol.* 4 (ed. Hermann 148.12–17; see Nüsser 1991). The final clause runs thus: ἀρχὴν καὶ διάταξιν διδασκαλίας τῆς κατὰ σοφίαν εὑρεῖν. The date (and identity) of Dercyllides remain in doubt. Some have assumed that since Albinus uses the phrase "Dercyllides and Thrasyllus," Dercyllides must precede Thrasyllus chronologically (e.g., Alline 1915: 15).

30 *Alc., Gorg., Phd., Crat., Tht., Soph., Pol., Phdr., Sym., Phileb., Tim., Parm.* For details, see Westerink 1962: xxxvii–xxxviii.

31 *Prol.* 5 (149.31–150.12 ed. Hermann; see Nüsser 1991). It is a challenging sequence, and does indeed seem suited to more experienced readers who needed less preparation or assistance. Dunn (1974: 179) suggests that this fourfold curriculum was a conscious reaction to the tetralogies, which Albinus says are not suited for readers wishing to approach the dialogues "according to wisdom."

32 Dunn 1976: 70–1.

33 Moreschini (1990: 29) overstates the case when he claims that commentaries to Platonic dialogues are "scarcely attested in the second century," considering the works of Galen, the anonymous commentator on the *Tht.*, Harpocration, Taurus, and others.

34 Plutarch, *De Gen. An.* (*Mor.* 1013B).

35 Proclus, *in Remp.* ed. Kroll 1901: 2:96.12; Porphyry, *Life* 14.12.

36 *Prol.* ed. Hiller [1878] 1987: 146.3–4.

37 Aulus Gellius, *NA* 7.14.5; Philoponus, *De Aet. Mundi* ed. Rabe 1963: 520.4; both noted by Dillon 1996: 240. A commentary on the *Republic* is mentioned by Ps.-Heron., *Definitiones* 137.4 (= Dörrie and Baltes 1993: 80.7). See Lakmann 1995: 211.

38 Procl. *in Remp.* ed. Kroll 1901: 2:96.12; Tertullian, *De an.* 28–9. See Dillon 1996: 270.

39 Procl., *in Remp.* ed. Kroll 1901: 2:96.12. According to Porphyry, *Life* 14.12, Numenius was an author of commentaries.

40 Porphyry, *Life* 14.12. Proclus mentions Cronius at *in Remp.* ed. Kroll 1901: 2:96.12 as having treated the Myth of Er.

41 Proclus (*in Tim*. ed. Diehl 1903: 3:247.15) describes Atticus as "the one who interpreted the *Phaedrus*," and often refers to his commentary on the *Tim*. See des Places 1977: 9.

42 *Sym*., 70.10–12, *Tim*., 35.10–12, *Phaed*., 48.7–11 (references are to columns in *Anon. Tht*.).

43 Dillon 1971 gives excerpts and references.

44 Procl., *in Tim*. ed. Diehl 1903: 1:204.17.

45 Quoted by Olympiodorus, Damascius, and Proclus in their commentaries on these dialogues; for references, see Brisson *et al.* 1982: 78–9.

46 Plutarch, *Mor*. 1012D; Galen, *On the Doctrines of Hippocrates and Plato* (ed. De Lacy 1980: 508.7). One interesting omission from the list is Plutarch himself. Neither the catalogue of Lamprias nor the fragments make any mention of ὑπομνήματα on any Platonic dialogue. From a strictly formal standpoint, Plutarch's *Generation of the Soul* is really a Type II commentary dealing with only two texts from the *Timaeus* (*Tim*. 35A1–B4, and 35B4–36B5). In fact, it is more of a monograph than a commentary.

47 See *Corpus* (1995) Vol. 3 for papyrus commentaries on *Alc*. 1 and *Pol*., both dating from the second century.

48 *Editio princeps* by Diels and Schubart (1905); the most recent edition with commentary and Italian translation is by Bastianini and Sedley 1995.

49 Diels and Schubart proposed a date "prior to the third century A.D." (p. vi), and very tentatively suggest Albinus as the author. Tarrant 1983 pushes the date forward to the first century BCE, arguing for Eudorus as the author; Bastianini and Sedley (1995: 256) agree with the earlier date, proposing the last part of the first century BCE, without following Tarrant's claims about Eudorus. For another recent treatment, see Sedley 1997.

50 E.g., 46.49–47.7 paraphrases *Tht*. 148e1–5; this is noted by Praechter 1909: 540 (= 1973: 274).

51 Cols 21–2.

52 Bastianini and Sedley highlight paraphrase by guillemets.

53 There are nine exceptions, according to Bastianini and Sedley 1995: 241. In some cases, *diple* signs are applied to lines that do not contain lemmata, though they seem to mark paraphrase of the text, or places where the commentator speaks in the voice of one of the characters (e.g., 45.47–46.3; 47.27–9; 57.2–7).

54 It is not clear, however, if the *paragraphoi* derive from the original scribe or from a later user of the text. See Bastianini and Sedley 1995: 240–1 for a discussion of other critical signs.

55 Space before: 4.27, 12.16, 14.42, 21.24, 22.24, 23.12, etc.; space after: 5.14, 9.6, 22.7, 22.27, etc. Occasionally, a space may appear before and after (e.g., 36.35 and 36.45), though this is unusual.

56 *Ekthesis* is also used in *PBerol*. inv. 11749, a papyrus commentary on Plato's *Statesman*. See *Corpus* 3:221–6.

57 33.1, 58.39, 66.12.

58 See 22.28–30 for comment on word order. In 12.21–4, the archaic usage Εὖ ἀγγέλλεις is glossed. See also 48.45, regarding ἄλοχος.

59 E.g., 17.32ff. (on *Tht.* 146a2–5), where Socrates alludes to a type of ball game played by children.

60 See 8.23–45 for another problem and its explanation; Bastianini and Sedley mention 19.47–21.13, 24.30ff., 52.44–53.36, among others as instances of *aporiai*.

61 11.23ff. (Stoics), 15.23ff., 22.39 (Epicureans). At 6.30, he mentions the *Akademikoi*, who take a more skeptical approach as opposed to the *Platonikoi*, who scrutinized Plato's dialogues for dogmatic statements (see 54.14ff., 70.14). The author does not place himself in either of these factions.

62 Sometimes alternative solutions to problems are proposed only to be dismissed, as in 19.47–21.13, 24.30ff., 52.44–53.36, 56.14–31, 57.15–42, and 59.2–34. The references are from Bastianini and Sedley 1995: 258.

63 Philoponus, *De Aet. Mundi* (ed. Rabe 1963: 145–7) preserves remarks on the generation of the cosmos taken from Taurus' commentaries on the *Timaeus*, which must have been quite detailed. Unfortunately, these four pages in Rabe's edition are the only fragments of this commentary that survive.

64 Discussing the sequence of thought in 37.39–38.37, Bastianini and Sedley observe that the author "presumes that the readers are making reference to the text in the lemmata, not to a separate copy of the *Theaetetus*" (1995: 531).

65 Diels and Schubart 1905: vi.

66 *Hist. Phil.* 2 (text in Diels [1879] 1965: 598.7–9): ἵνα οἱ φιλομαθεῖς τούτοις προεντυγχάνοντες μὴ δέοιντο τῶν ἐξηγουμένων, ἀλλὰ δι᾽ ἑαυτῶν γιγνώσκοιεν τὰ καθ᾽ ἕκαστα τῶν εἰρημένων σφέστερον.

67 For details (the little that is known), see Dillon 1996: 258–9. All the extant fragments of Harpocration may be found in Dillon 1971. They include comments on *Alc.* 1, *Phd.*, *Phdr.*, *Tim.*, and *Rep.*

68 Olymp. *in Phaed.* 41.17: καὶ διὰ τί τὸ φιλήδονον παρῆκεν; ὁ μὲν Ἁρποκρατίων ἀπορήσας οὐκ ἐπελύσατο . . . The text is taken from Dillon 1971: 130.

69 Quoted by Olymp. *In Phaed* 113.1ff.: οὕτως μὲν Ἁρποκρατίων ἐξηγεῖται. The text derives from an anonymous commentator quoted by Olymp. (*in Phaed.* 113.1ff.) and is taken from Dillon 1971: 130–1.

70 Dillon 1971: 130.

71 We have seen how Simplicius *in Cat.* 1.12–14 distinguishes between those commentators who wish only to exhibit Aristotle's own thought clearly and concisely, and other commentators who apply themselves in a moderate degree to answering questions (ζητήματα), presumably questions of a higher order, of the sort encountered in Harpocration.

72 Critical edition by Hiller 1878 (repr. 1987); text with French translation by J. Dupuis (1892); English translation of Dupuis in Lawlor and Lawlor 1979.

73 1.5–16 Hiller: τὸ μὲν οὖν συμπάσης γεωμετρίας καὶ συμπάσης μουσικῆς καὶ ἀστρονομίας ἔμπειρον γενόμενον τοῖς Πλάτωνος συγγράμμασιν ἐντυγχάνειν μακαριστὸν μὲν ἔτι τῷ γένοιτο, οὐ μὴν εὔπορον οὐδὲ ῥᾴδιον ἀλλὰ πάνυ πολλοῦ τοῦ ἐκ παίδων πόνου δεόμενον. ὥστε δὲ τοὺς διημαρτηκότας τοῦ ἐν τοῖς μαθήμασιν ἀσκηθῆναι,

ὀρεγομένους δὲ τῆς γνώσεως τῶν συγγραμμάτων αὐτοῦ μὴ παντάπασιν ὧν
ποθοῦσι διαμαρτεῖν, κεφαλαιώδη καὶ σύντομον ποιησόμεθα τῶν
ἀναγκαίων καὶ ὧν δεῖ μάλιστα τοῖς ἐντευξομένοις Πλάτωνι μαθημα-
τικῶν θεωρημάτων παράδοσιν . . .

74 Outside of the references in the introductory section, where Platonic
texts are adduced that advocate mathematical study, we find the following explicit references to the dialogues: 21.15 (*Phileb.*); 84.8 (*Epin.*);
96.5, 103.17 (*Tim.* 35B–C). Some discussions in Theon are quite germane to passages in Plato, e.g., 66.19ff. to *Tim.* 36B, but the connection
is not made explicit. There are also allusions to Platonic doctrines or
statements, e.g., cf. 73.11–15 and *Soph.* 263E; 200.8 and *Phdr.* 247A.

75 Ταῦτα μὲν οὖν καὶ ὁ Πλάτων. ὧν τὴν ἐξήγησιν ἐν τοῖς τῆς Πολιτείας
ποιούμεθα ὑπομνήμασιν (ed. Hiller 1878: 146.3). As we have seen, the
author of *Anon. Tht.* also makes statements of this kind; it seems the
authors of both works assume that the readers would have had access to
their other works as well.

76 Κατασκεύασται δ᾽ ἡμῖν σφαιροποιία κατὰ τὰ εἰρημένα (ed. Hiller
1878: 146.4–5). The model is mentioned again in 151.5. A sphere
answering this description actually appears in the famous Pompeian
mosaic called "the School of Plato" (see Kraus 1975, Plate 215). Lucian
mentions a "reed globe" (σφαῖρα καλάμου) in the house of the Platonist teacher Nigrinus (*Nigr.* 2).

77 Galen, *De aff. et pec.* 1.1 (ed. Marquardt 1884), quoted in the previous
chapter. Galen himself takes pride in the fact that he learned from
teachers, not δι᾽ ὑπομνήματα (*Loc. Aff.* 8.144K).

78 Perhaps Harpocration's commentaries were of this sort: based on the
types of questions posed, they seem to derive from the classroom.

79 Critical edition and German translation in Marg 1972; detailed commentary in Baltes 1972. Marg's text is reprinted with an English translation in Tobin 1985; see Harder 1939 for a useful summation of the
contents of the *Tim.* and *Tim. Locr.*

80 Details about the fabrication of the body (*Tim.* 72E–79A) are omitted, as
are concluding remarks about the origin of animals and of gender. For
other omissions, see Baltes 1972: 7–8; for additions and alterations, see
9–10.

81 Tim. 47E: "The foregoing part of our discourse [27–47] has been an
exposition of the operations of Reason; but we must also furnish an
account of what comes into existence through Necessity [47ff.]" – that
is, through natural causation.

82 See Tobin 1985: 12–13.

83 *Tim.* 72D. The *Tim. Locr.* is entirely lacking in this type of "methodo-
logical reserve" (Tobin 1985: 8).

84 *Tim. Locr.* 102b (221.8–10). Translation by Tobin 1985: 63.

85 Baltes says of *Tim. Locr.* 217.6–12, "aus *Tim.* 32a7-b8, z.T. mit wört-
licher Übereinstimmung" (p. 127). But comparison of the two passages
shows a few coincidences of vocabulary, but hardly more.

86 See Harder 1939: 1220–6 and Baltes 1972: 25: the *Tim. Locr.* is "a
synthesis of an epitome and a 'Timaiosinterpretation,' more precisely a
set of lecture notes." Baltes (1972: 19) speaks of "Schuldefinitionen,"
e.g., expressions like that in 205.12: "whatever motions, then, do

violence to something's nature are pains, and those that restore it to its proper nature are called pleasures" (tr. Tobin); see also 215.3–4, 219.3–4, 219.14, 221.9–10.

87 A partial exception is §33 (98a–9), where the *Tim. Locr.* gives an explanation of isosceles and scalene triangles.

88 See Cicero, *De Fin.* 2.5: "obscurity may be due to the abstruseness of the subject and not of the style – an instance of this is Plato's *Timaeus*" (tr. Rackham, LCL).

89 In this topical ordering, the *Didaskalikos* resembles Apuleius' *De Platone et eius dogmate*, which I leave aside at present. See Siniscalco and Albert 1981 for text of the latter and German translation. For a discussion of authorship, see Redfors 1960.

90 In particular, see Whittaker 1990 and Dillon 1993: xiii–xvi.

91 Platonic borrowings are italicized in Whittaker's Budé edition (Whittaker 1990).

92 As, for example, in the remarks on syllogisms: "Plato, in propounding arguments, frequently makes use of the first figure, and also of the second and the third. He uses the first figure in the *Alcibiades* thus . . . The second figure he uses in the *Parmenides*, as follows . . . " (158.39–43, tr. Dillon). Explicit reference to the dialogues is found only in 158–9, 181, and 188.

93 These are only a few of the many examples cited in Whittaker 1989: 72.

94 See Dillon 1993: xxix, and 1996: 269.

95 E.g., 162.42ff.

96 Dillon (1993: xiv) suggests that the work is actually intended as a "manual for teachers, or at least amateurs, of Platonism," not a manual for beginners. See also Whittaker 1990: xvii and 1989: 67.

97 Diogenes Laertius (3.65–6) speaks of manuscripts furnished with special critical signs to help the reader locate Platonic doctrines, apparently an editorial device to achieve the same end.

98 *Did.* 189.31, tr. Dillon. The Greek runs as follows: ὥστε μέντοι ἀπὸ τῶν εἰρημένων θεωρητικούς τε καὶ εὑρετικοὺς ἐξ ἀκολουθίας καὶ τῶν λοιπῶν αὐτοῦ δογμάτων γενέσθαι (ed. Whittaker 1990).

99 *NA* 2.2.2; that the "room" in question is in Taurus' house is evident from 2.2.10. On Taurus generally, see Lakmann 1995: 28–45.

100 Lucian, *Nigr.* 2. Satire or not, the literary conceit relies on a realistic portrayal of a philosopher's house.

101 On Taurus' pedagogy, see Lakmann 1995: 216–20 and Sandy 1997: 27–31.

102 *NA* 1.26, tr. Rolfe (LCL). Rolfe has "discourses" for *lectiones*, which seems to obscure the sense of something being read, whether Taurus' own lectures or an ancient text. *Lectio* typically refers to the reading of a text; for Quintilian (*I.O.* 10.1.19), it is explicitly juxtaposed to *ex tempore* oral utterance.

103 Lakmann (1995: 30) believes that *lectio* refers to the reading of Platonic dialogues, as in *NA* 17.20. Taurus probably did not restrict himself to Plato's dialogues; Gellius mentions a time when "I read this [a selection from Aristotle's *Problems*] at Athens with our friend Taurus" (*NA* 18.6).

NOTES

104 Quoted by Eusebius, *Pr. Ev.* 177.4–17 ed. Mras; tr. Gifford.
105 *On Listening to Lectures* 43F, tr. Babbitt (LCL).
106 Seneca, *Ep. Mor.* 95.2: Recitator historiam ingentem attulit minutissime scriptam, artissime plicatam, et magna parte perlecta "desinam," inquit, "si vultis." *Scripta artissime plicata* suggests a folded medium of some kind rather than a roll. Bellincioni (1979: 91) translates, "fascio compatto di cartelle." She does not discuss this in her extensive commentary. Gardthausen (1911: 133–4) cites several examples of elaborately folded sheets of paper. *Plicata* may refer to something wound around a staff; see Aulus Gellius, *NA* 17.9.9. However, it is difficult to know what it would mean to roll something "artissime."
107 *NA* 7.13; 17.8. These students were not simply boys fresh from the *grammaticus*, but *homines docti*, according to 18.10.5.
108 *NA* 19.13.1 (tr. Rolfe, LCL).
109 *NA* 12.5, where Aulus Gellius accompanies Taurus for a trip from Athens to Delphi, on the occasion of the Pythian Games.
110 See especially Goulet-Cazé 1982: 1:231–327; also Lim 1995: 37–47, and Fowden 1977: 370–3.
111 *Enn.* 3.7.1 tr. Armstrong (LCL), slightly modified. See also 5.1.8 where Plotinus states that his basic ideas are just interpretations of Plato.
112 *Life* 14.5.
113 When Plotinus says, "this is what Plato says," we often find an account of what Plotinus thinks Plato means, rather than a piece of actual text cited from a dialogue; see the note to *Enn.* 2.1.7 in Armstrong's LCL edition (vol. 2, p. 28).
114 E.g., *Enn.* V.1.1: "But Parmenides in Plato speaks more accurately . . ." In Bréhier's edition (5.8.5) this is treated as an explicit citation of *Parm.* On Plotinus' frequent allusions to the dialogues, see Goulet-Cazé 1982: 2:270.
115 See Proclus, *in Tim.* 2 300.24 ed. Diehl.
116 *Life* 14.10–16: Ἐν δὲ ταῖς συνουσίαις ἀνεγινώσκετο μὲν αὐτῷ τὰ ὑπομνήματα, εἴτε Σεβήρου εἴη, εἴτε Κρονίου ἢ Νουμηνίου ἢ Γαίου ἢ Ἀττικοῦ, κἀν τοῖς Περιπατητικοῖς τά τε Ἀσπασίου καὶ Ἀλεξάνδρου Ἀδράστου τε καὶ τῶν ἐμπεσόντων. Ἐλέγετο δὲ ἐκ τούτων οὐδὲν καθάπαξ, ἀλλ' ἴδιος ἦν καὶ ἐξηλλαγμένος ἐν τῇ θεωρίᾳ καὶ τὸν Ἀμμωνίου φέρων νοῦν ἐν ταῖς ἐξετάσεσιν. My translation owes much to Armstrong. Some problems of translation attend the passage: the sense of καθάπαξ, for example, and whether it refers to λέγειν or οὐδέν. My translation associates it with the verb, as does the translation of Bréhier (p. 15): "mais jamais on ne lisait un passage simplement et sans plus"; so also Armstrong: "he did not just speak straight out of these books." Goulet-Cazé takes καθάπαξ with οὐδέν, which would imply that Plotinus took nothing at all from these commentaries: "Plotin n'empruntait absolument rien à ces commentaires."
117 Compositions by members of the group might also be read, as, for example, Porphyry's recantation of his previous philosophical beliefs, in *Life* 18.19.
118 *Life* 13.10–17.

119 *How to Listen to Lectures* 42F; see especially chs 10–12 (*Mor.* 42F–44A) on the posing of questions.

120 Later Neoplatonic commentators divided exegesis itself into two parts, θεωρία (general theory) and λέξις (detailed remarks on texts), but this curricular division is probably not yet in place. See Praechter 1990: 48–9. Ἐξέτασις carries the sense of a word-by-word explication in Procl., *in Tim.* ed. Diehl 1903: 1.299.19–21: ἡμᾶς δὲ πρῶτον χρὴ τὴν λέξιν αὐτὴν καθ᾽ αὑτὴν ἐξετάσαντας ἔπειτα οὕτω πρὸς τὴν ὅλην θεωρίαν ἀναδραμεῖν.

121 In a lengthy note, Goulet-Cazé (1982: 2:263, n. 1) argues against a strict distinction between two types or stages of exegesis, but suggests (based on *Life* 14.16) that ἐξέτασις should be more closely tied to analysis, rather than an initial reading: "les ἐξετάσεις apparaissent comme les particularisations de la θεωρία; ce sont les investigations, les examens auxquels se livre le commentateur à propos d'un problème précis soulevé par le text."

122 See *Life* 20.49ff., regarding the Peripatetics Ammonius and Ptolemaeus, "both the greatest scholars of their time, especially Ammonius; there has been no one who has come near him in learning: but they did not write any work of professional philosophy (οὐδὲν τεχνικόν), only poems and show speeches" (λόγοι ἐπιδεικτικοί).

123 See Aulus Gellius, *NA* 17.20, on people reading Plato for the sake of "acquiring phrases." On the dialogues as after-dinner entertainment, see Plutarch, *Mor.* 711C.

124 Zanker 1988: 337.

125 *Philosophies for Sale* 15, 26.

5 JEWISH AND CHRISTIAN GROUPS
Part 1 Philo

1 See Hay 1979 on Philo's opponents, and Mack 1984 on Philo's intellectual milieu.

2 In what follows, I have generally used the LCL text and translation of Colson and Whittaker. To keep references as streamlined as possible, I have also utilized the traditional Latin abbreviations, e.g., *Her.* for *Quis rerum divinarum heres sit* (*Who Is the Heir of Divine Things*). A list of these abbreviations may be found in Vol. 1 of the LCL edition, pp. xxiii–xxiv.

3 Works termed συντάξεις: *Op.* (*Abr.* 2, 14), *Mos.* (*Mos.* 2.1, *Virt.* 52), *Decal.* (*Spec.* 1.1), *Spec. Leg.* (*Virt.* 101, *Praem.* 3); a lost work on rewards is called a σύνταξις (*Her.*1). It is interesting that with the exception of *Op.*, none of the Allegorical Commentaries is ever called a σύνταξις. Works termed βιβλίοι: *Agr.* (*Plant.* 1), *Plant.* (*Ebr.* 1). Works called γραφή: the lost first work on dreams (*Somn.* 1.1); presumably the term would apply to the rest of *Somn.* Philo never uses the term συγγράμματα of his works.

4 At *Ebr.* 1, he uses ὑπομιμνήσκειν to refer to a set of observations made within the previous treatise; at *Flacc.* 131, ὑπομνηματίζειν describes courtroom stenography.

5 For example, there may have been no breaks between the three volumes

of *L.A.*, or between *Gig.* and *Deus*. At times Philo explicitly signals a break, as at the beginning of *Plant.*: "We have said in the former book . . . " This is the first such remark encountered in the Allegorical Commentaries. *Ebr.*, *Sobr.*, and *Conf.* likewise begin with similar remarks.

6 *Conf.* begins with Gen. 11:1–9; *Fug.* begins with Gen. 16:6–9, 11–12 (Gen. 16:10 is never cited by Philo in any of his works; it may have been missing in his text).

7 E.g., at *L.A.* 1.63, Gen. 2:10–14 is quoted in full; v. 11 is repeated in 1.66, v. 13 in 1.68, v. 14 in 1.72.

8 Colson (1940: 239) calls these "direct" and "illustrative" quotations.

9 *Conf.*, for example, begins with an introductory sentence; at §142, the lemma is worked into a sentence ("This is the reason we assign for the words, 'God came down to see the city and the tower,' but the phrase which follows, 'which the sons of men built,' is no idle addition though perhaps . . . "); again, in §168: "we should give careful consideration to the question of what is implied by the words which came from the mouth of God: 'Come let us go down and confuse their tongue.' "

10 *Gig.* 67; *Det.* 57.

11 Colson (1940: 250) describes Philo as an "inveterate rambler," and likens him to Mrs Nickleby. Nikiprowetzky (1977, 1983) finds the *quaestio–solutio* pattern to be the "cellule mère" of Philo's exegesis. Christiansen (1969) finds the key to Philo's exegetical procedure in the process of diaeresis. Cazeaux (1983) finds a supremely subtle and pervasive pattern in Philo's seemingly disordered style. For strong criticism of the latter, see Runia 1984. This article and others by Runia on Philo are reprinted in Runia 1990.

12 *L.A.* 1.65: "Let us look at the particular words used" (ἴδωμεν δὲ καὶ τὰς λέξεις); he explains an apparent barbarism in *L.A.* 3.188; *Deus* 141 deals with an apparent solecism; *Plant.* 113: "The expression is equivocal" (ἡ δὲ λέξις ἐστὶν ἀμφίβολος); at *Her.* 17, he discusses the use of the imperfect vs. the aorist; *Fug.* 39: τὰς δὲ λέξεις ἀκριβωτέον; at *Fug.* 51, how Bethuel, a feminine word by derivation, can be the name of Rebecca's father.

13 E.g., *QG* 1.74, where Philo discusses Cain's fear that anyone who meets him will kill him; but Philo observes that only Adam and Eve are present in the world at this time. Raising questions of this type is a familiar critical tactic of the sort known as κατασκεύσις. See the *Progymnasmata* of Aelius Theon (ed. Spengel 1854: 2:93ff.) on refutation and confirmation.

14 *L.A.* 3.51–3; *Cher.* 21–30, *Quis Rer.* 280–3, *QG* 1.30.

15 *Conf.* 190. Other such occasions: *L.A.* 3.206; *Det.* 156: μήποτε οὖν, a common phrase; see Runia 1987: 115, with references in n. 27.

16 See Leopold 1983: 141–54, and Thyen 1955, especially 9–10 on rhetorical features in Philo.

17 Some passages are particularly rich with these figures, for example, *Gig.* 25–57, which Leopold (1983: 147–50) analyzes in detail. Leopold points out that diatribe was not a recognized type of speech in antiquity. But while an ancient listener might not have said "that's diatribe," he or she might have said "that sounds like school language."

This is the position of Halbauer 1911 as described by Stowers 1981: 28–9.

18 Leopold 1983: 144.

19 See Stowers 1981: 69–75.

20 E.g., there are no *Quaestiones* on Gen. 1, or on 28:10–50:26, nor on Gen. 21:1–22:24, or 25:9–18. See Wan 1993: 22, n. 1.

21 E.g., *QG* 2.32: "Why does (Scripture) say, 'In the tenth month, on the first (day of the month), the summits of the mountains appeared?'" Wan (1993) observes that nearly half (45 percent) of the *Quaestiones* take this form.

22 Out of 636 *quaestio et solutio* segments, 156 feature both literal and allegorical interpretations, while 188 contain only allegorical interpretation. It is interesting, however, that 226 include only literal interpretation, a surprising number for a famous allegorist. The figures are from Wan 1993: 35. Sterling (1991: 104–5) makes the same observation.

23 E.g., *QG* 3.1: "The literal meaning is clear"; 3.45: "The literal meaning is clear, so that the passage does not require any interpretation."

24 See *CAG* 4,1. Some answers are long, but most are quite short, even admitting of one-word answers, e.g., "not at all" (οὐδαμῶς).

25 See Nicole 1903: 1–3 and Zalateo 1964: 52–7. On the Homerica, see Wan 1993: 27.

26 Nikiprowetzky (1977: 180) sees the *Quaestiones* as establishing the basic grid for the Allegorical Commentaries; Marcus (*QG*, p. x), however, believes the question and answer commentaries came later. Philo refers to the Allegorical Commentaries at *QG* 2.4 (a reference to *Ebr.* 88–90) and in *QE* 2.34, a reference to Philo's lost treatise on the divine covenant mentioned here and in *Mut. Nom.* 53. See also Terian 1991 and Sterling 1991.

27 See Runia 1991: 76: there is "practically no correlation in the choice of secondary texts when the two series [the Allegorical Commentaries and the *Quaestiones*] expound the same main text."

28 Sterling (1991: 112) believes that the *Quaestiones* are "either a distillation of the *Allegoriae* or a prolegomena to it."

29 Wan (1993) argues that the *Quaestiones* and the Allegorical Commentaries developed independently.

30 Galen describes how mistakes arise when copyists try to incorporate marginal annotations into already existing texts. See *in Hp. Epid.* 3 (ed. Wenkebach 1934: 1.36 = 17A.80K) and *in Hp. Off.* 3.22 (18B.863K). Both texts are adduced by Emonds 1941, who gives a full discussion of the subject with reference to many ancient authors. Jaeger's remarks about the compilation of Aristotle's works are appropriate to keep in mind with respect to Philo: "We must always bear in mind the fact that the *Metaphysics* is not a literary work edited by its author but a text that gradually changed under his hands as he used it for his lectures in the Peripatus [*sic*]" (Jaeger 1956: 152).

31 See Dorandi 1991 on the literary evidence of Pliny's scholarly methods in light of *PHerc.* 1021, which appears to be in an intermediate stage of composition.

32 Bousset 1915. Bousset located sources in Philo by looking for

philosophical inconsistencies. Critics of Bousset agree that this approach insisted on too much homogeneity for a thinker such as Philo.

33 See Hamerton-Kelly 1972, Mack 1984, Tobin 1983. Tobin, for example, shows that Philo's exegesis stands in a tradition of anti-anthropomorphic interpretation. Dawson (1992: 74–82) discusses Aristeas and Aristobulus, two of Philo's predecessors in Alexandria.

34 Völker (1938: 10) and Wolfson (1947: 1:79) both argue that Philo's written work is based on synagogue homilies and that the expositions are just sermons on the lectionary readings. Völker is discussed and quoted by Nikiprowetzky (1977: 174–7, 205).

35 Nikiprowetzky (1977: 179) speaks of this sub-group within the synagogue as a "School of Wisdom." The question and answer commentaries on Genesis and Exodus mirror the activities of this school.

36 Sterling 1997.

37 *Spec.* 4.140. That Philo considers himself to be such a person, capable of divine utterance, is evident at various points in the text, e.g., *Cher.* 27, where he speaks of a "voice in my own soul, which oftentimes is god-possessed and divines where it does not know."

38 All the references to προσευχή occur in the apologetic treatises in *Flacc.* and *ad Gaium*, which suggests that Philo tailors his usage according to his audience. On προσευχή and συναγώγιον, see Hengel 1971 (pp. 168–9 for Philo's use of the term), and Kee 1992.

39 *Cont.* 75–7: ὁ πρόεδρος αὐτῶν ... ζητεῖται τι τῶν ἐν τοῖς ἱεροῖς γράμμασιν ἢ καὶ ὑπ' ἄλλου προταθὲν ἐπιλύεται ... καὶ ὁ μὲν σχολαιοτέρᾳ χρῆται τῇ διδασκαλίᾳ, διαμέλλων καὶ βραδύνων ταῖς ἐπαναλήψεσιν, ἐγχαράττων ταῖς ψυχαῖς τὰ νοήματα ... Αἱ δὲ ἐξηγήσεις τῶν ἱερῶν γραμμάτων γίνονται δι' ὑπονοιῶν ἐν ἀλληγορίαις· ἅπασα γὰρ ἡ νομοθεσία δοκεῖ τοῖς ἀνδράσι τούτοις ἐοικέναι ζῴῳ καὶ σῶμα μὲν ἔχειν τὰς ῥητὰς διατάξεις, ψυχὴν δὲ τὸν ἐναποκείμενον ταῖς λέξεσιν ἀόρατον νοῦν.

40 E.g., for the law as a living creature, see *QG* 3.3. Careful judgment is necessary when reading a description such as this, where stock elements of ideal philosophical group behavior are so much in evidence.

41 Som.2.127: καὶ καθεδεῖσθε ἐν τοῖς συναγωγίοις ὑμῶν, τὸν εἰωθότα θίασον ἀγείροντες καὶ ἀσφαλῶς τὰς ἱερὰς βίβλους ἀναγινώσκοντες κἂν εἴ τι μὴ τρανὲς εἶ διαπτύσσοντες καὶ τῇ πατρίῳ φιλοσοφίᾳ διὰ μακρηγορίας ἐνευκαιροῦντές τε καὶ ἐνσχολάζοντεσι.

42 *Cong.* 64–5. On the ἀκροατήρια as a venue for musicians, lecturing physicians, philosophers, astronomers, and poets, see Robert 1937: 79–81. It was not always a low-brow situation: Plutarch lectured in the ἀκροατήρια in Rome to an audience of high standing (*De curiositate* 15, *Mor.* 522E).

43 Nikiprowetzky 1977: 175.

44 Porphyry states that Plotinus too wrote under the "inspection and supervision of the gods" (*Life* 23.20). Another prolific author of a later day who wrote in a state of elevation was Thomas Aquinas: capable of occupying several secretaries at once, Aquinas dictated "as if a great torrent of truth were pouring into him from God (quoted in Carruthers 1990: 6).

45 Most people of means, such as Pliny the Elder, "wrote" by means of secretaries (*NH* 25.92); see also Plutarch, *Caesar* 17.5, Eusebius, *HE*

6.23. On the practice of writing by upper-class Romans (and their slaves), see McDonnell 1996.
46 E.g., the Younger Pliny. See *Ep.* 9.36.
47 *Abr.* 22–4; see also the delightful reverie at *Spec.* 3.1–7.
48 One might translate here, "if you *read* someone who has been initiated," given the common sense of ἐντυγχάνειν as "to read." See *Sac.* 79: "we should make it our aim to read the writings of the sages and listen to proverbs and old-world stories from the lips of those who know antiquity and ever seek for knowledge about the men and deeds of old" (ὡς δέον πολιὸν μὲν μάθημα χρόνῳ μηδὲν ἀρνεῖσθαι πειρωμένους καὶ γράμμασι σοφῶν ἀνδρῶν ἐντυγχάνειν).
49 It is striking that two verbs typically used for "to read" are ἀναγιγνώσκειν and ἐντυγχάνειν, verbs meaning "to recognize," and "to encounter," respectively. The latter term especially is a term denoting interaction; indeed, as if Philo and Jeremiah did "encounter" one another on the street. So while Philo's image of meeting Jeremiah and following him home may seem like colorful exaggeration, it may in fact conform to ancient ideas about reading as encounter, a point that I pose in what follows.
50 As with all the *Quaestiones*, this passage is extant only in Armenian, which prevents closer linguistic analysis of its contents.
51 The translation that follows is that of Grenfell and Hunt (1915). The papyrus dates from the second century CE.
52 Πᾶσα γὰρ ἀναθήματος ἢ θυσίας δωρεὰ τὸν παραυτίκα μόνον ἀκμάζει καιρόν, ἔφθαρται δὲ τὸν μέλλοντα, γραφὴ δὲ ἀθάνατος χάρις κατὰ καιρὸν ἀνηβάσκουσα τὴν μνήμην.
53 *Cont.* 25. Conceivably, these might have been texts committed to memory, but the sequence, "laws, prophets, psalms," sounds like a description of the Bible.
54 Ἕκαστοι μονούμενοι παρ᾽ ἑαυτοῖς ἐν τοῖς λεχθεῖσι μοναστηρίοις φιλοσοφοῦσι.
55 *Spec.* 4.160–4. See also Quintilian *I.O.* 11.2.32: "There is one thing which will be of assistance to everyone, namely, to learn a passage by heart from the same tablets on which he has committed it to writing."
56 ὦ ψυχή (*L.A.* 3.74, 164); ὦ διάνοια (*L.A.* 3.17, 36; *Deus* 4). This type of interior address recalls Augustine's style in his *Confessions*.
57 *Life* 4.10: "From the first year of Gallienus, Plotinus had begun to write on subjects that came up in the meetings of the school"; also 5.6: "many discussions took place in the meetings of the school and Amelius and I kept urging him to write." In both cases, writing was parasitic on class activity.
58 So also Runia 1986: 190: "Philo is writing his long series of treatises in the first place for himself."

Part 2 Qumran

1 *1QS* 8.11–15, tr. García Martínez (1996: 12). I have drawn on several different translations: García Martínez 1996, Vermes 1995, Knibb 1987, Charlesworth 1994, and the volumes in the DJD series. García Martínez 1996 is especially useful in view of its organization and com-

pleteness. A word on scroll nomenclature: references may begin with a number (almost always 1, 4, or 11); this refers to the cave in which the document was first discovered. The *"Q"* that almost always follows stands for "Qumran," a designation that distinguishes the Qumran texts from other desert collections such as those found at Nahal Hever. The next letter (or letters) usually represents a Hebrew word describing the content of the scroll, e.g., "Serekh," or "Rule" for the *Community Rule*, or *"p"* for pesher. So the reader will encounter references to *1QS* (*Community Rule*, or *Rule of the Community*), *4QpHab* (the Habakkuk pesher), *11QTemple* (the *Temple Scroll*). "CD" is an abbreviation for the so-called "Damascus Document," discovered in a Cairo synagogue in the nineteenth century. Sometimes a superscript letter is found that refers to separate copies of the same (or a similar) text, e.g., *4QpIsa^a*, *4QpIsa^b*, etc., for the different pesher commentaries on Isaiah. Well-preserved texts are then referenced by column and line number in arabic numerals (e.g., *1QS* 8.15). References to fragmentary scrolls employ the fragment numbers (arabic numerals), roman numerals for the column, and arabic numerals for the line, e.g. 4 ii 3 (fragment 4, column 2, line 3). So, for example, one might encounter a reference to *4QpNah* 3–4 iii 3, which refers to the Nahum pesher from Qumran Cave 4, joined fragments 3 and 4, column 3, line 3. For a complete treatment of these subjects, see Fitzmyer 1990.

2 *1QS* 9.16–17.

3 For the full version, see Snyder 2000.

4 For the "standard view" on Qumran archeology, see De Vaux 1973. His private notes together with many photographs may be found in De Vaux 1994. Disagreements persist about the nature of the compound. Robert Donceel and Pauline Donceel-Voûte have proposed that the site is not a monastic hermitage at all, but rather a Roman country villa. In particular, Locus 30, which De Vaux called "the Scriptorium" is supposed by Donceel and Donceel-Voûte to have been a dining room; see Donceel and Donceel-Voûte 1994. For a rejoinder, see Reich 1994. Hirschfeld (1998) follows the villa hypothesis of Donceel and Donceel-Voûte. I do not believe the challengers have seriously threatened the standard view. Neither Hirschfeld nor Donceel and Donceel-Voûte explain why a country villa should require a cemetery containing hundreds of graves.

5 These figures are based on the number of graves in the nearby graveyard, and on the seating capacity of the refectory. See Broshi 1992: 113–14.

6 De Vaux argues for the existence of two distinct cemeteries; Steckoll (1969: 37) claims there is only one. The presence of female skeletons would bear strongly on whether the community proper was composed entirely of celibate males. On the current *status quaestionis* of the cemetery, see Kapera 1994.

7 Josephus, *BJ* 2.124: "They (the Essenes) occupy no one city, but settle in large numbers in every town." Philo claims that "they live in many cities of Judaea and in many villages and grouped in great societies of many members" (*Hyp.* 11.1); elsewhere, he says that the Essenes number

more than 4000, and they live in villages and avoid the cities (*Prob.* 75–6). For an argument that the Qumran sectarians may be identified as Essenes, see VanderKam 1994: 71–98; for a dissenting view, see Cansdale 1997.

8 See the map of the site in De Vaux 1973.

9 Bernstein 1994a: 4. Fragments of four separate commentaries on Genesis have recently been published by Brooke (1996a). In only one of them (*4Q252* col. 5.5) does the characteristic term פשר appear, and its use there is rather more commonplace than in the pesher commentaries since it does not introduce an interpretation having to do with the sect or its future.

10 See Brooke 1996b and Bernstein 1994a.

11 See Rabinowitz 1973 and Basser 1988.

12 A rare exception is found in *4QpIsa*ᵇ ii 6, which launches immediately into the interpretation: "These are the Scoffers in Jerusalem." As noted above, when referring to citations within the scrolls, convention has it that roman numerals refer to columns, arabic numerals to lines: thus, ii 6 refers to column two, line six of a given text. Often, it will be necessary to specify a fragment number (fr.) as well.

13 See Bernstein 1994b.

14 *Editio princeps* in Brownlee 1950. See especially Horgan 1979 for analysis and commentary. Elliger (1953) is careful to preserve the various paleographic features in his transcription.

15 The book of Psalms, traditionally designated as wisdom literature, was considered prophetic by the Qumran sectarians. The pesher commentaries on Micah, Nahum, Zephaniah, Hosea, Isaiah, and Psalms may be found in Allegro 1968.

16 The few fragments of the Malachi commentary may be found in Brooke 1996a: 213–16.

17 *4QpNah* 1.1–5, tr. Vermes 1995: 337. Lemmata from Nahum are italicized; material in brackets is missing in the ancient manuscript and represents modern reconstruction.

18 See the commentary on the passage by Knibb 1987: 210–11 and the introduction to Qumran history in Vermes 1995: 23–40.

19 Horgan (1979: 245) mentions plays on words, reading the lemma in terms of alternate grammatical forms, use of synonyms for words in the lemma, and transposition of characters (in *1QpHab* 2.5–6, the root עמל, or "work" becomes מעל, "transgression") as instances of such exegetical techniques. The remark about transposition is from Fishbane 1988: 375.

20 *1QpHab* 4.8–12; translation by Knibb (1987: 227).

21 On the use of different textual traditions, see Horgan 1979: 245, n. 69. Another example is found in *4QpPs*ᵃ fr. 3–10 iii 5, where the lemma reads, "those who love the Lord will be like the glory of the pastures," which is interpreted positively as shepherds of the flock. The Masoretic Text, however, reads, "those who hate the Lord are like the glory of the pastures," i.e., transient and fleeting.

22 Knibb (1987: 229) calls this the "principle of atomization."

23 Knibb's translation (1987: 231).

24 A view first suggested by Elliger (1953: 154–7). See also Fröhlich 1986.

A recent treatment, with comparisons to dream interpretation in biblical and rabbinic materials, is that of Niehoff 1992.

25 Dan. 5:26: דְּנָה פְּשַׁר־מִלְּתָא. Not every use of the term פְּשַׁר, however, signals oracular utterance. In the recently published *4QCommentary on Genesis* (Brooke 1996a) fr. 5 iv 5, the curse on Reuben (Gen. 49:3–4a) is explained: "Its interpretation (פִּשְׁרוֹ) is that he reproved him [Reuben] for when he slept with Bilhah his [Jacob's] concubine." This information is readily available in Gen. 35:22; nothing oracular is involved.

26 See Daumas 1961.

27 The term "discontinuous pesharim" was originally proposed in Carmignac 1969–71: 361. Dimant (1984: 504) calls these "thematic pesharim."

28 This is the translation of Brooke 1985: 93, although he uses the term "midrash" for explanation, consistent with his view that exegesis at Qumran may be seen as continuous with rabbinic exegesis.

29 See Fraade 1991: 3–12 for a comparison of the pesher commentaries and the commentaries of Philo.

30 I find one possible exception in the Habakkuk pesher; see Snyder 2000.

31 The Greek manuscripts found at Qumran, however, are written *scriptio continua*. See the plates in Skehan *et al.* (1992).

32 For a detailed discussion of these matters, see Snyder 2000.

33 There are twelve such marks: 3:12,14, 4:11,14, 6:4,12, 8:1, 9:1,13,16 (probable), 10:3, and 12:2. The function of this mark is different than the slightly larger "X" found in the Isaiah scroll. On these marks, see Tov 1996: 65–8.

34 Only two such marks in *11QTemple^b* survive; see Yadin 1977: plates 36 and 37. Van der Ploeg (1985: 9) maintains that the same scribe is responsible for *1QpHab* and for *11QTemple^b*.

35 Dionysius Thrax, for example, describes the raised dot (στιγμὴ μέση) as a place where it is necessary to take a breath (Johnson 1994: 68). Johnson observes, "Dionysius in the second century BC is thinking of punctuation dots not as grammatical dividers but as practical aids to reading aloud." Indeed, since reading aloud was the normal way of appropriating a written text in antiquity, it stands to reason that punctuation marks are intrinsically cues for performance.

36 These points are developed in Snyder 2000.

37 *Prob.* 80–3.

38 *4Q266* fr. 5 ii: [   ] יֵן וכול אֲ[שר נקל בלשונו או בקול טרוד
דבר לו ו]לֹא פצל דברו להשמיע [קולו איש מאלה לא יקרא בספר]
[התורה]למה ישוג בדבר מות[
Text and translation in Baumgarten 1996: 50 (see also p. 102).

39 Baumgarten's rendering, "with a staccato voice not dividing words" seems implicitly contradictory; מדד in the sense of "be continuous" works more intelligibly with what follows. Outside of Prov. 19:13 and 27:15, which refer to a "continual dripping," the word is not attested in the biblical materials. It occurs in *1QM* 8.9,12,16, *4QM1* fr. 11 2.6, and fr. 13 1.6, all of which refer to the blowing of horns, something that may be either continuous or intermittent.

40 *1QS* 7.1, tr. Baumgarten in Charlesworth 1994.

41 On this practice and the rabbinic strictures controlling it, see Fraade 1992 and Alexander 1985.

42 For Leviticus, see Milik 1977: 85–91; for Job, see van der Ploeg and van der Woude 1971. See also the edition by Sokoloff 1974. Two copies of the Job targum have surfaced, one from Cave 4, another from Cave 11.

43 Van der Ploeg and van der Woude 1971: 4.

44 These remarks are from Sokoloff 1974: 7–8.

45 Tov (1988: 19) claims that all the Greek and Aramaic works found at Qumran were brought in from outside the community.

46 This argument is tentatively advanced by Tov (1995b: 109).

47 See Tov's table (1995b: 90–1) and his article (1995a).

48 Compare *4QEzek^a* at roughly 29 centimeters in height.

49 Of the twenty *tefillin* fragments labeled A through U, roughly fifteen exhibit this trait. See plates 7–25 in De Vaux and Milik 1977.

50 See White 1990. She calls it an anthology based on the harmonizing tendency of the text and its small dimensions.

51 Phylacteries typically contain four selections, two from Exodus and two from Deuteronomy, often Exod. 13:1–10 and 13:11–16, as well as Deut. 6:4–9 and 11:13–21. See Tov 1995a: 586–8 for a list of texts with references.

52 Ezek. 10:5–15, 10:17–11:11, 23:14–18, 23:44–7, and 41:3–6. Sanderson (1997: 216) describes *4QEzek^a* as "a brief scroll of excerpts."

53 See Stanley 1992: 76–7.

54 Duncan *et al.* 1995: 79.

55 See Tov 1995a: 598. Tov divides this literature into three types: texts for liturgy, personal reading, and exegetical-ideological anthologies.

56 Milik (De Vaux and Milik 1977: 86–8) questions whether this manuscript, which contained only seven lines of text per column, could possibly have contained the whole book of Leviticus. He terms this work an "ouvrage liturgique ou rituel" (p. 86).

57 See Weinfeld 1992.

58 The text with plates may be found in Allegro 1968: 57–60 and plate 21. For a basic introduction, see Fitzmyer 1957.

59 Though at the end of Deut. 5:28, a backslash mark is written in the left column, designating the boundary between the two texts.

60 See Albright 1937: 175 on the Nash papyrus, also on a single leaf, a format which would lend itself to "lectionary or teaching purposes."

61 Newsom 1987.

62 See Aulus Gellius, *NA* 19.1, for the Stoic philosopher who carried Book Five of Epictetus' *Discourses* in his *sarcinula*, or "small pouch."

63 Tov (1994: 112) distinguishes between "reworking/rewriting," which involves limited intervention in the biblical text, and "rephrasing," involving major intervention even to the point of rendering the underlying biblical text hardly recognizable.

64 This observation was made by Sidnie White-Crawford in a presentation given at the 1997 Society of Biblical Literature Meeting.

65 See VanderKam *et al.* 1994. VanderKam and Milik term three of these manuscripts as "Pseudo-Jubilees." Many papyrus fragments were also recovered, which may indicate drafts or scholarly working papers, as

well as a text in which *Jubilees* is cited with "thus it is written," a formula often used to introduce scripture citations.

66 For recent studies of the Temple Scroll and its language, see Swanson 1995: 9–16 and Wise 1990. Wise claims that the author of the Temple Scroll did not use Deuteronomy directly, but rather, a "Deuteronomy Source." For a close examination of the *Hodayot* and their use of biblical vocabulary and phraseology, see Kittel 1981, especially pp. 48–53, where she touches on the use of biblical quotations.

67 Tov and White 1994: 187–351. Allegro published *4Q158* in Allegro 1968, though it now appears to belong with *4Q364–7*.

68 This would make *4QRP* the longest text of any of the preserved scrolls from Qumran, according to Tov and White (1994: 191).

69 See Tov and White 1994: 187–96 for facts on textual affinities, orthography, and paleography.

70 Strikingly, the same juxtaposition of texts also appears in the biblical manuscript *4QNum^b*.

71 For these and other juxtapositions, see Tov 1992: 50–1.

72 So Tov and White 1994: 207, though the subject of the second-person utterance is not clear from what remains of the text.

73 The latter, however, is known from *11QTemple*.

74 Translation by O.S. Wintermute (1985: 2:83). Originally written in Hebrew, *Jubilees* is now extant in full only in Ethiopic. Some traces of Greek and Latin translations are also extant. Its date of authorship predates the Qumran community.

75 E.g., the meeting between the angels and Abraham at the Oaks of Mamre and the destruction of Sodom.

76 The banishment of Hagar in *Jub.* 17.

77 This latter story may be inspired by Abraham's actions in Gen. 15:11.

78 Translation by Fitzmyer (1971b). The text is extant in Aramaic, the original language in which it was composed, and probably dates from the first century BCE. The text is somewhat lacunose, and I have not reproduced all of Fitzmyer's brackets and conjectures. The text in italics represents Fitzmyer's judgment about direct borrowings of biblical expressions.

79 See Bernstein 1996. For example, the mention of Hagar at the end of the story anticipates Genesis 16:1, where Hagar is described as an Egyptian maidservant.

80 Indeed, the language and orthography of the *GenAp* (of which only a single copy was recovered) suggest it was not generated within the Qumran scribal community. See Tov 1986 and Tov 1988.

81 Twenty different copies, including three "pseudo-Jubilees" texts. See VanderKam 1994. I shall return to *Jubilees* below.

82 On study practices at Qumran, see Fraade 1993. *CD* and *1QS* may derive from different but related communities. *CD* has often been taken to refer to the wider Essene movement, while *1QS* may refer more specifically to the sectarian polity at Qumran proper. See Fraade 1993: 46, n. 1, on the possibility of different practices between the central group and its satellites.

83 *1QS* 6.6–7 (tr. Baumgarten in Charlesworth 1994). Another

NOTES

permissible translation of על יפות איש לרעהו would be "concerning the
right conduct of a man with his companion." See Fraade 1998: 66, n. 24.
84 On דרש, see Fraade 1998: 66–7.
85 *1QS* 6.7–8 (tr. Baumgarten in Charlesworth 1994).
86 In general, the five books of Moses were referred to as the "Book" of
Moses, e.g., *4QMMT* (= *4Q397* fr. 7–8). In *1QS* 7.1–2, however,
immediately after the remark about stumbling while reading the book
or saying prayers, it is stated that the person who speaks against "one of
the priests who are registered in the book" shall be punished for one
year. This certainly does not refer to the Torah.
87 *1QS* was a popular document at Qumran, being found in twelve copies
from Caves 1 and 4, and in scripts dating from different times; two
copies on papyrus were also discovered. On the study of משפט, see
Fraade 1993: 57, 66–7.
88 The Examiner (המבקר) may be distinguished from the Overseer
(האיש הפקוד), who appears in *1QS* 6.14. The Examiner appears also
in *CD* 15.14, 9.18–19, 22, 13.6–7, 13. In *CD* 14.11, the Examiner
has the same moderating prerogative: "By his word shall all the members of the congregation enter each in his turn. And any matter about
which a person may wish to speak, let him address the Examiner . . . "
89 See *1QS* 6.10–12: "No-one should talk during the speech of his fellow
before his brother has finished speaking. And neither should he speak
before one whose rank is listed before his own" (tr. García Martínez).
This tightly controlled scenario is not unlike the scene described by
Philo in *Prob.* 81.
90 *1QSa* 1.4–5, tr. García Martínez (1995: 126).
91 So Fraade 1993: 46.
92 Perhaps *4QMMT* was itself read in the context of study or liturgy. One
could cite the letters of Paul as a parallel for such an activity, or the
study of letters from community leaders among Epicureans. See the
discussion of *PHerc.* 1005 in Ch. 2, esp. col. 17.5–11 ed. Angeli (1988:
181).
93 Tr. Qimron and Strugnell 1994: 59 (= *4Q397* 14–21 i 10). Strugnell
(1994) offers a partial retraction of some of the assertions made in the
DJD volume. He believes it represents an early stage of the sect, perhaps
even antecedent to it, and that claims about the Teacher of Righteousness as the author cannot be maintained.
94 *CD* MS A 7.17. See Knibb 1987: 57, 62–3, on this difficult text.
95 *CD* 10.6, 13.2, 14.7, *1QSa* 1.7. For Schiffman (1975: 44), the term
refers to the Torah; Joseph Baumgarten and Daniel Schwartz consider
this to have been "a book of Torah interpretations by Qumran teachers"
(in Charlesworth 1994: 2:45, n. 153). Charlesworth (1994: 1:111, n.
14) draws attention to *4Q417* fr. 2 col. 1.16–17, which speaks of the
"meditation on a book of memorial" (הגוי לספר זכרון) as something
engraved by God "through all times for the Sons of Seth." On this, see
Harrington 1994: 144–5. Yadin (1983: 1:393–4) tentatively advances
the Temple Scroll as a possible candidate for the *Book of Hagu*.
96 *CD* 20.19. A list of community members censured for various offenses
has been published by Eshel 1994; see also Reed 1996: 147–8.
97 I have used the English translation of Wintermute (1985) throughout.

98 *Jub*. 1.4; in 1.27, 30.12,21, and 50.6, it appears that the Angel of the Presence does the writing. In 50.13, Moses speaks of the tablets which "he (the Angel of the Presence) placed in my hands so that I might write for you the law of each time and according to each division of its days." In 23.32 and 33.18, we find the Angel of the Presence again commanding Moses to write what is set down on the heavenly tablets. Based on a reading from 4*QJub*ᵃ fr. 1, col. 4.6–8, VanderKam (1992: 646) observes that the original Hebrew text probably had the Angel of the Presence "cause" Moses to write, i.e., dictated to him.

99 For further remarks about Enoch as a writer, see *1 Enoch* 12–14.

100 See also *Jub*. 8.11 for the document containing Noah's will. The Book of Discipline and the Book of Life are mentioned in 36.10.

101 Heavenly tablets with legal material are found in *Jub*. 3.10,31, 4.5, 6.17,22,29,31, 15.26, 16.29, 18.19, 30.8,21, 32.10–15, 33.10–12, 49.8,17; heavenly tablets containing judgments, both positive and negative, of people and their deeds occur at 5.12,15, 16.3, 19.9, 24.33, 30.12,17–20,22–3, 31.32, and 39.6–7. There are also tablets containing the division of years from the time of creation until the renewed creation in Jerusalem.

102 4*Q pPs*ᵃ iv 7–9; the translation is from Yadin 1983: 1:396.

103 So Yadin 1983: 1:396.

104 4*QCatena*ᵃ fr. 1–4, line 14 (= 4*Q*177), in Allegro 1968: 67–74. Both Allegro and Yadin translate "second law." But as Strugnell observes (1969–71: 238, 241), the clearly preserved text reads התורה שנית ("the law again"), rather than התורה השנית ("the second law"). Yadin believes the initial ה was omitted by haplography.

105 Text in Charlesworth 1994: 2:39. A note to this text reads, "As suggested by L. Ginzberg, lines 3–4 (in brackets) appear to be a gloss inserted by someone who wished to point out that, while the law is specified (מדוקדק) in the Torah, the periods of blindness to the law are specified (מדוקדק) only in the book of *Jubilees*." If this is a gloss, it would strengthen my case. Presumably, the gloss was added by a sectarian, and reflects prevailing ideas about *Jubilees*.

106 See Yadin 1983: 1:396.

107 So Neusner 1971: 3:178. See also Sanders 1990: 97–130.

108 Cribiore 1996: 148–52.

109 *1QSa* 1.7–8.

Part 3 Judaism in Palestine

1 Kugel (1994: 264) comments on this surprising lack; so, too, Fraade 1991: 2; with the exception of Philo and the Qumran pesharim, commentary "does not appear to have been the favored mode of scriptural interpretation."

2 See Alexander 1988b: 99, for the range of texts often termed "rewritten Bible."

3 See Neusner 1971 for a systematic attempt to evaluate the historical value of the rabbinic evidence.

4 By skirting the rabbinic evidence, I have also left out of account scholarship based on this, most prominently Gerhardsson 1961. Gerhardsson's

conjectures about a "college of the apostles" engaged in midrashic exegesis have been rightly criticized as quite anachronistic; see Smith 1963. Gerhardsson's assertions appear even less plausible in light of recent form-critical studies of rabbinic materials.

5 *De Fin.* 1.3.8; Quintilian, *I.O.*, 10.4.2. On Cicero's work as a translator, see Cuendet 1933 and Boyancé 1956.

6 The Elder Pliny, *HN* 29.17: "If medical treatises are written in a language other than Greek they have no prestige even among unlearned men ignorant of Greek" (tr. Jones, LCL).

7 Consider the following text from the Hermetic Corpus, *C.H.* 16.1–2: "Translation will greatly distort the sense of the writings and cause much obscurity. Expressed in our language [the Egyptian language], the teaching conveys its meaning clearly; for the very quality of the sounds . . . [lacuna]; and when the Egyptian words are spoken the force of the things signified appears in them."

8 I owe this suggestion to Steven Fraade.

9 The prologue of Ben Sira contains a remark on the difficulty of translation: "The Law and the prophets and the rest of the books have no small difference when they are expressed in the original language." For conflicting attitudes towards translation, see Brock 1992.

10 See Shutt 1985.

11 By "Septuagint," I mean the Greek Bible as a whole, not just the Greek version of the Pentateuch.

12 One of these contested renderings was παρθένος in Isa. 7:14, which translated the Hebrew *'almah*, or young woman, with no presuppositions about virginity necessarily implied. Justin's *Dialogue with Trypho*, ch. 43, registers this change and Justin's implicit objection to it: "your teachers dare to say that it is not said in the prophecy of Isaiah, 'Behold, a virgin will conceive' (ἡ παρθένος ἐν γαστρὶ ἕξει), but 'Behold a young woman will become pregnant and bear a son'" (ἡ νεᾶνις ἐν γαστρὶ λήψεται καὶ τέξεται υἱόν).

13 Thackery (1923: 14) speaks of Aquila's "monstrosities."

14 So Barthélemy (1963: ix), who observes that LXX Ecclesiastes is several centuries later than LXX Genesis.

15 Several monographs have appeared that treat the textual history of individual books, among them Shenkel 1968, O'Connell 1972, and Bodine 1980.

16 Based on the different Hebrew text types that surfaced at Qumran, W.F. Albright writes, "We now know that in the fragments so far described from the Pentateuch and the Former Prophets . . . the Greek translators were almost slavish in their literalism" (Albright 1974: 329).

17 The seminal work on the subject is by Barthélemy (1963), who bases his claims on a roll of the Minor Prophets discovered in 1952. Barthélemy argued convincingly that the version of the Minor Prophets contained in this scroll proved the existence of a pre-Aquilan revision of the LXX. Jellicoe (1973) provides a short review of the history of scholarship before Barthélemy; Munnich (1987) provides a review and assessment of the questions raised by Barthélemy, and presses his own claims for a "pre-καίγε" overhaul of the LXX based on the text of Psalms.

18 Barthélemy dates the roll on which his discovery of the καίγε recension

is based to the end of the first century CE, though C.H. Roberts places it earlier, from 50 BCE to 50 CE; Schubart leans towards a date late in the first century BCE. See Barthélemy 1953: 19; so also Kahle 1959: 226–7. As to the span of time over which καίγε texts were generated, Kraft (1965: 479–80) gives a suitably cautious answer: "Neither can the καίγε group as a whole be so confidently and schematically dated before Aquila, although probably the Aquila school must be seen as commencing its work after the earlier representatives of the καίγε group . . . have begun their labors."

19 Barthélemy 1963: 267.

20 So Munnich 1987: 217: "les «devanciers d'Aquila» possèdent eux-mêmes dans le Psautier grec un devancier . . . "

21 Some scholars have referred to "Ur-Theodotion" or "Proto-Theodotion," e.g., Thackery 1923: 24–8. Barthélemy (1963: 148–56) identifies this figure as Jonathan ben Uzziel, a rabbi from the first half of the first century CE, though this particular claim has been contested; see Kraft 1965: 480.

22 See, for example, Tov 1971. Another contender for an early recension of the Greek Bible is the "proto-Lucianic" recension, which some scholars claim predates καίγε. See Cross 1964; but cf. Tov 1972: 302: "the existence of a proto-Lucianic revision of the LXX has not been established." A fairly recent review of the proto-Lucian debate is that of Fernández Marcos 1984.

23 Based on the work of Barthélemy and others, Bodine (1980: 11–30) lists thirty characteristics of the καίγε recension; Hyvärinen (1977: 86–7) distills ten distinct characteristics of Aquila's translating habits.

24 E.g., Hebrew employs two forms of the first-person pronoun, אֲנִי and אָנוֹכִי, with no clear difference in meaning, and the Septuagint renders both by ἐγώ. The καίγε version, however, translates the former by ἐγώ, the latter by ἐγὼ εἰμί; the Septuagint translates the preposition מֵעַל by ἀπὸ or ἐπάνω; καίγε employs ἐπάνωθεν only.

25 On Symmachus' style, see Salvesen 1991. Fernández Marcos 1979: 110–13 also gives a concise summary of Symmachus' stylistic tendencies.

26 Brock 1979: 73: "the *sensus de sensu* approach can be seen as bringing the original to the reader, whereas in the *verbum e verbo* translation . . . the effect is to bring the reader to the original." Barr (1979: 311) describes this as an "imitative" style of translation: "Here translation is conceived not so much as a statement in Greek of the *sense* of the Hebrew: rather, or at least in addition, it is a guide in Greek to the *form* of the Hebrew . . . ," in other words, *verbum de verbo*, rather than *sensus e sensu*. But as Barr points out (p. 312), Aquila is not rigidly consistent in this area.

27 In a school setting, time was available to solve exegetical difficulties, and a teacher or more experienced student (see Epictetus, *Disc.* 2.17.35, 1.26.13) would have been on hand to explain problems that arose. See Brock 1979: 74: "The availability of such an expositor is essential if the techniques of literal translation are to be pushed to the extreme." Barthélemy suggested that such literalistic texts were produced by rabbinic schools (specifically, that of Akiva) which were practicing a detailed style of exegesis for which such texts might have been especially suited.

28 Alexander (1992: 147) remarks that Aquila's translation may have functioned as a "crib" for Greek speakers who wanted to follow the Hebrew original.

29 Conventional wisdom has it that the targums were for the benefit of the Aramaic-speakers who no longer understood biblical Hebrew. Another view is that the language situation in Galilee was in fact more multilingual than hitherto suspected, and that the audience may have been able to attend to both the Hebrew and the Aramaic. Fraade (1992: 283) describes the practice of targum as a "mediating accompaniment" to scripture.

30 Veltri (1994: 108) describes Aquila's translation as a targum since it is clearly used in tandem with a Hebrew text.

31 Fraade (1992: 254) observes that while Josephus, Philo, and the New Testament all mention public reading of scripture, there is no mention of its translation into Aramaic.

32 "Onkelos" may be a corrupted version of "Aquilas." The Babylonian Talmud (B) *Megilla* 3a assigns the targum of the Pentateuch to "Onkelos the proselyte under the guidance of R. Eliezer and R. Yehoshua," while the Palestinian Talmud (P) *Megilla* 71a attributes the Greek translation to Aquila: "Aquilas the proselyte translated the Pentateuch before R. Eliezer and R. Yehoshua." According to Silverstone (1931), Aquila wrote both the Greek and Aramaic translations; Barthélemy (1963: 152–3) believes that the reference in the Babylonian Talmud is simply mistaken. But recently, the Palestinian provenance of Onkelos and its traditional attribution has come into question; see Cook 1994.

33 Arguments for a second-century date are based on the similarity between the Aramaic of these targums and other extant literature. See Alexander 1988a: 247; so too Cook 1994: 150 ("preceding 200 CE").

34 Kahle (1959) and his students have argued strenuously that the so-called "Palestinian Targums," which include *Neofiti*, the *Fragmentary Targum*, and (sometimes) *Pseudo-Jonathan* are pre-Christian. So, for example, Díez Macho 1959, closely followed by Le Déaut 1978: 17. But see York 1974 and Kaufman 1985 for rejoinders.

35 Alexander 1988a: 217.

36 Useful tools for comparison are the editions containing Aramaic text and English translation of *Onkelos* in Aberbach and Grossfeld 1982, Drazin 1990 and 1994. Extensive footnotes document the differences between the Aramaic translation and the Masoretic Text (MT). In the examples that follow, I have used the translation and notes of Aberbach and Grossfeld. Other differences and additions are noted in Vermes 1963 and Bowker 1967.

37 Here and in what follows, "Glory of the Lord" is substituted for "Lord," in order to distance God from direct action; similarly in v. 15 with "Memra" (Aramaic for "word").

38 Aberbach and Grossfeld remark that this emphasizes the power and inexorability of the Conquest (1982: 170, n. 8).

39 Locating God at Beth-el might have implicitly demoted Jerusalem as the true cult center of Jewish religion. Furthermore, Beth-el had gained a reputation as a center of the calf-cult, and the Aramaic translator apparently does not wish to locate the divine presence so specifically.

40 *T.O.* replaces metaphorical language with concrete language.
41 "Eyes darker than wine" in the Masoretic Text would also support the translation "his eyes shall be red from or dull with wine." While clearly metaphorical, the translator/rewriter takes the opportunity to sanitize a biblical text that might appear to justify drunkenness.
42 See Aberbach and Grossfeld 1976 for detailed commentary.
43 At *T.O. Gen.* 18:23 it is God's anger that will destroy Sodom, not God himself; *T.O. Gen.* 18:33 has "the Glory of the Lord ascended," where the MT has "the Lord went his way"; the "Word of the Lord" comes to Abimelech in *T.O. Gen.* 20:3, rather than God himself; in *T.O. Gen.* 21.17, the cry of Ishmael "comes" to the Lord; in the MT, the Lord "hears" it.
44 *T.O. Gen.* 18.30, 32 modifies the typically Hebrew phrase for God's anger (God's nose became hot); Abimelech speaks "before" his servants, rather than "into their ears," as the Hebrew has it in *T.O. Gen.* 20.8.
45 *T.O.* has Rekem and Hagra for MT Kadesh and Shur in Gen. 20:1; modernizing of terms for currency in 20.16; Mount Moriah, the site of the sacrifice of Isaac, is termed "the land of worship" in *T.O.*; see Aberbach and Grossfeld 1982: 128, n. 1: "Since Mt. Moriah later became the site of the Temple of Jerusalem (cf. II Chron. 3:1), [Onkelos'] anachronistic rendering is an attempt to depict Mt. Moriah as a cult center even in the Patriarchal Age." Similarly in *T.O. Gen.* 22.14: "here shall (future) generations worship," a phrase missing from MT.
46 In Gen. 20.17, the MT seems to say that God kept Abimelech from bearing children.
47 *T.O. Gen.* 19.15 adds the comment that Lot's daughters were faithful to him.
48 In *T.O. Gen.* 18.1, God is revealed in the plain of Mamre, rather than by the oak trees, in order to distance God from sacred groves; at *T.O. Gen.* 18.12, Sarah's reference to sexual pleasure is altered; at 18.25, Abraham's rather saucy address to God is muted; in *T.O. Gen.* 20.13, God brings Moses "near to the fear of Him"; *T.O.* changes the phrase אֹתִי הִתְעוּ, which means literally "God caused me to err"; a phrase which might be interpreted as a bribe paid to Sarah is reworked in *T.O. Gen.* 20:16.
49 E.g., *T.O. Gen.* 2:7, where the "Lord reveals himself," an expression which *T.O.* usually avoids.
50 Silverstone (1931) argued that Aquila wrote both the Greek translation bearing his name and *T.O.* as well, but there is widespread skepticism regarding this claim.
51 Barthélemy (1963) linked Aquila with the conservative school of Akiva, and "Ur-Theodotion" with Hillel.
52 Though Thackery (1923: 24–8) and Jellicoe (1973: 23) believe that the reviser whose text lies behind the late second-century Theodotion may have worked in Ephesus.
53 On literature that might be described as "rewritten Bible," see Nickelsburg 1984, Harrington 1986, Fishbane 1988, and Alexander 1988b.
54 See Attridge 1984: 212–13.
55 See the introductions to the work by Murphy (1993: 1–8), who draws

on the insights afforded by narrative criticism, Harrington (1985: 297–303), and the introduction in Perrot and Bogaert (1976).

56 Harrington believes the work originated "around the time of Jesus" (Harrington 1985: 299).

57 Murphy (1993: 20) also finds four basic categories of material, similar to the ones I have proposed.

58 See also 64:7, where, in an effort to discourage the apparent efficacy of magical practices portrayed in the biblical story, Samuel *redivivus* says to Saul and the medium, "do not boast, King, nor you, woman; for you have not brought me forth."

59 See Barton 1994. I will return to this subject in the following section.

60 Perrot and Bogaert 1976: 33–9. Perrot's arguments have merit, but do not command unqualified assent. His claim that *LAB* focuses on certain texts of importance to the festal calendar seems overstated. *LAB* devotes far more attention to things other than narratives read on feast days. These receive treatment because they are important in liturgy and in life, but they do not receive special emphasis relative to other themes in the text.

61 On the recent discovery of the Jericho synagogue with an attached dining area, see the account of Ehud Netzer in a *New York Times* article from March 30, 1998. The article from *The Times* and from the *Jerusalem Post* may be retrieved from Donald G. Binder, "Second Temple Synagogues," <http://www.smu.edu/~dbinder/index.html>.

62 *CPJ* 138, 139.

63 See Pliny, *Ep.* 3.1.9; Aulus Gellius, *NA* 3.19, 13.11, 15.2, 19.7.

64 See Seneca, *Ep. Mor.* 88.40.

65 Allen Hilton drew my attention to this passage.

66 2 Macc. 2:25: ἐφροντίσαμεν τοῖς μὲν βουλομένοις ἀναγινώσκειν ψυχαγωγίαν, τοῖς δὲ φιλοφρονοῦσιν εἰς τὸ διὰ μνήμης ἀναλαβεῖν εὐκοπίαν, πᾶσιν δὲ τοῖς ἐντυγχάνουσιν ὠφέλειαν. There appears to be a distinct difference here between ἀναγιγνώσκειν and ἐντυγκάνειν. The latter seems to be inclusive of the other terms that describe the reading.

67 See also Quintilian, *I.O.* 10.7.28: "As regards writing, this is certainly never more necessary than when we have frequently to speak *ex tempore.*" Another germane parallel, which post-dates our period of interest, is the use of written ὑπομνήματα by Jewish students learning the Oral Law. See Lieberman 1962: 83–99.

68 See Perrot 1988 for a useful introduction and bibliography.

69 *SEG* 8 (1936) §170. However, Kee (1992: 4–7) questions the pre-70 date, based on the dislocation of the stone bearing the inscription.

70 *CIJ* 1.327, 343, 401, 516, 517, 522. These chests are typically shown with their doors open, Torah Scrolls resting inside. Generally, six or nine scrolls (1.327, 401) are shown, though 1.522 features twenty-four scrolls. The epitaphs, however, are datable only to the third or fourth century CE.

71 On the *'aron*, and the inscription, see White (1997: 37), who suggests that the ark for the scrolls did not come into use until the second century CE.

72 On the inscription, see Ameling 1993; on 498–9, Ameling discusses other evidence on reading in synagogues.

73 It was Mishnaic practice to read while standing as a sign of respect. See *Yoma* 7.1 and *Sotah* 7.8.

74 Kraabel (1979: 487) suggests that the "Eagle Table" in the Sardis synagogue may have functioned as a "monumental and imposing lectern."

75 See Birt [1907] 1976 and Marrou 1937 for artistic representations of readers. See also Beazley 1948 with plates of readers on red-figure vases.

76 Perhaps it is called Moses' seat because it is from such a seat that "Moses' voice," i.e., in the reading of Torah, proceeds. An ornate marble chair with a footstool was found in the synagogue at Delos, though its position on the West wall does not recommend it as a place suitable for addressing the rest of the room. It was probably the seat of honor accorded to the leader of the synagogue or perhaps an honored guest. See Matt. 23:6, regarding the scribes and Pharisees who φιλοῦσιν τὰς πρωτοκαθεδρίας ἐν ταῖς συναγωγαῖς.

77 "Unfold" is the clear sense of the term, and seems to suggest a book in codex form: πτύχες is the basic word for writing tablets (e.g., Eur. *IA* 98: ἐν ... δέλτου πτυχαῖς γράψας); Luke 4:17 is the only usage of πτύσσω or ἀναπτύσσω with βιβλίον in the first century. Clement of Alexandria (*Strom.* 6.15) quotes a section from the *Preaching of Peter* which uses similar language: ἀναπτύξαντες τὰς βίβλους ἃς εἴχομεν τῶν προφητῶν. At a slightly later date, the action is applied to γραμματεῖα, wooden tablets bound together (Ps.-Lucian, *Dem.* 25.10). It would be anachronistic to assume, however, that codices were in use in Palestinian synagogues at this early date. In fact, this may be a Lucan slip for later Christian practice. Even so, it may count as an early testimony to the use of the codex in public reading. It is also used for the "spreading out" of entrails before the haruspex (Epictetus, *Disc.* 1.17.21). I am grateful to Roger Bagnall for drawing my attention to this word.

78 In the Qumran Isaiah scroll, Isa. 61:1 is marked only by a short intralinear space, which would not easily catch the eye of a reader.

79 Based on his personal experiments with rolls of wallpaper, Skeat (1981) estimates that a practiced individual might roll up a long roll in the space of two minutes while standing; with the help of a table, the same operation requires forty-five seconds.

80 A similar impulse may be at work in Luke 2:46, where Jesus is found at the Temple "sitting in the midst of the teachers, listening and questioning them." Sitting and questioning is a posture more appropriate to a teacher than a student. There is an interesting contrast here to the presentation of Peter and John as ἀγράμματοι καὶ ἰδιῶται. As argued by Allen Hilton (1997), the author of Acts gains a rhetorical advantage by having illiterates produce παρρησία in Acts 4:13, but there would be no advantage, at least for a Greco-Roman audience, by portraying Jesus as illiterate.

81 See Perrot 1988: 138–44.

82 The paragraphing of the Isaiah scroll is suggestive here, since the sections delineated by *paragraphoi* often coincide with the blocks of text that appear in later lectionaries. See Perrot 1988: 156.

83 See Sanders 1992: 170–82 for sober reflections on the identity of the scribes and their profession, corrected for the tendentiousness of the Gospels and Josephus; also Saldarini 1988, Schwartz 1992, and Schams 1998.

84 Grabbe 1996: 39. So too, Goodman 1994: 104: "what in the Jewish background could have come through to the early Church to encourage them to depict Jewish scribes as they did?"

85 The substitution of "teacher" for "ruler's staff" is probably based on the similarity between מחוקק (staff) and חק (statute, law). In Sir. 10:5, γραμματεύς was used to render מחוקק. Interestingly, the Qumran sectarians made a similar move in CD 6:7–8: "And the scepter (מחוקק) is the Interpreter of the Torah." See Fraade 1993: 60.

86 Mark 8:31, 10:33, 14:1.

87 Stendahl (1968) finds evidence of scribal activity in the use of quotations from the Old Testament.

88 Ezra is called ὁ γραμματεύς in LXX 2 Esdr. 18:1 (= Neh. 8:1). The sequence σοφός–γραμματεύς also appears in 1 Cor. 1:20.

89 Scribes are in the employ of Pharaoh (AJ 2.205, 209, 234); of Saul the King of Israel (AJ 7.110); of David (AJ 7.293), of Joash (AJ 9.164), and of Josiah (AJ 10.55); at AJ 11.248, while suffering insomnia, King Artaxerxes of Persia summons a scribe to read to him from his records; in AJ 11.271, royal scribes draft a letter; at AJ 11.128 and 12.142, Josephus speaks of the "scribes of the temple"; in AJ 20.208–9, Zealots kidnap the γραμματεύς serving Eleazar, captain of the Temple.

90 E.g., forging documents, in AJ 16.319. Philo (Flac. 3) speaks of scribes in the employ of Flaccus as "instructors" or "advisors" (ὑφηγήται).

91 See EAH (1990) [1991] 29–31 or SEG 41 (1991) §323 for an inscription from Messenia which mentions οἱ σύνεδροι καὶ ὁ γραμματεύς, apparently connected with τὸ ἱερὸν τᾶς Μεσσάνας; a γραμματεύς is connected with the temple of the cult of the Lion in Leontopolis: see Bernand 1990: 71–2 (synopsis in SEG 40 [1990]); a decree in honor of the Emperor Tiberius set up in 14 CE mentions ὁ γραμματέος Συνέδρων, where the plural Συνέσρων means simply ἡ βουλή, according to LSJ (s.v. σύνεδρος II.2); an epitaph from Arnaut-Keni in Bithynia bears the name of Sanbatis, γραμματεὺς καὶ ἐπιστάτης τῶν παλαιῶν.

92 E.g., TAM V,2 #1031 (see synopsis in SEG 41 §1008); a glance at the index of OGIS discloses many other examples. This was true also of Jewish organizations: see CIJ 1:253 (§138).

93 SEG 43 (1993) §743.

94 The title was bestowed on children as young as six years of age. See Leon 1960: 186.

95 Leon 1960: 185, n. 1, notes the egregious misspellings in an epitaph written by a scribe for his daughter (CIJ 102).

96 This might explain the (by Greco-Roman standards) puzzling use of the term γραμματεῖς instead of γραμματικοί, which would have been much more appropriate to their role as interpreters of texts. The use of the term γραμματεῖς instead of γραμματικοί is one of the "oddities" of the New Testament depiction of scribes, according to Goodman 1994: 103.

NOTES

97 Barthélemy 1963: 148–56. Thackery (1923) located his "Ur-Theodotion" in Asia Minor, based on the use of certain words of Asian provenance.
98 See Kraft 1965: 480, who calls it an "intriguing possibility" which "does not rise to the level of a historical probability."
99 Goodman 1994: 107.
100 Sedley 1997: 113.
101 Scholars disagree over the degree to which Hebrew was used and understood. See the discussions by Fraade 1992: 269–82 and Smelik 1995: 2–14.
102 Noted by Kugel (1994: 264–66) and Fraade (1991: 2).
103 For appropriate cautions on the Oral Law and its stature relative to Torah, see Sanders 1992: 97–130. He concludes that a body of interpretation existed that went beyond the Torah, but that it was not of greater or even equal standing with the written law.
104 The Hebrew text and this translation may be found in Lieberman 1962: 207.
105 Schwartz (1992) downplays the importance of scribes.
106 Sanders 1985: 23–58 discusses the views of Käsemann, Bornkamm, Kümmel, and others on this point.
107 So Sanders 1985.

Part 4 Christian groups

1 A point made by James Robinson at the Society of Biblical Literature Conference in 1997, in the context of a panel review of Gamble 1995.
2 For a recent treatment of Patristic exegesis, see Young 1997.
3 Roberts 1979 is a distinguished attempt in this direction.
4 Many aspects of Christian literary culture, namely, the preference for the codex, the circulation of Christian literature, bibliographic habits, etc., have been the subject of a study by Harry Gamble (Gamble 1995); Alexander 1998 is also important. Essays in Bauckham 1998 discuss the circulation of and audience for texts in the early stages of the Christian movement; see also Kenyon 1932.
5 See Harris 1989 and the responses in Beard 1991; for Christians specifically, see Gamble 1995: 1–41 and Hilton 1997.
6 Stock 1983 and 1990; McKenzie 1987.
7 See M. Parry 1930 and 1932, A. Parry 1971, Lord 1960 and 1991, and Havelock 1963, 1982 and 1986. The studies of Ong (1967 and 1982) and Kelber (1983 and 1986) have been seminal within biblical studies; essays in *Semeia* (1994) follow and develop these studies further. Achtemeier 1990, for example, brings insights from orality theory to bear on exegesis; he differs from Kelber at significant points.
8 Lucian, *Double Indictment* 11 (tr. Harmon, LCL).
9 See Quintilian *I.O.* 1.5–6 on correctness with the forms of words; 1.11 on delivery; on tone and breathing, 11.3.30–65.
10 Quintilian *I.O.*1.11.15–18, 11.3.65–160.
11 Philostratus, *Lives of the Sophists* 601.
12 See Sandy 1997, Stanton 1973, and Dill 1956: 334–83. Galen, no friend of the sophists, participates enthusiastically in the rhetorical

283

culture of the second century, as demonstrated in von Staden 1997. Judge (1960: 126) claims that ancient observers would have viewed Paul as a sophist, with the understanding that a sophist is simply a traveling public speaker or teacher with a reputation and a retinue of students.

13 This quotation from Collart is taken from Sandy 1997: 182.

14 See Porphyry, *Life* 20.51, and Philostratus, *Lives of the Sophists* 628. For philosophical debate and disputation in a slightly later period than that of the present study, see Lim 1995.

15 On Galen's public displays of medical expertise, see von Staden 1994 and 1997.

16 *De libr. propr.* 2 (19.22K = *Scr. Min.* 2:101 ed. Müller): ὁπότε προῆλθον ἐπιδείξων ἐμαυτὸν οὐδὲν ἐψευσμένον ἐν τοῖς ἀνατομικοῖς ὑπομνήμασιν, εἰς τὸ μέσον ἀνέθηκα τὰ τῶν ἀνατομικῶν ἁπάντων βιβλία τὴν ἐξουσίαν δοὺς ἑκάστῳ τῶν παρόντων ὃ βούλεται μόριον ἀνατμηθῆναι προβάλλειν, κτλ. The reference and translation are from von Staden 1997: 43.

17 This is the translation of P.N. Singer (1997: 10).

18 *De libr. propr.* 1 (*Scr. Min.* 2:95 ed. Müller). The reference is from von Staden 1997: 49. Cf. Singer 1997: 6.

19 See Galen, *On Examinations by Which the Best Physicians Are Recognized*, ed. Iskander 1988: 69, 115–17.

20 Barton (1994) explores agonal motifs in the fields of astrology, physiognomics, and medicine.

21 ". . . the schematic nature of this elaboration [i.e., the types of pulse] is understandable when its genesis is set in the two contexts of the apprenticeship and the ἀγών" (Barton 1994: 162).

22 How did education in a Jewish school in Palestine in 10–20 CE take place? Paul is the product of such a milieu. People have assessed his level of education based on his use of rhetorical devices; on this, see Malherbe 1983: 34–45, 55–9. But I am unaware of any study which considers the way Paul deploys and explains written texts as evidence for the nature of Jewish education in the first century.

23 Biblical scholars have long been interested in Paul's use of scripture. Four major studies are Stanley 1992, Hays 1989, Koch 1986, and Ellis 1957.

24 On social stratification in Corinth, see Theissen 1988.

25 Harris (1989: 323–32) claims that general literacy rates in ancient Greece were probably around 10 percent of the general population, slightly higher for men, lower for women; higher for the upper classes, falling off rapidly for lower classes.

26 See also Acts 13:5,14, 14:1, 17:10,17, 18:4, 19:8. Acts 13:14–43 features Luke's account of a Pauline sermon, which features a narrative retelling of the Hebrew bible that centers on Jesus the Messiah as its keystone, followed by several scripture proof-texts drawn from the Prophets.

27 See Stowers 1984 for the argument that Paul's teaching took place largely in private homes, not in synagogues.

28 Fr. 8 ed. Des Places (1973).

29 Προσεποιεῖτο ἐξηγεῖσθαι σοφίαν νόμων τῶν Μωυσέως.

30 *AJ* 18.81–2, tr. Feldman (LCL). The verb φοιτᾶν has schoolish connotations; the phrase ἐς διδασκάλου φοιτᾶν means "go to school" (e.g., Philostratus, *Lives of the Sophists* 557).

31 See Scott 1995: 115: "To attract the reader's (and buyer's) attention, they [books] were filled with claims that the work in hand had been discovered in a tomb, dug up out of the ground, dictated in a vision, copied from a stele, translated from the Egyptian, etc." Georgi (1986: 162–4) gives examples drawn from the Hermetic Corpus, the Book of Elchasai, and others.

32 The text reads: ὃς κατʼ ὀφθαλμοὺς Ἰησοῦς Χριστὸς προεγράφη ἐσταυρωμένος.

33 This is the NRSV translation; the text reads as follows: ὅσα γὰρ προεγράφη, εἰς τὴν ἡμετέραν διδασκαλίαν ἐγράφη, ἵνα διὰ τῆς ὑπομονῆς καὶ διὰ τῆς παρακλήσεως τῶν γραφῶν τὴν ἐλπίδα ἔχωμεν.

34 A similar use of the term is found in Eph. 3:3. In Jude 4, it has the sense of "foretold."

35 E.g., Lightfoot (1870: 248): "This sense, however, is excluded here, as the words κατʼ ὀφθαλμούς forbid the supposition that the apostle is here speaking of the *predictions* of the Old Testament, even if such a sense were otherwise likely"; Zahn (1905: 139) takes a similar approach. Lagrange (1950: 57) agrees that the normal sense is "écrire d'avance," but believes this cannot be the meaning here because "les Écritures n'ont point été écrites pour les Galates . . . et la prédication n'est point une écriture"; cf. 1 Cor. 9:10.

36 See Betz 1979: 131. Later commentators, e.g., Martyn (1998: 283) and Matera (1992: 112) are content to quote Betz.

37 For references, see Schlier 1965: 120, n. 1 and Betz 1979: 131. Of the texts cited there, Quintilian *I.O.* 6.2.29–32 is most apropos. Here the speaker who wishes to persuade a jury will call before his mind the images or φαντασίαι that will generate emotions of horror or pity in himself: "From such impressions arises that ἐνάργεια which . . . makes us seem not so much to narrate as to exhibit the actual scene, while our emotions will be no less actively stirred than if we were present at the actual occurrence" (tr. Butler, LCL). To this, one might add *I.O.* 2.15.7, not adduced by Betz: "Thus, when Antonius in the course of his defence of Manius Aquilius tore open his client's robe and revealed the honourable scars which he had acquired while facing his country's foes, he relied no longer on the power of his eloquence, but appealed directly to the eyes of the Roman people" (tr. Butler).

38 As its lexical entry in LSJ s.v. ὀφθαλμός indicates.

39 So also Ephraim the Syrian, according to Zahn 1905: 139. Some Latin writers, Victorinus and Ambrosiaster, for instance, employed *proscribere*, which carries the sense of "post publicly."

40 As at Quintilian, *I.O.* 1.1.27.

41 Martyn 1998: 301 (on Gen. 12:3), 304, 434 on the Sarah–Hagar material in ch. 4, and 309 on Deut. 27:26. Barrett (1982) makes the same point with reference to Gen. 21:1–10.

42 Hays 1989: 112.

43 See Cribiore 1996: 152. Cf. Betz (1979: 314), who believes the letters were written in large characters as a way of adding stress.

44 I owe this observation to Allen Hilton.

45 Since it bears so crucially on the theological interpretation of the letter, the question of Paul's audience in Rome has been the subject of much study. The collection of articles in Donfried 1991 is most useful, Wiefel's article in particular. Scholarly opinion currently favors a gentile majority in the Roman church. Stowers 1994 argues that "the Jew" addressed in Rom. 2:17–29 is a rhetorically constructed Jewish teacher, and does not represent actual Jewish readers.

46 In 2 Cor. 3:14–15, Paul does refer to the reading of the "old covenant," which he implicitly equates with the reading of Moses. This, however, refers to the reading performed by Jews, probably in a synagogue context. Singing is also mentioned by Pliny the Younger (*Ep.* 10.96); nothing is said about the reading of scripture.

47 On the question of factions in Corinth, see Dahl 1967 and Meeks 1983: 117–18.

48 Acts 18:24: ἀνὴρ λόγιος, κατήντησεν εἰς Ἔφεσον, δυνατὸς ὢν ἐν ταῖς γραφαῖς . . . ἐλάλει καὶ ἐδίδασκεν ἀκριβῶς τὰ περὶ τοῦ Ἰησοῦ.

49 When looking at Paul's letters for "types" of language reflective of actual discourse, biblical scholars have fixed on the so-called diatribal aspects of Paul's letters. Direct address, counter-address, rhetorical questions directed at fictive and sometimes foolish opponents and a paratactic style that mimics actual speech are generally taken to constitute diatribal utterance. The landmark study within biblical studies is Bultmann 1910. For a précis of Bultmann's claims, see Donfried 1974; above all, see Stowers, 1981: 1–78 on the history of diatribe scholarship before and after Bultmann; further discussion in Leopold 1983, Gottschalk 1982 and 1983, Jocelyn 1982 and 1983, and Kern 1998: 110–11, 242.

50 This is implicit in the expression καθὼς γέγραπται, his favorite citation formula, which typically follows a theological assertion or ethical appeal. He uses it sixteen times; other variants utilizing καθὼς are not uncommon, e.g., καθὼς προείρηκεν Ἡσαΐας, in Rom. 9:29.

51 Hays 1989: 79: "Adopting an uncharacteristic exegetical format, Paul offers a running line-by-line pesher commentary on the passage." I would demur from describing this as pesher commentary, though one can see a family resemblance.

52 It figures prominently in the articles by Ward, Dewey, and Wire in *Semeia* 1994; see also Hays 1989: 73–83, and Suggs 1967.

53 E.g., in Alexander of Aphrodisias, where it very often introduces the paraphrase that immediately follows a lemma, e.g., *in An Pr.* 208.8, 256.32, 281.15, 288.29, 302.18, 302.33,34, 304.19, 308.6, 311.2, *et passim*; *in Top.* 88.25. Philo also employs the term on occasion (*Leg All.* 3.57, *Her.* 33, 214) though he prefers the more dramatic "what is this?" (τί δὲ τοῦτ᾽ ἐστίν, at *Leg. All.* 2.98, *Her.* 274, *Cong.* 81, *Mos.* 1.111, *Spec. Leg.* 4.59, *Virt.* 166, *Praem.* 111, *Prov.* 2.48).

54 In 1 Cor. 15:27, Paul does not say what the scripture means, but what it does not mean: "'For God has put all things in subjection under his feet.' But when it says, 'All things are put in subjection,' it is plain that this does not include the one who put all things in subjection under him."

55 Suggs 1967: 303, following Kirk 1950.
56 On this passage, see Hays 1989: 111–21.
57 For a detailed treatment of this passage, see Meeks 1982.
58 The author of the *Gospel of Truth* has gone one step farther with the notion of "Christ as text" with his meditation on Jesus as "the living book" (*GTr* 19:34–20:38). This passage also features the same descent–ascent pattern as the "Christ hymn" in Philippians 2:6–11.
59 Meeks (1982: 65, 73) sees the passage as a pre-existing homily.
60 Stanley 1992: 78; Stanley is preceded in this judgment by Koch 1986: 253.
61 Römer 1996.
62 The editors of this text note the presence of three types of punctuation, the low stop, the middle stop, and the high stop (στιγμὴ κάτω, στιγμὴ μέση, and στιγμὴ ἄνω). On the στιγμή, see Johnson 1994.
63 Von Staden 1997: 44–5 discusses Galen's alternating teaching venues of δημοσίαι and ἰδίαι.
64 Von Staden 1997.
65 This polemic rests on certain attitudes about writing as a surrogate for personal presence. In some quarters, writing was viewed as the work of a suspicious anti-social individual who was unwilling to engage in dialogue with fellow citizens or to risk cross-examination. Off in a corner with their books and tablets, writers were up to no good. See Steiner 1994.
66 Georgi (1986: 89–101) points to the exegesis of texts as one strategy employed by traveling teachers, though the evidence he compiles is not overwhelming. His reconstruction makes much of the so-called "divine man" idea, and the claims of Paul's opponents to be such individuals. In light of the waning fortunes of the divine man concept (see Holladay 1977), it is preferable to see the polemic in 2 Corinthians against the backdrop of agonal competition among teachers anxious to make a positive impression on students and patrons.
67 The first known example, no longer extant, is a commentary on Proverbs by Theophilus of Antioch, *c.* 180 CE.
68 See Löhr 1996 and Layton 1987: 438–42.
69 See Brooke 1891, Pagels 1973.
70 The letter is difficult to date precisely. It may be placed with certainty before the time of Clement of Alexandria, who quotes it as scripture, and after the destruction of the temple. Prigent (Prigent and Kraft 1971: 27) believes that the degree of evident separation from Judaism and the embryonic ecclesiastical organization suggest a date in the second half of the second century. But certainly these criteria obtained at different places at different times. The letters of Ignatius testify to a Christianity separate from Judaism and a fairly developed ecclesiastical apparatus already in the early part of the second century. Following K. Wengst, Neymyer (1989: 169, n. 1) dates it *c.* 130, based on the remarks in *Barn.* 16 about the reconstruction of the Temple. Lake (LCL edition of the Apostolic Fathers) places it at the end of the first or beginning of the second century.
71 On the various allusions and exegetical maneuvers, see the notes in

Prigent and Kraft 1971. The translation produced here follows that of Lake, with some alterations.

72 See Lake's note in the LCL edition of *Barnabas*, p. 361.

73 Prigent and Kraft (1971: 125, n. 1) class it as an *agraphon*, an extra-canonical saying of Jesus.

74 Some of the mixing and melding of texts, however, may derive from the author, and nothing would have prevented "Barnabas" from adding texts from his own notes, those of his teacher(s), or from memory. See Prigent and Kraft 1971: 10–11 and Prigent 1961: 16–28. In the latter, Prigent points to five kinds of evidence in favor of the source hypothesis: (1) groups of citations, (2) incorrect attribution, (3) textual variants shared by authors working in different milieux, (4) similar series of citations in separate authors, and (5) a citation group which is put to different uses in different contexts.

75 A full bibliography on the Testimony Book Hypothesis would be ponderous. See Fitzmyer 1957 and Gamble 1995: 24–8; Hodgson (1979) gives a history of the issue and supplies bibliography.

76 Von Campenhausen 1969: 195.

77 See Neymyer, 1989: 172–6. He points to other early Christian literature where the same remark occurs.

78 Justin is one example of a person who worships with other Christians but also styles himself as a teacher and speaks of the "employment of teachers" (χρησθεῖν διδασκάλῳ). He also mentions a certain Ptolemy who was a "teacher of Christian doctrines" (*2 Ap.* 2). In Eusebius *HE* 7.7.4, Eusebius alludes to members of congregations who were simultaneously patronizing teachers that Eusebius considers heterodox.

79 Hatch [1889] 1970: 203–7 argues for the use of such books, as does Jaubert (1971: 43–4), while Clarke (1937: 31) rather breezily asserts that Clement is not using such sources.

80 A convenient introduction to the question is given by Gamble 1995: 54–66; he also advances the claim that the codex was especially suitable for the Corpus Paulinum and that this accounts for Christian adoption of the codex for its texts. Roberts 1954 also contains a great deal of information on the subject.

81 A theologically tendentious version of this was originally proposed by Katz (1945); Gamble (1995: 270, n. 60) is unconvinced: "it is not obvious why such a differentiation should have been thought necessary or desirable."

82 The convenience aspects of the codex, ease of use, suitability for reference, compactness, etc., have often been noted. McCormick (1985) argues that codices were especially suited for the traveling lifestyle of Christian teachers.

83 Roberts 1979: 20. In an earlier work, Roberts (1954) argued that the Gospel of Mark was committed to papyrus notebooks and that this cleared the way for Christian adoption of the codex, a view that is modified in Roberts 1979. As noted, Gamble may be numbered among the "big cause" theorists: he believes that Paul's letters were committed to codices, and that this led to the use of codices by Christians.

GENERAL CONCLUSIONS

1 As tutor to the young Nero, he was probably not acting in the capacity of a teacher of philosophy.

2 *PHerc.* 1005 col. 14.13–18 ed. Angeli 1988.

3 Thus Cicero: "I judged that any persons from our nation that felt an interest in the subject, if they were learned in the teachings of the Greeks, would sooner read Greek writings than ours, and if on the other hand they shrank from the sciences and systems of the Greeks, they would not care even for philosophy . . . " (*Acad.* 1.2.5 tr. Rackham).

4 On the popularity of Plato in the second century, see De Lacy 1974 and Trapp 1990.

5 Hadot 1987. Although Hadot does not mention it, a partial parallel may be drawn here between the philosophical Schools after the crisis of 88 BCE and that of the Jews after the destruction of Jerusalem in 70 CE.

6 Dillon 1996: 338. Alexander (1990: 233) remarks that "books are of secondary importance in the passing on of a school tradition," and that this was common to all the Hellenistic schools. Thomas (1992: 162) follows Dillon and Alexander, when she states, "while written texts were certainly not forbidden in the philosophical schools, they might be seen as subordinate to the oral methods of teaching."

7 *Ep. Mor.* 33.9.

BIBLIOGRAPHY

Aberbach, M. and Grossfeld, B. (1982) *Targum Onkelos to Genesis*, New York: Ktav.
—— (1976) *Targum Onqelos to Genesis 49*, SBL Aramaic Studies 1, Missoula, Mont.: Scholars Press.
Achtemeier, P.J. (1990) "Omne Verbum Sonat: The New Testament and the Oral Environment of Late Western Antiquity," *JBL* 109: 3–27.
Albright, W.F. (1974) "New Light on Early Recensions of the Hebrew Bible," *BASOR* 140 (1955). Reprinted in S.Z. Leiman (ed.) *Canon and Masorah of the Hebrew Bible*, New York: Ktav, pp. 327–33.
—— (1937) "The Nash Papyrus," *JBL* 56: 145–76.
Alexander of Aphrodisias. *CAG* Vols 1–3.
Alexander, L. (1998) "Ancient Book Production and the Circulation of the Gospels," in R. Bauckham 1998, pp. 71–111.
—— (1995) "Paul and the Hellenistic Schools: The Evidence of Galen," in T. Engberg-Pedersen (ed.) *Paul in His Hellenistic Context*, Minneapolis: Fortress Press.
—— (1990) "The Living Voice: Scepticism Towards the Written Word in Early Christian and in Graeco-Roman Texts," in D.J. Clines *et al.* (eds) *The Bible in Three Dimensions*, Sheffield: JSOT Press, pp. 221–47.
Alexander, P.S. (1992) "Alison Salvesen, *Symmachus* . . .," *JJS* 43: 145–7.
—— (1988a) "Jewish Aramaic Translations," in *Mikra*, pp. 217–53.
—— (1988b) "Retelling the Old Testament," in D. Carson and H. Williamson (eds) *It Is Written: Scripture Citing Scripture. Essays in Honor of Barnabas Lindars*, Cambridge: Cambridge University Press, pp. 99–121.
—— (1985) "Targums and Rabbinic Rules for the Delivery of Targum," in J.A. Emerton (ed.) *Congress Volume: Salamanca, 1983*, Suppl. to VT 36, Leiden: E.J. Brill, pp. 14–28.
Allan, D.J. (1980) "ΑΝΑΓΙΓΝΩΣΚΩ and some Cognate Words," *CQ* 30: 245–51.
Allegro, J. (1968) *Qumrân Cave 4, I*, DJDJ 5, Oxford: Clarendon Press.

—— (1959) *The People of the Dead Sea Scrolls*, London: Routledge & Kegan Paul.

Alline, H. (1915) *Histoire du texte de Platon*, Paris: Librairie ancienne Honoré Champion.

Ameling, W. (1993) "Eine liturgische Inschrift aus der Synagoge von Sardes," in K. Dietz *et al.* (eds) *Klassisches Altertum, Spätantike und frühes Christentum. Adolf Lippold zum 65. Geburtstag gewidmet*, Würzburg: Selbstverlag des Seminars für Alte Geschichte der Universität Würzburg, pp. 494–508.

Ammonius. Vols 4.3, 4.4, 4.5, and 4.6 in *CAG*.

Anderson, G. (1993) *The Second Sophistic: A Cultural Phenomenon in the Roman Empire*, London: Routledge.

Angeli, A. (1988) *Agli amici di scuola*, La Scuola di Epicuro 7, Naples: Bibliopolis.

—— (1983) "Filodemo: le altre opere," in *ΣΥΖΗΤΗΣΙΣ*.

Angeli, A. and Colaizzo, M. (1979) "I frammenti di Zenone Sidone," *CErc* 9: 47–133.

Arrighetti, G. (ed.) (1973) *Epicuro: Opere*, Torino: Giulio Einaudi.

Ascough, R. (1998) *What Are They Saying About the Formation of Pauline Churches?* New York and Mahwah, N.J.: Paulist Press.

Asmis, E. (1990) "Philodemus' Epicureanism," in *ANRW II* 36.4, pp. 2369–2406.

Attridge, H.W. (1984) "Josephus and his Works," in Stone 1984, pp. 185–232.

Attridge, H.W. *et al.* (1994) *Qumran Cave 4.VIII. Parabiblical Texts, Part 1*, DJD 13, Oxford: Clarendon Press.

Bailey, C. (1926) *Epicurus: The Extant Remains*, Oxford: Clarendon Press.

Balogh, J. (1927) "Voces Paginarum," *Philologus* 82, N.F. 36: 84–109, 202–40.

Baltes, M. (1972) *Timaios Lokros, Über die Natur des Kosmos und der Seele*, Philosophia Antiqua 21, Leiden: E.J. Brill.

Bar-Ilan, M. (1988) "Scribes and Books in the Late Second Commonwealth and Rabbinic Period," in *Mikra*, pp. 21–37.

Barnes, J. (1997) "Roman Aristotle," in J. Barnes and M. Griffin (eds) *Philosophia Togata II*, Oxford: Clarendon Press, 1–69.

—— (1991) "The Hellenistic Platos," *Apeiron* 24: 115–28.

—— (ed.) (1980) "POxy. 3320," in R.A. Coles and M.W. Haslam (eds) *The Oxyrhynchus Papyri*, London: Egypt Exploration Society.

Barnes, J. and Griffin, M. (eds) (1997) *Philosophia Togata II*, Oxford: Clarendon Press.

Barnes, J. *et al.* (tr.) (1991) *Alexander of Aphrodisias, On Aristotle Prior Analytics 1.1–7*, London: Duckworth.

Barr, J. (1979) "The Typology of Literalism in Ancient Biblical Translations," in *Nachrichten der Akademie der Wissenschaften in Göttingen*, Ph.-Hist. Kl., Jahrg 1979.

Barrett, C.K. (1982) "The Allegory of Abraham, Sarah, and Hagar in the Argument of Galatians," in *Essays on Paul*, Philadelphia: Fortress Press, pp. 154–70.

Barthélemy, D. (1963) *Les Devanciers de Aquila*, Supplements to VT 10, Leiden: E.J. Brill.

—— (1953) "Redécouverte d'un chaînon manquant de l'histoire de la septante," *RB* 60: 18–29.

Barton, T. (1994) *Power and Knowledge: Astrology, Physiognomics, and Medicine under the Roman Empire*, Ann Arbor: University of Michigan Press.

Basser, H. (1988) "Pesher Hadavar: The Truth of the Matter," *RQ* 13: 389–404.

Bastianini, G. and Sedley, D. (1995) "Commentarium in Platonis «Theaetetum»," in *Corpus*, Vol. 3, pp. 203–562.

Bauckham, R. (ed.) (1998) *The Gospels for All Christians*, Grand Rapids, Mich.: William B. Eerdmans.

Baumgarten, J. (1996) *Qumran Cave 4.XIII. The Damascus Document (4Q266–273)*, DJD 18, Oxford: Clarendon Press.

—— (1992) "The Disqualifications of Priests in 4Q Fragments of the 'Damascus Document,' a Specimen of the Recovery of pre-Rabbinic Halakha," in Trebolle Barrera and Vegas Montaner 1992, Vol. 2, pp. 503–13.

Beard, M. (ed.) (1991) *Literacy in the Roman World*, Ann Arbor, Mich.: University of Michigan Press.

Beazley, J.D. (1948) "Hymn to Hermes," *AJA* 52: 336–40.

Becchi, F. (1994) "Aspasio commentatore di Aristotele," in *ANRW II* 36.7, pp. 5365–96.

Bellincioni, M. (1979) *Lettere a Lucilio, Libro XV: le lettere 94 e 95*, Brescia: Paideia.

Benko, S. (1980) "Pagan Criticisms of Early Christians," in *ANRW II* 23.2, pp. 1055–118.

Bernand, É. (1990) "Le Culte du lion en basse Égypte d'après les documents grecs," *Dialogues d'histoire ancienne* 16: 63–94.

Bernstein, M. (1996) "Re-arrangement, Anticipation and Harmonization as Exegetical Features in the Genesis Apocryphon," *Dead Sea Discoveries* 3: 37–57.

—— (1994a) "4Q252: From Re-Written Bible to Biblical Commentary," *JJS* 45: 1–27.

—— (1994b) "Introductory Formulas for Citation and Re-citation of Biblical Verses in the Qumran Pesharim: Observations on a Pesher Technique," *Dead Sea Discoveries* 1: 30–70.

Betz, H.D. (1979) *Galatians: A Commentary on Paul's Letter to the Churches in Galatia*, Philadelphia: Fortress Press.

Bickel, E. (1944) "Geschichte und Recension des Platontextes," *RM* 92: 97–159.

Binder, Donald G. "Second Temple Synagogues" <http://www.smu.edu/~dbinder/index.html>

Birt, T. ([1907] 1976) *Die Buchrolle in der Kunst*, Leipzig: Teubner; repr. Hildesheim: George Olms.

Blumenthal, H.J. (1979) "Photius on Themistius (Cod. 74): did Themistius Write Commentaries on Aristotle?," *Hermes* 107: 168–82.

Bodine, W. (1980) *The Greek Text of Judges*, Harvard Semitic Monographs 23, Chico, Calif.: Scholars Press.

Bömer, F. (1953) "Der Commentarius," *Hermes* 81: 210–50.

Bonhöffer, A. ([1894] 1968) *Die Ethik des Stoikers Epiktet*, Stuttgart: F. Enke; repr. Stuttgart: Fromann.

Bott, H. (1920) *De epitomis antiquis*, Marburg: J. Hamel.

Bourdieu, P. (1990) *In Other Words: Essays Towards a Reflexive Sociology*, tr. M. Adamson, Stanford: Stanford University Press.

Bousset, W. (1915) *Jüdisch-christlicher Schulbetrieb in Alexandria und Rom. Literarische Untersuchungen zu Philo, Clemens von Alexandria, Justin und Irenäus*, Forschungen zur Religion und Literatur des Alten und Neuen Testaments 23, Göttingen: Vandenhoeck & Ruprecht.

Bowersock, G. (ed.) (1974) *Approaches to the Second Sophistic. Papers Presented at the 105th Annual Meeting of the American Philological Association*, University Park, Pa.: American Philological Society.

Bowie, E.L. (1974) "Greeks and Their Past in the Second Sophistic," in M.I. Finley (ed.) *Studies in Ancient Society*, London: Routledge and Kegan Paul, pp. 166–209.

Bowker, J. (1967) "Haggadah in the Targum Onqelos," *JSS* 12: 51–64.

Bowman, A.K. *et al.* (eds) (1975) "POxy. 3219," in *The Oxyrhynchus Papyri*, Vol. 45, London: Egypt Exploration Society.

Bowman, A.K. and Woolf, G. (eds) (1994) *Literacy and Power*, Cambridge: Cambridge University Press.

Boyancé, P. (1963) "Études philoniennes," *REG* 76: 64–110.

—— (1956) "La Connaissance du grec a Rome," *REL* 34: 111–31.

Bréhier, E. (1924–38) *Plotin*, Paris: Les Belles Lettres.

Brilliant, R. (1984) *Visual Narratives: Storytelling in Etruscan and Roman Art*, Ithaca, N.Y.: Cornell University Press.

Brisson, L. *et al.* (1982) *Porphyre, La Vie de Plotin*, 2 Vols, Paris: J. Vrin.

Broccia, G. (1979) *Enchiridion: per la storia di una denominazione libraria*, Rome: Edizione di storia e letteratura.

Brock, S. (1992) "To Revise or not to Revise: Attitudes to Jewish Biblical Translation," in G. Brooke and B. Lindars (eds) *Septuagint, Scrolls and Cognate Writings*, Atlanta, Ga.: Scholars Press, pp. 301–38.

—— (1979) "Aspects of Translation Technique in Antiquity," *GRBS* 20: 69–87.

Brooke, A.E. (1891) *The Fragments of Heracleon*, Cambridge: At the University Press.

Brooke, G. (1996a) "4Q252," in J. VanderKam (ed.) *Qumran Cave 4.XVII. Parabiblical Texts, Part 3*, DJD 22, Oxford: Clarendon Press.
—— (1996b) "4Q252 As Early Jewish Commentary," *RQ* 17: 385–401.
—— (1992) "Ezekiel in Some Qumran and New Testament Texts," in Trebolle Barrera and Vegas Montaner 1992, Vol. 1, pp. 317–38.
—— (1985) *Exegesis at Qumran. 4Q Florilegium in its Jewish Context*, JSOT Suppl. 29, Sheffield: JSOT Press.
Broshi, M. (1992) "The Archeology of Qumran – a Reconsideration," in D. Dimant and U. Rappaport (eds) *The Dead Sea Scrolls. Forty Years of Research*, Studies on the Texts of the Desert of Judah 10, Leiden: E.J. Brill, pp. 103–15.
Brownlee, W.H. (ed.) (1950) "The Habakkuk Commentary," in *The Dead Sea Scrolls of St Mark's Monastery*, 2 Vols, New Haven, Conn.: American Schools of Oriental Research.
—— (1949a) "Further Corrections of the Translation of the Habakkuk Scroll," *BASOR* 116: 14–16.
—— (1949b) "Further Light on Habakkuk," *BASOR* 114: 9–10.
Bruns, I. (1897) *De Schola Epicteti*, Kiel: Schmidt & Klaunig.
—— (1892) *Supplementum Aristotelicum* 2.2. Reprinted with translation and commentary in Sharples 1983.
Buffière, F. (1956) *Les Mythes d'Homère et la pensée grecque*, Paris: Société d'édition «Les Belles Lettres».
Bühler, W. (1977) "Die Philologie der Griechen und ihre Methoden," *Jahrbuch der Akadamie der Wissenschaften in Göttingen*: 44–62.
Bultmann, R. (1910) *Der Stil der paulinischen Predigt und die kynisch–stoische Diatribe*, Göttingen: Vandenhoeck & Ruprecht.
Busse, A. (ed.) (1887) *In Categorias*, CAG 4.1.
Cansdale, L. (1997) *Qumran and the Essenes*, Texte und Studien zum Antiken Judentum 60, Tübingen: J.C.B. Mohr.
Cantarella, R. and Arrighetti, G. (1972) "Il libro «sul tempo» (*PHerc.* 1413) dell'opera di Epicuro «sulla natura»," *CErc* 2: 5–46.
Capasso, M. (1991) *Manuale del papirologico herculanese*, Galatina: Congedo Editore.
—— (1989) "Primo supplemento al catalogo dei papiri ercolanesi," *CErc* 19: 193–265.
—— (1988) "Un libro filodemeo in due esemplari," *CErc* 18: 139–48.
—— (1981) "I «Problemi di filologia filosofica» di Mario Untersteiner," *Elenchos* 2: 375–404.
—— (1980) "PHerc. 671: un altro libro «de Signis»?," *CErc* 10: 125–8.
Carlini, A. (1972) *Studi sulla tradizione antica e medievale del Fedone*, Bibliotheca Athena 10, Rome: Edizioni dell'Ateneo.
Carmignac, J. (1969–71) "Le Document de Qumran sur Melkisédeq," *RQ* 7: 343–78.
Carruthers, M. (1990) *The Book of Memory*, Cambridge: Cambridge University Press.

Castner, C. (1988) *Prosopography of Roman Epicureans*, Frankfurt am Main: P. Lang.

Cavallo, G. (1984) "I rotoli di Ercolano come prodotti scritti. Quattro riflessione," *Scrittura e Civiltà* 8: 5–30.

—— (1983) *Libri scritture scribi a Ercolano*, First Supplement to *CErc* 13.

Cazeaux, J. (1983) *La Trame et la chaîne: ou les structures littéraires et l'exégèse dans cinq des traités de Philon d'Alexandrie*, Arbeiten zur Literatur und Geschichte des hellenistischen Judentums 15, Leiden: E.J. Brill.

Chantraine, P. (1950) "Les Verbes signifiant 'lire,'" in *Mélanges Henri Grégoire*, Annuaire del'Institut de Philologie et d'Histoire Orientales et Slaves, Tome X, Bruxelles: Secrétariat des Éditions de l'Institut.

Charlesworth, J. (ed.) (1994) *The Dead Sea Scrolls: Hebrew, Aramaic, and Greek Texts with English Translations*, 2 Vols, Tübingen: J.C.B. Mohr.

—— (1985) *The Old Testament Pseudepigrapha*, 2 Vols, Garden City, N.Y.: Doubleday.

Chartier, R. (1995) *Forms and Meanings: Texts, Performances, and Audiences from Codex to Computer*, Philadelphia: University of Pennsylvania Press.

—— (1994) *The Order of Books*, tr. L. Cochrane, Cambridge: Polity Press.

Chilton, C.W. (1971) *Diogenes of Oenoanda*, London: Oxford University Press.

—— (1967) *Diogenis Oenoandensis Fragmenta*, Leipzig: Teubner.

Christiansen, I. (1969) *Die Technik der allegorischen Auslegungswissenschaft bei Philon von Alexandrien*, Beiträge zur Geschichte der biblischen Hermeneutik 7, Tübingen: J.C.B. Mohr.

Chroust, A.-H. (1965) "The Organization of the Corpus Platonicum in Antiquity," *Hermes* 93: 34–46.

Clarke, W.K.L. (1937) *The First Epistle of Clement to the Corinthians*, London: SPCK.

Clay, D. (1990) "The Philosophical Inscription of Diogenes of Oenoanda: New Discoveries 1969–1983," in *ANRW II* 36.4, pp. 2446–559.

—— (1982) "Epicurus in the Archives of Athens," in *Studies in Attic Epigraphy, History and Topography presented to E. Vanderpool*, Hesperia Suppl. 19, Princeton, N.J.: The American Classical School at Athens, pp. 17–26.

Colardeau, T. (1903) *Étude sur Épictète*, Paris: Librairie Thorin & Fils.

Colson, F. (1940) "Philo's Quotations from the Old Testament," *JTS* 41: 237–51.

Comparetti, D. (1910) "La Bibliothèque de Philodème," in *Mélanges oferts a M. Émile Chatelain*, Paris: Librairie ancienne; repr. Geneva: Slatkine Reprints, 1976, pp. 118–29.

Conzelmann, H. (1965) "Paulus und die Weisheit," *NTS* 12: 231–44.

Cook, E.M. (1994) "A New Perspective on the Language of Onqelos and Jonathan," in D. Beattie and M. McNamara (eds) *The Aramaic Bible: Targums in their Historical Context*, JSOT Suppl. 166, Sheffield: JSOT Press, pp. 142–56.

Corpus (1995) *Corpus dei papiri filosofici greci i latini*, 5 Vols, Florence: Leo S. Olschki.

Cribiore, R. (1996) *Writing, Teachers, and Students in Greco-Roman Egypt*, Atlanta, Ga.: Scholars Press.

Crönert, W. (1975) *Studi Ercolanesi*, It. tr. Enrico Livrea, Naples: Morano.

—— (1906) *Kolotes und Menedemos*, Munich: Albert Langen Georg Müller; repr. Amsterdam: Hakkert, 1965.

—— (1903) *Memoria Graeca Herculanensis*, Leipzig: Teubner.

Cross, F.M. (1964) "The History of the Biblical Text in Light of Discoveries in the Judaean Desert," *HTR* 57: 281–9, reprinted in Cross and Talmon 1975.

Cross, F.M. and Talmon, S. (eds) (1975) *Qumran and the History of the Biblical Text*, Cambridge, Mass.: Harvard University Press, pp. 177–95.

Cuendet, G. (1933) "Cicéron et Saint Jérome traducteurs," *REL* 11: 381–400.

Dagenais, J. (1994) *The Ethics of Reading in Manuscript Culture: Glossing the Libro De Buen Amor*, Princeton, N.J.: Princeton University Press.

Dahl, N. (1967) "Paul and the Church in Corinth in 1 Cor. 1:10–4:21," in Farmer *et al.* 1967, pp. 313–35.

Daumas, F. (1961) "Littérature prophétique et exégétique égyptienne et commentaires esséniens," in *A la Rencontre de Dieu. Mémorial Albert Gelan*, Le Puy: Editions Xavier Mappus, pp. 203–21.

Davies, P. (1982) *Qumran*, Guildford, Surrey: Lutterworth Press.

Dawson, D. (1992) *Allegorical Readers and Cultural Revision in Ancient Alexandria*, Berkeley: University of California Press.

De Lacy, P. (1980) *On the Doctrines of Hippocrates and Plato*, CMG V 4,1,2, Berlin: Akademie-Verlag.

—— (1974) "Plato and the Intellectual Life of the Second Century A.D.," in Bowersock 1974, pp. 4–10.

—— (1948) "Lucretius and the History of Epicureanism," *TAPA* 79: 12–23.

—— (1943) "The Logical Structure of the Ethics of Epictetus," *CP* 38: 112–35.

De Lacy, P. and De Lacy, E. (1978) *Philodemus, On Methods of Inference*, La Scuola di Epicuro 1, Naples: Bibliopolis.

Delattre, D. (1996) "Les Mentions de titres d'oeuvres dans les livres de Philodème," *CErc* 26: 143–68.

Del Fabbro, M. (1979) "Il commentario nella tradizione papiracea," *Studia Papyrologica* 18: 69–132.

Des Places, E. (1977) *Atticus*, Paris: Société d'édition «Les Belles Lettres».

—— (1973) *Numenius; Fragments*, Paris: Société d'édition «Les Belles Lettres».

De Vaux, R. (1994) *Fouilles de Khirbet Qumrân et de Ain Feshkha*, J. Humbert and A. Chambon (eds), Novum Testamentum et Orbis Antiquus, Series Archaeologica 1, Göttingen: Vandenhoeck & Ruprecht.

—— (1973) *Archeology and the Dead Sea Scrolls*, The Schweich Lectures of the British Academy 1959, London: The British Academy.

De Vaux, R. and Milik, J. (eds) (1977) *Qumran Grotte 4, II*, DJD 6, Oxford: Clarendon Press.

De Witt, N. (1936) "Organization and Procedure in Epicurean Groups," *CP* 31: 205–11.

Dexippus. *CAG* Vol. 4.2.

Diehl, E. (1903) *Procli Diadochi in Platonis Timaeum commentaria*, Leipzig: Teubner.

Diels, H. (1917) "Philodemos Über die Götter drittes Buch, I," *Abhandlungen der königlichen preussischen Akademie der Wissenschaft, phil.-hist. Kl.*, Jahrg. 1916, Nr. 4, pp. 3–69.

—— ([1879] 1965) *Doxographi Graeci*, Berlin.

Diels, H. and Schubart, W. (1905) *Anonymer Kommentar zu Platons Theaetet (Papyrus 9782), nebst drei Bruchstücken philosophischen Inhalts (Pap. N.8; P.9766, 9569)*, Berliner Klassikertexte II, Berlin: Weidmann.

Díez Macho, F. (1959) "The Recently Discovered Palestinian Targum: Its Antiquity and Relationship with the Other Targums," *VT Suppl.* 7: 222–45.

Dill, S. (1956) *Roman Society from Nero to Marcus Aurelius*, New York: Meridian Books.

Dillon, J. (1996) *The Middle Platonists*, 2nd edn, Ithaca, N.Y.: Cornell University Press.

—— (1993) *Alcinous. The Handbook of Platonism*, Oxford: Clarendon Press.

—— (1971) "Harpocration's Commentary on Plato: Fragments of a Middle Platonic Commentary," *California Studies in Classical Antiquity* 4: 125–46.

Dillon, J. and Long, A. (eds) (1988) *The Question of "Eclecticism,"* Berkeley: University of California Press.

Dimant, D. (1984) "Qumran Sectarian Literature," in Stone 1984, pp. 483–550.

Dodge, B. (1970) *The Fihrist of al-Nadîm*, New York: Columbia University Press.

Donceel, R. and Donceel-Voûte, P. (1994) "The Archaeology of Khirbet Qumran," in M.O. Wise *et al.* (eds) *Methods of Investigation of the Dead Sea Scrolls and the Khirbet Qumran Site*, Annals of the New York Academy of Sciences 722, New York: New York Academy of Sciences, pp. 1–38.

Donfried, K. (1991) *The Romans Debate*, 2nd edn rev. and expanded, Peabody, Mass.: Hendrickson.

—— (1974) "False Presuppositions in the Study of Romans," *CBQ* 36: 332–58; repr. in Donfried (1991).

Donini, P. (1994) "Testi e commenti, manuali e insegnamento: la forma sistematica e i metodi della filosofia in età postellenistica," in *ANRW II* 36.7, pp. 5027–100.

Dooley, W., SJ (tr.) (1989) *Alexander of Aphrodisias, On Aristotle Metaphysics 1*, Ithaca, N.Y.: Cornell University Press.

Dooley, W., SJ and Madigan, A., SJ (tr.) (1992) *Alexander of Aphrodisias, On Aristotle Metaphysics 2 & 3*, London: Duckworth.

Dorandi, T. (1991) "Den Autoren über die Schulter geschaut. Arbeitsweise und Autographie bei den antiken Schriftstellern," *ZPE* 87: 11–33.

—— (1990) "Per una ricomposizione dello scritto di Filodemo sulla retorica," *ZPE* 82: 59–87.

—— (1988) "Una 'ri-edizione' antica del Περὶ εὐσεβείας di Filodemo," *ZPE* 73: 25–9.

—— (1983) "G. Cavallo, *Libri scritture scribi a Ercolano*," *Parola della Pasato* 208: 71–80.

—— (1982) "Filodemo. Gli stoici (*PHerc.* 155 e 339)," *CErc* 12: 91–133.

—— (1980) "La rassegna dei filosofi di Filodemo," *RAAN* 55: 31–49.

Dörrie, H. (1990) *Der hellenistische Rahmen des kaiserzeitlichen Platonismus: Bausteine 36–72, Text, Übersetzung, Kommentar*, Der Platonismus in der Antike Vol. 2, Stuttgart/Bad Cannstatt: Frommann-Holzboog.

Dörrie, H. and Baltes, M. (1993) *Der Platonismus im 2. und 3. Jahrhundert nach Christus: Bausteine 73–100, Text, Übersetzung, Kommentar*, Der Platonismus in der Antike Vol. 3, Stuttgart/Bad Cannstatt: Frommann-Holzboog.

Drazin, I. (1994) *Targum Onkelos to Leviticus*, New York: Ktav.

—— (1990) *Targum Onkelos to Exodus*, New York: Ktav.

Drossaart Lulofs, H.J. (1965) *Nicolaus Damascenus on the Philosophy of Aristotle*, Leiden: E.J. Brill.

Dunn, M. (1976) "Iamblichus, Thrasyllus, and the Reading Order of the Platonic Dialogues," in R. Baine Harris (ed.) *The Significance of Neoplatonism*, Norfolk, Va.: International Society for Neoplatonic Studies, pp. 59–80.

—— (1974) "The Organization of the Platonic Corpus Between the First Century B.C. and the Second Century A.D," Ph.D. diss., Yale University.

Dupuis, J. (1892) *Théon de Smyrne, exposition des connaissances mathématiques utiles pour la lecture de Platon*, Paris: Hachette et Cie.

Düring, I. (1971) "Ptolemy's Vita Aristotelis Rediscovered," in Robert B. Palmer and Robert Hamerton-Kelly (eds) *Philomathes. Studies and Essays in the Humanities in Memory of Philip Merlan*, The Hague: Martins Nijhoff, pp. 264–9.

—— ([1957] 1987) *Aristotle in the Ancient Biographical Tradition*, Göteborgs Universitets Årsskrift 63, Göteborg; repr. New York: Garland Publishing, 1987.

—— (1950) "Notes on the History of the Transmission of Aristotle's Writings," *Göteborgs Högskolas Årsskrift* 56: 37–70.

Edelstein, L. (1966) *Plato's Seventh Letter*, Philosophia Antiqua 14, Leiden: E.J. Brill.

Elias. *CAG* Vol. 18.1.

Elliger, K. (1953) *Studien zum Habakuk-Kommentar vom Toten Meer*, Beiträge zur historischen Theologie 15, Tübingen: J.C.B. Mohr.

Ellis, E. (1957) *Paul's Use of the Old Testament*, Edinburgh: Oliver & Boyd.

Emonds, H. (1941) *Zweite Auflage im Altertum*, Leipzig: Harrassowitz.

Eshel, E. (1994) "4Q477: The Rebukes of the Overseer," *JJS* 45: 111–22.

Fantham, E. (1996) *Roman Literary Culture; From Cicero to Apuleius*, Baltimore and London: The Johns Hopkins University Press.

Farmer, W.R., Moule, C.F.D., and Niebuhr, R. (1967) *Christian History and Interpretation: Studies Presented to John Knox*, Cambridge: At the University Press.

Farrington, B. (1939) *Science and Politics in the Ancient World*, London: George Allen & Unwin.

Fernández Marcos, N. (1984) "The Lucianic Text in the Books of Kingdoms," in A. Pietersma and C. Cox (eds) *De Septuaginta*, Mississauga, Ontario: Benben Books, pp. 163–74.

—— (1979) *Introduccion a las Versiones Griegas de la Biblia*, Textos y Estudios «Cardenal Cisneros» 23, Madrid.

Festugière, A.-J. (1949) *La Révélation d'Hermès Trismégiste*, Paris: Librairie Lecoffre.

Fishbane, M. (1988) "Use, Authority and Interpretation of Mikra at Qumran," in *Mikra*, pp. 339–77.

Fitzmyer, J. (1990) *The Dead Sea Scrolls. Major Publications and Tools for Study*, 2nd rev. edn, Atlanta, Ga.: Scholars Press.

—— (1971a) *Essays on the Semitic Background of the New Testament*, London: Geoffrey Chapman.

—— (1971b) *The Genesis Apocryphon of Qumran Cave 1*, 2nd rev. edn, Rome: Biblical Institute Press.

—— (1957) "'4QTestimonia' and the New Testament," *TS* 18: 513–37; repr. in Fitzmyer 1971a, pp. 59–89.

Forbes, C. (1955) "The Education and Training of Slaves in Antiquity," *TAPA* 86: 321–60.

Fosse, B., Kleve, K., and Störmer, F. (1984) "Unrolling the Herculaneum Papyri," *CErc* 14: 9–15.

Fowden, G. (1977) "The Platonist Philosopher and his Circle in Late Antiquity," *Philosophia* 7: 359–83.

Fox, R.L. (1994) "Literacy and Power in Early Christianity," in A.K. Bowman and G. Woolf (eds) *Literacy and Power in the Ancient World*, Cambridge: Cambridge University Press, pp. 126–48.

Fraade, S. (1998) "Looking for Legal Midrash at Qumran," in Stone and Chazon 1998, pp. 59–79.

—— (1993) "Interpretive Authority in the Studying Community at Qumran," *JJS* 44: 46–69.

—— (1992) "Rabbinic Views on the Practice of Targum, and Multilingualism in the Jewish Galilee of the Third–Sixth Centuries," in Levine 1992, pp. 253–86.

—— (1991) *From Tradition to Commentary*, Albany, N.Y.: State University of New York Press.

Frede, M. (1989) "Chaeremon der Stoiker," in *ANRW II* 36.3, pp. 2067–103.

Frischer, B. (1982) *The Sculpted Word*, Berkeley: University of California Press.

Fröhlich, I. (1986) "Le Genre littéraire des pesharim de Qumrân," *RQ* 12: 383–98.

Funaioli, H. (1964) *Grammaticae Romanae Fragmenta*, Roma: L'Erma de Bretschneider.

Gallo, I. (ed.) (1975) *Frammenti biografici da papiri*, 2 Vols, Rome: Ateneo & Bizarri.

Gamble, H. (1995) *Books and Readers in the Early Church*, New Haven, Conn.: Yale University Press.

García Martínez, F. (1996) *The Dead Sea Scrolls Translated*, 2nd edn, tr. W. Watson, Leiden: E.J. Brill; Grand Rapids, Mich.: William B. Eerdmans.

Gardthausen, V. (1911) *Das Buchwesen im Altertum und im byzantinischen Mittelalter*, 2nd edn, Leipzig: Von Veit.

Gavrilov, A. (1997) "Techniques of Reading in Classical Antiquity," *Classical Quarterly* 47: 56–73.

Gemelli, B. (1983) "Il primo epicureismo romano ed il problema della sua diffusione," in *ΣΥΖΗΤΗΣΙΣ*, pp. 281–90.

Georgi, D. (1986) *The Opponents of Paul in Second Corinthians*, rev. edn, Philadelphia: Fortress Press.

Gerhardsson, B. (1961) *Memory and Manuscript*, Lund: Gleerup.

Gifford, E.H. (tr.) (1903) *Eusebius: Preparation for the Gospel*, Oxford: Clarendon Press; repr. Grand Rapids, Mich.: Baker Book House, 1981.

Gigante, M. (1995) *Philodemus in Italy*, tr. D. Obbink, Ann Arbor: University of Michigan Press.

—— (1986) "Biografia e dossografia in Diogene Laerzio," *Elenchos* 7: 7–102.

—— (1983a) "Filodemo sulla libertà di parola," in *Ricerche Filodemee*, 2nd edn, rev. and exp., Naples: Gaetano Macchiaroli, pp. 55–113.

—— (1983b) "L'Epicureismo a Roma da Alcio e Filisco a Fedro," in *Ricerche Filodemee*, 2nd edn, rev. and exp., Naples: Gaetano Macchiaroli, pp. 25–34.

—— (1979) *Catalogo dei papiri ercolanesi*, Naples: Bibliopolis.

Goodman, M. (1994) "Texts, Scribes and Power in Roman Judaea," in Bowman and Woolf 1994, pp. 99–108.

Gottschalk, H.B. (1987) "Aristotelian Philosophy in the Roman World," in *ANRW II* 36.2, pp. 1079–174.

—— (1983) "More on DIATRIBAI," *Liverpool Classical Monthly* 8: 91–2.

—— (1982) "Diatribe Again," *Liverpool Classical Monthly* 7: 91–2.

Goulet-Cazé, M.O. (1982) "L'Arrière-plan scolaire de la vie de Plotin," in L. Brisson *et al.* (eds) *Porphyre, La Vie de Plotin*, 2 Vols, Paris: J. Vrin, pp. 231–327.

Grabbe, L. (1996) *An Introduction to First Century Judaism*, Edinburgh: T. & T. Clark.

Grenfell, B.P. and Hunt, A.S. (1915) *The Oxyrhynchus Papyri*, Vol. 11, London: Egypt Exploration Society.

—— (1900) *Fayûm Towns and their Papyri*, London: Egypt Exploration Fund.

Hadot, I. (1996) *Simplicius. Commentaire sur le* Manuel *d'Épictète*, Leiden: E.J. Brill.

Hadot, P. (1987) "Théologie, exégèse, révélation, écriture, dans la philosophie grecque," in M. Tardieu (ed.) *Les Règles de l'interpretation*, Paris: Les Éditions du Cerf, pp. 13–34.

Hagen, C. (tr.) (1994) *Simplicius, On Aristotle Physics 7*, London: Duckworth.

Halbauer, O. (1911) *De Diatribis Epicteti*, Leipzig: Robert Norske Bornen.

Hamerton-Kelly, R.G. (1972) "Sources and Traditions in Philo Judaeus: Prolegomena to an Analysis of His Writings," *Studia Philonica* 1: 3–26.

Hanson, A.E. (1996) "A Petition and Court Proceedings: P. Michigan inv. 6060," *ZPE* 111: 175–82.

Hanson, A.E. and Gagos, T. (1997) "Well Articulated Spaces: Hippocrates, Epidemics II 6,7–22," in *'Specimina' per il Corpus dei Papiri Greci di Medicina. Atti dell'Incontro di studio, Firenze, 28–29 marzo 1996*, Florence: Istituto Papirologico «G. Vitelli», pp. 117–40.

Harder, R. (1958) *Plotins Schriften*, Hamburg: Felix Meiner Verlag.

—— (1939) "Timaios," *RE* 6A.2: 1203–26.

Harrington, D. (1994) "Wisdom at Qumran," in Ulrich and VanderKam 1994, pp. 137–52.

—— (1986) "Palestinian Adaptations of Biblical Narratives and Prophecies," in R. Kraft and G. Nickelsburg (eds) *Early Judaism and its Modern Interpreters*, Philadelphia: Fortress Press, pp. 239–47.

—— (1985) "Pseudo-Philo," in Charlesworth 1985, Vol. 2, pp. 297–377.

Harris, W. (1989) *Ancient Literacy*, Cambridge, Mass.: Harvard University Press.

Hatch, E. ([1889] 1970) *Essays in Biblical Greek*, Oxford: Clarendon Press; repr. Amsterdam: Philo Press, 1970.

Havelock, E.A. (1986) *The Muse Learns to Write: Reflections on Orality and Literacy from Antiquity to the Present*, New Haven, Conn.: Yale University Press.

—— (1982) *The Literate Revolution in Greece and its Cultural Consequences*, Princeton, N.J.: Princeton University Press.

—— (1963) *Preface to Plato*, New Haven, Conn.: Yale University Press.

Hay, D. (ed.) (1991) *Both Literal and Allegorical: Studies in Philo of Alexandria's Questions and Answers on Genesis and Exodus*, Brown Judaic Studies 232, Atlanta, Ga.: Scholars Press.

Hay, D. (1979) "Philo's References to Other Allegorists," *Studia Philonica* 6: 41–75.

Hays, R. (1989) *Echoes of Scripture in the Letters of Paul*, New Haven, Conn.: Yale University Press.

—— (1983) "Lucius Annaeus Cornutus' Epidrome. Introduction to the Traditions of Greek Theology: Introduction, Translation, and Notes," Ph.D. Diss., University of Texas at Austin.

Hellman, M.-C. (1988) "A propos d'un lexique des termes d'architecture grecque," in D. Knoepfler (ed.) *Comptes et inventaires dans la cité grecque. Actes du colloque international d'épigraphie tenu à Neuchâtel du 23 au 26 septembre 1986 en l'honneur de Jacques Tréheux*, Neuchâtel: Faculté des Lettres, pp. 239–61.

Helmreich, G. (ed.) (1907–9) *Galeni De usu partium libri XVII*, 2 Vols, Leipzig: Teubner.

Hendrickson, G.L. (1929) "Ancient Reading," *CJ* 25: 182–96.

Hengel, M. (1971) "Proseuche und Synagoge," in G. Jeremias *et al.* (eds) *Tradition und Glaube: Das frühe Christentum in seiner Umwelt. Festgabe für Karl Georg Kuhn zum 65. Geburtstag*, Göttingen: Vandenhoeck & Ruprecht, pp. 157–84.

Hermann. See Nüsser.

Hershbell, J. (1989) "The Stoicism of Epictetus: Twentieth Century Perspectives," in *ANRW II* 36.3, pp. 2152–63.

Hijmans, B.L. (1959) *ΑΣΚΗΣΙΣ*, Assen: Van Gorcum & Company.

Hiller, E. ([1878] 1987) *Theonis Smyrnaei, Philosophi platonici expositio rerum mathematicarum ad legendum Platonem utilium*, Leipzig: Teubner; repr. New York: Garland Publishing, 1987.

Hilton, A. (1997) "The Dumb Speak: Early Christian Illiteracy and Pagan Criticism," Ph.D. diss., Yale University.

Hirschfeld, Y. (1998) "Early Roman Manor Houses in Judea and the Site of Khirbet Qumran," *JNES* 57: 161–89.

Hodgson, R. (1979) "The Testimony Book Hypothesis," *JBL* 98: 361–78.

Holladay, C. (1977) *Theios Aner in Hellenistic Judaism*, Missoula, Mont.: Scholars Press.

Horgan, M. (1979) *Pesharim: Qumran Interpretations of Biblical Books*, Washington, D.C.: Catholic Biblical Association of America.

Horna, K. (1931) "Zur epikurischen Spruchsammlung," *WS* 49: 32–9.

Howe, H. (1948) "Three Groups of Roman Epicureans," *TAPA* 79: 341–2.

Hülser, K. (1987–8) *Die Fragmente zur Dialektik der Stoiker*, 4 Vols, Stuttgart: Frommann-Holzboog.

Hyvärinen, K. (1977) *Die Übersetzung von Aquila*, Uppsala: Gleerup.

Indelli, G. (1988) *Filodemo, L'Ira*, La Scuola di Epicuro 5, Naples: Bibliopolis.

Inwood, B. (1984) "Hierocles: Theory and Argument in the Second Century AD," *OSAPh* 2: 151–83.

Irigoin, J. (1994) "Les Éditions de textes," in Franco Montanari (ed.) *La Philologie grecque à l'époque hellénistique et romaine*, Entretiens sur l'antiquité classique 40, Geneva: Fondation Hardt, pp. 39–93.

Iskander, A.Z. (ed.) (1988) *Galen. On Examinations by Which the Best Physicians Are Recognized*, CMG 4, Leipzig: Akademie Verlag.

Isnardi Parente, M. (1989) "Ierocle Stoico. Oikeiosis e doveri sociali," in *ANRW II* 36.3, pp. 2201–26.

Jachmann, G. (1941) "Der Platontext," in *Nachrichten von der Akademie der Wissenschaften in Göttingen*, Ph.-Hist. Kl.; repr. in Christian Gnilka (ed.) *Textgeschichtliche Studien*, Beiträge zur klassischen Philologie Bd. 142, Königstein: Anton Hain, 1982.

Jaeger, W. (1956) "Contemporary Evidence on the Text of the First Chapters of Aristotle's Metaphysics," *SIFC* 27–8: 150–6.

—— (1948) *Aristotle. Fundamentals of the History of his Development*, 2nd edn, tr. R. Robinson, Oxford: At the Clarendon Press.

—— (1912) *Studien zur Entstehungsgeschichte der Metaphysik des Aristoteles*, Berlin: Weidmann.

Jambert, A. (1971) *Épître aux Corinthians (par) Clément de Rome*, Paris: Les Éditions du Cerf.

Jellicoe, S. (1973) "Some Reflections on the KAIΓE Recension," *VT* 23: 15–24.

Jocelyn, H. (1983) "'Diatribes' and the Greek Book-Title Διατριβαί," *Liverpool Classical Monthly* 8: 89–91.

—— (1982) "Diatribes and Sermons," *Liverpool Classical Monthly* 7: 3–7.

Johnson, W. (1994) "The Function of the Paragraphus in Greek Literary Prose Texts," *ZPE* 100: 65–8.

Jones, A.H.M. *et al.* (1971) *Prosopography of the Later Roman Empire*, 3 Vols, Cambridge: Cambridge University Press.

Judge, E.A. (1960) "The Early Christians as a Scholastic Community," *JRH* 1: 4–15, 125–37.

Kahle, P. (1959) *Cairo Geniza*, 2nd edn, Oxford: Basil Blackwell.

Kapera, Z. (1994) "Some Remarks on the Qumran Cemetery," in Wise *et al.* 1994, pp. 97–113.

Kaster, R.A. (1988) *Guardians of Language: the Grammarian and Society in Late Antiquity*, Berkeley: University of California Press.

Katz, P. (1945) "The Early Christians' Use of Codices Instead of Rolls," *JTS* 46: 63–5.

Kaufman, S. (1985) "On Methodology in the Study of the Targums and Their Chronology," *JSNT* 23: 117–24.

Kee, H.C. (1992) "Early Christianity in the Galilee: Reassessing the Evidence from the Gospels," in Levine 1992, pp. 3–14.

Keenan, J.G. (1977) "A Papyrus Letter about Epicurean Philosophy Books," *J. Paul Getty Museum Journal* 5: 91–4.

Keil, H. (1857–80) *Grammatici Latini*, 7 Vols, Leipzig: Teubner; repr. Hildesheim: Georg Olms, 1961.

Kelber, W. (1986) "Writing is a Technology that Restructures Thought," in G. Baumann (ed.) *The Written Word*, Oxford: Oxford University Press.

—— (1983) *The Oral and the Written Gospel: The Hermeneutics of Speaking and Writing in the Synoptic Tradition, Mark, Paul, and Q*, Bloomington, Ind.: Indiana University Press (a revised edition, with a new foreword appeared in 1997).

Kennedy, G. (1984) *New Testament Interpretation through Rhetorical Criticism*, Chapel Hill/London: University of North Carolina Press.

—— (1980) *Classical Rhetoric and its Christian and Secular Tradition from Ancient to Modern Times*, Chapel Hill: The University of North Carolina Press.

—— (1963) *The Art of Persuasion in Greece*, Princeton, N.J.: Princeton University Press.

Kenny, A. (1978) *The Aristotelian Ethics*, Oxford: Clarendon Press.

Kenyon, F.G. (1951) *Books and Readers in Ancient Greece and Rome*, 2nd edn, Oxford: Oxford University Press.

Kern, P. (1998) *Rhetoric and Galatians*, Cambridge: Cambridge University Press.

Kirk, K. (1950) *The Epistle to the Romans in the Revised Edition*, The Clarendon Bible, Oxford: Clarendon Press.

Kittel, B. (1981) *Hymns of Qumran*, Chico, Calif.: Scholars Press.

Kleve, K. (1996) "How to Read an Illegible Papyrus. Towards an Edition of PHerc. 78, Caecilius Statius, *Obolostates Sive Faenerator*," *CErc* 26: 5–14.

—— (1989) "Lucretius in Herculaneum," *CErc* 19: 5–27.

—— (1979) "What Kind of Work did Lucretius Write?," *SO* 54: 81–5.

Knibb, M. (1987) *The Qumran Community*, Cambridge: Cambridge University Press.

Knox, B. (1968) "Silent Reading in Antiquity," *GRBS* 9: 421–35.

Koch, D.-A. (1986) *Die Schrift als Zeuge des Evangeliums*, Tübingen: J.C.B. Mohr.

Konstan, D., Clay, D., Glad, C., Thom, J., and Ware, J. (1998) *Philodemus, On Frank Criticism*, Society of Biblical Literature Texts and Translations 43, Atlanta, Ga.: Scholars Press.

Kraabel, A.T. (1979) "The Diaspora Synagogue: Archaeological and Epigraphic Evidence Since Sukenik," in *ANRW II* 19.1, pp. 477–510.

Kraft, R. (1965) "D. Barthélemy, *Devanciers* . . . ," *Gnomon* 37: 474–83.

Kraus, T. (1975) *Pompeii and Herculaneum*, tr. R. Wolf, New York: Harry N. Abrams.

Kroll, W. (1901) *Procli Diadochi in Platonis Rem Publicam commentarii*, Leipzig: Teubner.

Kugel, J. (1994) *In Potiphar's House: The Interpretive Life of Biblical Texts*, Cambridge, Mass.: Harvard University Press.

Lagrange, M.-J. (1950) *Saint Paul Épitre aux Galates*, Paris: Librairie Lecoffre.

Lakmann, M.-L. (1995) *Der Platoniker Tauros in der Darstellung des Aulus Gellius*, Leiden: E.J. Brill.

Lang, K. (1881) *Cornuti Theologiae Graecae Compendium*, Leipzig: Teubner.

Lasserre, F. (1991) "Anonyme. Commentaire de l'«Alcibiade I» de Platon," *Studi e testi per il corpus dei papiri filosofici greci i latini 5*, Florence: Leo S. Olschki, pp. 7–23.

Lawlor, R. and Lawlor, D. (1979) *Mathematics Useful for Understanding Plato*, San Diego: Wizards Bookshelf.

Layton, B. (1987) *The Gnostic Scriptures*, Garden City, N.Y.: Doubleday & Company.

Le Déaut, R. (1978) *Targum de Pentateuque*, SC 245, Paris: Les Éditions du Cerf.

Leon, H.J. (1960) *The Jews of Ancient Rome*, Philadelphia: Jewish Publication Society.

Leopold, J. (1983) "Characteristics of Philo's Style in the *De Gigantibus* and *Quod Deus*," in Winston and Dillon 1983, pp. 141–54.

Levine, L. (ed.) (1992) *The Galilee in Late Antiquity*, New York: Jewish Theological Seminary.

Lieberman, S. (1962) "The Publication of the Mishnah," in *Hellenism in Jewish Palestine*, 2nd rev. edn, New York: Jewish Theological Seminary, pp. 83–99.

Lightfoot, J. (1870) *St. Paul's Epistle to the Galatians*, Andover: Warren F. Draper.

Lim, R. (1995) *Public Disputation, Power, and Social Order in Late Antiquity*, Berkeley: University of California Press.

—— (1993) "The Auditor Thaumasius in the *Vita Plotini*," *JHS* 113: 157–60.

Löhr, W. (1996) *Basilides und seine Schule; Eine Studie zur Theologie-und Kirchengeschichte des zweiten Jahrhunderts*, Tübingen: J.C.B. Mohr.

Long, A.A. (1992) "Stoic Readings of Homer," in R. Lamberton and J.J. Keany (eds) *Homer's Ancient Readers: The Hermeneutics of Greek Epic's Earliest Exegetes*, Princeton, N.J.: Princeton University Press, pp. 41–66.

Long, A.A. and Sedley, D.N. (eds) (1987) *The Hellenistic Philosophers*, 2 Vols, Cambridge: Cambridge University Press.

Longo Auricchio, F. (1977) *ΦΙΛΟΔΗΜΟΥ ΠΕΡΙ ΡΗΤΟΡΙΚΗΣ libros primum et secundum*, Naples: Giannini.

—— (1971) "Su alcune liste di libri restituite dai papiri," *RAAN* 46: 143–50.

—— (1970) "Per una nuova edizione del secondo libro della «Retorica» di Filodemo," *RAAN* 45: 119–28.

Longo Auricchio, F. and Capasso, M. (1987) "I rotoli della villa Ercolanese: dislocazione e ritrovamento," *CErc* 17: 37–47.

Longo Auricchio, F. and Tepedino Guerra, A. (1981) "Aspetti e problemi della dissidenza epicurea," *CErc* 11: 25–40.

Lord, A.B. (1991) *Epic Singers and Oral Tradition*, Ithaca, N.Y.: Cornell University Press.

—— (1960) *The Singer of Tales*, Cambridge, Mass.: Harvard University Press.

Lutz, C. (1947) *Musonius Rufus. "The Roman Socrates,"* reprinted from Yale Classical Studies Volume 10, New Haven, Conn.: Yale University Press.

Lynch, J.P. (1972) *Aristotle's School*, Berkeley: University of California Press.

McCormick, M. (1985) "The Birth of the Codex and the Apostolic Lifestyle," *Scriptorium* 39: 150–8.

McDonnell, M. (1996) "Writing, Copying, and Autograph Manuscripts in Ancient Rome," *Classical Quarterly* 46: 469–91.

Mack, B. (1984) "Philo Judaeus and Exegetical Traditions in Alexandria," in *ANRW II* 21.1, pp. 228–71.

McKenzie, D.F. (1987) "The Sociology of a Text: Oral Culture, Literacy and Print in Early New Zealand," in P. Burke and R. Porter, *The Social History of Language*, Cambridge: Cambridge University Press, pp. 161–97.

—— (1986) *Bibliography and the Sociology of Texts*, The Panizzi Lectures 1985, London: The British Library.

McNamee, K. (1992) *Sigla and Select Marginalia in Greek Literary Papyri*, Papyrologica Bruxellensia 26, Brussels: Fondation égyptologique reine Élisabeth.

Madigan, A. (tr.) (1993) *Alexander of Aphrodisias, On Aristotle Metaphysics 4*, London: Duckworth.

Mahaffy, J. (1891–3) *The Flinders Petrie Papyri*, 2 Vols, Dublin: Academy House.

Mahdi, M. (1962) *Alfarabi's Philosophy of Plato and Aristotle*, New York: Free Press of Glencoe.

Malherbe, A.J. (1983) *Social Aspects of Early Christianity*, Philadelphia: Fortress Press.

Manetti, D. and Roselli, A. (1994) "Galeno commentatore di Ippocrate," in *ANRW II* 37.2, pp. 1529–635.

Mansfeld, J. (1994) *Prolegomena: Questions to be Settled before the Study of an Author, or a Text*, Leiden: E.J. Brill.

Marg, W. (1972) *De natura mundi et animae*, Philosophia Antiqua 24, Leiden: E.J. Brill.

Marquardt, J., Müller, I., and Helmreich, G. (eds) (1884–93) *Claudii Galeni Pergameni Scripta minora*, 3 Vols, Leipzig: Teubner; repr. Amsterdam, 1967.

Marrou, H.I. (1956) *A History of Education in Antiquity*, tr. G. Lamb, Madison, Wis.: University of Wisconsin Press.

—— (1937) *Μουσικος Ανηρ*, Grenoble: Allier.

Martin, D. (1995) *The Corinthian Body*, New Haven, Conn.: Yale University Press.

Martin, M. (1958) *The Scribal Character of the Dead Sea Scrolls*, Louvain: University of Louvain.

Martyn, J.L. (1998) *Galatians*, Anchor Bible Commentary 33A, New York: Doubleday.

Mason, H. (1974) *Greek Terms for Roman Institutions. A Lexicon and Analysis*, Toronto: Hakkert.

Matera, F. (1992) *Galatians*, Sacra Pagina Series 9, Collegeville, Minn.: The Liturgical Press.

Mazzoli, G. (1989) "Le 'Epistula Morales ad Lucilium' di Seneca," in *ANRW II* 36.3, pp. 1823–77.

Meeks, W. (1985) "Breaking Away: Three New Testament Pictures of Christianity's Separation from the Jewish Communities," in J. Neusner and E. Frerichs (eds) *To See Ourselves as Others See Us*, Chico, Calif.: Scholars Press.

—— (1983) *The First Urban Christians*, New Haven, Conn.: Yale University Press.

—— (1982) "'And Rose up to Play': Midrash and Paraenesis in 1 Corinthians 10:1–22," *JSNT* 16: 64–78.

Meiser, K. (1880) *Anicii Manlii Severini Boetii commentarii in librum Peri hermeneias*, Leipzig: Teubner; repr. New York: Garland, 1987.

Mejer, J. (1978) *Diogenes Laertius and his Hellenistic Background*, Hermes Einzelschriften 40, Wiesbaden: Franz Steiner.

Mercken, H.P.F. (1990) "The Greek Commentators on Aristotle's Ethics," in Sorabji 1990, pp. 407–33.

Mewaldt, J. (1914) *In Hippocratis de natura hominis commentarii*, CMG 5,9,1, Leipzig/Berlin, 1914.

Mikra (1988) *Mikra. Text, Translation, Reading and Interpretation of the Hebrew Bible in Ancient Judaism and Early Christianity*, Assen/Maastricht: Van Gorcum; Philadelphia: Fortress Press.

Milik, J.T. (1977) *Qumran Grotte 11*, DJD 6, Oxford: Clarendon Press.

—— (1959) *Ten Years of Discovery in the Wilderness of Judea*, tr. J.M. Strugnell, London: SCM Press.

Momigliano, A. (1941) "Benjamin Farrington, *Science and Politics in the Ancient World*," *JRS* 31: 149–57.

Moraux, P. (1986a) "Les Débuts de la philologie aristotélicienne," in G. Cambiano (ed.) *Storiografia e dossografia nella filosofia antica*, Torino: Tirrenia, pp. 127–47.

—— (1986b) "Diogène Laërce et le Péripatos," *Elenchos* 7: 247–96.

—— (1984) *Der Aristotelismus bei den Griechen von Andronikos bis Alexander von Aphrodisias II*, Berlin: Walter de Gruyter.

—— (1974) "La Critique d'authenticité chez les commentateurs grecs d'Aristote," in *Mélanges Mansel*, Ankara: Türk Tarih Kurumu, pp. 265–88.

—— (1973) *Der Aristotelismus bei den Griechen von Andronikos bis Alexander von Aphrodisias I*, Berlin: Walter De Gruyter.

—— (1970) *D'Aristote à Bessarion*, Laval: Les Presses de l'Université Laval.

—— (1969) "Eine Korrektur des Mittelplatonikers Eudoros zum Text der Metaphysik des Aristoteles," in R. Stiehl and H.E. Stier (eds) *Beiträge zur alten Geschichte und deren Nachleben. Festschrift für Franz Altheim um 6.10.1968*, Berlin: Walter de Gruyter, pp. 492–504.

—— (1967) "Alexander von Aphrodisias Quaest. 2.3," *Hermes* 95: 159–69.

—— (1951) *Les Listes anciennes des ouvrages d'Aristote*, Louvain: Éditions Universitaires de Louvain.

—— (1942) *Alexandre d'Aphrodise. Exégète de la Noétique d'Aristote*, Bibliothèque de la Faculté de Philosophie et Lettres de l'Université de Liège 99, Liège: Faculté de Philosophie et Lettres.

Moraux, P. and Wiesner, J. (eds) (1983) *Zweifelhaftes im Corpus Aristotelicum*, Berlin: Walter de Gruyter.

Moreschini, C. (1990) "L'esegesi del *Fedro* e il medioplatonismo," *Koinonia* 14: 29–39.

Most, G. (1989) "Cornutus and Stoic Allegoresis," in *ANRW II* 36.3, pp. 2014–65.

Müller, C.W. (1975) *Die Kurzdialoge der Appendix Platonica*, Munich: W. Fink.

Müller, I. (ed.) (1884–93). See Marquardt *et al.* 1884–93.

Munnich, O. (1987) "La Première Révision de la Septante," in *ANRW II* 20.1, pp. 190–220.

Murphy, F.J. (1993) *Pseudo-Philo, Rewriting the Bible*, Oxford: Clarendon Press.

Naveh, J. (1986) "A Medical Document or a Writing Exercise? The So-Called 4QTherapeia," *IEJ* 36: 52–5.

Neusner, J. (1971) *The Rabbinic Traditions About the Pharisees Before 70*, 3 Vols, Leiden: E.J. Brill.

Newsom, C. (1987) "Merkabah Exegesis in the Qumran Sabbath Shirot," *JJS* 38: 11–30.

Neymyer, U. (1989) *Die Christlichen Lehrer im zweiten Jahrhundert*, Leiden: E.J. Brill.

Nickelsburg, G. (1984) "The Bible Rewritten and Expanded," in Stone 1984, pp. 89–156.

Nicole, J. (1903) "Un Questionnaire de chirurgie," *Archiv für Papyrusforschung* 2: 1–3.

Niehoff, M. (1992) "A Dream Which Is Not Interpreted Is Like a Letter Which Is Not Read," *JJS* 43: 58–84.

Nikiprowetzky, V. (1983) "L'Exégèse de Philon d'Alexandrie dans le *De Gigantibus* et le *Quod Deus sit Immutabilis*," in D. Winston and J. Dillon (eds) *Two Treatises of Philo of Alexandria*, Chico, Calif.: Scholars Press, pp. 5–75.

—— (1977) *Le Commentaire de l'écriture chez Philon d'Alexandrie*, Leiden: E.J. Brill.

Nock, A.D. (1933) *Conversion*, London: Oxford University Press.

—— (1931) "Kornutos," *RE Suppl.* 5: cols 995–1005.

Nüsser, O. (1991) *Albins Prolog und die Dialogtheorie des Platonismus*, Stuttgart: B.G. Teubner. (Uses pagination of Hermann's earlier critical edition.)

Obbink, D. (ed.) (1996) *Philodemus, On Piety, Part 1*, Oxford: Clarendon Press.

O'Connell, K. (1972) *The Theodotionic Revision of the Book of Exodus*, Cambridge, Mass.: Harvard University Press.

Olbricht, T. (1990) "An Aristotelian Rhetorical Analysis of 1 Thessalonians," in D. Balch *et al.* (eds) *Greeks, Romans, and Christians; Essays in Honor of Abraham J. Malherbe*, Minneapolis: Fortress Press, pp. 216–36.

Olivieri, A. (ed.) (1914) *Philodemi ΠΕΡΙ ΠΑΡΡΗΣΙΑΣ*, Berlin: Teubner. (Cited as *De lib. dic.* [*De libertate dicendi*].)

Olympiodorus. *CAG* Vols 12.1 and 12.2.

Ong, W. (1982) *Orality and Literacy: The Technologizing of the Word*, London and New York: Methuen.

—— (1967) *The Presence of the Word: Some Prolegomena for Cultural and Religious History*, New Haven, Conn.: Yale University Press.

Osann, F. (1844) *L. Annaeus Cornuti De Natura Deorum*, Göttingen: Libraria Dieterichiana.

Oswiecimski, S. (1978) "The Enigmatic Character of Some of Plato's Apocrypha," *Eos* 66: 31–40.

Owens, J. (1984) "The Present Status of Alpha Elatton in the Aristotelian Metaphysics," *Archiv für Geschichte der Philosophie* 66: 148–69.

Pagels, E. (1973) *The Johannine Gospel in Gnostic Exegesis: Heracleon's Commentary on John*, Society of Biblical Literature Monograph Series 17, Nashville, Tenn.: Abingdon Press.

Parente, M.I. (1989) "Ierocle Stoico. Oikeiosis e doveri sociali," in *ANRW* II 36.3, pp. 2201–26.

Parry, A. (1971) *The Making of Homeric Verse*, Oxford: Clarendon Press.

Parry, M. (1930) "Studies in the Epic Technique of Oral Verse-Making. I. Homer and Homeric Style," *HSCP* 41: 73–147.

—— (1932) "Studies in the Epic Technique of Oral Verse-Making. II. The Homeric Language as the Language of an Oral Poetry," *HSCP* 43: 1–50.

Pasquali, G. (1988) *Storia della traduzione e critica del testo*, Florence: Casa Editrice le Lettere.

Perrot, C. (1988) "The Reading of the Bible in the Ancient Synagogue," in *Mikra*, pp. 137–59.

—— (1969) "Petuhot et Setumot. Étude sur les alinéas du Pentateuque," *RB* 76: 50–91.

Perrot, C. and Bogaert, P.-M. (eds) (1976) *Pseudo-Philon, Les Antiquités bibliques*, Vol. 2, SC 230, Paris: Les Éditions du Cerf.

Pfann, S. (1996) "4QDaniel^d (4Q115): A Preliminary Edition with Critical Notes," *RQ* 17: 39–71.

Pfeiffer, R. (1968) *History of Classical Scholarship*, Oxford: Clarendon Press.

Philip, J.A. (1976) "The Platonic Corpus," *Phoenix* 24: 296–308.

Philippson, R. (1941) "Philonides," *RE* 20, 1, cols 63–73.

—— (1939) "Die Quelle der epikureische Götterlehre in Ciceros erstem Buche de natura deorum," *SO* 19: 36–40.

—— (1921) "Zu Philodems Schrift Über die Frömmigkeit," *Hermes* 56: 355–410.

Philoponus. *CAG* Vols 13–17.

Pigeaud, J. (1981) *La Maladie de l'âme. Étude sur la relation de l'âme et du corps dans la tradition médico-philosophique antique*, Paris: Société d'édition «Les Belles Lettres».

Pine-Coffin, R.S. (tr.) (1961) *Saint Augustine, Confessions*, Harmondsworth: Penguin Books.

Plezia, M. (1946) *De Andronici Rhodii Studiis Aristotelicis*, Archiwum Filologisczne 20, Krakow: Polska Akademi Umiejetnosci.

Pohlenz, M. (1964) *Die Stoa*, Göttingen: Vandenhoeck & Ruprecht.

Praechter, K. (1990) "Review of the Commentaria in Aristotelem Graeca," tr. V. Caston, in Sorabji 1990, pp. 31–54. (A translation of Praechter [1937] "Die griechischen Aristoteleskommentare," *ByzZ* 37.)

—— (1909) "Rez. Anonymer Kommentar zu Platons Theaetet (Papyrus 9782), hrsg. von H. Diels und W. W. Schubart," *GGA* 171: 530–47; repr in H. Dörrie (ed.) *Kleine Schriften*, Hildesheim: Georg Olms, 1973, pp. 264–81.

—— (1908) "Rez. Davidis prolegomena et in Porphyrii Isagogen commentarium," *GGA* 170: 209–39.

—— (1906) "Rez. CAG 22.2," *GGA* 168: 861–907.

—— (1905) "Rez. Procli Diadochi in Platonis Timaeum commentaria ed. Diehl," *GGA* 167: 505–35.

—— (1904) "Rez. Olympiodori prolegomena et in categ. comm. ed. Busse," *GGA* 166: 374–91.

Prigent, P. (1961) *Les Testimonia dans le Christianisme primitif. L'Épître de Barnabé (I–XVI) et ses sources*, Paris: Gabalda.

Prigent, P. and Kraft, R. (1971) *Épître de Barnabé*, SC 172, Paris: Les Éditions du Cerf.

Puglia, E. (1988) *Demetrio Lacone, Aporie testuali ed esegetiche in Epicuro*, La Scuola di Epicuro 8, Naples: Bibliopolis.

—— (1987) "*PHerc.* 1420/1056: un volume dell'opera «Della natura» di Epicuro," *CErc* 17: 81–3.

—— (1986) "L''enchiridion' di Demetrio Lacone," *CErc* 16: 45–51.

—— (1982) "La filologia degli Epicurei," *CErc* 12: 19–34.

Purcell, N. (1983) "The *Apparitores*: A Study in Social Mobility," *Papers of the British School at Rome* 51: 125–73.

Qimron, E., and Strugnell, J. (1994) *Qumran Cave 4.V. Miqsat Ma'ase ha-Torah*, DJD 10, Oxford: Clarendon Press.

Rabe, H. (1963) *Ioannes Philoponus de aeternitate mundi contra Proclum*, Hildesheim: Georg Olms.

Rabinowitz, I. (1973) "Pesher/Pittaron. Its Biblical Meaning and Its Significance in the Qumran Literature," *RQ* 8: 219–32.

Radaway, Janice (1991) *Reading the Romance: Women, Patriarchy, and Popular Literature*, 2nd edn, Chapel Hill, N.C.: University of North Carolina Press.

Rawson, E. (1985) *Intellectual Life in the Late Roman Republic*, London: Duckworth.

Reale, G. (1974) *Aristotele, Trattato sul cosmo*, Naples: Luigi Loffredo.

Redfors, J. (1960) *Echtheitskritische Untersuchung der apuleischen Schriften De Platone und De mundo*, Lund: C.W.K. Gleerup.

Reed, S. (1996) "Genre, Setting, and Title of 4Q77," *JJS* 47: 147–8.

Regenbogen, O. (1950) "Πίναξ," *RE* 20, 2, cols 1408–82.

Reich, R. (1994) "A Note on the Function of Room 30 (the 'Scriptorium') at Khirbet Qumran," *JJS* 44: 157–60.

Renehan, R. (1990) "Werner Jaeger: The Oxford Classical Text of Aristotelis Metaphysica (1957)," in W.M. Calder III (ed.) *Werner Jaeger Reconsidered*, Illinois Classical Studies Suppl. 3, Atlanta, Ga.: Scholars Press, pp. 147–60.

Reppe, R. (1906) *De L. Annaeo Cornuto*, Leipzig: Norske.

Rist, J. (1965) "Neopythagoreanism and 'Plato's' Second Letter," *Phronesis* 10: 78–81.

—— (1964) "Demetrius the Stylist and Artemon the Compiler," *Phoenix* 18: 2–8.

Robert, L. (1937) *Études anatoliennes*, Paris: De Boccard.

Roberts, C.H. (1979) *Manuscript, Society and Belief in Early Christian Egypt*, Schweich Lectures 1977, London: Oxford University Press.

—— (1954) "The Codex," *Proceedings of the British Academy* 40: 169–204.

Romeo, C. (1988) *Demetrio Lacone, La poesia (PHerc. 188 e 1014)*, La Scuola di Epicuro 9, Naples: Bibliopolis.

—— (1979) "Demetrio Lacone sulla grandezza del sole (PHerc. 1013)," *CErc* 9: 11–35.

Römer, C.E. (1996) "Gemeindebrief, Predigt oder Homilie über den Menschen im Angesicht des Jüngsten Gerichts," in C. Römer and T. Gagos (eds) *P. Michigan Koenen. Michigan Texts Published in Honor of Ludwig Koenen*, Amsterdam: J.C. Giessen, pp. 35–43.

Rosenthal, F. and Walzer, R. (1943) *Plato Arabus*, London: Warburg Institute.

Runia, D. (1991) "Secondary Texts in Philo's *Quaestiones*," in Hay 1991, pp. 41–79.

—— (1990) *Exegesis and Philosophy. Studies on Philo of Alexandria*, Aldershot: Variorum.

—— (1987) "Further Observations on the Structure of Philo's Allegorical Treatises," *VC* 41: 105–38.

—— (1986) "How to Read Philo," *Nederlands Theologisch Tijdschrift* 40: 185–98; repr. in Runia 1990.

—— (1984) "The Structure of Philo's Allegorical Treatises", *VC* 38: 211–26; repr. in Runia 1990.

Russell, D. (1990) *Antonine Literature*, Oxford: Oxford University Press.

Rutgers, L. *et al.* (eds) (1998) *The Use of Sacred Books in the Ancient World*, Leuven: Peeters.

Said, E. (1979) "The Text, the World, the Critic," in J. Harari (ed.) *Textual Strategies. Perspectives in Post-Structuralist Criticism*, Ithaca, N.Y.: Cornell University Press, pp. 161–88.

Saldarini, A. (1988) *Pharisees, Scribes, and Sadducees in Palestinian Society*, Wilmington, Del.: Michael Glazier.

Salvesen, A. (1991) *Symmachus in the Pentateuch*, Manchester: University of Manchester.

Sanders, E. (1992) *Judaism: Practice and Belief, 63 BCE–55 CE*, London: SCM Press.

—— (1990) *Jewish Law from Jesus to the Mishnah*, London: SCM Press.

—— (1985) *Jesus and Judaism*, Philadelphia: Fortress Press.

Sanderson, J. (1997) "4QEzek^{a-c}," in Ulrich *et al.* 1997.

Sandy, G. (1997) *The Greek World of Apuleius: Apuleius and the Second Sophistic*, Leiden: E.J. Brill.

Sawyer, J. (1999) *Sacred Languages, Sacred Texts*, London: Routledge.

Sbordone, F. (1947) *Philodemi Adversus {Sophistas}*, Naples: Luigi Loffredo.

Scarpat, G. (1975) *Lettere a Lucilio*, Brescia: Paidea Editrice.

Schäfer, K. (1959) "Eisagoge," *RAC* 4: 862–904.

Schams, C. (1998) *Jewish Scribes in the Second-Temple Period*, JSOT Suppl. 291, Sheffield: Sheffield Academic Press.

Schenkl, H. (1916) *Epicteti Dissertationes*, Leipzig: Teubner.

Schiffman, L. (1975) *The Halakah at Qumran*, Leiden: E.J. Brill.

Schissel, O. (1926) "Der Studenplan des neuplatonikers Proklos," *ByzZ* 26: 265–72.

Schlier, H. (1965) *Der Brief an die Galater*, Meyers Kommentar VII, Göttingen: Vandenhoeck & Ruprecht.

Schmidt, E.A. (1965) *Aristoteles. Über die Tugend*, Aristoteles Werke in Deutscher Übersetzung 18.1, Berlin: Akademie Verlag.

Schwartz, D.R. (1992) "'Scribes and Pharisees, Hypocrites': Who are the 'Scribes' in the New Testament," in *Studies in the Jewish Background of Christianity*, Tübingen: Mohr, pp. 89–101. (Hebrew original: *Zion* 50 [1984/85 = *Zion Jubilee Volume L (1935–1985)*], pp. 121–32).

Schweighäuser, J. (1799–1800) *Epicteteae Philosophiae Monumenta*, Leipzig.

Scott, A. (1995) "Churches or Books? Sethian Social Organization," *JECS* 3: 109–22.

Scott, W. (1885) *Fragmenta Herculanensia*, Oxford: Clarendon Press.

Sedley, D. (1997) "Plato's Auctoritas and the Rebirth of the Commentary Tradition," in J. Barnes and M. Griffin (eds) *Philosophia Togata II*, Oxford: Clarendon Press, pp. 110–29.

—— (1989) "Philosophical Allegiance in the Greco-Roman World," in

M. Griffith and J. Barnes (eds) *Philosophia Togata*, Oxford: Clarendon Press, pp. 97–119.

—— (1973) "Epicurus, On Nature, Book XXVIII," *CErc* 3: 5–83.

Semeia (1994) "Orality and Textuality in Early Christian Literature," *Semeia* 65.

Serena Funghi, M. and Cavini, W. (eds) (1995) "Commentarium in Aristotelis «Topica»," in *Corpus* 3:14–18.

Setaioli, A. (1988) *Seneca e i greci*, Bologna: Pàtron.

Sharples, R.W. (tr.) (1994) *Alexander of Aphrodisias, Quaestiones 2.16–3.15*, Ithaca, N.Y.: Cornell University Press.

—— (tr.) (1992) *Alexander of Aphrodisias, Quaestiones 1.1–2.15*, London: Duckworth.

—— (1990) "The School of Alexander?" in Sorabji 1990, pp. 83–111.

—— (1987) "Alexander of Aphrodisias: Scholasticism and Innovation," in *ANRW II* 36.2, pp. 1176–243.

—— (1985) "Ambiguity and Opposition: Alexander of Aphrodisias, *Ethical Problems* 11," *BICS* 32: 113–19.

—— (1983) *Alexander of Aphrodisias on Fate*, London: Duckworth.

Shenkel, J. (1968) *Chronology and Recensional Development in the Greek Text of Kings*, Cambridge, Mass.: Harvard University Press.

Shiel, J. (1957) "Boethius and Andronicus of Rhodes," *VC* 11: 179–85.

Shinan, A. (1983) "On the Nature of the Aramaic Targums to the Pentateuch," *Prooftexts* 3: 41–9.

Shutt, R.J.H. (1985) "Letter of Aristeas," in Charlesworth 1985, Vol. 2.

Silverstone, A.E. (1931) *Aquila and Onkelos*, Manchester: Manchester University Press.

Simplicius. *CAG* Vols 7–11.

Singer, P.N. (tr.) (1997) *Galen; Selected Works*, Oxford: Oxford University Press.

Siniscalco, P. and Albert, K. (1981) *Platon und seine Lehre*, Ger. tr. K. Albert, Sankt Augustin: Hans Richarz.

Skeat, T.C. (1981) "Was Rerolling a Papyrus Roll an Irksome and Time Consuming Task?," in Edda Bresciani *et al.* (eds) *Scritti in onore Orsolina Montevecchi*, Bologna: Editrice Clueb, pp. 373–86.

Skehan, P., Ulrich, E., and Sanderson, J. (eds) (1992) *Qumran Cave 4.IV. Paleo-Hebrew and Greek Biblical Manuscripts*, DJD 9, Oxford: Clarendon Press.

Skydsgaard, J.E. (1968) *Varro the Scholar*, Analecta Romana Instituti Danici IV Supplementum, Copenhagen: Einar Munksgaard.

Smelik, W.F. (1995) *The Targum of Judges*, Leiden: E.J. Brill.

Smith, J.Z. (1982) *Imagining Religion*, Chicago and London: University of Chicago Press.

Smith, M. (1963) "A Comparison of Early Christian and Early Rabbinic Tradition," *JBL* 82: 169–76.

Smith, M.F. (1993) *Diogenes of Oinoanda, The Epicurean Inscription*, La Scuola di Epicuro, Suppl. 1, Naples: Bibliopolis.

Snyder, H.G. (2000) "Naughts and Crosses: Pesher Manuscripts and Their Significance for Reading Practices at Qumran," *Dead Sea Discoveries* 7 (in press).

Sokoloff, M. (1974) *The Targum to Job from Qumran Cave XI*, Jerusalem: At Ahva Press.

Solmsen, F. (1981) "The Academic and the Alexandrian Editions of Plato's Works," *ICS* 6: 102–11.

Sorabji, R. (ed.) (1997) *Aristotle and After*, London: Institute of Classical Studies.

—— (ed.) (1990) *Aristotle Transformed*, London: Duckworth.

Souilhé, J. (1948) *Épictète: Entretiens*, Paris: Société d'édition «Les Belles Lettres».

Spengel, L. (1854) *Rhetores Graeci*, 3 Vols, Leipzig: Teubner.

Spina, L. (1977) "Il trattato di Filodemo su Epicuro ed altri (PHerc 1418)," *CErc* 7: 43–83.

Stanley, C. (1992) *Paul and the Language of Scripture: Citation Technique in the Pauline Epistles and Contemporary Literature*, SNTSMS 69, Cambridge: Cambridge University Press.

Stanton, G. (1973) "Sophists and Philosophers: Problems of Classification," *AJP* 94: 350–64.

Starr, R. J. (1987) "The Circulation of Literary Texts in the Roman World," *CQ* 37: 213–23.

—— (1991) "Reading Aloud: Lectores and Roman Reading," *CJ* 86: 337–43.

Steckel, H. (1968) "Epikuros," *RE* Suppl. 11, cols 579–652.

Steckoll, S. (1969) "Marginal Notes on the Qumran Excavations," *RQ* 7: 33–40.

Steiner, D.T. (1994) *The Tyrant's Writ*, Princeton, N.J.: Princeton University Press.

Stellwag, H.W.F. (1933) *Epictetus, Het Eerste Boek der Diatriben*, Amsterdam: H.J. Paris.

Stendahl, K. (1968) *The School of St. Matthew*, Acta Seminarii Neotestamentici Upsaliensis Vol. 20, Lund: C.W.K. Gleerup; repr. Philadelphia: Fortress Press.

Sterling, G. (1997) "'The School of Sacred Laws': The Social Setting of Philo's Treatises," unpublished paper delivered at the 1997 Society of Biblical Literature Conference.

—— (1991) "Philo's *Quaestiones*, Prolegomena or Afterthought?," in Hay 1991, pp. 99–123.

Stock, B. (1983) *The Implications of Literacy*, Princeton, N.J.: Princeton University Press.

—— (1990) *Listening for the Text*, Baltimore, Md.: Johns Hopkins University Press.

Stone, M. (ed.) (1984) *Jewish Writings of the Second Temple Period*, Assen: Van Gorcum; Philadelphia: Fortress Press.

Stone, M. and Chazon, E. (eds) (1998) *Biblical Perspectives: Early Use and Interpretation of the Bible in Light of the Dead Sea Scrolls. Proceedings of the First International Symposium of the Orion Center for the Study of the Dead Sea Scrolls and Associated Literature, 12–14 May, 1996*, Leiden: E.J. Brill.

Stowers, S. (1994) *A Rereading of Romans*, New Haven, Conn.: Yale University Press.

—— (1984) "Social Status, Public Speaking and Private Teaching: The Circumstances of Paul's Preaching Activity," *NT* 26: 59–82.

—— (1981) *The Diatribe and Paul's Letter to the Romans*, Chico, Calif.: Scholars Press.

Stroumsa, G. (1998) "The Christian Hermeneutical Revolution and Its Double Helix," in L. Rutgers *et al.* 1998.

Strugnell, J. (1994) "MMT: Second Thoughts on a Forthcoming Edition," in Ulrich and VanderKam 1994, pp. 57–73.

—— (1969–71) "Notes en marge du volume V des 'Discoveries in the Judaean Desert of Jordan,'" *RevQ* 7: 163–276.

Sudhaus, S. (1895) "Exkurse zu Philodem. 1. Ein litterarischer Streit in der epikureischen Schule," *Philologus* 54: 80–5.

—— (1892) *Philodemi Volumina Rhetorica*, Leipzig: Teubner; repr. Amsterdam: Hakkert, 1964.

Suggs, M.J. (1967) " 'The Word Is Near You': Romans 10:6–10 Within the Purpose of the Letter," in Farmer *et al.* 1967, pp. 289–312.

ΣΥΖΗΤΗΣΙΣ (1983) *ΣΥΖΗΤΗΣΙΣ: Studi sull'epicureismo greco e romano offerti a Marcello Gigante*, Naples: Gaetano Macchiaroli.

Svenbro, J. (1993) *Phrasikleia: An Anthropology of Reading in Ancient Greece*, tr. J. Lloyd, Ithaca, N.Y.: Cornell University Press.

Swanson, D. (1995) *The Temple Scroll and the Bible*, Leiden: E.J. Brill.

Szlezak, T. (1972) *Pseudo-Archytas, Über die Kategorien*, Berlin: Walter de Gruyter.

Tarán, L. (1981a) *Speusippus of Athens*. Leiden: E.J. Brill.

—— (1981b) "Paul Moraux, *Der Aristotelismus bei den Griechen von Andronikos bis Alexander von Aphrodisias*," *Gnomon* 53: 721–50.

—— (1976) "Carlini, *Studi sulla tradizione antica e medievale del Fedone*," *Gnomon* 48: 760–8.

—— (1975) *Academica: Plato, Philip of Opus, and the Pseudo-Platonic Epinomis*, Memoirs of the American Philosophical Society 107, Philadelphia.

Tarrant, H. (1993) *Thrasyllan Platonism*, Ithaca, N.Y.: Cornell University Press.

—— (1983) "The Date of Anon. in Theaetetum," *CQ* 33: 161–87.

Terian, A. (1991) "The Priority of the *Quaestiones* among Philo's Exegetical Commentaries," in Hay 1991, pp. 29–46.

Thackery, H. (1923) *The Septuagint and Jewish Worship*, The Schweich Lectures 30, London: Oxford University Press.

Theissen, G. (1988) *The Social Setting of Pauline Christianity*, tr. J. Schütz, Philadelphia: Fortress Press.

Thesleff, H. (1965) "The Pythagorean Texts of the Hellenistic Period," *Acta Academiae Aboensis*, Humaniora 30.1: 15–19.

Thomas, R. (1992) *Literacy and Orality in Ancient Greece*, Cambridge: Cambridge University Press.

Thyen, H. (1955) *Der Stil der Jüdisch-Hellenistischen Homilie*, Göttingen: Vandenhoeck & Ruprecht.

Tobin, T. (1985) *Timaios of Locri, On the Nature of the World and the Soul*, Chico, Calif.: Scholars Press.

—— (1983) *The Creation of Man: Philo and the History of Interpretation*, Washington, D.C.: Catholic Biblical Association.

Tov, E. (1996) "Scribal Markings in the Texts from the Judean Desert," in D.W. Parry and S.D. Ricks (eds) *Current Research and Technological Developments on the Dead Sea Scrolls. Conference on the Texts from the Judean Desert, Jerusalem, 30 April 1995*, Leiden: E.J. Brill, pp. 41–77.

—— (1995a) "Excerpted and Abbreviated Biblical Texts," *RQ* 16: 581–600.

—— (1995b) "Three Manuscripts (Abbreviated Texts?) of Canticles from Qumran Cave 4," *JJS* 46: 88–111.

—— (1994) "Biblical Texts as Reworked in some Qumran Manuscripts with Special Attention to 4QRP and 4QParaGen-Exod," in E. Ulrich and J. VanderKam (eds) *Community of the Renewed Covenant*, Notre Dame, Ind.: Notre Dame University Press, pp. 111–34.

—— (1992) "The Textual Status of 4Q364–367 (4QPP)," in Trebolle Barrera and Vegas Montaner 1992, Vol. 1, pp. 43–82.

—— (1988) "Hebrew Biblical Manuscripts from the Judaean Desert: Their Contribution to Textual Criticism," *JJS* 39: 1–37.

—— (1986) "The Orthography and Language of the Hebrew Scrolls Found at Qumran and the Origin of These Scrolls," *Textus* 13: 31–57.

—— (1972) "Lucian and Proto-Lucian," *RB* 79: 101–13.

—— (1971) "Pap. Giessen 13, 19, 22, 26: A Revision of the LXX?," *RB* 78: 355–83.

Tov, E. and White, S. (1994) "4QReworked Pentateuch," in Attridge *et al.* 1994.

Trapp, M.B. (1990) "Plato's *Phaedrus* in Second-Century Greek Literature," in D.A. Russell (ed.) *Antonine Literature*, Oxford: Clarendon Press, pp. 141–73.

Trebolle Barrera, J. and Vegas Montaner, L. (eds) (1992) *The Madrid Qumran Congress. Proceedings of the International Congress on the Dead Sea Scrolls, Madrid 18–21 March, 1991*, 2 Vols, Studies on the Texts of the Desert of Judah 11, Leiden: E.J. Brill.

Turner, E.G. (1987) *Greek Manuscripts of the Ancient World*, 2nd rev. edn by P.J. Parsons, Bulletin Supplement 46, London: University of London Institute of Classical Studies.

—— (1975) "Oxyrhynchus and Rome," *HSCP* 79: 1–24.

—— (1968) *Greek Papyri: an Introduction*, Oxford: Clarendon Press.

—— (1962) "L'Érudition alexandrine et les papyrus," *ChrEg* 37: 135–52.

Ulrich, E. (1994) "The Bible in the Making: the Scriptures at Qumran," in Ulrich and VanderKam 1994, pp. 77–93.

Ulrich, E. and VanderKam, J. (1994) *Community of the Renewed Covenant*, Notre Dame, Ind.: Notre Dame University Press.

Ulrich, E. *et al.* (eds) (1995) *Qumran Cave 4.IX. Deuteronomy to Kings*, DJD 14, Oxford: Clarendon Press.

Ulrich, E. *et al.* (eds) (1997) *Qumran Cave 4.X. The Prophets*, DJD 15, Oxford: Clarendon Press.

Untersteiner, M. (1980) *Problemi di filologia filosofica*, L. Sichirollo and M. Venturi Ferriolo (eds), Milan: Cisalpino-La Goliardica.

Urman, D. and Flesher, P. (eds) (1995) *Ancient Synagogues*, Leiden: E.J. Brill.

Usener, H. (1977) *Glossarium Epicureum*, rev. and ed. by M. Gigante and W. Schmid, Rome: Ateneo & Bizarri.

—— (1965) *Kleine Schriften*, 3 Vols, Osnabrück: Otto Zeller.

—— (1901) "Philonides," *RhM* 56: 145–8.

—— (1892) "Unser Platontext," in *Göttingen Nachrichten*, 2:25–50; 6:181–215; repr. in his *Kleine Schriften* 3:104–62.

—— (1887) *Epicurea*, Leipzig.

Van der Horst, P.W. (1984) *Chaeremon, Egyptian Priest and Stoic Philosopher*, Études préliminaires aux religions orientaux dans l'Empire romain 101, Leiden: E.J. Brill.

VanderKam, J. (1994) *The Dead Sea Scrolls Today*, Grand Rapids, Mich.: Eerdmans.

—— (1992) "The Jubilees Fragments from Qumran Cave 4," in Trebolle Barrera and Vegas Montaner 1992, Vol. 2, pp. 635–48.

—— (1978) "The Textual Affinities of the Biblical Citations in the *GAp*," *JBL* 97: 45–55.

VanderKam, J. *et al.* (eds) (1994) *Qumran Cave 4.VIII, Parabiblical Texts, Part 1*, DJD 13, Oxford: Clarendon Press.

Van der Ploeg, P.M. (1985) "Les Manuscrits de la grotte XI de Qumrân," *RQ* 12: 3–15.

Van der Ploeg, P.M. and van der Woude, A.S. (1971) *Le Targum de Job de la grotte XI de Qumrân*, Leiden: E.J. Brill.

Van Groningen, B.A. (1963) "ΕΚΔΟΣΙΣ," *Mnemosyne*, Ser. 4, Vol. 16: 1–17.

Veltri, G. (1994) "Der griechische Targum Aquilas," in M. Hengel and A.M. Schwemer (eds) *Die Septuaginta zwischen Judentum und Christentum*, Tübingen: J.C.B. Mohr, pp. 92–115.

Vermes, G. (1995) *The Dead Sea Scrolls in English*, 4th rev. edn, Harmondsworth: Penguin.

—— (1963) "Haggadah in the Onkelos Targum," *JSS* 8: 159–69.

Vogliano, A. (1954) "Gli studi filologici epicurei nell'ultimo cinquantennio," *MH* 11: 188–94.

—— (1928) *Epicurei et Epicureorum Scripta in Herculensibus papyris servata*, Berlin: Weidmann.

—— (1926) "Nuovi testi epicurei," *RIFC* 54: 37–48.

Völker, W. (1938) *Fortschritt und Vollendung bei Philo von Alexandrien. Eine Studie zur Geschichte der Frömmigkeit*, Leipzig: J.C. Hinrich.

Von Arnim, H. (1913) "Hierocles," *RE* 8.2: 1479.

Von Campenhausen, H. (1969) *Ecclesiastical Authority and Spiritual Power*, tr. J.A. Baker, Stanford: Stanford University Press.

Von Leutsch, E.L. and Schneidewin, F.G. (1958) *Corpus Paroemiographorum Graecorum*, Vol. 1, Hildesheim: Georg Olms.

Von Staden, H. (1997) "Galen and the 'Second Sophistic,'" in Sorabji 1997, pp. 33–54.

—— (1994) "Anatomy as Rhetoric: Galen on Dissection and Persuasion," *JHM* 50: 47–66.

Von Wilamowitz-Möllendorf, U. (1962) *Platon: Beilage und Textkritik*, 2 Vols, 3rd edn, Berlin: Weidmann.

—— (1881) *Antigonos von Karystos*, Berlin: Weidmann.

Vooys, C.J. (1934) *Lexicon Philodemeum*, Purmerend: J. Muusses.

Wachsmuth, C. and Hense, O. (1884–1912) *Ioannes Stobaei Anthologium*, repr. Berlin: Weidmann, 1961.

Walzer, R. (1949) *Galen on Jews and Christians*, London: Oxford University Press.

Wan, S. (1993) "Philo's *Quaestiones et solutiones in Genesim*: A Synoptic Approach," *SBLSP* 32: 22–53.

Weinfeld, M. (1992) "Grace after Meals in Qumran," *JBL* 111: 427–40.

Wellmann, M. (1895) *Pneumatische Schule bis auf Archigenes*, Philologische Untersuchungen 14, Berlin: Weidmann.

Wenkebach, E. (1934) *Galeni In Hippocratis Epidemiarum libr. I comm. III*, CMG 5.10.2.1, Leipzig/Berlin: Teubner.

Westerink, L.G. (1962) *Anonymous Prolegomena to Platonic Philosophy*, Amsterdam: North-Holland Publishing Company.

White, L.M. (1997) "Synagogue and Society in Imperial Ostia: Archaeological and Epigraphic Evidence," *HTR* 90: 23–58.

White, S.A. (1990) "4QDt^n: Biblical Manuscript or Excerpted Text?" in H. Attridge *et al.* (eds) *Of Scribes and Scrolls. Studies on Hebrew Bible, Intertestamental Judaism, and Christian Origins Presented to John Strugnell*, Lanham, Md.: University Press of America, pp. 13–19.

Whittaker, J. (1990) *Alcinoos: Enseignement des doctrines de Platon*, Paris: Société d'édition «Les Belles Lettres».

—— (1989) "The Value of Indirect Tradition in the Establishment of Greek Philosophical Texts or the Art of Misquotation," in J.N. Grant (ed.) *Editing Greek and Latin Texts. Papers given at the Twenty-Third Annual*

Conference on Editorial Problems, University of Toronto, 6–7 November, 1987, New York: AMS Press.

—— (1987) "Platonic Philosophy in the Early Centuries of the Empire," in *ANRW II* 36.1, Berlin: de Gruyter.

Wiefel, W. (1991) "The Jewish Community in Ancient Rome and the Origins of Roman Christianity," in Donfried 1991.

Wilken, R. (1984) *The Christians as the Romans Saw Them*, New Haven. Conn.: Yale University Press.

Wilpert, P. (1940) "Die Reste verlorener Aristotelesschriften bei Alexander von Aphrodisias," *Hermes* 75: 367–96.

Winston, D. and Dillon, J. (eds) (1983) *Two Treatises of Philo of Alexandria*, Chico, Calif.: Scholars Press.

Wintermute, O.S. (1985) "Jubilees," in Charlesworth 1985, Vol. 2, pp. 35–142.

Wirth, T. (1967) "Arrians Erinnerungen an Epiktet," *MH* 24: 149–89, 197–216.

Wise, M.O. (1990) *A Critical Study of the Temple Scroll from Qumran Cave 11*, Chicago: The Oriental Institute.

Wise, M.O. *et al.* (eds) (1994) *Methods of Investigation of the Dead Sea Scrolls and the Khirbet Qumran Site: Present Realities and Future Prospects*, New York: New York Academy of Sciences.

Wolfson, H.A. (1947) *Philo: Foundations of Religious Philosophy in Judaism, Christianity, and Islam*, 2 Vols, Cambridge, Mass.: Harvard University Press.

Yadin, Y. (1983) *The Temple Scroll*, 3 Vols, Jerusalem: The Israel Exploration Society.

—— (1977) *The Temple Scroll, Vol. 3, Supplementary Plates*, Jerusalem: The Israel Exploration Society.

—— (1962) "Expedition D – The Cave of Letters," *IEJ* 12: 204–36.

York, A. (1974) "The Dating of Targumic Literature," *JSJ* 5: 49–62.

Young, F. (1997) *Biblical Exegesis and the Formation of Christian Culture*, Cambridge: Cambridge University Press.

Zahn, T. (1905) *Der Brief des Paulus an die Galater*, Leipzig: A. Deichert.

Zalateo, G. (1964) "Papirio di argomento medico redatti in forma di domanda e resposta," *Aegyptus* 44: 52–7.

Zanker, P. (1995) *The Mask of Socrates: the Image of the Intellectual in Antiquity*, tr. A. Shapiro, Berkeley: University of California Press.

—— (1988) *The Power of Images in the Age of Augustus*, tr. A. Shapiro, Ann Arbor, Mich.: The University of Michigan Press.

INDEX